TEACHING MUSIC IN THE TWENTIETH CENTURY

Lois Choksy, *The University of Calgary*

Robert M. Abramson, *Manhattan School of Music*

Avon Gillespie, *North Texas State University*

David Woods, *University of Arizona*

Prentice-Hall, Inc. Englewood Cliffs, New Jersey 07632

Library of Congress Cataloging in Publication Data

Choksy, Lois.
   Teaching music in the twentieth century.

   Includes bibliographical notes.
   1. School music—Instruction and study.   I. Title.
II. Title: Teaching music in the 20th century.
MT1.C5375 1986   780'.7'2   85-6340
ISBN 0-13-892662-X

ACKNOWLEDGMENTS

Goals for Music Education (pp. 113–115); Outcomes of the Music Education Program (p. 115); and Program Cone (p. 116), copyright © 1972 by Music Educators National Conference. Reprinted by permission.   "Hush Little Minnie" from ENGLISH FOLK SONGS FROM THE SOUTHERN APPALACHIANS. Collected by Cecil J. Sharp. By permission of Oxford University Press.   "Un Canadien Errant" ("Once a Canadian Lad," pp. 220–221); "I's the B'y that Builds the Boat" (pp. 224–225); "The Ryans and the Pittmans" ("We'll Rant and We'll Roar," p. 269), arranged by Richard Johnston. © 1954 by Waterloo Music Company Limited, Waterloo, Ontario, Canada. International & United States Copyright Secured. All rights reserved by copyright owners. Used by permission.   "Xtoles" (p. 243); "Stone Pounding" (pp. 248–249); "The Street," Tchaikovsky (pp. 287–288) reprinted from the Julliard Repertory Library by permission of Canyon Press, Inc.   "Hey, Tswana" (p. 286) from *The Melody Book* by Patricia Hackett. © 1983 by Prentice-Hall, Inc.   "Nachtanz" (pp. 289–290) by J. H. Schein. Copyright CONSORT MUSIC, INC., 1976. *Quartet Recorder*, Book 2 (Burakoff & Strickland). Used by permission of publisher.   "Titi-Toria" (p. 292) English by Max V. Exner, from *Tent and Trail Songs*. Copyright © 1962 by World Around Songs, Inc. Used with permission.   BICINIA HUNGARICA, Vol. III (pp. 230, 319), © copyright 1941 by Zoltan Kodály; renewed 1969. Revised versions © 1962, 1967 by Boosey & Co., Ltd. Reprinted by permission of Boosey & Hawkes, Inc.   15 TWO PART EXERCISES, Kodály (p. 319), © copyright 1952 by Boosey & Co., Ltd.; renewed 1980. Reprinted by permission of Boosey & Hawkes, Inc.   DON'T LEAVE ME, Bartok (p. 323), © copyright 1942, 1955, 1957 by Hawkes & Son, London, Ltd.; renewed 1969, 1983, 1985. Reprinted by permission.

Cover design: Ben Santora
Manufacturing buyer: Raymond Keating
Page layout: Peter J. Ticola

© 1986 by Prentice-Hall
A Division of Simon & Schuster, Inc.
Englewood Cliffs, New Jersey 07632

Printed in the United States of America

10   9   8   7   6   5   4   3

ISBN-0-13-892662-X   01

Prentice-Hall International (UK) Limited, *London*
Prentice-Hall of Australia Pty. Limited, *Sydney*
Prentice-Hall of Canada Inc., *Toronto*
Prentice-Hall Hispanoamericana, S.A., *Mexico*
Prentice-Hall of India Private Limited, *New Delhi*
Prentice-Hall of Japan, Inc., *Tokyo*
Prentice-Hall of Southeast Asia Pte. Ltd., *Singapore*
Editora Prentice-Hall do Brasil, Ltda., *Rio de Janeiro*
Whitehall Books Limited, *Wellington, New Zealand*

CONTENTS

FOREWORD   *x*

PREFACE   *xii*

1
METHOD IN NORTH AMERICAN MUSIC TEACHING: The Beginnings   *1*

WHAT IS METHOD?   *2*

LOOKING BACK   *2*

The Contributions of Horace Mann, *2*   Introduction

of Music Into Public Schools, *5*   The Influence of

Lowell Mason, *5*

LOOKING AT THE PRESENT   *11*

2
INFLUENCES ON METHODS, APPROACHES, AND PHILOSOPHIES OF TEACHING MUSIC IN THE LATTER HALF OF THE TWENTIETH CENTURY   *12*

THE WOODS HOLE CONFERENCE   *12*

THE YOUNG COMPOSERS PROJECT   *13*

THE YALE SEMINAR   *14*

Music Materials, *14*   Music Performance, *15*

THE MANHATTANVILLE MUSIC CURRICULUM PROGRAM   *16*

THE TANGLEWOOD SYMPOSIUM   *17*

THE ANN ARBOR SYMPOSIUM   *21*

THE INFLUENCE OF MODERN TECHNOLOGY ON MUSIC EDUCATION   *22*

SUMMARY   *23*

APPENDIX TO CHAPTER 2 *25*

PANEL OF THE ANN ARBOR SYMPOSIUM *25*

PANEL OF PSYCHOLOGISTS FOR SESSIONS I AND II *25*

PANEL OF MUSIC EDUCATORS FOR SESSIONS I AND II *26*

PANEL OF PSYCHOLOGISTS FOR SESSION III *26*

3
THE APPROACH OF EMILE JAQUES-DALCROZE *27*

THE EDUCATIONAL PHILOSOPHY OF JAQUES-DALCROZE *29*

The Reasons for Training in Rhythm, *31*   The Birth of Eurhythmics: First Experiences and Discoveries, *32* Kinesthesia: The Missing Link, *33*

TECHNIQUES OF EURHYTHMICS *36*

The Use of Improvisation in Eurhythmics Classes, *36*   The Use of Movement in Eurhythmics, *37*   The Development of Inner Hearing, *39*

CONTENT OF EURHYTHMICS *40*

THE THIRTY-FOUR JAQUES-DALCROZE ELEMENTS OF RHYTHM *41*

JAQUES-DALCROZE'S CONTRIBUTION TO RHYTHMIC THEORY   *50*

SOLFÈGE–SOLFÈGE-RYTHMIQUE AND IMPROVISATION   *51*

Solfège, *52*

MUSICAL INTERPRETATION   *54*

Phrasing, Nuance, and Expression, *54*   Numbered
Melodies, *55*   Scales, Tonalities, Intonation,
and Hearing, *55*   Syllables and Numbers, *57*
Solfège, Tonality, Nuance, Phrasing, *58*
Solfège-Rythmique, *61*

IMPROVISATION   *61*

Beginning Keyboard Improvisation, *66*
Improvisation and the Printed Page, *68*

CONCLUSION   *68*

4
THE KODÁLY
METHOD   *70*

Objectives of Kodály Musical Training, *72*   A Child-
Developmental Approach, *72*   The Tools of the
Kodály Method, *73*   Sequencing for
Learning, *78*   Some Possible Kodály Sequences

in Rhythm, Melody, Form, and Harmony, *79*

Combining the Elements, *90*

SUMMARY AND CONCLUSIONS *90*

5

THE ORFF
APPROACH *92*

THE ORFF PROCESS *96*

Support Systems for the Process: Orff

Instruments, *98*   The Musical Materials, *102*

SUMMARY *103*

6

COMPREHENSIVE
MUSICIANSHIP: An
American Technique and
Philosophy for Teaching
Music *104*

The Young Composers Project, *105*

The Contemporary Music Project, *105*

THE COMPREHENSIVE MUSICIANSHIP APPROACH *106*

Common Elements, *108*   Musical

Functions, *110*   Educational Strategies, *111*

SUMMARY AND CONCLUSIONS   *112*

7
ACHIEVING GOALS AND OBJECTIVES IN SCHOOL MUSIC PROGRAMS VIA THE PRINCIPLES OF JAQUES-DALCROZE, KODÁLY, ORFF, AND COMPREHENSIVE MUSICIANSHIP   *113*

GOALS FOR MUSIC EDUCATION   *113*

OUTCOMES OF THE MUSIC EDUCATION PROGRAM   *115*

FRAMEWORK FOR A MUSIC EDUCATION PROGRAM   *115*

PHYSICAL SETTINGS, EQUIPMENT NEEDS, LESSON PLANNING, AND TEACHING STYLES   *117*

JAQUES-DALCROZE   *117*

Teaching Style, *117*   Space, Equipment, and Costume, *118*   Musical Materials, *119*   Lesson Planning, *120*   Exercise and Game Plans, *123*

Three Types of Lesson Plans, *125*

The Process of Eurhythmics, *127*

KODÁLY   *130*

Lesson Planning, *132*   Pedagogical

Process, *132*   Musical Materials, *136*

ORFF   137

Lesson Planning, *138*   Musical

Materials, *143*   Physical Setting, *143*

COMPREHENSIVE MUSICIANSHIP   144

Classroom Objectives, *145*   Role of the

Teacher, *145*   Planning for Musical

Learning, *147*   Application of CM

in the Upper Elementary Grades

and in the Junior High School General Music

Program, *148*   Application of CM in High School

Performing Ensembles, *151*

CONCLUSIONS   152

8

GRADES K-1-2   *153*

INTRODUCTION   153

JAQUES-DALCROZE   154

Preschool, *154*   Nursery School through

Grade 2, *154*   Lesson for Primary Grades, *157*

KODÁLY   169

Lesson for an Early Stage, *169*   Lesson for the End
of Grade 2, *174*   Conclusion, *180*

ORFF *180*

Movement, *181*   Voice, *181*   Form, *181*

Suggested Orff Experiences, *182*

COMPREHENSIVE MUSICIANSHIP *189*

Learning Objectives, *189*   Lesson Plans, *190*

Summary, *196*

CONCLUSIONS *196*

9
GRADES 3-4-5   *197*

INTRODUCTION *197*

JAQUES-DALCROZE *198*

Rhythmics, *198*   Lesson Plan, *199*

Conclusion, *215*

KODÁLY *215*

Lesson for Grade 3, *215*   Lesson for Grade 5, *222*

ORFF *230*

Movement, *231*   Voice, *231*

Form, *231*   Instruments, *232*   Lesson Cycle, *235*

COMPREHENSIVE MUSICIANSHIP *240*

Learning Objectives, *240*   The Organization of Pitch,

Duration, Intensity, and Timbre, *241*   Lesson Plans

Emphasizing the Comprehensive Musicianship Approach

to Teaching in the Intermediate Grades, *242*

Summary, *249*

CONCLUSIONS   250

10
GRADES 6-7-8   *251*

INTRODUCTION   251

Preprofessional Training, *251*   Avocational and

Recreational Training, *251*

JAQUES-DALCROZE   253

Lesson on Group Improvisation, *254*

Conclusion, *265*

KODÁLY   265

Lesson for Twelve- and Thirteen-Year-Olds, *267*

ORFF   274

Movement, *274*   Voice, *274*   Organization

and Materials of Music, *275*   Instruments, *275*

Evaluation, *275*   Lesson Cycle, *276*

COMPREHENSIVE MUSICIANSHIP   *282*

Learning Objectives, *282*   The Organization of Pitch, Duration, Intensity, and Timbre, *283*   Lesson Plans, *284*   Summary, *293*

CONCLUSION   *294*

11
METHOD IN MUSIC FOR OLDER STUDENTS   *295*

INTRODUCTION   *295*

JAQUES-DALCROZE   *297*

Lessons on *Solfège* and *Solfège-Rhythmique, 297*

Conclusion, *314*

KODÁLY   *314*

Lesson, Example 1, *316*   Lesson, Example 2, *321*

ORFF   *324*

Lesson Cycle, *325*   Conclusion, *330*

COMPREHENSIVE MUSICIANSHIP   *330*

Learning Objectives, *330*   The Organization of Pitch, Duration, Intensity, and Timbre, *331*   Summary, *333*

CONCLUSION   *334*

12
SPECIFIC METHOD OR
ECLECTICISM?   *335*

Creativity, *337*   Movement, *338*   Instrumental
Training, *338*   Musical Reading and Writing, *339*
Music Used in Teaching, *341*   Inferences, *342*

FOREWORD

One evening in February, 1982, after the closing meetings of the Music Educators National Conference in San Antonio, Texas, to which we had both been invited as speakers, Robert Abramson and I had dinner together. We had known one another for more than thirty years, since our student days at the Peabody Conservatory of Music in Baltimore, even though we rarely saw each other unless, as occasionally happened, we were invited to speak at the same conference.

Over dinner we talked of our work. Comparison of methodologies is a subject that has fascinated me for many years, and I have never lost an opportunity to discuss the similarities and differences of the various approaches with people whose work is considered excellent in fields other than mine. We drew triangles on the tablecloth, representing the three basic functions of music

and tried to describe to each other how our own teaching methods (his: Jaques-Dalcroze; mine: Kodály) approached each of these dimensions. The conversation went on well into the evening and left both of us feeling that we had not even skimmed the surface of the topic.

Two days later, back at my desk at The University of Calgary, I received a telephone call from my editor at Prentice-Hall, asking if I would be interested in writing a book combining the various methods. I recall saying rather acerbically that there were already too many such books on the market, purporting to explain everything about every method, written by people who knew nothing about any method. The conversation ended with him asking me to think about it. I had hardly put the telephone down when the thought occurred to me that probably there were many people as interested in an authoritative comparison of methodologies as I, and that the solution was not for one author—any *one* author—to write such a book, but for a group of persons, each with impeccable credentials in his or her own area, to do it together.

I decided to take on the project and to include in the proposed book the four most commonly used approaches in North American schools: Jaques-Dalcroze, Kodály, Orff, and Comprehensive Musicianship. I chose not to include the widely-known Suzuki method only because it is purely instrumental and is, therefore, not as closely associated with public school general music teaching.

Having chosen the methods, the choice of authors was, for me, obvious. I placed a call immediately to Abramson at the Manhattan School of Music, where he is Professor of Music and Director of the Jaques-Dalcroze Program, and asked what he thought of the idea. He was enthusiastic and agreed at once to write the Jaques-Dalcroze sections of the book. I knew I could get no one more highly skilled than this composer and music educator who had spent two post-graduate years studying at the Jaques-Dalcroze Institute in Geneva and had achieved the highest level of certification possible in the field.

I had discussed with many Orff clinicians the philosophies and principles underlying the Orff and Kodály approaches. Only one had ever really been able to express fluently to me the qualities of Orff teaching; Avon Gillespie, Associate Professor of Music at North Texas State University, and formerly a teacher at the Orff Institute in Salzburg. Gillespie expressed some sincere concerns about writing the Orff chapters for such a book. In one letter he wrote: "... there is a real need for this philosophy to be elusive and abstract. . . ."Fortunately, I was able to convince him that his writing would not be molded into any "pattern" and that I believed that only he, in North American practice, could represent the Orff approach in both an uncompromised and uncompromising way.

By electing to include Comprehensive Musicianship in this volume I found myself under fire, even at the earliest stages. There were those prepublication reviewers who said that as an approach it was "dead," or indeed, had never "lived." I believe, to the contrary, that Comprehensive Musicianship is the culmination of more than thirty years of exploratory work at the highest levels in North American music education, and that to exclude it would be to ignore the whole structure of organized music education. Far more music teacher-training institutions claim to take a Comprehensive approach than to take the Jaques-Dalcroze, Kodály, and Orff approaches together. I felt that to disregard a practice so widely claimed and so little understood would have been a glaring omission.

My choice to write the Comprehensive Musicianship sections was a longtime friend who has been involved in this approach since its earliest days— David Woods, Head of Music Education at the University of Arizona. Again, my choice was made against a background of many years of discussion with Woods on exactly the topic of this book.

The actual assembling of this volume has not been easy. Each of us has a natural bias for his or her own way of teaching, and to describe that way without expressing that bias has been one of our most difficult tasks. We hope we have succeeded.

Lois Choksy
Professor of Music
The University of Calgary

PREFACE

The four methods discussed in this book were initiated, and their philosophies were evolved, in the minds of composers, not teachers. The fact that these innovators *did* sometimes teach was of secondary consideration. Kodály and Orff are known to this day primarily as composers; Jaques-Dalcroze, while not so known now, *was* very well known in his time and composed several hundred works, large and small. The movers in the United States and Canada in the Tanglewood Symposium and behind the Manhattanville Music Curriculum Program, the Contemporary Music Project, and the John Adaskin Project also were composers of international stature.

Many levels of creativity go into the evolution of a method. Each of the four methods considered here was originally conceived by people who were brilliant—who perhaps even possessed genius. Around them, in every instance, were others, highly talented people, who helped to bring the conceptions to fruition. In some cases the names of the members of these coteries are well known: Keetman and Günther, the two women who brought Orff's concept to reality; Szőnyi, Nemesszeghy, and Forrai, women Kodály referred to as his "Amazons." Dancers, well-known in their day, did much to influence Jaques-Dalcroze's thinking at Hellerau. From its inception, Comprehensive Musicianship involved many people including the composers Norman Dello Joio, Grant Beglarian, and Samuel Adler.

The most talented teacher does not have the vision, nor, in all fairness, the time to create something better than that which has already been created by genius. Teaching is both an art and a science, and the complete teacher must be both an artist and a scientist. The artistic component produces the musicality and beauty in a music lesson and the scientific ability makes it possible for the teacher to apply problem-solving approaches to lessons.

But, just as not every physician can or has to reinvent the heart-transplant technique in order for it to benefit humanity, not every teacher can or has to invent his or her own teaching method in order to teach most effectively. This book should help teachers make intelligent and knowledgeable choices among methods.

TEACHING MUSIC IN THE TWENTIETH CENTURY

1

METHOD IN NORTH AMERICAN MUSIC TEACHING:
The Beginnings

Music education is alive and well in North America. In spite of periodic economic setbacks, shifts in educational focus, and "back to basics" movements, more children are receiving more music lessons in more schools than ever before in the history of the North American school music movement. The question has changed from "shall we have music in our schools?" to "how should music be taught in our schools?" What is the best, the most efficient, the most effective way to teach music?

The music student entering teaching today is faced with a plethora of curriculum choices. Not only are there the methods being considered in this book—Orff, Jaques-Dalcroze, Kodály, and Comprehensive Musicianship—but there are also the *related arts* approach, the *eclectic* curriculum, the *integrated* curriculum, the *generalist* approach, to mention only a few. Every music series purports either to *be* a method or to *combine* several methods. Teachers are encouraged to dabble with techniques from this approach or from that approach, without understanding the fundamental principles underlying any one of them. Choices are made for superficial reasons, and methods thus unknowledgeably employed are discarded when they do not produce instant success.

There is obviously a need for method in the teaching of music in North America. But there is not necessarily a need for everyone to practice the same method. The teacher who has a clear idea of musical goals and an understanding of the underlying principles of each method will be more likely to choose the one method best suited to his or her own talents and teaching style.

WHAT IS METHOD?

Perhaps it would be well to define what is meant by *method* in music education. For the purposes of this book the word *method* shall be applied only to a teaching approach which has (1) an identifiable underlying philosophy (in other words, a specific set of *principles*); (2) a unified body of pedagogy unique to it (a body of well-defined *practice*); (3) goals and objectives worthy of pursuit; and (4) integrity (it's *raison d'être* must not be commercial).

Under this definition the four most widely practiced methods in North America today are the Kodály Method, the Jaques-Dalcroze Method, the Orff Approach, and the Comprehensive Musicianship Approach. Although the practitioners of each of the above sometimes take exception to the word *method* in connection with their practices, these approaches all fall fully within the definition of method given here: they each have specific sets of principles, uniquely identifiable practices, precise sets of goals for music education, and none was originated for commercial purposes.

Of the four, three—Kodály, Orff, Jaques-Dalcroze—had their origins in Europe; only Comprehensive Musicianship had its inception in North America. However, some of the best Kodály practice, Orff classes, and Jaques-Dalcroze work in the world are taking place in North American schools: there is nothing foreign about the practice of these methods in the United States and Canada. They have become North American as surely as if they had originated here. While this book will occasionally discuss practice in Austria, Germany, Switzerland, or Hungary, its focus will be on practice in North America. The Kodály method in North America has, of necessity, a different sequence and uses different musical materials than it does in Hungarian schools. In varying degrees the same may be said of Orff and Jaques-Dalcroze. In actuality, Comprehensive Musicianship, the *American* approach, with its world music orientation, uses more foreign material in teaching than do any of the three "foreign" methods.

LOOKING BACK

In order to understand the development of school music in twentieth-century North America, and the logical position occupied by each of the above methodologies in that development, it is necessary first to look back to the milieu from which American music teaching came.

The Contributions of Horace Mann

The schools in the United States were in a state of disarray during the early 1800s. Many of their problems had been caused by local control of the community school systems. Local control was first set up by the first school law of Massachusetts in 1789, which established a district system of school organization.

In 1800 these districts were granted the authority to tax the local citizens for support of the community schools. But instead of encouraging local interest and support for the schools, local financial involvement caused community disagreements and public feuds.

Because the schools were still not free to most of the students, problems also occurred in the area of attendance. Many districts levied taxes on all of the parents of school-age children. In order to continue in school yet avoid paying the school tax poor families in these districts were required to take a "pauper's oath." The oath was considered so insulting by most poor people that they avoided the schools altogether and received no education at all.

By the 1830s these and other problems regarding education had intensified so much that there were movements for school reform in almost all of the states outside of the South. Andrew Jackson was the President at the time, and a new era of the common man had started to take hold in all facets of society. Legislators in many of the states led or responded to the call for public responsibility for the schools. Massachusetts was the first state to make a viable effort to improve school organization.

In 1827, Horace Mann (1796–1859), a young lawyer in the state of Massachusetts, was elected to the House of Representatives in Massachusetts, where he served until he was elected to the state Senate in 1833. He was elected President of the Senate in 1836 and again in 1837. While in the legislature, Mann worked diligently and successfully for three major concerns: humane treatment of the insane, temperance, and public education. He was particularly influential in encouraging educational reform and revitalization. On April 29, 1837, as President of the Massachusetts Senate, Mann signed a bill entitled An Act Relating to Common Schools. This bill provided that a state Board of Education be established in Massachusetts and that the Board appoint a secretary for the administration of the act. The law authorized the board to distribute throughout the state information on the "most approved and successful methods of arranging the studies and conducting the education of the young." The bill also charged the Board "to make a detailed report to the legislature of all its doings with such observations as its experience and relection might suggest, on the condition and efficiency of the system of popular education, and the most practical means of improving and extending it."

James G. Carter, Chairman of the Committee on Education of the state House of Representatives and an activist for education reform, was responsible for drafting the bill and pushing it through the legislature. As a former district school teacher, Carter was bitter about the prevailing district system of school organization in the state. Carter was appointed by the governor to serve on the state Board of Education and he worked vigorously to upgrade pedagogical standards. Other members of the first Board of Education in the state of Massachusetts included: Horace Mann; Emerson Davis, a Congregational pastor; Edmund Dwight, a wealthy merchant and a strong supporter of education reform; Thomas Robbins, a Congregational pastor; Edward Newton, a business man; Robert Rantoul, a leading Democrat in the House of Representatives; and Jared Sparks, a former Unitarian minister and the President of Harvard College. Governor Everett and Lieutenant Governor George were both *ex officio* members of the Board.

Mainly because of the insistence of Edmund Dwight, Horace Mann was asked to accept the position of first secretary of the Board of Education of the state of Massachusetts. To the surprise of his friends and colleagues, the young lawyer with a promising political career ahead of him accepted the position. Mann seemed to be fully aware of the enormity of the task of being the secretary to the Board of Education. He wrote in his journal, "The interests of a client are small compared with the interests of the next generation. Let the next generation, then, be my client."[1]

Horace Mann served as the secretary for the Board of Education in Massachusetts from 1837 to 1847. With determination he set out to improve school attendance, curriculum development, teacher education, school building conditions, and the acquisition of materials, books, and supplies for the students. The bill that had established the Board of Education was a rather weak one in that it did not allow the Board of Education to establish or administer schools in the state. It could build and persuade, but it could not command reform. Undaunted by the limited powers of his position, Mann began his campaign against the inadequacies of the schools in the state. In August of 1837, he began to travel to communities throughout the state of Massachusetts giving lectures and speeches on the improvements of education for children. In November, 1838, he published the first issue of *The Common School Journal,* which contained articles on the need for improvement in the public schools. Subscriptions from the journal did not even pay the printing and mailing costs, so Mann subsidized the publication out of his own small salary. He continued the publication until he resigned as secretary in 1848.

After only five months in office, Mann submitted the first of the annual reports required by the bill which established the Board of Education. From that year until 1848, he submitted twelve annual reports. The reports focused on the state of the schools in Massachusetts and gave Mann an opportunity to express his own views on the need for improvement in education. His reports were written for legislators as well as for school administrators and teachers. Mann distributed the reports to every school in the state at his own expense. Of these reports, the seventh (1843) was the most important to music education and was the most important in spreading the philosophies and ideas of Johann Pestalozzi. In fact, the seventh annual report has been termed "the most important single influence in spreading Pestalozzian ideas of method, discipline, school management, and curriculum throughout the United States."[2]

The seventh annual report was written in 1844, after Mann had spent six months in Europe observing schools in Great Britain and the continent. It describes many examples of European teaching and educational organization. Regarding music, Mann stated, "all Prussian teachers are masters not only of vocal, but of instrumental music." Mann also stated that "music brings the whole mind, as it were, into a state of fusion, from which condition the teacher can mould it into what forms he will, as it cools and hardens."[3]

[1]"Horace Mann's Journal," October, 1837, in *Life and Works of Horace Mann,* Vol. 3, Mary Peabody Mann and George Combe Mann, eds. (Boston: Lee and Shepard, 1891).

[2]Paul Monroe, *Founding of the American Public School System* (New York: Macmillan, 1940), p. 384.

[3]Horace Mann, *Annual Reports on Education* (Boston: Horace B. Fuller, 1968), pp. 345–46.

Mann believed that music instruction must form an essential element in any school curriculum. He also believed that music instruction in the schools must develop a love of music and sincere desire to sing, believing that singing should become a natural and enjoyable activity in the school. In his seventh annual report, Mann called for "the introduction of music, drawing and the study of natural objects" to enrich the curriculum in the schools.[4]

Introduction of Music Into Public Schools

If there is one moment that can be heralded as the beginning of public school music in North America, that would probably be August 28, 1838. On that day the School Board of Boston made music a part of the regular curriculum, with the following stern warnings: Music should not occupy more than two hours a week; Music should be given at the same stated and fixed times throughout the city; and The classroom teacher must be present during lessons to "discipline" the class.[5] The salary for the music teacher was $100 a year, out of which the teacher was expected to supply the piano. (Although the program was originally approved on August 24, 1837, its implementation was delayed a full year because of budget considerations—a gambit still familiar to music teachers today.)

Schools in the United States had occasionally offered instruction in music before this, but never in an organized fashion and never with a teacher paid by a Board of Education. This seemingly insignificant beginning was in reality a giant step forward, and may be attributed almost entirely to the efforts of Horace Mann and one other music educator—Lowell Mason (1792–1872).

The Influence of Lowell Mason

Mason came from a musical family and at an early age was conducting choirs, composing, and organizing singing schools and instrumental groups. He was both a music teacher of some repute and a prolific writer on musical subjects. Among his many publications were the first American songbook written especially for children, *The Juvenile Psalmist, or, The Child's Introduction to Sacred Music,* prepared at the request of the Boston Sabbath School Union,[6] and *Juvenile Lyre,*[7] said by Mason to be "the first school song book to be published in this country."[8] Still, his impact on American music education might have been limited had he not come into contact with the pedagogical principles of the great Swiss education reformer Johann Heinrich Pestalozzi (1746–1827).

PESTALOZZIAN PRINCIPLES OF EDUCATION   Pestalozzi rejected the school practices of memorization and recitation that were then common, and substituted for them observation, experimentation, and reasoning. He was the first to attempt to link the educational process to the natural development of the child. His dictum was: "Read nothing; Discover everything; Prove all things." He believed in the "harmonious development of all the faculties of the child," "the whole child: mentally, physically and morally," "training the *head, hand* and

---

[4]Edgar W. Knight, *Education in the United States* (Boston: Ginn, 1941). p. 319.
[5]Boston Academy of Music, *Annual Reports,* 7 (1839), 12–13.
[6]Boston: Richardson, Lord, and Holbrook, 1829.
[7]Written with a colleague, Elam Ives, Jr., in 1830–1831.
[8]*An Address on Church Music* (New York: Mason and Law, 1851).

heart." He was convinced that the only way to develop the abilities of the child was to create situations in which those abilities would have to be used. He said that the teacher's job was to stimulate and direct the child to self-activity.

Education, according to Pestalozzi, should be so sequenced and structured that each stage could grow naturally out of the preceding and into the succeeding stage. A corollary of this approach, which was at that time revolutionary, was a discarding of the often brutal discipline of the past and the substituting of strict but loving classroom management. He deeply believed in the power of this kind of education to regenerate society.

Pestalozzi was not a musician. Although he made reference to the value of music, he made no attempt to apply his educational philosophy to the teaching of music.[9]

Lowell Mason's Adaptation of Pestalozzian Principles   Lowell Mason was introduced in the United States to the Pestalozzian philosophy by an associate who had studied in Switzerland and saw possibilities of its application to the teaching of music. Mason found Pestalozzi's theories interesting and challenging. He was at that time involved with a group of music-loving merchants and businessmen in founding the Boston Academy of Music, a private music school. Some of its stated aims were

1. to make vocal musical training available to both children and adults;
2. to train teachers of music;
3. to form an association of performers and conductors of sacred music;
4. to provide exhibitions and concerts of children's and adults' classes (to show the results of the teaching) and of large groups assembled annually or semiannually (festivals);
5. to introduce vocal music into the schools;
6. to publish books of instruction.

In 1834, for use in this school, Mason wrote the *Manual of the Boston Academy of Music, for Instruction in the Elements of Vocal Singing, on the System of Pestalozzi*.[10] This was followed by a series of sixty-one articles—"Pestalozzian Music Teaching"—published by the *New York Musical Review and Gazette* between 1855 and 1857.[11] These two works set forth a method that is specific both in its educational principles and in its pedagogical practices, that has reached into the twentieth century and influenced music education throughout North America.

Principles and Practice of Lowell Mason's Pestalozzian Method

It is not the *mere knowledge* which is desired, but it is the expansion of the human powers which is the result of the acquisition of knowledge.[12]

[9]*Gesangbildungslehre nach Pestalozzischen Grundsätzen* (*The Theory of Instruction in Singing, on Pestalozzian Principles*) (Zürich: H. G. Nägeli, 1810).

[10]Boston: Carter, Hendee, 1834.

[11]These articles were collected and issued as the book *The Pestalozzian Music Teacher* (New York: Ditson, 1871).

[12]Daniel Gregory Mason, "A Glimpse of Lowell Mason from an Old Bundle of Letters," *The New Music Review and Church Music Review*, 26 (January, 1927), 50.

Only the most choice songs and melodies [must] be admitted into our families and schools . . . [good music tends] to *improve the heart,* and thus be instrumental in promoting the cause of human happiness, virtue, and religion.[13]

. . . if music be not taught in childhood, much progress must not be expected afterwards.[14]

[The purpose of music in the schools] is not to form the musician, [but to give all students] the power of understanding and appreciating music.[15]

[Music] is itself a discipline of the highest order, a subordination of mind, eye, ear, unitedly tending to one object.[16]

. . . the development of the musical faculty contributes to the development of the whole man.[17]

No talent, however vigorous, springs spontaneously into action. Some labor is necessary to unfold its latent energies, as well as to improve it.[18]

[Good teaching does not] commence with book rules, nor attempt to lead from general laws to particular facts, but rather from particular facts to general laws; not from theory to practice, but from practice to theory.[19]

[The first medium of instruction should be the voice and early teaching should be by rote.] This is the natural process of learning to sing, just as it is natural for children to learn to talk before they learn spelling, reading, or grammar.[20]

. . . experience proves that large classes of young persons, capable of reading music with much accuracy, may be easily gathered in almost any part of New England, or indeed of the United States.[21]

A capacity for music is much more common than is generally supposed. Children must be taught music, as they are taught to read.[22]

The philosophy of Lowell Mason, gleaned from his many publications, may be summarized as follows:

1. The purpose of music in the schools is to create musically intelligent adults rather than to train professional musicians.
2. The quality of music used in teaching is of vital importance. Only music of artistic value should be used in the music class.
3. The process used in teaching is of greater importance and more lasting value than the product of that teaching.

[13]*Manual of the Boston Academy of Music,* pp. 21–22.

[14]Lowell Mason, *Address on Church Music* (Boston: Hilliard, Gray, 1826), pp. 23–30.

[15]City of Boston, School Committee, *Report of the Committee on Music,* August 24, 1837.

[16]*Report of the Committee* (1837).

[17]Arthur Lowndes Rich, *Lowell Mason* (Chapel Hill: University of North Carolina, 1946), p. 62.

[18]Lowell Mason, *Address on Church Music.*

[19]Lowell Mason, *How Shall I Teach?* (New York: Mason Brothers, 1860), p. 166.

[20]Lowell Mason, *The Song-Garden,* Vol. 1 (New York: Mason Brothers, 1864), pp. ii–iv.

[21]Lowell Mason, *An Address on Church Music* (New York), p. 16.

[22]Lowell Mason, *Address on Church Music* (Boston), pp. 23–30.

4. To be most effective, music education must begin with the young child.
5. Music is a discipline involving all the senses and contributing to the total development of the human being.
6. To achieve in music, work is necessary.
7. Practical experience must come before theory; and theory must grow out of that practical experience.
8. Musical literacy is both a possible and desirable goal for most people.

The *practice* based on these *principles* was "an inductive method, exercising actively the reasoning powers of the mind."[23] Its *pedagogy* was summarized by Mason as (1) sounds before symbols; (2) principles before rules; and (3) practice before theory.[24]

Knowledge, according to Mason, is to be "acquired by the pupils themselves, rather than from the dictation of the teacher. He should seldom tell them anything, which, by a series of questions, he can lead them to find out by themselves. His object is so to *lead* them to the desired information, as to excite their curiosity, and fix their attention. Knowledge acquired in this manner, is deeply impressed on the mind, and therefore durable."[25]

Mason believed that learning occurs in three ways:

1. through self-activity
   Learning by doing. Pupils are expected to acquire knowledge through their own observations, experiences and actions, rather than being told by a teacher.
2. through reasoning
   Observation, comparison, judgment, and decision. Students are to arrive at conclusions based on their experiences.
3. through testimony and faith
   Certain universal usages, certain definitions simply exist. Students cannot arrive at these through reasoning or self-activity. These they simply have to accept on faith from their teachers.

The Mason–Pestalozzi process is from the known to the unknown and from general knowledge through analysis to particular knowledge: "The thing to be understood is first examined, then taken to pieces, then put together again,—the whole being done with interest, thought, understanding."[26]

On the material through which children were to learn, Mason expressed the concerns that

the words and music be of interest to the students,

the ranges be suitable for young voices,

it be within the students' music reading capacities,

it be appropriate to the students' maturity level.

[23]Boston Academy of Music, *Annual Reports*, 11, 1843.
[24]Mason and Seward, *The Pestalozzian Music Teacher*, p. 11.
[25]*Manual of the Boston Academy of Music*, p. 14.
[26]Mason and Seward, *The Pestalozzian Music Teacher*, p. 8.

He saw the overlapping stages of a child's music literacy training as follows:

1. rote-singing stage, in which all songs are first sung by the teacher and then learned by imitation, without books
2. rote song–note-reading stage, in which songs sung previously by rote are now sung following notes; simple notational skills are introduced
3. note-reading stage, in which songs and exercises containing the notes and patterns taught in stage 2 are read and more advanced new reading material is gradually introduced
4. part-singing and choral-singing stage, in which students move through rounds and canons to two-part singing in thirds and sixths to chordal harmony

Tonic *solfa*, the system in which *do* is the tonal center or key note in all major keys and *la* is the tonal center or key note in all minor keys, was the principal tool used by Mason and his colleagues in their teaching at the Boston Academy and in the public schools of Boston. It was, however, not the only tool: they also used both numbers and absolute note names in their singing classes. Other devices to aid in the acquisition of sight-singing skills were tone ladders, aural dictation, time beating, and large movements to indicate rhythmic feeling. The cultivation of a simple form of perfect pitch—the ability to recall one note accurately and find others from it—was also encouraged.

Rhythm was taught by short patterns which were chanted on a neutral syllable while keeping the beat by tapping or conducting. Mason also suggested that the students should be made to feel rhythm through body movement. For the study of melody short tonal patterns of three-note range were introduced first. These were extended to the lower tetrachord (*do–re–mi–fa*) and later to the upper tetrachord (*so–la–ti–do*) and to the complete major diatonic scale. Although in his guides to teachers Mason separated the elements of music, he strongly suggested that teachers integrate them in their teaching from the first days of class.

Creativity was also a part of Mason's method. He gave specific instructions for leading children with even minimal notational skills to simple composition. He obviously did not consider a person musically literate who could not write and create music as well as read it.

In summary, the practices of Lowell Mason and his collaborators at the Boston Academy of Music involved

1. vocal music as the basis for all music education
2. a recognition of the limitations of the child voice
3. the principle of experience before abstraction
4. a sequential approach to elementary note reading
5. the use of tonic *solfa* for melodic reading
6. an approach to rhythm reading based on patterns rather than on simple note durations
7. the use of beating time and of body movement for teaching rhythm

Between 1837 and 1852 public school music based on these ideas spread across the United States and by 1900 music was established as a regular school subject in most of America. Some of these practices instituted by Mason are so common in the schools today that it is difficult to realize that there was a time when they represented a dramatic departure from the norm.

MUSIC EDUCATION AFTER MASON   When Mason himself ceased to be actively involved in the school music movement it gradually changed character. The Mason–Pestalozzian principles that had produced such excellence were misunderstood or deliberately ignored, while the surface elements of the approach—melodic and rhythmic patterning, the use of *solfa* as a tool—became reasons rather than means. By the end of the nineteenth century little practice existed that could be said to have fallen genuinely within Mason's philosophy.

A reaction against unthinking drills and music education aimed solely at technical proficiency showed itself in the child study movement and in stress on the instructional aspect of teaching, with emphasis on developing teaching techniques. Along with this came a demand for real music, high-quality songs to replace the endless exercises that had become the working material of Mason's successors in the late 1800s. The approach that arose from these concerns was referred to as "the song method."[27]

Less emphasis was placed on music reading as a goal. The idea that the classroom teacher could and should handle music in the schools began to find acceptance. Definite courses of study in music were written and songbook series were published in conjunction with those courses of study, for use by the classroom teacher. From *doing* in the nineteenth century, children were moved to *enjoying* early in the twentieth century: "*The specific or musical aim* is to develop appreciation of the beauty that is in music."[28] Music as a discipline, with skill and concept content, suffered.

It is an anomaly that this same period which saw the undermining of music as a legitimate subject for serious study also saw the rise of organizations and programs for special training of music specialists. The year 1922 saw "the organization of the first real four-year school music training course at Oberlin [College]."[29] Oberlin's program became the pattern for many others in succeeding years. States began to regulate qualifications for music teaching, and certification in music was instituted.

Gradually the pendulum again began to swing and by 1936 references were made in the literature, if somewhat obliquely, to skill teaching: "Our music curriculum must find a place for three types of musical projects—listening projects, performance projects, and creative projects."[30]

During this period music reading was ostensibly valued and sought

[27]Benjamin Jepson, "The Science of Music vs Rote Practice in Public Schools," *Official Report of the Eleventh Annual Meeting of the Music Teachers National Association,* 1887, pp. 174–87.

[28]National Education Association, Department of Superintendence, "The Nation at Work on the Public School Curriculum," *Fourth Yearbook.* Washington, D.C., 1926, p. 300.

[29]Karl W. Gehrkens, "Public School Music," *The International Cyclopedia of Music and Musicians,* 9th ed., Robert Sabin, ed. (New York: Dodd, Mead, and Co., 1964), p. 1703.

[30]James L. Mursell, "A Balanced Curriculum in Music Education," *Education,* 56 (May, 1936), 521.

after, but only when a need for it was felt by a student. The extent of musical illiteracy in the following generation is mute evidence of how few felt that need. It is fortunate that linguistic literacy was not treated so cavalierly.

The early twentieth century saw two other developments that were to have far-reaching effects on the teaching of music. The first of these was the invention of the phonograph, which made possible the introduction of music of the highest quality to the classroom. The ramifications of the electronic age on music teaching are only beginning to be realized today, not only with record players but also with tape recorders, video cassettes, and synthesizers, the last now a part of many schools' facilities. Music education is at present only at the cutting edge of the age of technology. It will surely revolutionize music teaching in the years to come.

Second, the twentieth century has seen an increasing sophistication in research techniques and extensive publication of research results. Much has been ascertained that was only conjecture in the nineteenth century. There can no longer be any excuse for music curricula that do not take into account child development or the nature of learning.

LOOKING AT THE PRESENT

Against this backdrop several ways of teaching music arose in the United States. The ones that have become predominant are the Kodály Method from Hungary, the Jaques-Dalcroze Method from Switzerland, the Orff Approach from Germany, and the Comprehensive Musicianship philosophy from within the United States. It is interesting to observe that traces of the Pestalozzi–Mason philosophy and pedagogy may be discerned in all of these twentieth-century music methods.

The chapters that follow will discuss the recent history of music education in North America, the methods and approaches that have emerged, and the principles and practices of each of these in detail.

2

INFLUENCES ON METHODS, APPROACHES, AND PHILOSOPHIES OF TEACHING MUSIC IN THE LATTER HALF OF THE TWENTIETH CENTURY

Music education in contemporary America has been influenced by numerous research studies, projects, experiments, and ideas. These educational activities, concepts, and theories have provided music teachers with new insights into the nature of music learning. These forces have also provided many alternatives and options for encouraging musical growth in young people.

THE WOODS HOLE CONFERENCE

The major catalyst for change and reform in contemporary education was the Woods Hole Conference which took place in September, 1959, at Woods Hole, Cape Cod, Massachusetts. Thirty-five scientists, scholars, and educators met to discuss how education in science could be improved in the public schools. The ten-day meeting was called by the National Academy of Sciences, which, through its education committee, had been examining for several years the long-range problem of improving the dissemination of scientific knowledge in America.

The purpose of the meeting was to examine the fundamental processes involved in imparting to young students a sense of the substance and method of science. Throughout the United States major curricular projects in science had been developed and implemented. It was time for scientists and educators to examine the progress of these projects and to provide direction for the future course of science education in America. The urgency for such a plan was stimulated by the recent advances in scientific technology by the Soviet Union. A few days after the Conference opened, its members were divided into five work groups—one concerned with "The Sequence of Curriculum," a second with "The Apparatus of Teaching," a third with "The Motivation of Learning," a fourth with "The Role of Intuition in Learning and Thinking," and a fifth with "Cognitive Processes in Learning." Each group prepared a lengthy report which was presented to the whole Conference for debate. Major themes from these reports and debates were later adopted as guidelines for education development in the sciences. These themes were designed to help promote higher standards of excellence in science education at all levels of instruction.

The Woods Hole Conference generated many curriculum studies in a diversity of academic and artistic subject areas. Because of the practical and valuable results of the Woods Hole Conference, its structural organization soon became a model for educational evaluation and revitalization in many fields, including music.

THE YOUNG COMPOSERS PROJECT

In the same year that the Woods Hole Conference took place (1959), changes and experimental programs began to occur in music education. One of the most significant programs was the Young Composers Project which was funded by The Ford Foundation and administered by the National Music Council. In this project composers went into the schools as music teachers and music resource people.[1] The ultimate success of placing composers in classrooms and rehearsal halls in schools throughout the country led to the establishment of the Contemporary Music Project for Creativity in Music Education (CMP) in 1962. The CMP helped to broaden the scope of music education by encouraging teachers to utilize a synthesis of performance, analysis, and composition in all instructional activities in music. The CMP also encouraged teachers to use music from all periods and from all cultures both in performing groups and in general music classes.[2]

[1]In Canada, the John Adaskin Project performed the same function. This project was begun by the Canadian Music Centre in the early 1960s. The centre and the Canadian Music Educators' Association are continuing the John Adaskin Project; this new project is designed (1) to acquaint music educators with good Canadian music currently available and suitable for school use; (2) to promote the publication of additional repertoire; (3) to encourage composers to add to the repertoire.

[2]The goals, objectives, and results of the Young Composers Project and the CMP are reviewed in Chapter 6.

THE YALE SEMINAR

In June of 1963 a seminar on music education took place at Yale University. Following the example set at the Woods Hole Conference in 1959, the Seminar at Yale focused on the problems facing contemporary music education and on possible solutions for those problems. Claude V. Palisca, Professor of Music at Yale University, was appointed the Director of the Yale Seminar. The thirty-one participants, mostly professional musicians, professors, and scholars, defined two areas of music education that required close examination: music materials and music performance.

Music Materials

The participants at the Yale Seminar outlined six major criticisms of the musical material being used in the instructional programs in music in schools throughout the country:

1. It is of appalling quality, representing little of the heritage of significant music.
2. It is constricted in scope. Even the classics of Western music—such as the great works of Bach, Mozart, Beethoven—do not occupy the central place they should in singing, playing, and listening. Non-Western music, early Western music, and certain forms of jazz, popular, and folk music have been almost altogether neglected.
3. It stunts the growth of musical feeling because it is so often not sufficiently interesting to enchant or involve a child to whom it is presumed to be accessible. [Children's potentials are constantly underestimated.]
4. It is corrupted by arrangements, touched-up editions, erroneous transcriptions, and tasteless parodies to such an extent that authentic work is rare. A whole range of songbook arrangements, weak derivative semipopular children's pieces, and a variety of "educational" recordings containing music of similar value are to be strongly condemned as "pseudo-music." To the extent artificial music is taught to children, to that extent are they invited to hate it. There is no need to use artificial or pseudo-music in any of its forms.
5. Songs are chosen and graded more on the basis of the limited technical skills of classroom teachers than the needs of the children or the ultimate goal of improved hearing and listening skills. This is one of the causes of the proliferation of feeble piano and autoharp accompaniments and of "sing-along" recordings.
6. A major fault of the repertory of vocal music stems from the desire to appeal to the least common denominator and to offend the least possible number. More attention is often paid to the subject matter of the text, both in choice and arrangement of material, than to the place of a song as music in the educational scheme. Texts are banal and lack regional inflection.[3]

[3]Irving Lowens, "Music: Juilliard Repertory Project and the Schools," *The Sunday Star.* Washington D.C., May 30, 1971, sec. E, p.4.

Music Performance

The participants at the Yale Seminar agreed that the performance standards in American music education were high, but that the music programs in the schools often concentrated on performance drill and neglected activities which promote musical understanding and musical growth.

To counteract their criticisms of the materials used in music education in the schools and the criticisms of the unbalanced emphasis on performance drill in school ensembles, the participants at the Yale Seminar proposed ten recommendations for the improvement of music education:

1. The basic goal of a K–12 music curriculum should be on the development of musicality through performance, movement, musical creativity, ear training, and listening. Creativity in this case includes original compositions by students.
2. The school music repertory should be broadened to include the best of Western and non-Western music of all periods.
3. A continuous and sequential program of guided music listening for K–12 should be developed.
4. Performance experiences should include ensembles for which authentic and varied repertory has been developed.
5. Advanced theory and literature courses should be available for students with high musical aptitude and achievement.
6. Musicians, composers, and scholars should be encouraged to go into the schools to help develop musicality in young people.
7. School music programs should take advantage of community music resources.
8. Opportunities for advanced music study which exist in major cities in America should be made available to all talented students in the country. Such a program should help establish a national network of schools or academies of music, art, drama, and dance throughout the country.
9. Films, recordings, and television should be used more in music education. A national education media system in music should be established.
10. Through regional workshops and clinics, programs should be initiated to improve teaching skills and techniques.[4]

Because there were few professional music educators participating in the Yale Seminar and because the ideas had little publicity, the ten recommendations were not immediately implemented at the grassroots level. It was not until the Tanglewood Symposium in 1967 that many of these issues were confronted by the leaders of music education.

One immediate result, however, of the Yale Seminar was the establishment of the Juilliard Repertory Project. In 1964, the Juilliard School of Music, under the auspices of the United States Office of Education, began a project to collect a repertory of authentic and meaningful music materials to be used in school music programs. The purpose of the Juilliard Repertory Project was to

[4]Michael L. Mark, *Contemporary Music Education* (New York: Schirmer, 1978), pp. 31–34.

research and compile the highest quality music for students at all levels of instruction.

Under the direction of Vittorio Giannini, over 400 compositions were tested and evaluated. Of these, 230 were ultimately included in the Juilliard Repertory Library.[5] The works in the collection are divided into style categories which include pre-Renaissance, Renaissance, Baroque, Classic, Romantic, contemporary, and folk.

In April, 1965, the Contemporary Music Project for Creativity in Music Education sponsored the Northwestern University Seminar on Comprehensive Musicianship. The four-day seminar was held at Northwestern University in Evanston, Illinois. The participants included scholars, historians, music educators, theorists, composers, and performers. The seminar focused on the examination of the content and the organization of basic college music courses in theory and in history. The participants also examined precollege instruction in music and made specific recommendations regarding the content and the orientation of precollege music experiences. It was at the Northwestern University Seminar that the concept of *Comprehensive Musicianship* became formalized.[6]

THE MANHATTANVILLE MUSIC CURRICULUM PROGRAM

Also in 1965, the Manhattanville Music Curriculum Program began under the direction of Ronald B. Thomas. The Manhattanville Music Curriculum Program (MMCP) was funded by a grant from the United States Office of Education and was named for the Manhattanville College of the Sacred Heart in Purchase, New York, where it originated. The objectives of the program were to develop a music curriculum and related materials for a sequential music program for primary grades through high school.

The project resulted in the development of a comprehensive curriculum in music for Grades 3 through 12 called the *synthesis* and an early childhood curriculum in music called *interaction*. Three feasibility studies, including the Electronic Keyboard Laboratory, the Science Music Program, and the Instrumental Program, were also completed during the MMCP.

The MMCP encourages students to experiment with both environmental and musical sounds in order to discover the inherent nature of sound and the structure and function of the elements of music. Students are urged to draw their own conclusions about sound and music based on the results of their experiences in an MMCP-oriented classroom.

The MMCP divides musical concepts into two major categories—inherent concepts and idiomatic concepts. Inherent concepts are defined as those that apply to all types of music and include form, melodic direction, timbre, texture, dynamics, harmony, and rhythm. Idiomatic concepts are those that apply only to the music of a specific historical period or music from a specific area of the world. The originators of the MMCP believed that if music education

---

[5](Cincinnati, OH: Canyon Press, 1970), 383 pages.
[6]More detailed information about the Northwestern University Seminar and Comprehensive Musicianship can be found in Chapter 6.

began with inherent concepts which pertain to all music, then students would not make specific value judgments which apply only to some music (idiomatic concepts) but would be able to consider all music without bias.

The MMCP utilizes three types of skills: aural (listening), dextrous (performance), and translative (notational). It focuses on all contemporary musical forms, including popular music, and it requires the students to experience every aspect of music as an art form.

The students involved in a Manhattanville Music Curriculum Program are expected to become composers, conductors, performers, listeners, and critics in the classroom activities. The MMCP is designed as a curriculum concept spiral and includes a sequenced series of problem-solving situations for the students to encounter.

THE TANGLEWOOD SYMPOSIUM

In 1967, the Music Educators National Conference in cooperation with the Berkshire Music Center, the Theodore Presser Foundation, and the School of Fine and Applied Arts of Boston University sponsored the Tanglewood Symposium. The theme of the Symposium was "Music in American Society." The participants at the Symposium included musicians, scholars, educators, labor leaders, philosophers, theologians, music educators, and industrialists. These participants evaluated the role of music in American society and in education and concluded that "education must have as major goals the art of living, the building of personal identity, and the nurturing of creativity."[7]

The music educators at the Tanglewood Symposium formulated the following eight declarations for the improvement of music education:

1. Music serves best when its integrity as an art is maintained.
2. Music of all periods, styles, forms, and cultures belongs to the curriculum. The musical repertory should be expanded to involve music of our time in its rich variety, including currently popular teenage music and avant-garde music, American folk music, and the music of other cultures.
3. Schools and colleges should provide adequate time for music programs ranging from preschool to adult or continuing education.
4. Instruction in the arts should be a general and important part of education in the senior high school.
5. Developments in educational technology, educational television, programmed instruction, and computer-assisted instruction should be applied to music study and research.
6. Greater emphasis should be placed on helping the individual student to fulfill his needs, goals, and potentials.
7. The music education profession must contribute its skills, proficiencies, and insights toward assisting in the solution of urgent social problems

[7]Robert A. Choate, ed., *Documentary Report of the Tanglewood Symposium.* (Washington, D.C.: Music Educators National Conference, 1968), p. 139.

such as those in the inner city or other areas with culturally deprived individuals.

8. Programs of teacher education must be expanded and improved to provide music teachers who are specially equipped to teach high school courses in the history and literature of music, courses in the humanities and related arts, as well as teachers equipped to work with the very young, with adults, with the disadvantaged, and with the emotionally disturbed.[8]

One of the first steps in realizing the recommendations of the Tanglewood Symposium was the establishment of the Goals and Objectives Project (GO Project) in 1969 by the Music Educators National Conference (MENC). A steering committee and eighteen subcommittees were organized by MENC to evaluate present activities and to establish additional viable programs in the following areas of music education:

Musical behaviors (identification and evaluation)
Comprehensive Musicianship (music study in the senior high school)
Music for youth
Inner city music education
Research
Logistics
Fact finding
Aesthetic education
Information science
Music for early childhood
Impact of technology
Music in higher education
Learning processes
Music enrichment for national life
MENC professional activities
Professional organization relationships
Music of non-Western cultures[9]

The reports from the committees were synthesized into a tentative statement of goals and objectives by Paul Lehman, Associate Dean of the School of Music at the University of Michigan, and presented to affiliate organizations and to the national committees of MENC for review.

In October 1970 the MENC National Executive Board officially adopted two major goals for the MENC and four for the profession from the recommendations and reports of the GO Project.

[8]Choate, *Tanglewood*, p. 139.
[9]Michael L. Mark, "The GO Project: Retrospective of a Decade," *Music Educators Journal*, 67, no. 4 (December, 1980), 43–47.

The MENC goals were that MENC should conduct programs and activities to build (1) a vital musical culture, and (2) an enlightened musical public.

The goals for the profession included (1) comprehensive music programs in all schools, (2) involvement of people of all ages in learning music, (3) high-quality preparation of teachers, and (4) use of the most effective techniques and resources in music instruction.[10]

Thirty-five objectives were also adopted by the MENC in 1970 from the report of the GO Project. These objectives outlined, rather specifically, the directions, activities, and subgoals that should be studied and implemented by the professional music educators. The thirty-five objectives are as follows:

1. Advocate the expansion of music education to include preschool children.
2. Lead efforts to ensure that every school system requires music from kindergarten through Grade 6 and for a minimum of two years beyond that level.
3. Promote challenging courses in music for the general college student.
4. Advocate the expansion of music education for adults both in and out of school.
5. Lead in efforts to ensure that every school system allocates sufficient staff, time, and funds to support a comprehensive and excellent music program.
6. Lead in efforts to ensure that every secondary school offers an array of music courses to meet the needs of all youth.
7. Lead in efforts to develop programs of music instruction challenging to all students, whatever their socio-cultural condition, and directed toward the needs of citizens in a pluralistic society.
8. Lead in the development of programs of study that correlate performing, creating, and listening to music and encompass a diversity of musical behaviors.
9. Advance the teaching of music of all periods, styles, forms, and cultures.
10. Promote the development of instructional programs in aesthetic education.
11. Develop standards to ensure that all music instruction is provided by teachers well prepared in music.
12. Assume leadership in the development of resources for music teaching and learning.
13. Cooperate in the development of exemplary models of desirable programs and practices in the teaching of music.
14. Expand programs to secure greater involvement and commitment of student members.
15. Strengthen the relationships·between the conference and its federated, associated, and auxiliary organizations.

[10]Mark, "GO Project," p. 43.

16. Establish procedures for organizational program planning and policy development.

17. Seek to expand membership to include all persons who, in any capacity, teach music.

18. Periodically evaluate the effectiveness of policies and programs.

19. Ensure systematic interaction with the membership concerning the goals and objectives of the conference.

20. Assist teachers in the identification of musical behaviors relevant to the needs of their students.

21. Promote the conduct of research-related activities in music education.

22. Disseminate news of research in order that research findings may be applied promptly and effectively.

23. Initiate efforts to establish information retrieval systems in music and education, and to develop databases for subsequent incorporation into such systems.

24. Provide advisory assistance where music programs are threatened by legislative, administrative, or other action.

25. Conduct public relations programs to build community support for music education.

26. Gather and disseminate information concerning music and music education.

27. Encourage other organizations, agencies, and communications media to gather and disseminate information about music and music education.

28. Pursue effective working relationships with organizations and groups having mutual interests.

29. Encourage the improvement and continuous updating of preservice and in-service education programs for all persons who teach music.

30. Assist graduate schools in developing curricula especially designed for the preparation of teachers.

31. Develop and recommend accreditation criteria for the use of recognized agencies in the approval of school and college music programs and in the certification of teachers.

32. Support the expansion of teacher education programs to include specializations designed to meet current needs.

33. Assume leadership in the application of significant new developments in curriculum, teaching-learning techniques and technology, instructional and staffing patterns, evaluation, and related topics to every area and level of music teaching.

34. Encourage maximum use of community music resources to enhance educational programs.

35. Determine the most urgent needs for information in music education.[11]

[11]Mark, "GO Project,' pp. 43–47.

The GO Project provided MENC and the profession of music education with a long-range plan for music instruction. This plan was based on a thorough assessment of the past activities of the profession and on present and future educational and societal needs in America.

THE ANN ARBOR SYMPOSIUM

Another worthy follow-up of the Tanglewood Symposium was the National Symposium on the Application of Psychology to the Teaching and Learning of Music held in three sessions at the University of Michigan in Ann Arbor. The funding for the three sessions came from the Presser Foundation, which in 1967 had joined with MENC to put on the Tanglewood Symposium. The Symposium on the Application of Psychology to the Teaching and Learning of Music, known as the Ann Arbor Symposium, was sponsored by the Music Educators National Conference, the School of Music of the University of Michigan, and the Center for Research on Learning and Teaching at the University of Michigan.[12] A panel of distinguished psychologists was organized by administrators of the Symposium to present papers on various topics of interest in the psychology of music teaching. A panel of prominent music teachers also was organized to present papers regarding research in music learning and learning theory. Members of both panels were assigned specific topics for the papers to write and present and specific papers to respond to.

The papers were presented first by music educators and then were responded to by psychologists, in Session I, and were organized under six topics: auditory perception, motor learning, cognitive skills, child development, memory and information processing, and affect and motivation. Judith Murphy has described the papers thus:

> . . . At the risk of ignoring individual differences, one might say that in general the music educators dealt with an assigned topic—auditory perception, affect and motivation, or whatever—and then used it to expound on many problems of music education. Some of them seized the chance to expound on their own particular knowledge. The psychologists thus found themselves confronted with full-scale exegeses on music education larded with citations from research findings old and new.
>
> Faced with this barrage of evidence, speculation and inquiry, the psychologists did what came naturally. Some responded by holding forth on their own particular interest, viewpoint, and knowledge. If they had their own more or less relevant experiments to report, they proceeded to do so, after some kind of graceful allusion to the untoward flood of questions.
>
> Others took the occasion to outline theories and hypotheses of their own and relate them in one way or another to music education. A few simply winged it, resorting to agreeable reflections on music, their own

[12]See Appendix to this chapter for lists of members of the various panels.

work, and elements of their musical biographies. Some took the offensive and offered rival questions, among them: "Is it possible that music means something?" One occasionally got the impression of two boxers shadowboxing one another in separate gyms.[13]

During Session II the psychologists made their presentations, with the music educators responding.

By and large, the presentations moved from the particular to the general—from presentations dealing with pitch and motor skills to presentations dealing broadly with instructional models and motivations and music's social context. Even the psychologists focusing on particular experiments, however, used them to project their views on larger matters. There was a tendency in these papers to stress listening over performing and learning over teaching.[14]

In Session III the focus was on creativity and motivation. Five papers on motivation and five on creativity were presented by eminent psychologists.

Many facts, theories, and speculations emerged from the three sessions of the Ann Arbor Symposium. However, some results of the symposium can be summarized in three important themes:

1. Music education must deal with the individual differences of the learners.
2. Teaching of music throughout should be done at several levels of learning at the same time. Students should be aware of the musical structures of pitch and rhythm, while relating those elements to aural, verbal, and symbolic associations. Students should also relate music to their own personal and educational environments.
3. Sequencing of musical concepts and skills should be done routinely in all educational processes.

The Ann Arbor Symposium allowed music educators to interact with each other and with leading psychologists in an attempt to bring about greater understanding of "how children learn when they learn music."

THE INFLUENCE OF MODERN TECHNOLOGY ON MUSIC EDUCATION

In addition to the practical and philosophical projects, seminars, and symposium sessions which have influenced music instruction in the American schools since the Woods Hole Conference, technological advances have also influenced and

---

[13]Judith Murphy, "Conflict, Consensus, and Communication—An Interpretive Report on the Applications of Psychology to the Teaching and Learning of Music," *Music Educators Journal,* 66, no. 7 (March, 1980), S-8–S-9.

[14]Murphy, "Applications," p. S-17.

improved music teaching. The computer society of the 1980s has presented new challenges and opportunities for music educators at all levels of instruction. The advent of computer-assisted learning has resulted in sweeping educational changes in many schools throughout America. A new literacy is now required of both teachers and students in all subject areas, including music.

This view was stated succinctly by Franklin:

> An educational change resulting from the development of the computer is the academic requirement of student computer literacy, a requirement that is being included in school and college curricula across the nation. Computer literacy, the ability to communicate with a computer, has become a basic skill in many schools, a skill that is taking its place alongside the traditional skills of reading, writing, and mathematics. Several colleges and universities and some high schools now have curricula requiring all students to gain computer literacy skills prior to graduation.[15]

The potential applications of microcomputers in music education are limited only by knowledge and creativity of the user or programmer. The use of the computer in music education is a growing discipline, one still in its infancy. However, it is clear that computer-assisted instruction in music can expand and improve teaching strategies through individualized instruction and through instant feedback so that students learn music more efficiently and effectively. The computer has been used to develop aural skills, to develop skills of symbolic association, and to provide information about the harmonic content of a piece of music. Students can compose, analyze, transpose, and even improvise with selected computer systems. As more musicians and music educators become familiar with computer application, the more advanced and the more convenient the systems will become.

SUMMARY

The Woods Hole Conference of 1959 established a model for educational reform and development in many subject areas, including music. It was the inspiration and the stimulation for the Yale Seminar of 1963. This Seminar addressed itself to the problems confronting music education. Recommendations for the solutions to the problems identified were made by the participants of the seminar. One immediate result of the Yale Seminar was the establishment of the Juilliard Repertory Project at the Juilliard School of Music in 1964. The Project developed a compilation of high-quality vocal and instrumental music for the classroom from a cross-section of musical styles and periods.

In 1959, the same year as the Woods Hole Conference, the Ford Foundation granted funds to establish the Young Composers Project in the public schools in America. This experiment of placing composers in classrooms and in rehearsal halls led to the establishment of the Contemporary Music Project for

[15]James L. Franklin, "What's a Computer Doing in My Music Room?" *Music Educators Journal,* 69, no. 5 (January, 1983), 29.

Creativity in Music Education (CMP) in 1962. The CMP held seminars, workshops, and clinics throughout the country to assist teachers in becoming familiar with contemporary music and improving their compositional and analytical skills. The CMP also supported projects in the public schools which tested and experimented with the synthesis of performance, analysis, and composition in music instruction. In 1965, the CMP sponsored the Northwestern University Seminar on Comprehensive Musicianship in Evanston, Illinois to set up a structure for comprehensive teaching at the college level. The participants also focused on curriculum design and materials for precollege music instruction. It was at the Northwestern University Seminar that the term *Comprehensive Musicianship* emerged to describe a broad-based and total approach to the teaching and learning of music of all cultures and of all periods.

During the same year the Manhattanville Music Curriculum Program (MMCP) was initiated. This project focused on sound discovery and sound exploration as avenues for the musical growth and development of children.

In 1967, the Tanglewood Symposium on "Music in American Society" resulted in eight major declarations for the improvement of music education. One of the first steps in realizing the recommendations made at the Tanglewood Symposium was the establishment of the Goals and Objectives Project (GO Project) in 1969 by the MENC. The participants in the project investigated and evaluated all facets of professional music education and formulated extensive goals and objectives for the profession to use in long-range planning for the improvement of music instruction in all areas of society.

Another follow-up of the Tanglewood Symposium was the Ann Arbor Symposium. This symposium was held in three sessions: the first was in 1978, the second in 1979, and the third in 1982. The purpose of the symposium was to translate the abstract thinking of psychologists into improved practice in the classroom.

In addition to the projects and studies which have influenced music education since the Woods Hole Conference in 1959, the profession has recently been influenced by advances in computer-assisted instruction. Computer programs have been developed to expand and improve aural skill development, compositional techniques, and harmonic analysis skills. The field of music education will be changed and modified by the computer society of the 1980s and 1990s.

Amid all the serious investigation, experimentation, and implementation during the later part of the twentieth century, four approaches to music education emerged in classrooms across North America in answer to the many questions, aims, and objectives brought to light. These four are the methodologies associated with Jaques-Dalcroze, Kodály, Orff, and Comprehensive Musicianship.

APPENDIX TO CHAPTER 2

The three sessions of the Ann Arbor Symposium were held on October 30–November 2, 1978 (Session I); July 30–August 2, 1979 (Session II); and August 2–6, 1982 (Session III).

PANEL OF THE ANN ARBOR SYMPOSIUM

Director: Paul Lehman, University of Michigan
Chairman: James A. Mason, Brigham Young University
Special consultant: Wilbert J. McKeachie, University of Michigan
Special consultant: Alvin C. Eurich, Academy for Educational Development (New York City)

PANEL OF PSYCHOLOGISTS FOR SESSIONS I AND II

Roger Brown, Harvard University
Ruth Day, Duke University
Diana Deutsch, University of California
W. Jay Dowling, University of Texas at Dallas
Howard E. Gardner, Harvard University
William Kessen, Yale University

David LaBerge, University of Minnesota
Joel O. Raynor, State University of New York at Buffalo
Frank Restle, Indiana University
Roger N. Shepherd, Stanford University
Jane A. Siegel, Toronto Board of Education (Ontario, Canada)
Edward L. Walker, retired, University of Michigan
Asahel D. Woodruff, emeritus, University of Utah

PANEL OF MUSIC EDUCATORS
FOR SESSIONS I AND II

Henry L. Cady, University of Delaware
James C. Carlson, University of Washington
Edwin E. Gordon, Temple University
R. Douglas Greer, Columbia University
Steven K. Hedden, University of Iowa
Jack J. Heller, University of Connecticut
Gerard L. Knieter, University of Akron
Robert G. Petzold, University of Wisconsin at Madison
Robert G. Sidnell, Stephen F. Austin State University
Malcolm J. Tait, Case Western Reserve University
David B. Williams, Illinois State University
Marilyn P. Zimmerman, Temple University

PANEL OF PSYCHOLOGISTS FOR
SESSION III

John G. Nicholls, Purdue University
Stanley S. Gryskiewicz, Center for Creative Leadership (Greensboro, North Carolina)
Martin L. Mehr, University of Illinois
Francis X. Barron, University of California at Santa Cruz
Joel O. Raynor, State University of New York at Buffalo
Michael A. Wallach, Duke University
Jacquelynne Eccles Parsons, University of Michigan
Irving Taylor, Lakehead University (Thunder Bay, Ontario, Canada)
Martin V. Covington, University of California at Berkeley
Donald J. Treffinger, State University College at Buffalo

3

THE APPROACH OF EMILE
JAQUES-DALCROZE

"Dalcroze Eurhythmics" is an approach to music education based on the premise that rhythm is the primary element in music, and that the source for all musical rhythm may be found in the natural rhythms of the human body. The total method consists of three parts—Eurhythmics, *Solfège,* and Improvisation—and is named after the Swiss pedagogue Emile Jaques-Dalcroze (1865–1950).

Although he is often referred to simply as "Dalcroze," the last name of this famous Swiss professor of theory is a hyphenated one, Jaques-Dalcroze;[1] and the method so misnamed "Eurhythmics" encompasses far more than just rhythm.

Jaques-Dalcroze was himself a product of Swiss and Viennese conservatories, with a sound traditional musical background. His mother was a Pestalozzian music teacher, and this, no doubt, also exerted some influence on his thinking when a young man.

It is difficult to pinpoint the exact beginnings of Jaques-Dalcroze's unique approach to music education, but possibly it can be traced to his appointment, at age twenty-five, as professor of harmony and *solfège* at the Conservatory of Music in Geneva.

This appointment drew him for the first time into close contact with large numbers of students, and he discovered that many of his pupils, although technically advanced on their instruments, were unable to feel and express mu-

[1]Although his correct original name was Emile Jaques, in 1888 he changed it to Emile Jaques-Dalcroze at the request of his publisher, in order to avoid confusion with two other composers named Emile Jaques.

sic. They could not deal with even the simplest problems of rhythm, and often their sense of pitch, tonality, and intonation was defective. They possesed a mechanical rather than a musical grasp of the art of music. They could not hear the harmonies they were writing in their theory assignments and were not able to invent simple melodies or chord sequences. When the students tried to follow the rules of harmony without understanding or sensing the reasons for the rules, the results were dull, awkward, and lacked smoothness of voice leading and clarity of expression.Frequently, their lack of sensitivity created problems in their individual performances.

The rest of Jaques-Dalcroze's life was spent inventing ways to help his students develop their abilities to feel, hear, invent; sense and imagine; connect, remember, read and write; perform and interpret music. He devoted himself to converting musical knowledge into musical understanding. He fought to change the teaching of *solfège* and theory from the abstractions represented by musical signs to a basic experience with musical sounds. He worked to free his students of conflicts between mind and body, between feeling and expression. He hoped to balance the interaction of the nervous system and the muscles, to train the body quickly and accurately to perform commands given by the brain. He hoped to create a harmony between the temperament and the will, between impulse and thought.

The problems Jaques-Dalcroze observed in his students were the same problems all perceptive teachers struggle with in their professional lives. His innovative solutions derived from the musical and educational factors in his early life.

Born in Vienna to a financially secure Swiss merchant family, Emile and his sister Hélène were fortunate in having their mother Julie support them in their early interest in music. She was a fine music teacher who had studied and taught the philosophy and methods of the educational innovator Pestalozzi. Julie Jaques stimulated her children's love for music. At an early age the children were singing duets and playing four-hand piano pieces. They lived in Vienna, a city of brilliant opera, concerts, and theater. The Jaques family enjoyed them all. Emile responded to these experiences by inventing and performing his own pantomimes and musical plays. At the age of seven he wrote his first march for the piano and the first of more than 600 songs. His love of singing, playing, moving, acting, and creating continued throughout his life, and the integration of all these aspects of music became the impetus for his educational philosophy and practice. His methods form a totality of music and invite students and teachers to experience the wholeness and aliveness of the art.

When Emile was ten years old the family moved to Geneva. He was enrolled at a private school dedicated to the development of the spirit, imagination, and responsibility. He loved this school because learning was fostered through joyful activity. In 1877 Emile, then twelve, was enrolled simultaneously at the Conservatory of Music, which he enjoyed, and the College of Geneva, which he hated. He found the teaching at the College dull, the discipline harsh. He could not wait to graduate from " . . . a prison where education consisted of rote drills, abstractions without explanations, as dry as possible, with no help, no attempt to interest the student."[2]

[2]Frank Marten et al., *Emile Jaques-Dalcroze—L'Homme, le Compositeur, le Créateur de la Rhythmique* (Neuchatel: 1965), unpublished translation by Robert Abramson.

In 1881 Emile joined the Belles-Lettres Society, a group of students dedicated to acting, writing, and music. While a member of this Society, he wrote many musicals in which he also acted, played, and sang before the public. The success of these performances encouraged him to develop his skills in composing and writing for the theater, and resulted in the composition of operas, concerts, and chansons for adults, and gesture-songs for children. The climax of his compositions was reached in his gigantic festival works for large choruses and crowds of actors that were grouped by designs based on rhythmic movement.

In 1884 Jaques-Dalcroze went to Paris to study music with composers Léo Delibes and Gabriel Fauré and to study acting with members of the Comédie Francaise. During this time he also studied with Mathis Lussy, the Swiss theorist whose novel theories of rhythm and musical expression contained the seeds of Jaques-Dalcroze's own later rhythmic and expressive processes. In 1886 he accepted a position as assistant conductor at the opera in Algiers. This was his first contact with Arabic folk music, which led him to the invention of a new music notation for music of unequal beats and unequal measures. For the first time he realized that there were several worlds of rhythmic expression and that each of these worlds required a unique reading, writing, and performance style.

Jaques-Dalcroze enrolled in the Vienna Conservatory in 1887 to study composition with symphony composer Anton Bruckner. After graduation he returned to Geneva as an actor, singer, conductor, poet, composer, pianist, and ethnomusicologist, ready to begin his new career as professor of music.

THE EDUCATIONAL PHILOSOPHY
OF JAQUES-DALCROZE

The musical, physical, and emotional problems which Jaques-Dalcroze discovered in his students, combined with the dullness of the teaching material, led him to question the philosophies and teaching methods of his time. Many of the same questions are still being asked by music educators today:

> Why are music theory and notation being taught as abstractions, divorced from the sounds, motions, and feelings they represent?
>
> Is there a way to arouse and develop musical awareness, understanding, and response simultaneously with training the musical ear?
>
> Can mere finger technique of a pianist be considered a complete musical education?
>
> Why are the various musical studies so fragmented and specialized?
>
> Why does the study of piano not lead to an understanding of harmony?
>
> Why does the study of harmony not lead to an understanding of musical styles?
>
> Why does the study of music history not reflect the movement of peoples, societies, or individuals?
>
> Why are so many textbooks on transposition, harmony, and counterpoint written in a technical style? Should they not aim first at the development of the ability to hear the effects they describe?

Why is it that the qualities that characterize a real musician are seldom felt in a music class?

What can be done about music lessons in which students are permitted to perform without understanding; students are permitted to read without comprehension; students are permitted to write that which they cannot hear or feel?

These questions, asked by Jaques-Dalcroze more than eighty years ago, could well pertain to the activities permitted in many music classrooms even today. Although present trends in music education for children have begun to address these problems, much can still be learned by studying the solutions offered by Emile Jaques-Dalcroze.

With all these questions in mind, Jaques-Dalcroze began a series of experiments with his students. He developed techniques combining hearing and physical response, singing and physical response, and reading–writing and physical response, in an attempt to arouse vivid sensations of sound. He used the results of these experiments to devise means to induce and then to develop *inner hearing*—the ability to summon musical sensations and impressions by thinking, reading, and writing music without the aid of an instrument.

In order to develop a better sense of intonation, tonality, and tonal centering, Jaques-Dalcroze used arm- and hand-levels to express the diatonic major scales. Further, he invented a technique of vocal improvisation, insisting that students "speak" the musical language to show their understanding of musical grammar and syntax. Within one year of his appointment to the Conservatory he had established a new course called "*Solfège Supérieur*," a fusion of sight singing, ear training and theory, and performance and improvisation. In 1894 he published his pedagogical books: *Exercises Pratique d'Intonation dans l'Étendue d'une Dixième* (Practical Exercises In Intonation)[3] and *Solfège avec Paroles Destinées aux Élèves de Chant* (Vocal Studies with Words for Students of Voice).[4]

Still, something was missing, something deep and mysterious about the musical process, something to unify vibrations and sensation, feeling and thought, temperament and spontaneity, imagination and willpower; that is, all those faculties found in truly talented musicians. Jaques-Dalcroze looked again at his students. He noticed something he had missed before. Students who could not *play* in tempo in the musical world were able to *walk* in tempo in the real world. Their walk was completely spontaneous and uninhibited by thought or any discernable action of the will. Next he observed that some of his best students tapped their feet or shook their heads and torsos in response to music. These were natural, automatic reactions common to all ages and cultures. Then he noticed that the students changed their movements when following a crescendo and sometimes physically demonstrated the accents they heard in the music. They also noticeably relaxed their muscles for a phrase ending. They appeared to be allowing the music to penetrate, feeling its effects. The students themselves were the instruments, he realized; not the piano, violin, flute, voice, or drum, but the students themselves.

[3]Lausanne: Jobin, 1894.
[4]Lausanne: Jobin, 1894.

Jaques-Dalcroze's thoughts then went beyond the subject of music teaching. The questions he asked and the answers he found foreshadowed more modern theories of learning and learning readiness:

What is the source of music? Where does music begin?
Human emotions are translated into musical motion.
Where do we sense emotions?
In various parts of the body.
How do we feel emotions?
By various sensations produced by different levels of muscular contraction and relaxation.[5]
How does the body express these internal feelings to the external world?
In postures, gestures, and movements of various kinds. Some of these are automatic, some are spontaneous, others are the results of thought and will.[6]
By what instrument does a human being translate inner emotions into music?
By human motion.
What is the first instrument that must be trained in music?
The human body! The base of all musical art is human emotion. It is not enough to train just the mind or the ear or the voice; the entire human body must be trained since the body contains all of the essentials for the development of sensibility, sensitivity and analysis of sound, music and feeling. Any musical idea can be performed by the body and any movement of the body can be transformed into its musical counterpart. There must be an immediate reaction between the mind that conceives and the body that acts.[7]

These answers seemed simple, but, in fact, they were profound insights that added a new dimension to stimulus-response behaviorism and became the basis for many twentieth-century ideas of affective behavioral studies and holistic learning.

The Reasons for Training in Rhythm

Thus far Jaques-Dalcroze's thinking seemed simple, logical, and firmly based in the reality of his observations and experiences in his classroom. Though his new techniques in ear training and sight singing had been successful up to a point, he understood that training the ears and eyes to discern pitch, scales, tonalities, and harmonies was not enough to make students feel or love music deeply. He perceived that the aspects of music that make the most definite appeal to the senses (in other words, the ones most clearly connected to the students' lives) were rhythm and movement. Of the three elements of music—pitch, rhythm, and dynamic energy—he realized that the last two were entirely dependent on move-

[5]Any of those sensations described by everyday phrases such as "butterflies in the stomach," "tight-lipped", or "pain in the neck."
[6]For example, "a warm handshake," "a sassy face," "a timid walk," "a sad goodbye," or "downcast eyes."
[7]Marten, *Jaques-Dalcroze*, unpublished translation by Robert Abramson.

ment and found their best model in muscular systems. All degrees of tempo—allegro, andante, accelerando and ritardando—could be experienced, understood, and expressed with the body. He sensed that the keenness of musical feelings depended on the keenness of physical sensations. He was convinced that combining intense listening with body responses would generate and release a powerful musical force.

The Birth of Eurhythmics: First Experiences and Discoveries

Now he needed a laboratory in which to test his theories. He needed students, space, and time. His requests for help rejected by the school authorities, Jaques-Dalcroze decided to hire his own workspace and enlist the aid of student volunteers. Together they began the search for principles, teaching strategies, teaching styles, and methods that would harness this musical power and convert it into a practical educational tool. They hoped to find the connection between the ear that hears; the body that performs, feels, and senses; and the brain that judges, imagines, and corrects. The principles and methods they developed were so original that they were given their own special name: in Europe, "Le Rythme"; in Asia, "Dalcroze-Rhythmics"; and in Great Britain and North America, "Eurhythmics."

At the beginning of this work Jaques-Dalcroze thought that the solution to many rhythmic problems would be a simple matter of teaching students by training the muscles to contract or relax

1. at a specific time (the speed or tempo of a sound)
2. in a specific space (the duration of a sound)
3. with a particular force (the dynamic energy of a sound)

This was a new application of the laws of mechanics of motion discovered by Sir Isaac Newton. The innovation was in using Newton's laws to train the human body to perform rhythms accurately and comfortably by using correct proportions of time, space, and energy in a gravity field. It was a kind of rhythmic gymnastics leading to the law of least effort for greatest effect, which is basic to all the arts. Exercises in regulating hearing and body movement responses through knowledge of the rules of time–space–energy proportions, coupled with special gravity exercises in the use of weight and balance, became the basis for diagnosing rhythmic movement problems. Without this diagnostic knowledge the teacher and student could become discouraged by clumsy or inaccurate performance and even give up the quest for rhythmic development and freedom. When accuracy and comfort of body movement had been achieved, Jaques-Dalcroze worked out a new series of exercises designed to help students strengthen their feeling for metrics and their instinct for the many flows of motion called rhythm. He began by playing musical rhythms suggesting the motion of walking and asked his students to respond to what they heard by regulating the positions and movements of their walk to express the speed, the durations, and the accents they heard in the music. Surprisingly, even the most physically and intellectually gifted students did not all react the same way. There were immediate problems. Some students responded by moving too quickly;

some, too slowly. Some students performed well only at certain tempi and not at others. Many students performed well at moderate tempi, but had difficulty when asked to change to a faster or slower speed, in spite of their obvious desire to make the change. Students had difficulty remembering a tempo or a duration. Sometimes the students would begin a walking exercise smoothly and confidently, then suddenly become confused and unable to continue accurately.

Jaques-Dalcroze recognized that something was still missing from his method. He formulated the principle that real teaching begins when the student has a problem—all else is simply instruction. He was determined to find the missing link in the chain of responses that begins with listening and ends with moving. He realized that it was not enough to understand a rhythm or to have a muscular system capable of interpreting a rhythm. His students had both, but still had trouble reaching the goals of quick, accurate, economical, and expressive rhythmic performance. He realized that there must also be some system of rapid communication between the brain, which conceives and analyzes, and the muscles which perform—a feedback system to and from the brain, which studies the body's performance and sends information for correction.

Kinesthesia: The Missing Link

Jaques-Dalcroze now returned to his earlier speculations on the role of muscular sensations in rhythmic learning. He postulated that whenever the body moves, the sensation of movement is converted into feelings that are sent through the nervous system to the brain which, in turn, converts that sensory information into knowledge. The brain converts feelings into sensory information about direction, weight, force, accent quality, speed, duration, points of arrival and departure, straight and curved flow paths, placements of limbs, angles of joints, and changes in the center of gravity. The brain judges the information and issues orders to the body again through the nervous system. These orders are given to protect the organism from injury and to find the most effective ways to move through the mental phenomena of attention, concentration, memory, willpower, and imagination.

Today this process is called the *kinesthetic sense*. It combines with the other organs to convert sensation into information regarding feeling. This was precisely the tool Jaques-Dalcroze needed to help his students control the rapid communications between the exterior senses of hearing, seeing, touching, and moving and the hidden, interior activities of the brain which control memory, memory retrieval, judgement, willpower, and imagination. The child learning to roller-skate, the artist drawing from a model, the musician studying a score, and the athlete practicing a high jump are all using this same combination of moving–feeling–sensing: *kinesthesia*.

Jaques-Dalcroze now understood the chain of connections essential to the success of his methods. Hearing could be linked to moving; movement could invoke feeling; and feeling could trigger kinesthetic sensing to bring information directly to the brain and then back to the body via the nervous system. This brain connection would lead to the analytic process necessary to improve, correct, and perfect expressive performance and to read, write, and improvise music. In this way the exterior forces of the body and the interior processes of the brain could be harmonized and coordinated. The following diagram summarizes the kinesthetic processes:

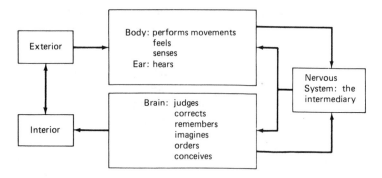

Jaques-Dalcroze's original discoveries regarding time–space–energy–balance (physiology and physics) could now be linked with kinesthesia and the training of feelings, emotions, and brain function (psychology). These basic connections of Jaques-Dalcroze's Method may be illustrated by the triangle

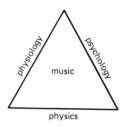

There was one major problem still to be resolved. Kinesthesia generally works on a subconscious level. One is seldom aware of the kinesthetic process during ordinary activities. One gets out of bed and walks; one bends over to pick up a piece of paper; one sings a tune or plays a piece without awareness of the connection between brain and body; one crosses a street, sees a car coming and decides to continue to walk, speed up, slow down, run, or stop; one moves through a room and, by subtle shifts of direction and balance, avoids bruises. These actions are improvised without conscious planning. All of these miracles of kinesthesia, movement, and rhythm that protect the organism from injury make life not only possible but also efficient and pleasurable. They are done without hard work or conscious reflection, imagination, or willpower. Such automatic responses are called *automatisms.*

The problem facing Jaques-Dalcroze was to make the students aware of the possibility of conscious control of their own kinesthesia. If he could teach them how to invoke and use their kinesthesia consciously, they would have all their faculties ready to work; they would be in a state of attention and concentration; they would be alerted to the slightest change in sound or rhythm; they would become aware of their own rhythms and the rhythms of others; they could consciously develop new responses or vary old ones; they could learn to put one rhythm "on automatic" while performing another consciously; they would become more aware of the differences between individual and ensemble performance; and they would be better able to solve the problems that arise when different people have different approaches to rhythmic movements that must be synchronized or harmonized by the group.

Through experimentation, and with the help of the Swiss psychologist Edouard Claparède,[8] Jaques-Dalcroze discovered the technique of *excitation and inhibition* in a constantly changing musical environment. This technique forces constant attention and creative improvised responses to musical changes and puts the kinesthetic process under the conscious control of the student. Together, Jaques-Dalcroze and Claparède formulated the primary goals of Eurhythmics training:

1. development of attention
2. conversion of attention to concentration
3. social integration (awareness of similarities and differences and appropriate responses between oneself and others)
4. responses to and expression of all nuances of sound–feeling

With these new goals added to the old, Jaques-Dalcroze realized that his training "in music by music" was more than a musical education. It was, in fact, a general education using music as a humanizing force. It was designed to teach students to use all of their faculties in solving problems. This aspect of the use of Eurhythmics as an educational force goes beyond music into the fields of therapy, rehabilitation, and special education. It also becomes valuable for the training of dancers, actors, athletes, poets, and painters. Perhaps this explains the wide differences of understanding, definition, range, interests, and goals of teachers using the methods of conscious kinesthesia invented by Jaques-Dalcroze. His methods are complementary to many other methods and fields of study.

After two years of experimentation, the methods, goals, principles, and techniques of Eurhythmics were finally put together.

SUMMARY OF THE GOALS OF
EURHYTHMICS

A. Mental and Emotional
1. awareness
2. concentration
3. social integration
4. realization and expression of nuances
B. Physical
1. ease of performance
2. accuracy of performance
3. personal expressiveness through performance, using the laws of

time—space—energy—weight—balance
gravity field

C. Musical: Quick, accurate, comfortable, expressive personal response to hearing, leading to performance, analysis, reading, writing, and improvising

---

[8]Founder of the Institut Jean-Jaques Rousseau for the study of child development, and teacher of Jean Piaget.

Jaques-Dalcroze and his associates had finally found the processes and methods that connected in a constant spiral of learning: hearing to moving; moving to feeling; feeling to sensing; sensing to analyzing; analyzing to reading; reading to writing; writing to improvising; and improvising to performance. In less than two years from the beginning of the experiments, the method was introduced into the regular curriculum of the Geneva Conservatory.

TECHNIQUES OF EURHYTHMICS

By 1905 Emile Jaques-Dalcroze had worked out thousands of exercises and games linking beautiful music, intense listening, and consciously improvised movement. By watching these movement responses, a well-trained teacher may observe the accuracy, personal expressive powers, and depth of the students' knowledge in the physical, mental, and emotional domains. The teacher may then respond to group or individual problems with appropriate activities and instruction to strengthen whichever areas—physical, mental, or emotional—need support.

The Use of Improvisation in Eurhythmics Classes

Jaques-Dalcroze himself improvised the music for the lessons he taught, and the best Eurhythmics teachers still use improvised music—vocal or instrumental—more often than composed music in the beginning stages of a lesson.[9] Improvisation allows the teacher to present one element or any combination of elements in serial order or in random combinations. It also permits the teacher the freedom to place rhythmic ideas in any style, any variety of phrase shapes, or with any variety of articulations of legato and staccato. Sudden stops and starts are used to obtain the quality of "effective surprise" within the lesson. This quality encourages both attention and creative action by promoting activity in a challenging and constantly changing musical environment. The use of improvised music enables the teacher to move gradually from simple to more complicated exercises as well as to vary the lesson plan at any point better to suit the students' needs. Improvised music also allows the teacher to present foreground and background information simultaneously and to permit the students to perceive, feel, and absorb the entire interaction going on in the music. In turn this helps students to grasp more complete information about musical relationships. In contrast, when using composed music the musical forces are already in place and the rhythmic, melodic, and harmonic forces are already in complex interactions.

Composed music is often used in later lessons, after principles and elements of music have been studied. However, in the early stages of learning, improvised music based on the element being studied is the most important teaching material, since it encourages personal and expressive application of the students' knowledge as well as the students' ability to make aesthetic judgments (such as "too long," "too short," "too loud," "too soft," or "just right") through their improvisational experiments.

[9]For specific improvisations see Tapes 1 and 2 of the cassette accompanying Robert M. Abramson, *Rhythm Games for Perception and Cognition* (Hialeah, FL: Columbia Pictures Publications, 1978).

The Use of Movement in Eurhythmics

Unlike dance, in which movement is stylized and is used to portray the images and ideas of a dancer or choreographer, Jaques-Dalcroze and his students improvised unstylized movements, postures, and gestures to express the speeds, durations, dynamics, accents, and other elements which produce musical rhythm.

MOVEMENT VOCABULARY   The particular movement vocabulary used by Jaques-Dalcroze is understandable to most children and adults without special training. Movements are classified into two types:

MOVEMENTS IN PLACE	MOVEMENTS IN SPACE
Clapping	Walking
Swinging	Running
Turning	Crawling
Conducting	Leaping
Bending	Sliding
Swaying	Galloping
Speaking	Skipping
Singing	

With this vocabulary an almost infinite number of combinations can be created to express everything from the simplest to the most complex rhythmical time–space combinations and flow qualities. Movements in place or space can be combined with high, low, or middle body position in space to show changes of weight and height of sound as well as melodic contour. Different parts of the body may coordinate to demonstrate the same rhythm, or may "disordinate," using head, torso, arms, hands, feet, and voice independently, to perform counterpoints of two to six different rhythms simultaneously.

By adding gestures and postures to these movement combinations, the student can express melody, harmony, polyrhythms, counterpoint, and phrasing. By using other movements, varieties of dissonance and accent can be explored and expressed. In Eurhythmics the body is used as an orchestra to express physical, vocal, and instrumental rhythms.

MOVEMENT PROBLEMS   The idea of using body movement in *space–time* to express music in *time–space* was revolutionary at the time of Jaques-Dalcroze's experiments. Today this theory has been absorbed in music curricula throughout the world and is particularly evident in the methodologies of Carl Orff, Maria Montessori, and Zoltán Kodály.

The easy acceptance of Jaques-Dalcroze's ideas without adequate training in the techniques, principles, and philosophy underlying them has, however, created serious problems for some music teachers using movement as a vehicle for teaching ear training and rhythm. Teachers who are trained in Jaques-Dalcroze techniques are able to observe, understand, and respond skillfully to problems of body-technique and of the proper use of time–space–energy, weight, and balance which are vital to good movement and thus to good rhythmic performance. Teachers who use movement but lack a clear understanding of Jaques-Dalcroze's methods in finding solutions to movement problems may unknowingly force their students into embarrassing, self-consciously inhibited, clumsy, and unsuccessful movement activities. This unfortunate result may occur despite the students' love of music and deep feeling for rhythm.

It is the walking and clapping exercises that Jaques-Dalcroze invented that have entered the general practice of music teaching but which are now often used ineffectively. The untrained teacher frequently succeeds in producing a sensation of tactility (touch) instead of the necessary sensation of kinesthesia (rhythmic movement). Such a teacher assumes that the goal of the exercises is to produce a unison ensemble centered on movement at the attack of a beat (at the instant the foot touches the floor at the beginning of a walking step or at the instant that the hands touch in a clap). This error prevents the student from developing a clear kinesthetic feeling for the process of *preparation, attack,* and *prolongation* involved in the performance of each musical beat.

TOTALITY OF MOVEMENT EXPERIENCE   A total kinesthetic sensation must be invoked in every Jaques-Dalcroze movement experience. The sequence of response is always from preparation, to attack, to prolongation, and then return to preparation.

With such a simple movement in place as clapping, this sequence would involve

1. *Preparation*
   breathe, along with a lifting swing of the arms and shoulders away from the center of the body measuring the tempo (time–space) of the beat (inhaling)
2. *Attack*
   the instant of striking the hands together (exhaling)
3. *Prolongation*
   pulling the hands apart to feel and measure kinesthetically the full length of the beat
4. *Return to preparation*
   lifting the arms upward and outward and breathing (inhaling for recycling of energy)

Using this four-step cycle the teacher may create exercises and games that prepare the students smoothly and easily to perform beats in any tempo, any dynamic level, and with any change in the nuances of tempo or dynamics.

In walking exercises, too, it is important not to allow tactility to replace kinesthesia. The instant the foot touches the floor in a walking step is only the attack of the beat; it is not the real rhythmic sensation which occurs in and around the attack of the beat. A true kinesthetic response involves the transfer of weight felt in the body during walking. This weight transfer originates and carries through the preparation, attack, and prolongation of the walking step and is created by motion in the foot, ankle, knee, and hip joints and in the movements in the muscles of the trunk, thigh, calf, and foot. The teacher well trained in Jaques-Dalcroze techniques prepares students for good walking techniques and is aware that students who use their bodies poorly (with dragging or slapping feet, slouching posture, or lack of balance) will not receive the proper kinesthetic sensation of a walking rhythm in music and will probably have difficulty in expressing clearly what they hear and feel in music.

Jaques-Dalcroze was an acute observer of rhythmic movement in the world-at-large. Besides the larger rhythms of the body (breathing, heartbeats, sleep, and temperature cycles), he observed the rhythms of peoples, discerning a kind of common language of rhythmic style similar to the idea of *lingua franca* in language. He observed the rhythms of children at play, of adults at work, and even the rhythmic gestures that accompany human communication and interaction. All these movements became possibilities for the lessons of the Eurhythmics teacher. The rhythmic movements of nature found in changes of seasons, weather, and the great natural forces of wind, rain, the seas, and the planets, were studied in order to connect them to music and movement. Also studied and utilized in movement exercises were the natural rhythmic movements found in the lives of animals and plants. These latter, in the hands of inadequately trained teachers, have sometimes become exercises of a purely imitative nature: "be a bird, a butterfly, a wave, a leaf." There is no doubt that students and teachers find this kind of activity enjoyable, but, although it may lead to the development of imaginative movement and even of some body skills, there is the danger that the music will be used merely as an accompaniment rather than as the motivating force for the movement. Such a use of Eurhythmics does not necessarily contribute to the development of musical or mental skills. The imitation of nature and life has its purpose in song, dance, and rhythmic studies, but unless there is also attention to increased movement perception and ear training, and a connection to cognitive musical understanding, such exercises may become simple imitation rather than education.

The rhythms of the other arts of visual design, like architecture, painting, and sculpture, with their many rhythmic motions based on the play of light and shadow, weight and balance, surface and volume, line, shape, and color, and the counterpoint of movement between background, middleground, and foreground, are further possibilities for the Eurhythmics teacher. Poetry and dance offer other sources for different rhythms. Finally, the rhythms of mechanical objects, toys, and machines are another source of creative and imaginative movement. The Eurhythmics teacher is trained to observe and respond to all worlds of rhythm, movement, and music and to engage in a lifetime study of them.

The Development of Inner-Hearing

The next step in a program of Jaques-Dalcroze's Eurhythmics training is to foster in the students the ability to *internalize* feelings of movements and sounds. This is the area of Eurhythmics study that develops kinesthetic imagination and kinesthetic memory by encouraging students to store a vocabulary of movement feelings, images, and sounds. This special use of motion and sound sensing is one that enables a musician to perfect performance without playing an instrument. It allows the performer to imagine and visualize performance and to make the necessary corrections. Jaques-Dalcroze called this inner-hearing—the memory of muscular sensations.

Inner-hearing is achieved through a transfer from overt action to imagined action by successively imposed inhibitions of the overt action. At the simplest level it may be demonstrated as:

1. Clap a pattern aloud, move the body in space, speak or sing aloud, or any combination of these three.
2. Clap silently, move in space, hum quietly, or any combination.
3. Eliminate (inhibit) parts of the movement and parts of the sound, but feel and hear internally in proper time and space.
4. Inhibit all external sound and motion, but feel and hear inside the body.

Internal feeling and hearing are the final goals. In this training the student may learn to internalize beat, meter, rhythm, melody, and form.

5. Try to replace the silent activities by externalizing parts of the original pattern of movement and sound.
6. Perform more of the original pattern externally.
7. Perform all of the original pattern externally.

The last three steps encourage the student to use memory retrieval as a perfomance tool, so that automatic learning may be brought back to consciousness for immediate use or for further development.

CONTENT OF EURHYTHMICS

Rhythm is the central subject of each and every Eurhythmics lesson. In Jaques-Dalcroze's view rhythm is not simply timing but is the constantly changing flow of motion that gives vitality, color, and interest to the regular events—the beat—in Western music. Like an electric current of varying intensity, rhythmic movements may vary in qualities of tension and release between the two poles of nonmovement—total tension and total relaxation. Jaques-Dalcroze used the word *rhythm* to mean a balance and ratio of the flow among body, mind, and feelings, as well as a balance between conscious and unconscious movement. In his theory, rhythm *exists* in a time–space–energy context, but is *produced* by complicated interactions among many elements of motion. Sometimes these elements work together (for example, the beat and its subdivision) and sometimes they are in strong opposition (syncopation and polyrhythm). Sometimes several different layers of rhythm may produce extremely complex waves of motion.

As in spoken language, rhythmic movement may have particular nationalistic characteristics. Some cultures foster the development of complex rhythmic games in very young children; others engender strong feelings for regular, heavily accented, even plodding rhythmic games. Jaques-Dalcroze's theories encourage the study of music from around the world and facilitate the teaching of many different styles of rhythm. They encompass both measured and unmeasured rhythm, and they introduce ways of studying Eastern music, with its unequal beats and measures, and jazz and Afro-Cuban-influenced music, with their additive rhythms. The basis for all these studies is a list of the elements of rhythm. Any one of these elements may be used to build an infinite variety of lessons in a spiral plan moving from simple to more and more complex experiences. The teacher may combine elements to show how the individual elements affect each other in creating more complex qualities of musical expression.

The list that follows is not in any specific order of study. Any of the elements in the list can and should be made into experiences suitable for a child, teenager, or adult.

THE THIRTY-FOUR JAQUES-DALCROZE ELEMENTS OF RHYTHM

1. TIME–SPACE–ENERGY–WEIGHT–BALANCE   There is a special affinity between time and space in that slow tempi generally require large movements; moderate tempi, moderate movements; fast tempi, small movements. The application of different amounts of energy and weight to these tempi creates a rhythmic flow and plasticity of rhythmic expression.

2. REGULAR BEATS–EXTRINSIC FORMS (CRUSIC, METACRUSIC, AND ANACRUSIC QUALITIES)   Extrinsic beat occurs in music when the regular beat is very forcefully presented (for example, in rock music). Jaques-Dalcroze's theory of rhythmic beat qualities goes on to classify beats as the *crusic beat,* seen as a release of energy; the *metacrusic beat,* seen as a gentle carryover or a dying away; and the *anacrusic beat,* seen as a preparation of energy for release. Human breathing in a relaxed state is the ideal basis for an understanding of the anacrusic (inhaling), metacrusic (holding the breath), and crusic (exhaling) qualities of a beat. This is the three-beat norm of human respiration. (In a highly excited state only anacrusis and crusis exist.) In any Eurhythmics class these qualities should be expressed even in the simplest clapping and walking exercises. Attack, prolongation and decay, and renewal of beats should be carefully studied.

3. TEMPO   All tempi are studied and responded to with movement.

4. NUANCES OF TEMPO (ACCELERANDO AND RITARDANDO)   Nuances of tempo can be measured: for example, ♩♩♩ ♩ ♩ ♩ ♩♩ ♫♫ ♫♫ ♫♫ ♫♫ or unmeasured: for example, ♩ ♩. ♩ ♩ ♫♫ ♫♫♫
The most important aspect of their study is the development of memory of an original tempo and the ability to regain an original tempo after accelerandos and ritardandos. In movement, nuances of tempo are expressed by the size of the step or other motion.

5. DYNAMICS (ALL LEVELS OF ENERGY AND WEIGHT)   Stronger dynamic levels tend to be more exciting, weaker dynamic levels less so, and movement must reflect this. It is important to deal with dynamic excitement skillfully, without loss of rhythmic control.

6. NUANCES OF DYNAMICS (CRESCENDO, DIMINUENDO, SUBITO PIANO, SU-

BITO FORTE)   Nuances of dynamics involve the control of energy and feeling as well as the ability to excite or inhibit physical action.

7. ARTICULATION (STACCATO, LEGATO, PORTAMENTO; ATTACK, RELEASE, SUSTAIN; VIBRATO POSSIBILITIES)   Different parts of the body have characteristics suitable to the expression of different articulations: for example, flicking, swinging, smacking, batting, and punching are some simple possibilities of articulation of the arms, hands, shoulders, and torso. Articulation requires the exploration of many ways and places to begin a motion and many ways and places to connect or stop motions.

8. ACCENTS (METRIC, AGOGIC, DYNAMIC, TONIC, ORNAMENTAL, HARMONIC)   Accents release energy in different ways. Metric accents release energy on the first beats of meters. Agogic accents involve a difference of weight when

applied to sounds because of their position and duration: for example, ♪ ♩ ♪ . Dynamic accents are places of unusual emphasis. They may be shown by an accent mark or indicated by words such as tenuto, sforzando, rinforzando. Appoggiatura, mordents, trills, and similar embellishments, when used to emphasize notes, are considered ornamental accents. Accents are considered harmonic when they are created by the level of dissonance of a chord. There are many other types of accents whose different qualities allow for a great variety in rhythmic color.

9. MEASURE (SIMPLE, STRAIGHT; COMPOUND, CURVED)   Beats in simple meters are usually performed with parts of the body moving in straight lines. Often the subdivision of ♩ into ♪ ♩ can be suggested by bending a knee while walking or an elbow when conducting. Compound meters are always curved or circular. This roundness may be expressed in movements of hips, torso or arm swings. Beats have specific qualities and normative functions according to their place within a measure:

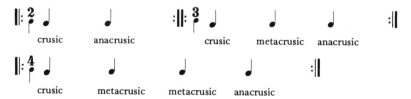

These qualities can be expressed in movement by the bend of a knee, a lift of the torso, or a step forward or backward. When clapping beats in measured form it is necessary to move the arms from left to right across the body to represent the place of each beat within the measure.

10. RESTS (ACTIVE SILENCE; QUALITIES OF SILENCE)   Rests always express inner activity. Although walking or clapping may cease, gestures of the face, shoulders, and torso may be used to express the different qualities pro-

duced by rests in different parts of a measure or pattern. The qualities range from violent rests producing syncopation to relaxing rests at the end of a phrase or period. The most important focus in the study of rests is to keep the beat internally while inhibiting outward motion.

11. DURATIONS (VARIATION OF LENGTH CREATED BY ADDITION) The quality of energy and weight must increase as sounds get longer. This produces the vivid shading of durations heard in the performance of fine artists. Without these nuances, the study of duration is reduced to timing, and becomes a mechanical experience instead of an aesthetic one.

12. SUBDIVISION In Eurhythmics, subdivision is first taught as a feeling experienced in changing the speed and quality of movement: for example, ♩ (walking) versus ♪♪ (running; twice as fast). In order to change from ♩ to ♪♪ and from ♪♪ to ♩ the student must be able to remember ♪♪ while doing ♩ . The careful measurement and adjustment of space to time is absolutely necessary. In compound meter the change of movement from ♩· to ♪♪♪ requires not only an adjustment from a larger to a smaller space but also the shaping of energy into a circular or curved path. In the performance of patterns requiring subdivision the student must learn quite early that subdivision of a beat produces a change not only in speed but also in lift, weight, and momentum (forward drive). The ability to change to any subdivision quickly and smoothly is a necessary and elemental skill.

13. PATTERNS Patterns are taught as constructions and applications of rhythmic elements. The position of a rhythmic element produces a change of meaning and, therefore, of expression. In this way the study of patterns becomes similar to the study of words in a language; certain placements of rhythmic elements become idiomatic forms of expression; for example, long durations at the ends of two-measure patterns produce phrasings and cadences

(⁴₄ ♩ ♩ ♩ ♩ | ♩ ♩ 𝅗𝅥 * |).

Rests on final beats (⁴₄ ♩ ♩ ♩ ♩ | ♩ ♩ ♩ 𝄽 * |)

or on first beats (⁴₄ ♩ ♪♪♩ ♩ | 𝄽 ♩ ♩ 𝄽 * |)

produce suspense. Subdivisions placed on final beats produce stronger anacrusic effects, a lifting feeling (| ♩ ♩ ♩ ♪♪ |).

There are specific rules of expression and phrasing for patterns involving anacrusic, metacrusic, and crusic forms of phrases.

14. INTRINSIC BEAT [EXTRACTING THE BEAT BACKGROUND FROM A PATTERN]   In art music the intrinsic or basic beat may be buried in a matrix of conflicting patterns. Locating and feeling the beat becomes a prime requirement for understanding these works, since the interplay between beat and meter is a very important process in this music. This analytic ability requires the skill to perform in movement a beat and a rhythmic pattern separately. Without constant attention to the measure and the beat there is difficulty in producing an authoritative sense of regularity. On the other hand, without equal attention to the nuances of rhythmic patterns there will be too little flow and vitality.

15. PHRASING   Patterns are joined to create phrases whose cadences are created by the appropriate placement of rests, accents, and durations. Crusic, metacrusic, and anacrusic forms of phrases are demonstrated. Both regular and irregular phrase lengths are studied. The ability to locate points of relaxation or arrest of motion in music is related to phrasing. Different kinds of phrase beginnings affect the continuity of movement.

16. ONE-VOICE FORMS (MOTIVE, PHRASE, PERIOD, THEME; THEME AND VARIATIONS; SONG AND DANCE PART-FORMS)   A movement study is made of two-, three-, and four-measure phrases, and balanced phrases which lead to periods. Periods are combined to produce simple binary and ternary forms with attention to the need for both unity and contrast. Forms are studied through movement before they are studied in music.

17. DIMINUTION   Students perform movements twice as fast, three times as fast, five times as fast, and so forth, in order to discover the effect of the diminution of time values.

18. AUGMENTATION   Students perform movements twice as slow, three times as slow, five times as slow, and so forth, in order to discover the effect of the augmentation of time values. The student's ability to perceive, imagine, and perform materials presented in formal tempo relationships leads to an understanding of the ways musicians may develop a basic idea. Thus

$\frac{4}{p}$ ♩ ♩ ♫ ♩ | can become $\frac{4}{p}$ ♪ ♪ ♬ ♪ | (diminution—twice as fast) or

$\frac{4}{p}$ 𝅗𝅥 𝅗𝅥 ♩ ♩ 𝅗𝅥 | (augmentation—twice as slow). In terms of movement, the

same basic rhythm may become a sprightly expression of joy or become grave and dignified.

19. RHYTHMIC COUNTERPOINT   The ability to perform two or more different patterns simultaneously while preserving their individual qualities and expressing the new qualities produced by their interaction is an extremely im-

portant study. The simplest exercises are contests in which the students maintain one pattern against the teacher's opposing ones. The teacher can add new and more challenging patterns as the game continues. Later, counterpoint is performed between two groups; then, in more advanced form, between a duet, trio, or quartet of students. More difficult versions of the same game involve speaking or singing well-known songs and accompanying the voice by counterpoints of clapping, playing percussion instruments, or walking.

20. SYNCOPATION (BY RETARDATION AND ANTICIPATION)   Syncopation can be described as an argument between a normal metric accent pattern and a pattern that begins too soon (anticipation) or too late (retardation):

Children play many games involving syncopation. Games of stepping on sidewalk cracks, hide and seek, hopscotch, and stepping stones involve changes from regular metric to antimetric movement. All such games require a good sense of physical and emotional balance. Easy quick-reaction games of clapping or speaking on beats, or of changing to clapping or speaking between beats, may be used to prepare syncopated behavior.

21. ONE-VOICE FORMS WITH ACCOMPANIMENT (WITH OSTINATO; WITH CONTRAPUNTAL ACCOMPANIMENT)   This is a more advanced study of rondo, phrase, period, and two- and three-part forms with the accompaniment of variable rhythmic counterpoints or simple counterpoint produced by ostinati techniques.

22. CONTRAPUNTAL FORMS (OSTINATO LAYERS; OSTINATO ACCOMPANIMENT WITH VARIATIONS: CHACONNE, PASSACAGLIA, MEDIEVAL AND BAROQUE DANCE VARIATIONS)   Groups of students invent, perform, and develop their own patterns based on forms in two, three, four, or more ostinati performed simultaneously to create layers over a beat given by the teacher. Various groups must be prepared to trade-off patterns upon command. The chaconne and passacaglia dance forms use a repeated bass ostinato, usually four to eight measures long, against continuous variations of the upper voices. Students perform movement improvisations in these and other dance forms.

23. CANON (INTERRUPTED; CONTINUOUS)   In the interrupted canon the teacher performs a pattern and then waits for the students to echo it, clapping or moving. The teacher then continues with a new pattern. In the continuous canon a leader performs uninterrupted rhythmic patterns of movements or sounds or both. The group follows at a specified distance, usually at either two or four beats after the leader.

24. FUGUE   Fugue is taught in advanced classes. Starting with two- and three-part invention forms, the students move to fugues, mixing strict canonic movement imitation with episodes of free rhythmic movement counterpoint.

25. COMPLEMENTARY RHYTHMS   The word "complementary" in this sense means "to complete." If the original rhythm is

♩   ♩ ♩ (positive space–time),

its complement might be

𝄽 ♪ ♫ 𝄽 ♪ 𝄽 ♪ (negative space–time).

In these exercises the original rhythmic pattern is performed by one part of the body and the complementary pattern by the voice or some other body part. The complement always follows the initial attack of the original pattern and is never simultaneous. Duration by space–size of movement is most important.

26. UNEQUAL MEASURES $\left(\dfrac{3+2+4+6+5}{\text{♩}}\right)$

Study of music with unequal measures provides entrance to a wide variety of styles ranging from Gregorian chant to the dance and song of eastern Europe. The preparation for these studies starts with quick-reaction games in perceiving and performing differences between series of accented and unaccented beats, then mixing $\frac{2}{4}$ and $\frac{4}{4}$ measures. A $\frac{5}{4}$ measure may be performed as $\frac{3}{4} + \frac{2}{4}$,

$\frac{3}{4} + \frac{2}{4}$, $\frac{4}{4} + \frac{1}{4}$, $\frac{1}{4} + \frac{4}{4}$ or $\frac{1}{4} + \frac{1}{4} + \frac{1}{4} + \frac{1}{4} + \frac{1}{4}$, using arm swings to study the changes in weight and balance produced by these asymetries. The iambic pen-

tameter $\frac{5}{4}$ ♪ | ♩ ♪♩ ♪♩ ♪♩ ♪♩ :‖ , so common in ordinary English

sentences, rhythms, and familiar from the poetry of Shakespeare, is an interesting model for studies in unequal measures.

27. UNEQUAL BEATS $\left(\frac{2}{4} + \frac{2}{4}. + \frac{2}{4} + \frac{2}{4}. + \frac{2}{4}\right)$ Here the measures are

equal but the beat unit is unequal. Unequal beats are common in the music of Latin America and are found in the music of North Africa, the Middle East, the

Caribbean, and in American jazz. Such rhythms are built on the principle of a fast *chronos* (or beat subdivision) as a basis for forming beats of different lengths by addition: for example, ♩ ♩ ♩ | ♩. ♩. ♩. |. In jazz the form is most frequently mixtures of ♩. and ♩ : (notation). In

Latin-American music it looks like this: (notation).

Although these rhythms look difficult in notation (Western notation does not express these motions easily), they are easy to study by returning to the original exercises of duration by addition, and practicing changes through a replacement exercise.

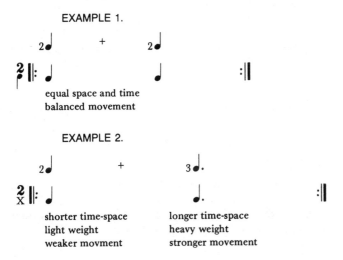

EXAMPLE 1.

equal space and time
balanced movement

EXAMPLE 2.

shorter time-space
light weight
weaker movment

longer time-space
heavy weight
stronger movement

(Here and in the next example, X = changing beat. This symbol is one of Jaques-Dalcroze's original contributions to rhythmic theory.)

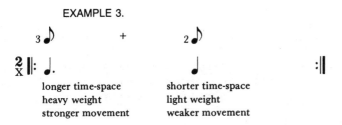

EXAMPLE 3.

longer time-space
heavy weight
stronger movement

shorter time-space
light weight
weaker movement

28. UNEQUAL MEASURES AND UNEQUAL BEATS   The combination of the above two rhythmic elements—unequal measure and unequal beat—exists in the

rhythms of the Far East, particularly India, and also in some contemporary Western music.

29. POLYMETRICS Polymeters combine two different meters simultaneously:

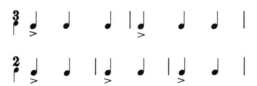

This in turn produces the crossing of accent patterns. This effect is typified by ragtime and other forms of jazz. The first movement of the Beethoven's *Symphony No. 3* (The "Eroica") also offers an example of polymeter.

30. POLYRHYTHMICS Polyrhythmics—2 against 3, 3 against 2, 3 against 4, 4 against 3, and so forth,—are created when straight simple meter and curved compound meter patterns in two different tempi occur simultaneously. Children unconsciously perform polyrhythms between the upper and lower parts of the body (for example, bouncing a ball and walking; walking while picking flowers or berries).

31. HEMIOLA Hemiola occurs in many forms, but it is most easily seen as a play of metrics and tempo proportions: really sounds like . Hemiola is common in early English madrigals and songs and in Baroque dances, both in the music and the dance step. For example, in a minuet:

music

dance

Hemiola is found also in the music of Brahms and in certain folk music.

32. RHYTHMIC TRANSFORMATION Rhythmic transformation is the changing of rhythm from simple to compound meter, producing a shift of accent and a quality change from straight to curved motion. For example, when changes to , the accents change as well as the

quality of flow, which changes from a straight line $\left(\begin{smallmatrix} 3 \\ \flat \end{smallmatrix}\right)$ to the curved flow of $\begin{smallmatrix} 2 \\ \flat \end{smallmatrix}$.

This effect is very common in French music of the late-nineteenth and early-twentieth centuries and in folk songs and dances of Hispanic cultures.

33. DIVISIONS OF TWELVE   By grouping or regrouping into divisions of twelve, one can better study possible shifts of beat and meter and more easily see the effect of performing two or more of the divisions together. The shifts of beat and meter available are:

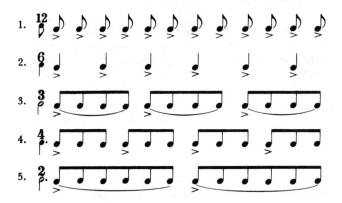

The never-changing *chronos* $\left(\begin{smallmatrix} \eighthnote \end{smallmatrix}\right)$ is equal in all measures and must be maintained in spite of changes of unit, measure length, or placements of anacrusic, metacrusic, or crusic beats.

34. RUBATO   Rubato is the lengthening or shortening of rhythmic values of a musical pattern for expressive purposes while continuing to maintain a steady beat. Use of rubato also involves the ability to vary lengths of beats and rhythmic patterns and still arrive at important harmonic cadences in tempo. For example:

JAQUES-DALCROZE'S CONTRIBUTION TO RHYTHMIC THEORY

A major problem in teaching rhythm is the lack of a strong unifying theory of rhythmics, which would account for the differences in quality and usage of rhythm between the Eastern and Western musical worlds, a theory which could help to explain differences in rhythmic style among various historical periods of music, and, finally, a theory which could help performers translate symbols on a page into expressive performance.

After studying the work of Jaques-Dalcroze, one may postulate that there are really five different worlds of rhythm.

1. THE WORLD OF NONMETRIC RHYTHMS   This consists of nonmetric chant and recitative in which the tempo or beat is provided by words and sylla-bles, and measurement is provided by syllable, word, phrase, or sentence. Rhyth-mic cadences are produced either by an introduction of a long sound followed by a breath or by a rest during which the singer breathes. Nonmetric works may be performed by a single group or by two groups antiphonally. Gregorian chant, some unaccompanied folk songs, and Hebraic cantillation are examples of nonmetric rhythms.

2. THE WORLD OF METRIC RHYTHMS   In metric rhythms beats can be subdivided into any number of smaller parts. Durations are derived from a long beat and are divided into smaller units: for example,

Harmonic or contrapuntal rhythms combine to produce homophonic, poly-phonic and heterophonic rhythmic textures. Examples of this rhythmic world may be found in classical art songs, symphonies, dance, music, and most accom-panied folk music of Western Europe.

3. THE WORLD OF ADDITIVE RHYTHMS   Additive rhythms are based on a short, fast beat called the *chronos protos*. The *chronos* is used to create different groupings and different-sized beats by addition instead of division. For example,

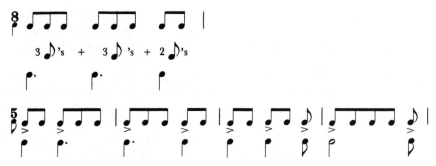

In art music some examples are *Jamaican Rumba,* by Arthur Benjamin; *Scaramouche,* by Darius Milhaud; and *El Salón México,* by Aaron Copland.

4. THE WORLD OF UNEQUAL MEASURES   In unequal measures the beat unit remains regular but the measuring of the beats changes. The constantly changing primary accent produces a quality of elasticity in the music. For example,

This world of rhythm is found in Eastern Europe, the Near East, and in contemporary Western art music. Some works that contain unequal measures are the *Douze Préludes* of Debussy; *Rumanian Dances for Piano* and *Divertimento for Strings,* by Bartók; and *The Rite of Spring,* by Stravinsky.

5. THE WORLD OF UNEQUAL BEATS   In this, a measure always contains the same number of beats but the size of the beat itself varies. This produces an effect similar to a rubato. Examples of this are found in the music of India, the Far East, and in the music of Olivier Messiaen, Ursula Mamlock, and others.

Each of these five worlds of rhythm can exist independently, although the Western music of the late-nineteenth and the early-twentieth centuries combines many of them. For performers trained in metrics—Western notation, which was devised essentially to express the second world of rhythm (metrics)—the notation of the other worlds of rhythm is often difficult to read and interpret. This is the reason for the difficulty a classically trained musician may encounter in translating notation of a jazz piece into correct performance, or the difficulty an ethnomusicologist may have in correctly notating an authentic version of certain national folk idioms.

SOLFÈGE–SOLFÈGE-RYTHMIQUE AND IMPROVISATION

Although the name Jaques-Dalcroze has come to be associated with the word "Eurhythmics," the Swiss pedagogue's method is actually a tripartite one, involving not only Eurhythmics but also *Solfège–Solfège-Rythmique* and Improvisation. The first aspect has been touched upon in the description of Eurhythmics: the ears and the body are used as the natural instruments for the study of rhythmic movement.

The second aspect of Jaques-Dalcroze's triad is his *solfège–solfège-rythmique*. This part of his method consists of thousands of graded and sequential exercises for the study of the theory and practice of scales, modes, intervals, melody, harmony, modulation, counterpoint, and vocal improvisation.[10] Through these the student is offered guidelines for choosing phrasings, dynamics, accents, and the other elements of musical expression.

Just as Eurhythmics suggests the ear and body as ideal instruments for the study of rhythm, *Solfège* suggests the ear and body combined with the speaking and singing voice as the ideal instruments for the study of musical tone, tonal combinations, and tonal relationships.

Solfège

All the pedagogical principles and techniques he discovered in Eurhythmics Jaques-Dalcroze reapplied to the study of sight-singing and ear training.

Special exercises for the development of perfect pitch,[11] accurate hearing, and refined intonations were combined with exercises in mental and musical alertness, concentration, and memory. Further exercises were given for the development of skills in breathing, postural balance, and muscular relaxation, which are required for good singing, as well as exercises to develop the visual skills required for quick musical reading and comprehension.

STAFF NOTATION AND READING   The beginning of Jaques-Dalcroze's *Solfège* is rooted in the study of staff notation. A one-line staff is used first to present ways of naming notes by speaking and singing syllables. For example,

The student studies the possibilities of *do* as a line or space note and the way notes are named in ascending or descending order. At first, notes are read with equal duration. Then the teacher introduces rhythms by pointing to the notes at different speeds. To develop visual and mental skills the teacher may use a pointer to repeat, omit, or change the reading direction (left to right; right to left).

The skill of reading leger lines is developed very early by erasing parts of the long line of the staff and interpreting the result as fragments of the original staff. For example,

[10]The following books of exercises were written by Jaques-Dalcroze: *L'Étude de la Portée Musicale* (Lausanne: Jobin, n.d.); *Solfège-Rythmique* (Lausanne; Jobin, n.d.); *Les Gammes, Les Tonalités, Le Phrase et less Nuances,* 3 vols. (Lausanne: Jobin, n.d.).

[11]Jaques-Dalcroze proved in his studies with children that perfect pitch can be acquired if instruction begins early enough and before a child begins the study of an instrument.

MOVABLE CLEF CONCEPTS The principles of clef reading are introduced quite early by naming any line or space on the staff *do, fa,* or *sol.* For example, read

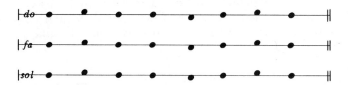

The children first practice naming lines and spaces on a two-line staff, and next on a two-line staff with rhythm. For example, read with syllables

Finally, the three clefs are presented to replace *do, fa,* and *sol,* and the three-, four-, and five-line staves are introduced:

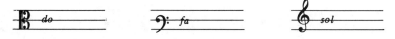

SCALES AS THE SOURCE OF MELODY In the sight-reading and dictation exercises of his *Solfège,* Jaques-Dalcroze used diatonic and chromatic *solfa* syllables to denote exact pitch (with C as *do*), roman numerals to identify position and function of a succession of pitches, and arabic numerals to indicate specific pitch within a scale. For example,

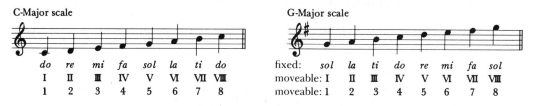

C-Major scale

do	re	mi	fa	sol	la	ti	do
I	II	III	IV	V	VI	VII	VIII
1	2	3	4	5	6	7	8

G-Major scale

fixed:	sol	la	ti	do	re	mi	fa	sol
moveable:	I	II	III	IV	V	VI	VII	VIII
moveable:	1	2	3	4	5	6	7	8

The C-Major scale is presented first as the "ideal" melody. It is sung with syllables and numbers. The student is then taught the order of whole steps and half steps:

Rhythms using 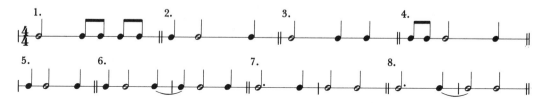, and are then added in order to practice the articulation of the syllables in increasingly fast tempi. Hand signals, body gestures, and conductor's arm beats are used with these exercises to coordinate aural and muscular sensations. The C-Major scale is then sung using specific rhythms to explore the process by which a scale may be changed into melody:

All major scales are used for singing these rhythms.

To accommodate children with limited vocal range, Jaques-Dalcroze suggested singing the scale in a range surrounding the key note rather than

from tonic to tonic. Using the rhythm pattern and the scale of A♭-Major, for example, an exercise might be constructed as follows:

etc.

MUSICAL INTERPRETATION

Phrasing, Nuance, and Expression

Principles of musical interpretation are always presented with melodies to illustrate their application:

1. Ascending melodies, with few exceptions, ought to be sung with a crescendo:

2. Descending melodies, with few exceptions, ought to be sung with a diminuendo:

The students study, conduct, and sing written melodies containing the

symbols   *(cresc.)*   and   *(dim.)*   in appropriate places in order to translate an image into accurate physical and musical expression. Since there are no words to the melodies given by Jaques-Dalcroze, students have to choose phrasing, nuance, and expression without the aid of a text. This increases the students' understanding of music as a language in its own right, and produces a musicianship applicable to students of voice or of any instrument.

As an assessment task, students are required to place the proper symbols in melodies from which they have been omitted; then the students perform their own completed versions.

Numbered Melodies

In order to help students to hear and remember the position of each tone in the scale as well as the relationships among various tones, they may be given a melody written with roman numerals representing scale tones. For example:

As training progresses through the circles of 5ths and 4ths, this same exercise will be resung in all the major and minor keys by translating the roman numerals into syllables or letter names of the new keys.

Scales, Tonalities, Intonation, and Hearing

Starting with all the conventional notions of Major-scale construction in whole- and half-steps from tonic to tonic, and the usual method of naming scales by syllable, roman numerals, and function names (tonic, dominant, mediant, and so forth), Jaques-Dalcroze noted several problems with the conventional methods and proposed some solutions.

Among the problems he noticed in his young students were a lack of feeling about tonal attraction and resolution and a tendency to wander from key to key. He noticed also that when Major scales were taught from tonic to tonic, they were experienced only as transpositions of the same simple melody. Moreover, some scales could not be experienced through singing because they extended beyond the students' vocal range.

These problems lead to difficulties in hearing the differences among the tonalities and in perceiving the relationship between one tonality and another. He felt that although tonic-to-tonic scale position brought a certain sense of security to very elementary study, it hindered the students' perceptions of the changes in gravity and posture when a melody began or ended on a tone of the scale other than the tonic. He proposed a solution to resolve the difficulties of experiencing, comparing, and measuring all the Major scales, while keeping all of them within a comfortable singing range. His method of fixed-*do* scales used the C-Major scale melody as the norm to which all other scales were compared. The C-Major scale (from middle C to the C above) became the frame which contained the C-Major, as well as all the other scales.

The system he invented may be used to

1. Compare differences between tonalities:

2. Find relationships between tonalities:

3. Develop a feeling for dominant motion, leading to a strong feeling for the tonic by accenting tones 2, 4, 5, 7.

Accompany throughout with V7 chord in the key of G.

4. Explain modulation:

5. Explain the harmonic difference in function when the same notes of a harmony are reinterpreted as tonic, dominant, subdominant, or other:

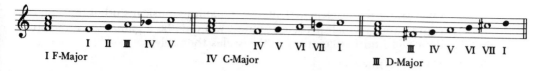

I F-Major   IV C-Major   III D-Major

6. Prepare the ear, eye, and voice to make quick changes from half- to whole-step at any moment and to define the result in any tonality:

C-Major   G-Major

In actual practice, the use of C-Major as a melodic measuring device is quite simple. The teacher sings the scale of C-Major, and then the intervals within that octave are altered by singing the scale of G-Major from C to C.[12] The students examine the differences in sound color and feel of the two scales and notice two important events: first, the lack of an ending in the G-Major scale and the need to ascend or descend to G to finish the melody; second, that the subdominant in C-Major has changed and become the leading tone in G-Major. The students sing the C-Major and then the G-Major scales, completing each with its appropriate tonic. The teacher may then sing melodies without a resolution and have the students finish the melody, determine the tonic, and name the scale. Jaques-Dalcroze asserted that within a few months of such practice students could determine the key of any melody in a major scale.

Students are introduced to modulating melodies through the simple device of joining one scale to another:

I   C-Major   Db-Major   I

Jaques-Dalcroze believed that children are not only creative, but also discerning, and capable of making intelligent and selective aesthetic judgments. He believed that teachers should, therefore, avoid presenting only the simplest materials, materials that tend to dull the glories of musical feelings and to hide the deep truths about music which children are capable of experiencing.

Syllables and Numbers

Jaques-Dalcroze used fixed-*do* syllables to present exact pitch and roman numerals to express their movable functions. He viewed scales as ideal melodies through which to explain all the processes of music. He felt that they offered a rational method for naming and classifying musical phenomena:

[12]In both scales the appropriate V_7 chord is emphasized by small accents on tones II, IV, and VII to exert maximum tonal pull. (These rhythmic accents prevent the scales from being perceived as a lydian mode on C.)

Once the scales are learned, all the remaining musical studies (except, of course, those which involve rhythm) will only be a game, since the student will find explanation in the scales themselves.

What are intervals?

They are simply fragments of scales with the interruptions of intermediary sounds.

What are chords?

They are only a superposition of the notes of a scale.

What are resolutions?

Simply the satisfaction given to suspended notes of a scale in order to continue their movement.

What is modulation?

The linking of one scale to another.

Everything which concerns melody and harmony is implicitly contained in the study of scales and is no more than a question of terminology and classification.[13]

Solfège, Tonality, Nuance, Phrasing

THE DIVISION OF THE SCALES.   Just as Jaques-Dalcroze realized that a lack of rhythmic theory in Western music prevented a rational approach to rhythmic training, so too he realized that the lack of a coherent theory of melody was preventing a rational and thorough pedagogy of melody. In order to help his students understand the way in which single scale tones could be combined to become melodic *cells,* he developed a technique which would compel the eyes to read, the ears to hear, and the brain to respond to meaningful groupings of several tones at a time rather than one tone at a time. These cells were created by dividing major scales into conjunct note groups with two, three, four, and five members. Two-note cells are called dichords, three-note cells are trichords, four-note cells are tetrachords, and five-note cells are pentachords.

DICHORDS.   Starting with the C-Major scale, Jaques-Dalcroze demonstrated how two adjacent notes could become the basic cells of a melody.[14]

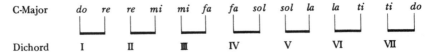

The students read, analyze, sing, and write melodies after studying the size of the dichords (major or minor) and the characteristics of their motion

---

[13]*Les Gammes, Les Tonalités, Le Phrase et les Nuances,* vol. I.

[14]These exercises, with dichords, trichords, and so on, may also be performed with movable-*do* syllables. Many exercises from *Solfège-Rythmique* and the other books cited have been incorporated into the Kodály Method in the works of E. Hegyi and E. Szönyi. The idea of scale segmentation may also be seen in Kodály training in the groupings of the tones of the pentatonic modes: for example, *sol-mi, sol-la.*

(resolving, requiring resolution, or cadencing). They also improvize melodies

1. with linked dichords: for example,

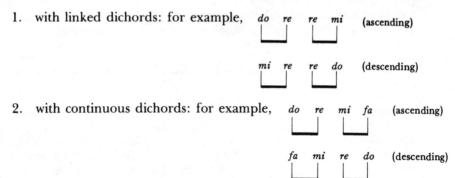

| | do | re | re | mi | | (ascending) |

| | mi | re | re | do | | (descending) |

2. with continuous dichords: for example,

| | do | re | mi | fa | | (ascending) |

| | fa | mi | re | do | | (descending) |

Finally, ascending and descending forms are combined into new melodic shapes:

for example, *do re re do fa mi re do*. The student now has

the pieces with which to construct melodies in all these forms.

TRICHORDS. These melodic cells are formed from three conjunct degrees of a scale. In the major scale they come in two sizes:

do re mi = major

re mi fa = minor

mi fa sol = minor

and in three shapes:

do re mi = whole step + whole step = major

re mi fa = whole step + half step = minor

mi fa sol = half step + whole step = minor

The students sing melodies based on trichords in conjunct, linked, continuous, and disjunct motions, and practice singing trichords in all scale degrees and in all keys.

CHROMATIC SCALE.   After much study of the diatonic forms of dichord and trichord, students are introduced to the concept of chromaticism and are led to distinguish between diatonic and chromatic half steps. Again, Jaques-Dalcroze uses the ascending diatonic scale as the reference and students are led

to discover the chromatic dichords between I and II ♩♩♩ as ♩♩♩♩ . It is

do - re   do do♯ re

important that the chromatic half step be on a weak beat. This aids in identifying the C♯ as a passing motion and not as a tone functioning as a leading tone of D-Major. The student then works in the same fashion with tones II, III, IV, V, VI, and VII and discovers that the dichord III cannot be filled with a chromatic half step. These experiences lead to the discovery of the chromatic scale.

PENTACHORDS AND HEXACHORDS.   Rhythmic groupings of these five- and six-note cells produce varieties of harmonies. Pentachords, when split into trichords, produce triads, and pentachords starting on various degrees of the scale produce different triads: for example

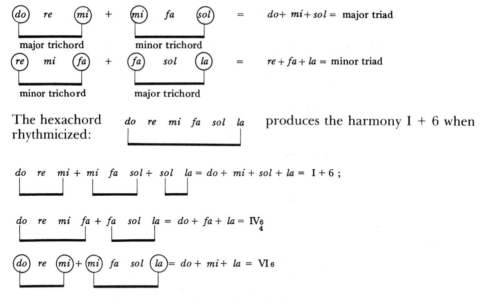

The hexachord rhythmicized: do re mi fa sol la   produces the harmony I + 6 when

do   re   mi + mi   fa   sol + sol   la = do + mi + sol + la = I + 6 ;

do   re   mi   fa + fa   sol   la = do + fa + la = IV$_4^6$

do   re   mi + mi   fa   sol   la = do + mi + la = VI$_6$

Building hexachords on other degrees of the scale produces new harmonies.
    By finishing with seven-note groups (heptachords) and their division into different varieties of trichords, the stage is set for the study of harmony and the various minor scales.
    Jaques-Dalcroze arrives at analysis and synthesis of harmony by using the various cells of the major scale to produce all kinds of triads and all the varieties of seventh chords. Students are taught to construct melodies on harmonies and to sing, read, write, and improvise with this material.

Solfège-Rythmique

Jaques-Dalcroze felt that the subject of rhythm was largely ignored in the existing texts on musical reading and writing:

> . . . other methods of solfège teach the rules of pitch, meter, intonation, and color, but do not introduce the subject of rhythm itself; nor do they deal with the relationship of rhythm to meter, dynamics, and melody.
>
> . . . most theorists concede that there is a distinction between meter and rhythm but they do not emphasize the distinction clearly enough.
>
> The study of rhythm necessitates a whole series of special bodily experiences (Eurhythmics) which form an indispensible basis for rhythmic manifestations on intellectual, sensory, and emotional levels. These experiences have been discussed thoroughly in my works on Rhythmics.[15]

With Eurhythmics experience assumed as a background, Jaques-Dalcroze devised a method for transforming all of the physical practices of Eurhythmics into equivalent experiences of vocal and instrumental sight reading. All of the techniques of Eurhythmics—excitation and inhibition, quick-response replacement of one value in a series of values—were translated into exercises to train students in reading, thinking, singing, or playing instruments.

Jaques-Dalcroze gave a total of 100 melodies and 450 exercises in the twenty-four chapters of his *Solfège-Rythmique*. These melodies, however, are not intrinsic to the method. The teacher may substitute scales; folk, popular, or classical music; or improvised melodies with equal effectiveness. The same melody may be used for hundreds of rhythmic exercises because each exercise transforms the original melody through infinite rhythmic and metric variations into a new melody containing the seeds of new ideas, problems, and solutions. Each exercise is a challenge to the students to pay attention, to develop concentration, to express changes of feelings, to maintain balance and poise, and to negotiate quick and accurate responses in order to produce the clearest effect with the least amount of effort.

The exploration and application of techniques of rhythmic variation to a simple melody or scale throughout the *Solfège-Rythmique* are the foundation for the development of imagination, and the groundwork for developing the musical analysis skills necessary to improvise music with the same ease as speaking one's mother tongue.

IMPROVISATION

Improvisation is the third and final part of Jaques-Dalcroze's complete method. Its goal is to produce skillful ways of using movement materials (rhythm) and sound materials (pitch, scale, harmony) in imaginative, spontaneous, and personally expressive combinations to create music.

THE TOOLS The tools of improvisation may be movement, speech, story, song, percussion, strings, winds, piano, or all of these combined.

[15]Emile Jaques-Dalcroze, *Solfège-Rythmique* (Lausanne: Jobin, n.d.).

THE HUMAN IMPETUS TO IMPROVISE   The beginnings of improvisation may come from the transformation of a spoken story into movement and sound, or the reverse, the transformation of movement and sound into poetry and story.

An improvisation can be built from movement, stories, poetry, noises, musical sounds, or even visual images. The driving force for motivating improvisation is limited only by a teacher's imagination and courage. An improvisational approach in the hands of a well-trained teacher allows for individual attention to discoveries made by students. It enables the teacher to find ways of expressing particular interests at various levels of musical sophistication. Any musical idea can be demonstrated in its simplest, most primitive form or in its most highly developed artistic form. Improvisational teaching allows the teacher to shift ideas and materials rapidly in response to student needs.

IMPROVISATION AND TEACHER TRAINING   The teacher of Jaques-Dalcroze's method must be trained to create and develop many variations of materials, techniques, exercises, and games through improvisation. The teacher must become a creative artist and a model of artistry for the students. Of course, to be able to teach in this way demands special training. The most important abilities developed in Jaques-Dalcroze training are the abilities to

> mirror movements exactly in improvised speech, song, sound, percussion, recorder, piano, and so forth
>
> accompany any movements, using the same tools
>
> analyze and perform the underlying meter and beats of given rhythmic movements
>
> express the varieties of dynamics in a flow of movement
>
> express the articulation and phrasing of any movement (legato, staccato, portamento)

The teacher must also be trained to tell a story, accompanying and illustrating it with clear, emotional, improvised musical expression, or, conversely, to improvise a piece of music while also improvising a story to fit the emotional, musical, and rhythmic content of a lesson.

The teacher must learn to use simple percussion instruments in extremely artistic ways. Even a drum or a rattle must be played with authority and sensitivity, so that the sound and message are never merely noisemaking. The teacher must also receive special training in ensemble percussion improvisation; in instrumental duets, trios, and quartets; and in choruses and orchestras with and without a conductor.

Since the art of gesture and movement is so important in Jaques-Dalcroze classes, learning how to direct an improvisation is most crucial, as is developing the ability to change gears quickly from being a director to being a follower in an improvisation. The twofold goal of improvisation training is the same for teacher and student: to develop the ability to express quickly and clearly ideas and feelings about any musical subject or combination of subjects, and to combine this ability with the ability to transform other people's music into lively, recreative performance.

At the highest level, Jaques-Dalcroze teachers are expected to be able to improvise in the styles of different composers, showing how the choice of materials, forms, and variational processes reflects the improviser's sensitivity to national qualities of language, religion, dance, and social organization;

develop one small musical pattern into a long and fully developed sonata or fugal movement;

remember and reproduce an improvisation after its first performance.

By mastering improvisational techniques, teachers develop the courage to explore new dimensions in their innate musicality. This, in turn, makes it possible for them to help their students to discover new dimensions in their musical personalities. Above all, teachers learn to balance the need for structure with the need for freedom of investigation, exploration, and expression.

Much musical training consists of perfecting performance by a stop–correct–replay–go-on style. Getting the correct notes, accents, and phrasing are the most important goals. Most students who have been trained this way have difficulty in being playful with and about music. Improvisational training supplies the hidden but necessary side of performance that prizes the ability to keep going, to make good use of unexpected accidents and changes in plan. Improvisational ability encourages spontaneity of expression in performance. It makes possible a balance between perfecting and letting go, between impulse and thought.

USE OF IMPROVISATION IN THE CLASSROOM   Students use improvisation in every lesson in many ways. They improvise movement expressions to demonstrate what they hear. They use speech, clapping, song, and percussion to develop and play with the ideas and materials of the lesson. If the early part of the lesson focuses on analysis by ear, body, and eye, the end of the lesson is often centered on a synthesis through improvised performance. Thus, improvisation is practiced in some form throughout the lesson. In more advanced lessons, rhythm and pitch are combined in increasingly complex variations of musical grammar and syntax, leading to studies of variations of phrases and periods. In turn, these lead to the simpler sectional forms (two-part, three-part, and compound song and dance forms); then to the rondo and theme and variations; and finally to the larger forms of sonata and concerto. Later, more sophisticated improvisations are made, combining rhythm and pitch; and finally, students progress to instrumental improvisation on recorders, strings, and piano.

Through these studies in improvisation, artistic impulses are released, and materials from the lesson are vitalized so that students can understand how life experiences may be converted into artistic impulses. In more controlled improvisation, students learn how the artist selects, varies, develops, and finishes musical materials.

Often the first steps in a beginner's improvisation are simple and amusing; like children's drawings, this simplicity may be fresh and charming. In music these "delightful accidents" due to inexperience will be enjoyed by teachers who have learned to control their anxiety so that they do not stand in the way of the students' development. The teacher's ability to be relaxed about errors while analyzing the reasons for the errors is very important. In this way the teacher can improvise techniques or methods to help the students gain more skill, without suppressing natural inventiveness. It is just as important to be patient with a child's first expression of musical language as it is to be patient with a child's early attempts at speaking, writing, reading, drawing, or painting.

In beginning improvisation, beat and tempo can help hold solo or group efforts together. In young children without special training, feeling for meter may vary widely or even be nonexistent. The temptation of the teacher to "make things fit" by insisting on evenness when evenness and regular proportions are not called for is very destructive. On the other hand, when accurate demonstration of meter is required, it should be worked on for perfection.

TECHNIQUES OF EXPERIMENTAL IMPROVISATION   In Jaques-Dalcroze's writings the practice and process of experimental improvisation is used first to invoke and later to strengthen the imagination. For the beginning student it is an ideal way to start the study of the elements of music theory; for the advanced student or professional musician it permits explorations and experiments with musical materials that help to illuminate the cold abstractions of music theory.

In Eurhythmics lessons the body and the ear are taught to perform efficiently. In *Solfège* lessons the ear is trained to listen, discern, select, and remember many qualities and combinations of sounds and motions through singing, reading, and writing. In early experimental improvisations students work to discover what can be done with the facts, concepts, feelings, techniques, and experiences of those lessons. In this way the real and practical materials can be transformed by imaginative variations into a personal expression of human feeling and musical art.

It is most important to the beginning pedagogy that it is made clear to the students that they improvise only for themselves and not for the pleasure or approval of the teacher or any other audience. This is often a difficult principle for performance-oriented teachers to grasp, but if it is not kept in mind, the improvisation lesson could become a lesson in how to immobilize a student by invoking the terror of the unknown. Students themselves must learn to treat improvisation practices as experiments and not to compare their productions with masterpieces of musical composition. Anything that produces fear or ridicule of experimental improvisation is irrelevant and harmful both to the process and to creative discovery. Later in the process, critiques are possible and, indeed, lead to a sharing of values and experiences.

FROM THE LITERAL TO THE ARTISTIC   The improvisational process often takes the literal materials of life, art, and science and treats them in nonliteral ways. By experimenting with variations of tempo, dynamics, and articulation (legato, staccato, portamento), everyday sounds and movements are transformed into the world of art. For example, the literal sound of a dog barking can be transformed into singing or piano playing; a human snore could be transformed into body movements that accurately reflect the details of the rhythms, timbres, pitches, dynamics, and articulations of the original snore. Using improvisational experiment (by making the tempo much slower or much faster), new variations can be invented and used as fresh ideas for creations totally divorced from the actual original sound. This can be even further removed from the literal snore by transferring the facts, feelings, and ideas of the snore to their representation by sound and movement gestures on percussion instrument, voice, or piano.

MOODS AND IMPROVISATION   Since moods affect human behavior and are revealed by breathing, posture, gestures and other symbolic rhythms, and even pitch qualities, they are useful tools for beginning an improvisation. Students can experiment to find the tempo, dynamics, or scale of a mood either by observation of other people or by allowing themselves to "turn on" their feelings to create the mood. These realizations about mood can then be exaggerated in size and tempo to reveal more information about all the small actions of the body that express a mood. Through improvisational experiment students can attempt to transform the motions of a mood into musical expression. Since emotion results in motion, the process may also be reversed, allowing the motions of rhythm, pitch, and harmony to reproduce emotion. The teacher may then introduce examples, in folk music and art songs, of the moods that have been studied, and help students to analyze the way in which musical materials may be used to evoke an emotional reaction in an audience.

FROM THE CONCRETE TO THE ABSTRACT   Improvisation and imagination do not develop in a vacuum. Anything that can be seen, heard, touched, felt, tasted, or moved can be a stimulus to improvisation. One's own memory is a treasure chest for exploration through improvisation. The study of solo or group improvisation permits imagination to grow and inhibition to fall away. By using improvisation as a problem-solving technique, Jaques-Dalcroze encouraged students to find many of their own ingenious solutions to practical musical problems and to develop the ability to think in concepts, the ability to formulate abstract images and ideas which go far beyond the factual.

In Jaques-Dalcroze's method, improvisation is used to teach theoretical facts and constructs and, at the same time, to show their infinite possibilities for reconstruction and recombination into new ideas. Above all, improvisation techniques must avoid imitation of mental structures that cut students off from the curiosity of how and why something is taught, thought, or practiced. When students only imitate a teacher's improvisation, they may fall into easy cliches of speech, sound, or movement, acceptable to the teacher but denying, and sometimes burying, the students' own individuality. By exercising the students' originality the teacher can strengthen their creative ability just as one can strengthen muscles by exercising them. Jaques-Dalcroze wrote

> Improvisation is the study of the direct relationship between cerebral commands and muscular interpretations in order to express *one's own* musical feelings. Performance is propelled by developing the students' power of sensation, imagination, and memory. It is not based on direct imitation of the teacher's performance.[16]

In other words, improvisation is the mind at play.

[16]Emile Jaques-Dalcroze, "Rhythmics and Pianoforte Improvisation," *Music and Letters*, 13, no. 4 (October, 1932), 371–80.

Beginning Keyboard Improvisation

The beginning techniques used by teachers of Jaques-Dalcroze's methods consist of experimental play with the strings of the piano: plucking, striking, gliding, strumming, and stopping the vibrations of the strings. These movements are combined with singing, speaking, or striking a percussion instrument or bell near the strings while using a sustaining pedal, thus producing sympathetic vibrations. The piano, as a vibrating instrument, can be studied from the inside out. Listening to the works of John Cage and Karlheinz Stockhausen can offer fine illustrations of music made by these techniques. Later, note clusters, played on the black keys with the whole palm of the hand, are used to avoid the harmful physical tensions produced by the single-finger note playing often seen in inexperienced players.

Various exercises in note-cluster improvising can be derived by combining

1. pitch patterns: high, medium, low
2. duration patterns: long, medium, short
3. tempo patterns: fast, moderate, slow
4. rhythm patterns: subdivisions, dotted rhythms, rests
5. dynamic patterns: loud, medium soft, getting louder, getting softer
6. articulation patterns: legato, staccato, portamento

These can be combined with the following physical and spatial coordinations:

1. alternating hands
    a. right hand, left hand
    b. left hand, right hand
    c. hands crossing (L–R–L or R–L–R)
    d. hands alternating and crossing
2. hands together
    a. parallel motion
    b. contrary motion
    c. oblique motion (one hand in place, the other moves)
    d. similar motion (both hands move up or down, but one moves further than the other)

These techniques can be used to improvise accompaniments to stories and poems (*melodramas*) or to accompany songs, by either following the rhythmic word patterns of the song or building an accompaniment of beat or ostinato patterns.

IMPROVISED DIALOGUES   Pieces built on conversational rhythms of speech can be used to develop improvisational dialogues between two students, a student and the teacher, or between two students at one piano in dialogue with a percussion orchestra. The dialogue approach can also be used by substituting gestures for speech. In these kinds of improvisations students use meaningful physical gestures toward a partner and then convert the gesture into musical gesture using note clusters.

Of great importance to the success of the improvisations is the necessity for partners to develop intense, concentrated listening to each other's "conversation." Especially important is clear projection of the qualities that express cadences. If a student indicates clearly that she or he has finished a gesture, the other student will know when to respond. Without strong indications of starting and finishing a series of gestures, the improvisation can become lifeless or shapeless. As in everyday life, students may interrupt or even finish a partner's phrase or sentence. Sometimes a partner may interject gestures of sound that represent expletives, or murmers of approval with sounds or rhythms, such as "a-huh," "hmmm," or "wow!" The student intending to finish the conversation must make that clear by using combinations of dynamics, rhythms, weight, gesture, or silence.

EXPERIMENTAL IMPROVISATION USING HARMONIC INTERVALS Another technique of simple keyboard improvisation is studied by exploring the effect of various styles of playing a single interval. The major second, for example, can be played smoothly and quietly, with an effect of floating enhanced by the sustaining pedal, but it can also be short and snappy when played without the pedal, with a dry staccato articulation. Many kinds of pieces can be constructed using just one interval for unity and different ones for variety.

THE FUNCTION OF IMPROVISATION On the function of improvisation, Jaques-Dalcroze wrote

> Improvisation's function is to develop rapidity of decision and interpretation, effortless concentration, the immediate conception of plans, and to set up direct communications between the soul that feels, the brain that imagines and coordinates, and fingers, arms, hands, and breath that interpret, thanks to the nervous system which unites all the particular senses—hearing, seeing, feeling, touching, and thinking in time, energy, and space.[17]

The interaction of the movement in time, space, and energy of rhythm and pitch is represented on the baseline of the triangles. Melody and harmony are created by the interaction and are represented as two sides of a large triangle. In the Jaques-Dalcroze Method, Improvisation is represented by the central vector and apex of the two smaller triangles.

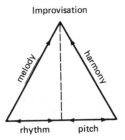

[17]Jaques-Dalcroze, "Rhythmics," p. 371.

Any lack of training or experience or lack of technique in those areas along the baseline of this triangle will lead to difficulties on the sides or at the apex.

When improvisation is added to Eurhythmics and *Solfège* there is a synthesis of all the elements which comprise the musical universe, and the study of music centers on the presentation of ideas and feelings through sound. Improvisation not only unites the first two branches of Jaques-Dalcroze's method but also acts as an assessment of the effectiveness of the whole.

Improvisation and the Printed Page

It is easy to understand the creative value of improvisation from a composer's point of view; but how does improvisational training aid performers who must play composed music from the printed page? The answer lies in two important truths:

> No written notation of music tells the performer everything about the playing of a piece.
>
> The notation in a printed composition cannot be read literally.

Improvisational practices applied to composed music help a performer make discoveries about nuances that must be heard and felt in addition to what actually appears on the printed page. They help a performer to understand and feel the different reasons for a composer's choice of variations and repetitions of ideas. This understanding makes available to a performer many possibilities for expressive interpretation. Whether music is classical, popular, or folk, each musical style generates its own materials and shapes. Through Jaques-Dalcroze's method, experimental improvisation gives students and teachers tools with which to understand and appreciate the whole world of music.

CONCLUSION

The combination of Eurhythmics, *Solfège*, and Improvisation, now known as the Jaques-Dalcroze Method, has obviously had a profound influence on educators in general and music educators in particular. His contribution answers the demand for a child-centered and experiential education such as that proposed by the American educational theorists John Dewey and Mortimer Adler.

Currently, cognitive psychology (a relatively new branch of the science that studies learning, memory, and the development of successful performance skills) is beginning to test and prove that Jaques-Dalcroze's original guesses, notions, and experiments, begun over eighty years ago, are valid and viable. Among his ideas now being proved by scientific experimental evidence are the following:

1. The use of imaginative kinesthesia as proposed and practiced in Eurhythmics. (It is now used in many fields of skill development outside of music.)
2. The idea that information, ordination, and classification are best learned, memorized, and retrieved by studying the manner in which

they are useful, as proposed and practiced in the *Solfège* and *Solfège-Rythmique* of Jaques-Dalcroze.

3. Techniques of heuristic (problem-solving) skills and higher-level thinking characterized by intuitive, inductive, and even illogical thinking. This kind of imaginative thinking is developed by the experimental and creative approaches as proposed and practiced in the Improvisation techniques of Jaques-Dalcroze.

Interest in the Jaques-Dalcroze Method is increasingly evident in North America and around the world. In many ways it represents some of the newest thinking in music education.

It was in 1905 that Emile Jaques-Dalcroze first gained public recognition, when he demonstrated his Eurhythmics before an international convention of music educators at Soleure, Switzerland. In 1906 he gave his first teacher-training course in Geneva.

In 1910 Wolf and Harald Dohrn, two German industrialists who were vitally interested in the problems of education, art, and social progress, invited Jaques-Dalcroze to establish a school and theater in Hellerau, Germany. At Hellerau Jaques-Dalcroze and his old friend Adolphe Appia (author of *L'oeuvre d'art vivant*) established what was to become the school and theater of the future. Together they discovered new methods of coordinating stage design, lighting, and choral movement, pointing the way towards new possibilities for opera, drama, and dance.

Many of the students at Hellerau became the leading artists of the next generation: Hanya Holm, Marie Rambert, and Vaslav Nijinsky were among the dancers and choreographers attracted to Hellerau; the director and producer Sergei Diaghilev was there also. These artists in turn have affected the dance and theater to the present day through their influence on Ted Shawn, Ruth St. Dénis, Doris Humphrey, Martha Graham, Paul Taylor, and Alvin Ailey. Among the musicians to come to Hellerau were Sergei Rachmaninoff, Ernest Bloch, and Ignace Paderewski; some writers were Paul Claudel, William James, George Bernard Shaw, and Upton Sinclair. The directors and actors Max Reinhardt, Gordon Craig, and Konstantin Stanislavsky visited and worked in the theater, and the future leaders in education Maria Montessori, Dorothee Günther, Gunild Keetman, and Carl Orff came to Hellerau to study and observe this unique experiment in education by the arts.

The success of Hellerau helped to spread the growth of Jaques-Dalcroze's work and the development of Eurhythmics schools in England, Russia, and many other countries in Europe. Unfortunately, the educational experiment was disrupted by the outbreak of World War I: Jaques-Dalcroze's liberal views forced him to flee Germany. In 1915 he returned to Geneva to found the Institut Jaques-Dalcroze. From this school his students have spread his method in Europe and to America, Australia, Japan, and throughout the world.

In 1924 he was made an officer of the French Legion of Honor; in 1930 he received an honorary Mus.D. from the University of Chicago. Emile Jaques-Dalcroze died July 1, 1950. He left behind a legacy of music and movement for the world.

4

THE KODÁLY METHOD

What is known in North America as the "Kodály Method" was developed in Hungary in the 1940s and 1950s by the composer Zoltán Kodály (1882–1967), his colleagues, and his students, as a comprehensive system of music education. It was not invented by Kodály, but rather it evolved in the Hungarian schools under his inspiration and guidance. The goals, the philosophy, and the principles were Kodály's. The pedagogy, the means through which to achieve these goals, was not. None of the *practices* associated with Kodály originated with him. *Solfa* was invented in Italy and *tonic solfa* came from England; rhythm syllables were the invention of Chevé in France, and many of the *solfa* techniques employed were taken from the work of Jaques-Dalcroze; hand-singing was adapted from John Curwen's approach in England and the teaching process was basically Pestalozzian. The uniqueness of the Kodály Method came in the way in which these previously separate techniques were combined into one unified approach, which itself supported a viable philosophy of music education.

In 1950 the first singing primary school was established in Kesckemet, Kodály's birthplace, under the direction of his longtime friend, the school principal Marta Nemesszeghy. Here children received music instruction every day of the school week, and the method was further developed and refined. As a result of the phenomenal success of Nemesszeghy and the children at the Kesckemet school, the next years saw a rapid rise in the development and dissemination of this method, from the nursery school level to the conservatories and the most advanced classes of the Franz Liszt Academy of Music in Budapest. Today there are more than 150 Singing Primary Schools in Hungary, and the method developed in them has spread all over the world. Classes trained in the principles of

Kodály exist in Japan, New Zealand, Australia, Africa, most countries of Europe, and North and South America.

The philosophy underlying the Kodály approach is as follows:

ALL PEOPLE CAPABLE OF LINGUAL LITERACY ARE ALSO CAPABLE OF MU-SICAL LITERACY.   Musical literacy should not be the property of a chosen few, but a general knowledge of all. It is not too many centuries ago that the ability to read words was the privilege of the elite. The common man was thought to be incapable of so erudite an exercise as reading. Today, in a time of universal lingual literacy, this viewpoint seems absurd. There is no reason to suppose that human beings are less capable of learning to read music than words. Music reading, like word reading, is a taught skill, a skill that not only can, but should, be taught. If the language of music becomes a known language, enjoyment of music will certainly increase, and the quality of life itself improve.

SINGING IS THE BEST FOUNDATION FOR MUSICIANSHIP.   The youngest infants produce musical sounds. Singing is as natural an activity to the child as speaking. To use this native ability, to foster and cultivate the voice—the instrument everyone has—is both practical and effective. Throughout history great musicians have known the importance of singing in music education. Musical knowledge acquired through singing is internalized in a way that musical knowledge acquired through an instrument—an external appendage—can never be.

MUSIC EDUCATION TO BE MOST EFFECTIVE MUST BEGIN WITH THE VERY YOUNG CHILD.   Studies undertaken in Hungary[1] with children under two years of age show marked differences in the acquisition of speech and music between children who are sung to every day and children who have no music in their environment. The importance of the early childhood years in general education has been long known; that importance is, if anything, even greater in music than in other areas.

THE FOLK SONGS OF A CHILD'S OWN LINGUISTIC HERITAGE CONSTITUTE A MUSICAL "MOTHER TONGUE" AND SHOULD THEREFORE BE THE VEHICLE FOR ALL EARLY INSTUCTION.   Language and music fit together in a special way in folk song. The natural stress patterns of a language are mirrored in melody and rhythm, so that the young child not only learns tunes and words, but also acquires greater fluency and understanding in his own language. Folk songs, themselves valuable as an art form, can give children a sense of cultural identity and continuity with the past.

ONLY MUSIC OF THE HIGHEST ARTISTIC VALUE, BOTH FOLK AND COM-POSED, SHOULD BE USED IN TEACHING.   In presenting any music to a class the teacher places an implied value on that music. Children, open-minded and impressionable, learn first by imitation and example. If the music offered to them has intrinsic value, if it is from the heritage of good music, they will learn to value good music.

[1]Under the direction of Katalin Forrai in the state-run daycare centers of Budapest.

MUSIC SHOULD BE AT THE HEART OF THE CURRICULUM, A CORE SUBJECT, USED AS A BASIS FOR EDUCATION.   Music, perhaps more than any other subject, can contribute to the development of the child in every way—emotionally, intellectually, aesthetically, and physically. The argument usually put forward against giving music equal importance with mathematics and reading in the elementary school is that "there isn't enough time in the school day . . ."; that time would have to be "stolen" from "more important" subjects. In places where music *has* been taught daily, following Kodály's principles, far from falling behind in other academic areas, children have tended to do at least as well as other children who receive music teaching less frequently.[2] Some research shows that classes in which music was taught daily as a core subject in the curriculum surpassed similar classes who received less frequent music instruction, surpassing them in the very academic areas that are generally put forward as the reason for not having more time for music—mathematics and reading.[3] However, the reason for music at the core of the curriculum is not to help children achieve higher scores on mathematics tests; it is to provide the coming generations with fuller lives, to open to them the limitless possibilities of participation in music as a means of filling some of the fifty hours a week (at a conservative estimate) of nonworking time the average adult now enjoys. Leisure time is increasing as work becomes even more automated. Education should prepare people for that time as well as for the 40 hours spent earning a living.

Objectives of Kodály Musical Training

The principal objectives of Kodály musical training may be stated as follows:

1. to develop to the fullest extent possible the innate musicality present in all children
2. to make the language of music known to children; to help them become musically literate in the fullest sense of the word—able to read, write, and create with the vocabulary of music
3. to make the children's musical heritage—the folk songs of their language and culture—known to them
4. to make available to children the great art music of the world, so that through performing, listening, studying, and analyzing masterworks they will come to a love and appreciation of music based on knowledge about music

A Child-Developmental Approach

The Kodály Method is highly structured and sequenced, with well-defined skill and concept hierarchies in every element of music. These sequences are both

---

[2]The San Jose Unified School District Project.

[3]Hurwitz, Wolf, Bortnick, and Kokas, "Nonmusical Effects of the Kodály Music Curriculum in Primary Grade Children," *Journal of Reading Disabilities,* 8, no. 3 (1975); Klara Kokas, "Psychological Tests in Connection with Music Education in Hungary." Presented at the *International Seminar on Experimental Research in Music Education,* The University of Reading, England, July 9–16, 1968.

drawn from and closely related to child development—the way in which young children progress naturally in music—as shown through research.

Three-note songs and chants (*la–so–mi*), tetratonic (*so–mi–re–do*), and pentatonic (*la–so–mi–re–do*) songs comprise most, but not all, of the earliest melodic teaching material. Early-childhood folk tunes made up primarily of Major seconds, minor thirds, and perfect fourths (such as "Ring Around the Rosy," "Bye, Baby Bunting") are considered ideally suited to young, insecure singers. These tunes are without minor seconds, an interval often difficult even for adults to sing in tune.

Later, as voices mature and musical abilities increase, musical materials are extended to include more songs in diatonic major and minor keys, modes, and altered scales.

However, at every stage in the child's musical training *some* diatonic music is included. From first grade some songs with minor seconds (*fa–mi, ti–do*) are attempted. If they are not, these sounds will be forever beyond children. Just as a child who cannot say an *r* correctly ("see the wabbit wun!") must hear that *r* sounded by others and must try to pronounce it himself if he or she is ever to pronounce it correctly, so must the first-grader hear and attempt to sing the minor second in some songs if he or she is ever to sing it correctly.

Child developmental as it applies to Kodály practice means that the major body of teaching material must lie within children's capabilities. However, at all times some musical materials must be included that are designed to expand those capabilities.

Rhythmically, the meter of young children's movements—walking, running, skipping, swaying, bouncing—is duple. It may be a simple duple $\frac{2}{4}$, quadruple $\frac{4}{4}$, or compound duple $\frac{6}{8}$; however, it *is* duple. Triple meter is extremely uncommon as a natural expression among young children in English-speaking cultures. Based on child-developmental patterns, the earliest rhythmic teaching material in a Kodály approach is duple. Triple meters are included later, when a firm foundation in duple has been established.

Form, harmony, tempo, and dynamics have been similarly examined and sequenced into hierarchies, so that the five-year-old may experience all aspects of music at his or her own level, the eight-year-old experience those same elements, but at a more advanced level, and the twelve-year-old, the high school student, or the adult still work with the same elements, but in even greater complexity. As the child develops physically, socially, emotionally, aesthetically, and intellectually, he or she is also led to develop musically in the acquisition of increasingly complex skills and more involved concepts.

The Tools of the Kodály Method

The tools employed in Kodály practice are (1) tonic *solfa,* (2) hand signs, and (3) rhythm duration syllables.

Other tools are employed as well and will be mentioned later; however, these three are the basic instruments through which Kodály teachers bring children to musical literacy.

1. TONIC *SOLFA.* Tonic *solfa* is a system of syllables—*do, re, mi, fa, so, la, ti, do*—in which *do* is considered to be the keynote or tonal center in all major

keys and *la* is considered to be the keynote or tonal center in all minor keys. For example,

Tonic *solfa* is without equal as a way to train the musical ear, since it focuses the attention initially not on a specific pitch but on pitch relationships and pitch functions within a tonal system. Once learned, *do* to *so* in any key immediately brings to mind the sound of the perfect fifth; *so* to *mi*, the sound of the minor third.

The songs and singing games of early childhood, the folk music, and much of the art music of the Western world is tonal in character and thus is eminently suitable for study via tonic *solfa*.

A possible limitation of the movable-*do* approach is that it is not useful for studying music that is *not* tonal in character; this includes the music of some non-Western societies and some music of the twentieth century. However, *solfa* in the Kodály approach is not used in isolation. Children are begun with relative-*do*, but once they are secure in that easier way of singing, reading, and writing music, letter names for the notes are introduced (usually around third grade) and are then sung interchangeably with *solfa* until they too are secure.

This singing of absolute note names (A–B–C's) in conjunction with *do–re–mi*'s (a common practice in Hungarian schools) is an aspect of Kodály practice that has not been sufficiently incorporated into Kodály teaching in North America. It is an important step, particularly for children who are studying instruments. If they sing only *solfa* syllables in class and then are asked to think only in letter names in a piano or trumpet lesson, they may never themselves make the connection between the two skills. Children will always be more facile in *solfa*—it is the best training for the voice and for the ear—but absolute note names must also be taught. They are the vocabulary of the professional musician.

2. HAND SIGNS.   If *solfa* is an aid to tonal memory, *solfa* combined with a system of hand signs appears to make that tonal memory both more quickly accomplished and more secure.

Originally developed by John Curwen in England in 1870 and somewhat changed and adapted for use in the Hungarian schools, the hand signs used in Kodály practice today are illustrated on pages 76–77.

They are performed in an area more or less between the top of the head and waist.

Some North American adaptations would have children use very much wider motions at the early *so–mi* stage; this is impractical since it involves relearning when additional notes are introduced; however, it does no real harm. A practice that does inhibit effective use of hand signs is the use of both hands. Only one hand should be used by the child—his or her writing hand, the dominant hand. No skill is accomplished as well with both hands as with the dominant hand. The right-handed child who learns hand-singing first with the right hand acquires tonal patterns more quickly and more securely than the child who uses both hands.

The teacher, however, can and should use both hands to show two different pitches. By showing a sustained *do* with the left hand and a *do–so–do* with the right, for example, the teacher can lead two halves of the class through practice in intervals and work on intonation. Later still the teacher can lead a class or choir through chord changes via hand signs. They are an invaluable teaching technique.

RHYTHM DURATION SYLLABLES.   Rhythm in a Kodály approach is taught by pattern and by relative durations over the beat as expressed in a series of syllables adapted from those invented by Jacques Chevé in the 1800s and still used in French conservatories.[4] These syllables are not names; they are merely a way of voicing rhythm. The names—quarter note, eighth note, half note, and so on, are also taught in Kodály classes, but not until later, after children are able to read rhythm duration syllables. Some changes in these syllables have been made in parts of the United States and Canada to compensate for problems arising from language (the *r* in Hungarian, for example, is a rolled, rhythmic sound, but in English it is a hard sound that actually seems to stop the flow of the rhythm).[5]

The following duration syllables are used widely in Kodály practice in North America:

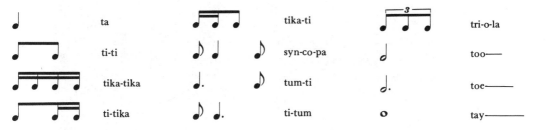

[4]For the syllables used in Hungary see Lois Choksy, *The Kodály Context* (Englewood Cliffs, NJ: Prentice-Hall, 1981, p. 190.
[5]Pierre Perron, Professor of Music at Dalhousie University in Halifax has developed a complete system of duration syllables, based on Chevé's, for use with North American children in Kodály programs. Some of these are included here.

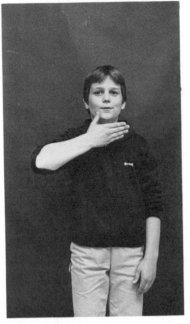

so

la

do

re

ti

do'

mi

fa

These syllables are taught by using patterns and phrases taken from songs. They are viewed as sounds and sound relationships rather than as mathematical values. It is important when having children perform rhythms with duration syllables to make sure that each sound continues to the next sound. *Ta* represents a quarter note. In $\frac{2}{4}$ it must sound for a full beat. Classes sometimes say it as if it

were an eighth note followed by an eighth rest: ♪⁷ ♪⁷ They have learned *ta* as
                                                 ta   ta

a name rather than as a relative duration. If children sing their rhythmic patterns, producing them on a pitch or pitches, this is less likely to occur.

Sequencing for Learning

Child-developmental characteristics in music, rather than the logic of the subject matter, determine the overall sequence in the Kodály Method. Duple meter is taught before triple; minor thirds and major seconds before minor seconds. These are decisions based upon what young children can do.

However, a study of child development cannot tell the teacher whether

the eighth note followed by a dotted quarter ♪ ♩. should be taught before or

after the dotted quarter followed by the eighth note ♩. ♪ . The minutiae of sequencing must come from some other source. The broad outlines of the Kodály sequence are designed to suit the maturity levels of the child; the small sequences within the overall sequence are based upon the frequency of occurrence of a particular rhythmic figure or melodic turn in the song material being used for teaching—the folk songs and art music from which new learnings are to

be drawn. In English-language folk music ♩. ♪ occurs more frequently than

♪ ♩. ; therefore, the former is taught before the latter. There are more songs containing a melodic turn using low *la* and low *so* than there are containing high *do*; therefore, high *do* is taught after low *la* and low *so*.

The first criterion in sequencing—child development—is universal. Children exhibit approximately the same ability at the same ages in Switzerland, in Australia, in Japan, and in North America. Those aspects of the sequence that are based on this criterion will be similar in all these places.

The second criterion—frequency of occurrence in the musical material—may very well cause major differences in sequencing among these same countries, or, indeed, from one place to another within a single country. The folk music of Iceland, for example, does not contain the same rhythmic figures and melodic turns as the folk music of the United States. Even within North America significant differences in sequence can occur, depending upon whether the teacher is working with predominantly Hispanic children in Texas

($\frac{3}{4}$ meter would surely be taught sooner), Black children in Mississippi (the initial melodic teaching might well use patterns based on *do–la·–so·* rather than on *la–so–mi*), or rural children in New England (the sixteenth-note patterns common to their singing game tradition taught earlier).

The broad outlines of sequence do not change since they are based on principles that do not change. However, within that outline it is vitally important that teachers view sequence as a flexible factor, to be adapted to the specific region, the specific culture, and the specific class.

Some Possible Kodály Sequences in Rhythm, Melody, Form, and Harmony

BEAT AND RHYTHM. There are a finite number of ideas or concepts necessary to understanding beat and rhythm:

1. Music moves to a steady BEAT.

Ring a-round the ro - sy
♡   ♡   ♡   ♡

2. Some beats have a feeling of stress or ACCENT.

Rain, rain, go a - way
♡   ♡   ♡   ♡

3. Music moves in groups of beats defined by accented beats. This is known as METER.

$\frac{2}{4}$ Rain, rain | go a - way |
♡   ♡ | ♡   ♡ |

4. All music moves in twos or in threes or in combinations of twos and threes.

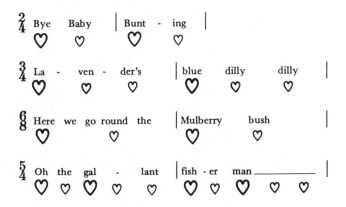

$\frac{2}{4}$ Bye   Baby | Bunt - ing |
♡   ♡   ♡   ♡

$\frac{3}{4}$ La - ven - der's | blue   dilly   dilly |
♡   ♡   ♡   ♡   ♡   ♡

$\frac{6}{8}$ Here we go round the | Mulberry   bush |
♡   ♡   ♡   ♡

$\frac{5}{4}$ Oh the gal - lant | fish - er man _____ |
♡   ♡ ♡   ♡   ♡   ♡   ♡ ♡   ♡   ♡

5. Over the beat, music moves in longer and shorter sounds and silences. This is known as RHYTHM.

| long | long | short | short | long | | short | short | short | short | long | | silence |

6. There can be *one* sound on a beat

,

two sounds on a beat

,

or *more* sounds on a beat.

7. Some sounds last longer than one beat.

8. Sounds over beats can be evenly () or unevenly ( ) arranged.

9. Longer and shorter sounds and silences may be grouped into patterns.

These concepts are basic to understanding patterns in duration. They are the generalizations that children must be led to draw as they work with beat, meter, and rhythm.

All teaching about beat, meter, and rhythm must be built on the children's ability to correctly perform and identify beat, accent, and rhythm in music. Feeling for these may be encouraged by having children step, clap, tap, and move in a variety of ways while singing. The terms *beat*, *accented beat*, and *rhythm* should be taught. When children can physically demonstrate that they can correctly identify and perform these three cornerstones of all rhythmic arrangement, the teacher may begin to introduce specific rhythmic patterns. These patterns are always four beats long at the early teaching stage, corresponding to the phrase length in young children's songs.[6]

---

[6]The natural phrase length in almost all traditional English-language children's music is four beats. If one encounters an eight-beat phrase or a phrase of another length, it is probably teacher-invented.

With each new rhythmic figure children are led first to sing man
containing that figure in various patterns, then to focus on one song to d
or derive the figure, then to put down symbols for the figure in various p
(write it or construct it with sticks), then to read it from flash cards, boar
tion, and books, and finally, to use it in improvisation or composition.

One new note value may actually give rise to five, six, or ten ne
terns. Children do not know eighth-note pairs just because they have en
tered them in one place in one song. They must have practice with them in

common placement in music. In presenting ♪♪ , for example, the teacher
actually introduces not one rhythmic figure but six or more rhythm patterns:

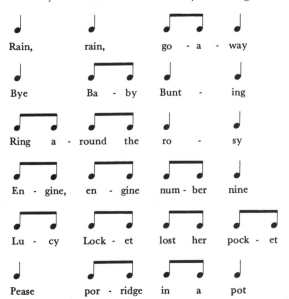

Rain,   rain,   go - a - way

Bye   Ba - by   Bunt - ing

Ring   a - round   the   ro - sy

En - gine,   en - gine   num - ber   nine

Lu - cy   Lock - et   lost   her   pock - et

Pease   por - ridge   in   a   pot

Each of these is carefully prepared through song material, and the position of ♩♩ in each is discovered aurally by the children before the notation is shown.

This process is multiplied by every rhythmic figure to be taught. One basic sequence for teaching rhythm in North American schools is given in the following table.

Rhythmic Figures in an Order from Simple to Complex, Based on Frequency of Occurrence in English-Language Folk Music

	Simple duple meter $\frac{2}{4}$ ($\frac{4}{4}$) ¢	Compound duple meter $\frac{6}{8}$ ($\frac{6}{4}$ $\frac{12}{8}$)	Simple triple meter $\frac{3}{4}$	Compound triple meter $\frac{9}{8}$	Asymmetric meters $\frac{5}{8}$ ($\frac{5}{4}$ $\frac{7}{8}$)
1.	♩				
2.	♫				
3.	𝄿				
4.	♩				
5.		♬♬ ♬♬			
6.	♩. ♪				
7.	𝅝				
8.		♩. ♩.			
9.	♪♩ ♪				
10.	♪♩.				
11.	♪♩ 𝄾				
12.		♩ ♪♩ ♪			
13.	𝅘𝅥𝅯𝅘𝅥𝅯𝅘𝅥𝅯𝅘𝅥𝅯				
14.	♩♫				
15.	𝅘𝅥𝅯𝅘𝅥𝅯♩				
16.			♩ ♩ ♩		
17.			♩ ♩		
18.			♩.		
19.	♩. ♩				

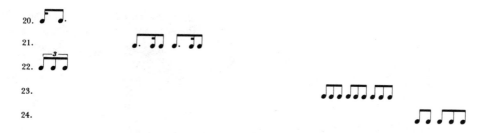

20.

21.

22.

23.

24.

MELODY. The number of concepts inherent in pitch movement—MELODY—are few. Pitches

> may move from higher to lower
> may move from lower to higher
> may be repeated
> may move by step, skip, or leap

Melodic movements create linear patterns or melodies.

These generalizations are important aids in teaching, but of themselves they are nonspecific and do not help children with tonal memory in the way that the generalizations about rhythm help with rhythmic memory. Knowing that G to E is a descending skip does not give one its relative sound or specific pitches.

Intervalic memory is approached, like rhythmic learning, through patterns—patterns from daily life, from infant songs and chants, and from folk songs. Developmentally, an approximation of the descending minor third is the earliest interval sung by most young children. It is an extension of the natural speech stress in English: "Mom'-my," "Dad'-dy." It is the basic interval of children's teasing chants:

Sus - ie   has   a   boy - friend!

It is the sound of a mother calling her child to dinner:

John - ny!

From the minor third, melodic sequence moves gradually through the patterns of pentatonic songs to diatonic, modal, and chromatically altered material. The sequence that emerges is the following, or some variation of it.

Melodic Groupings for Teaching in an Order from Simple to Complex, Based on Frequency of Occurrence in Folk Music from English-Speaking Countries (new notes are underlined and tonal centers are circled)

1. <u>s</u> <u>m</u>
2. <u>l</u> s m
3. m <u>r</u> (d)
4. s m r (d)
5. l s m r (d) (the *do*-pentatonic scale)
6. l s m r (d) l,
7. l s m r (d) l, s,
8. l s m r d (l,) (the *la*-pentatonic scale)
9. <u>d'</u> l s m r (d)
10. s m r d l, (s,) (the *so*-pentatonic scale)
11. <u>r'</u> d l s m (r) (the *re*-pentatonic scale)
12. l s <u>f</u> m r (d)
13. m r (d) <u>t,</u> l, s,
14. s f m r (d) t, l, s,
15. d' t l s f m r (d) (the diatonic major scale)
16. l s f m r d t (l) (the diatonic minor scale; the aeolian mode)
17. d <u>ta</u> l s f m r (d) (the mixolydian mode)
18. l s <u>fi</u> m r d t (l) (the dorian mode)
19. l <u>si</u> f m r d t (l) (the harmonic minor scale)
20. d di r ri m f fi s si l li t d (the ascending chromatic scale)
21. d t ta l lo so sa(w) f m ma r ra d (the descending chromatic scale)

Each of the above groupings may involve many melodic patterns. If only four notes *s, m, r, d* are known, there are at least five common patterns:

1. *s–m–r–d*
2. *d–r–m–s*
3. *m–r–d–s*
4. *s–r–m–d*
5. *r–s–m–d*

As more notes are added, the patterns to be mastered increase. New notes must be practiced in every position in which they occur in music. Knowing four notes in a descending order does *not* prepare children to sing those same four notes in an ascending order. Only experience singing songs with each pattern can do this.

One important point must be reiterated. The preceding chart gives an order for introducing new notes; it is not intended as a restriction on children's rote-singing material. The class working on identifying the new note *la* in songs containing only three notes—*la, so,* and *mi*—should at the same time in their rote-singing experiences be performing songs in both pentatonic and diatonic scales. Only in this way can students be ready for further melodic learning. As children always have a larger speaking vocabulary than reading vocabulary, so must they have a larger rote-singing vocabulary than note-singing vocabulary.

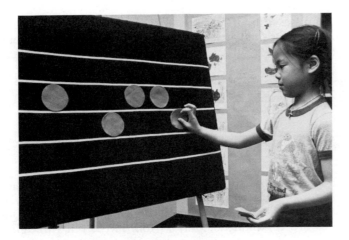

FORM.   If children are led to analyze the small forms of their songs from kindergarten age, they will not have difficulty analyzing larger forms later. Some of the principles are as follows:

1. Music has patterns.
2. Patterns are organized into phrases.
3. Sometimes two phrases are the same.
4. Sometimes two phrases are different.
5. Sometimes phrases are not the same, but are similar.
6. Similar phrases can give a feeling of question (incomplete) or answer (complete).
7. Same, different, and similar phrases are organized into FORMS.
8. Some common forms of songs are AABA, AABB, ABAC.

These eight principles are sequenced in order of presentation to young children.
    Pattern, the smallest unit, is focused on by the teacher in both rhythmic and melodic skill-work. Phrase, the implied punctuation in music, is taught every time a new rote song is taught. The teacher sings the whole song, phrasing it correctly, breathing at phrase endings, and then teaches it phrase by phrase. By imitation children learn the meaning of phrase.
    When *phrase* has specific meaning to children it is possible to listen to two phrases and identify whether they are the same or different. At this stage symbols may be attached to phrases to diagram the form:

Hot cross buns,	○	
Hot cross buns,	○	same
One a penny, two a penny,	□	different
Hot cross buns.	○	same as first two

Later, letter names are used to describe the likeness and unlikeness of phrases, and "Hot Cross Buns" becomes A–A–B–A—classic song form.

Sometimes phrases are not precisely alike, but similar. One phrase may have a feeling of being unfinished at its first statement, but sound complete at its second statement:

These are both B phrases, but the first ends on a note other than the tonal center—it feels incomplete. It is a *question* phrase. The second phrase is similar, but ends on *do*—it has a feeling of completeness. It is an *answer* phrase. Question and answer phrases are common not only in folk music but throughout art music.

The eight principles given here are simply enlarged upon when students begin to analyze larger forms. In a Beethoven symphony, a Bach fugue, or a Stravinsky chamber work the principles of repetition, contrast, and variation are as evident as in a four-phrase children's game song.

HARMONY AND THEORY. The teaching of harmony and theory begins of necessity only after children have had a large body of rote experience and have some proficiency in singing, reading, and writing simple rhythms and melodies. The earliest steps may be taken as soon as children know the *do-* and *la-* pentatonic scales. The tonal centers (*do* or *la*) are sung as drone accompaniments to known songs:

With most pentatonic songs a drone constructed on the tonal center produces a satisfactory accompaniment. However, as the melodic vocabulary increases to include *fa* and *ti* and more diatonic songs are sung, the tonal center does not always sound "right":

The children must be led to discover the need for another note in their accompaniments—*so* (the root of the V-chord).

If sufficient practice is given with singing the tonic and dominant chord roots—*do* and *so* in Major, *la* and *mi* in minor—the triads built on those tones present no difficulty when they are introduced. Chord inversion becomes necessary when young voices try to skip from one chord to another in root position.

I   V

Children discover that by keeping the upper voice on *so* the chord becomes more singable:

I   V

All elementary harmony and theory is taught in a similar manner, through singing and through derivation from the known. The following table gives a sequence for such theory teaching.

One Possible Sequence for Presenting Concepts in Harmony and Theory, Based on the Sequences Being Followed Concurrently in Rhythm and Melody

HARMONY	THEORY, SCALES, INTERVALS
1. Identify *do* as a tonal center in some songs of major character. Use it as a drone accompaniment.	
2. Identify *la* as a tonal center in some songs of minor character. Use it as a drone accompaniment.	
3.	Identify pentatonic scale patterns.
4.	Construct pentatonic scales.
5.	Aurally distinguish between major seconds and minor thirds.
6. Discover the need for another accompanying tone (V) in some songs (*so* in major; *mi* in minor).	
7.	Identify the diatonic major scale pattern and the two tetrachords of the major scale.
8.	Construct diatonic major scales beginning on different pitches.
9.	Aurally distinguish between major seconds and minor seconds; between major thirds and minor thirds.
10. Construct a triad (1–3–5) on *do* (I). Sing it as an accompaniment to *do*-pentatonic songs.	
11.	Identify the pure minor scale pattern (aeolian mode).
12.	Construct minor scales beginning on different pitches.
13. Construct a triad (1–3–5) on *la* (i). Sing it as an accompaniment to *la*-pentatonic songs.	

14.

Aurally identify the perfect fifth *do–so*. Locate and sing other perfect fifths in the scale.

15.

Distinguish between major and minor scales. Analyze the patterns of major and minor seconds to determine what gives a scale its major or minor sound. (1 to 3 is two major seconds in major scales but one major second and one minor second in minor scales.)

$$M_2 \begin{bmatrix} m \\ r \\ \end{bmatrix} \begin{array}{l} \text{major} \\ \text{scale} \end{array} \quad m_2 \Big< \begin{array}{l} d \\ t \end{array} \quad \begin{array}{l} \text{minor} \\ \text{scale} \end{array}$$
$$M_2 \begin{bmatrix} \\ d \\ \end{bmatrix} \text{pattern} \quad M_2 \begin{bmatrix} \\ l \\ \end{bmatrix} \text{pattern}$$

16. Build a triad on *so* (V) (*s–t–r'*) Sing the new triad to accompany diatonic major songs. Build one on *mi* (v) (*m–s–t*) for minor-mode songs.

17.

Aurally identify the major sixth *do–la*. Discover other major sixths in the scale.

18.

Aurally identify the minor sixth *mi–do'*. Discover other minor sixths in the scale. Rule: The inversion of a major interval is minor; the inversion of a minor interval is major: *do–mi* is a major third; *mi–do'* is a minor sixth.

19. Discover the need for chord inversion in order to produce good voice leading (I–V₆–I; or I⁶₄–V–I⁶₄).

20.

Aurally identify the perfect fourth *so–do*. Find, sing, and label other perfect fourths in the diatonic major scale.

21. Use *fa* (IV) in the accompaniments of diatonic songs.
22. Build a triad on *fa* (IV). Identify the inversions best for singing a I–IV–V–I progression.
23.

Identify the harmonic minor scale and the new note *si* (raised *so*).

24. Build the altered V chord in minor (*m–si–t*) and use it with the chord on *la* (i) in accompanying minor-mode songs.
25. Build triads on *re* (ii) and *la* (vi). Use chord progressions with these chords to accompany songs.
26. Aurally identify chords in art music.
27.

Identify the scale of mixolydian mode: *so* to *so'* or *do re mi fa so la ta do*.

28.

Identify the dorian mode: *r mf s l td r* or *la ti do re mi fi so la*.

29. Accompany mixolydian and dorian songs with triads built on the tonic and the seventh degree of the scale.
30.

Identify and perform the melodic minor scale.

31.

Identify and perform the chromatic scale and find its use in art music.

The work of this sequence is seen as encompassing four or more years. Through item 29 it has been done with elementary school children; however, if one had secondary school students or college students with little or no theory background, it would be necessary to begin with item 1 for them as well. The study of music theory is an important and all too often neglected aspect of basic musicianship, and it is very much a part of the Kodály Method.

THE EXPRESSIVE ELEMENTS.   Musical discrimination in the use of tempo, dynamics, and timbre is encouraged from the earliest lessons in a Kodály class. "How will this lullaby sound best, softer or louder? Why? Should the tempo be faster or slower? Why?" Children are asked to make decisions and to justify them. "If we want to keep the beat on a rhythm instrument, which instrument better suits this song, drum or triangle?" (All children like drums, for example, but drums are not the best instrument with which to accompany a lullaby.) Only with practice will children learn to make appropriate musical decisions regarding tempo, dynamics, and timbre.

INNER HEARING AND MUSICAL MEMORY.   In addition to the elements of music—melody, rhythm, form, harmony, tempo, dynamics, timbre—certain skill areas involving several of these elements at a time are a regular part of Kodály training. One of the most important of these is inner hearing—the ability to *think* musical sounds without external voicing. Children may be told, "Sing the first, second, and fourth phrases aloud; sing the third phrase inside your head." If they come in together and at the right moment, they have thought the music of the third phrase. Or "Sing the music of the first three phrases inside your head; sing the fourth phrase aloud." Later, students may "sing all the *re*'s" in a song silently, or "sing all the eighth notes inside." Children who can do this correctly are developing the ability to think musical sound. This ability is used whenever a person looks at a musical score, thinking the sounds. It is a mark of the literate musician, and it is a skill that can be systematically taught.

MUSICAL MEMORY.   Musical memory is trained in much the same way. Beginning with kindergarten and first-grade children the teacher, as a part of each class period, sings a song or a part of a song on a neutral syllable ("loo") and asks the children first to identify the song and then to check their answers against the repeated melody. At the beginning stages children's answers are little more than random guesses, but repetition of the check-and-see step gradually trains them to think and recall with intelligence.

At later stages the teacher may silently show hand signs for the first phrase of a song without naming it and expect the children to sing the correct song back with words, having inner-heard its melody and correctly identified it. Both inner hearing and musical memory play a part in this as well as in some exercises using a tone ladder, a scale written on the chalkboard vertically, as follows:

l
s

m
r
d

The teacher points out a familiar melody on the tone ladder and has the class follow the pointer, sing the melody "inside," and recall what song it is.

In another memory-training game a four-phrase rhythm is placed on the chalkboard and read aloud by the class. One phrase is erased and the exercise read aloud again, including the erased phrase. Another phrase is erased, and so on, until nothing remains on the board and the entire four-phrase rhythm has been committed to memory. Then the entire exercise can be reconstructed either on the chalkboard or in notebooks.

Combining the Elements

In the preceding pages specific teaching-learning sequences have been suggested for rhythm, melody, form, and harmony. In addition, teaching techniques have been suggested for tempo and dynamics and for developing inner hearing and memory.[7]

For clarity, each element has been presented here separately. However, they are not taught to children that way. In any lesson all the elements of music are intertwined. While the first-grade class is practicing known patterns of eighth notes and quarter notes, they are also singing rote songs with the soon-to-be-learned new note *la*. They are identifying phrases and deciding on tempo and dynamics for their songs.

The fourth-graders read songs in the *do*-hexachord (*la so fa mi re do*) and sing, by rote, songs with the next note to be taught, *ti*. They practice rhythms

with ♩．   ♪ and ♪ ♩ ♪ and will soon derive a new rhythmic figure ♪ ♩．   . They diagram the form of all songs they sing, using letters (AABA) and can improvise and compose with the *do*-pentatonic scale, incorporating principles of tempo, dynamics, and timbre.

Musical elements do not in reality exist in isolation, and they must not be taught that way.

SUMMARY AND CONCLUSIONS

The Kodály Method involves

> singing as the basis for music instruction
> the use of both folk and art music
> tonic *solfa*, hand signs, and rhythm duration syllables

The Kodály Method is

> child developmental
> highly sequential

---

[7]For a Kodály sequence intergrating the concepts of rhythm, melody, form, and harmony see Lois Choksy, *The Kodály Context* (Englewood Cliffs, NJ: Prentice-Hall, 1981), pp. 166–69.)

A primary goal of the Kodály Method is

to produce universal musical literacy.

Kodály musical training always involves active music making. Musical learning evolves from musical experience. Singing games and dances, folk songs, and art songs, songs sung in unison, rounds, canons, part songs, themes from great instrumental music—all these are the cornucopia from which musical concepts are drawn and through which musical skills are practiced. These musical concepts and skills are then applied to more complex music, and more involved concepts evolve and further musical skills are developed. It is a spiral curriculum process in the truest sense of the word—a spiral aimed at the fullest development of the musicianship inherent in all people.

Kodály himself said of it

> It is the richness of both the musical experiences themselves and the memory of them that makes a good musician. Individual singing plus listening to music (by means of active and passive well-arranged experiences) develops the ear to such an extent that one understands music one has heard with as much clarity as though one were looking at a score; if necessary—and if time permits—one should be able to reproduce such a score.
>
> This, and certainly no less, is what we expect from a student of a language; and music is a manifestation of the human spirit similar to a language. Its great men have conveyed to mankind things unutterable in any other language. If we do not want such things to remain dead treasures, we must do our utmost to make the greatest number of people understand their secrets.[8]

[8]Preface to Erzsébet Szőny, *Musical Reading and Writing* (New York: Boosey and Hawkes, 1954), p. 8.

5

THE ORFF
APPROACH

Carl Orff (1895–1982) was a German-born composer who introduced to the world a dynamic process which could ignite a fire in the imaginations and fantasies of children, inviting them into the world of music. But Orff did not originally set out to develop a program for the musical education of young children. Although today when one says "Orff" the word that immediately comes to mind is "instruments," he was not at the beginning primarily interested in the development of instruments.

The roots of Orff's works for the schools, or *Schulwerk* as it was to be known, may be traced to his love of dance and to his vision of an ultimate wedding of music to dance for the theater. As a young man Orff had occasion to meet and observe the great dancer and gymnast Mary Wigman. Wigman and another dancer, Dorothee Günther, were part of what was then referred to as "The New Dance Wave," a movement which included other such notables as Isadora Duncan and Ruth St. Dénis. The innovative styles and dance forms these artists developed were filled with opportunities for dancers to improvise and to use unusual techniques to express their art and craft. This intrigued Orff, who saw numerous possibilities for his compositions in conjunction with this modern dance.

Rather than imitating existing dance theater, in which the orchestra played in a pit and the dancers performed on a stage, Orff took his inspiration from folk traditions and brought the instruments on stage with the dancers, a startling innovation at that time. Later in the development of his music for dance, the dancers themselves played the instruments—drums, cymbals, tambourines, claves. Music became not just an addendum to movement, but a tool and motivating factor for the dancers. For them, music and movement became one and the same.

The music written by Orff during this period of his life was intended for professional dancers and musicians, not for children. His compositions were conceived in purely artistic rather than educational terms.

His involvement in music education began when his friend and colleague Dorothee Günther started to use these works in the training of dancers and gymnasts in her school, the Güntherschule, in Munich in 1924. Her basic courses combining music and movement were the forerunners of the process to be used in the Orff-Schulwerk.[1]

Orff and Günther based the curriculum of the new school on what Orff referred to as "elemental style." Music and dance were broken down into their simplest component parts and these parts were mastered through performance. This elemental style of teaching and learning was in sharp contrast to the subject–logic–content approach that was more usual in music school curricula. Their teaching reflected the biological theory that the development of the single individual retraces the development of all mankind: that ontogeny recapitulates phylogeny. The elemental style of Orff teaching begins with primal music—with the drum and the fundamental beat, man's earliest musical experiences. It was important to Orff and Günther from the very start that the students *physically* experience beat, meter, tempo, and rhythm, that they express these elements in dance and through instruments, *doing* rather than *learning about*.

In the school itself, Günther was responsible for the dance and theoretical training, while Orff composed the music to be used in the classes and performances. The reputation of the school spread quickly because of the quality of the work produced there. Both professional and nonprofessional dancers flocked to Munich for work in this new elemental style.

In 1926 Gunild Keetman became a student at the Güntherschule. Orff commented on her unusual talent for both music and movement, and said of her that she " . . . became after a short time my helper and colleague in the further expansion of the musical training. . . . I am not exaggerating when I say that without Keetman's decisive contribution . . . 'Schulwerk' could never have come into being."[2] It was to Keetman that Orff gave the responsibility of translating his ideas into techniques for playing his newly developed instruments, particularly xylophones.[3] And it was Keetman who composed the first pieces for these instruments in what has become known as the Orff style.

[1]Günther's method is detailed in Carl Orff and Gunild Keetman, *Music For Children*, (English version adapted from *Orff-Schulwerk* by Margaret Murray), 5 vols. (London and Mainz: Schott, 1974).

[2]Carl Orff, *Schulwerk: Elementare Music*, vol. 3 of *Carl Orff und Sein Werk* (Tutzing: Schneider, 1976), p. 67. Translation by Lee Choksy. Subsequent footnotes in this chapter naming Orff, *Schulwerk*, refer to this 1976 publication. The translations (of Choksy and Gillespie) are unpublished.

[3]In 1928 Karl Maendler, following Orff's design suggestions, built the first Orff xylophone for the Güntherschule.

The actual development of Orff instruments was a direct result of Orff's exposure to the African xylophone and to instruments from Indonesia. The primal sounds of these instruments so suited Orff's philosophy of elemental music and were so in keeping with the artistic goals of the Günther dance troupe that Orff began to incorporate them into his compositions. Drums, small percussion instruments, finger cymbals, and sticks had been used by the dancers and players previously. His works now were expanded to include barred instruments such as xylophones (wood sounds), metallophones (metal sounds), glockenspiels (clear, bell-like sounds), gambas, four-stringed instruments, and even recorders. The styles and sizes of the instruments were tailored to Orff's specifications, thus, these instruments are commonly referred to today as "Orff instruments."

This elemental style was the basis for several theater pieces by Gunild Keetman composed during this period and performed by dancers from the school. (These include, for example, *Nachtlied, Bolero, Stabetanz, Paukentanz,* all in 1930.) These works were seen and critically acclaimed throughout Germany and much of Europe.

The collaboration between Orff and Keetman, which began at the Güntherschule, would eventually produce the many volumes of *Musik für Kinder* (see footnote 1), the basic published material of the Orff approach. However, in the early days all their works were still sketched and designed with adults in mind and were aimed specifically at dance groups.

The first volumes of the Orff-Schulwerk to be published were not the *Musik für Kinder* (or *Music For Children,* as it is known today), but rather a compilation of the educational works that Keetman had used in the training of professional dancers and instrumentalists.[4] The rhythmic and melodic exercises in these volumes were intended to provide a basis for student improvisation. Although the music could be, and was, performed as written, its primary function was to provide a creative stimulus, a vehicle for individual musical expression. These volumes were important as forerunners of the Orff approach because they established the basic compositional techniques, the melodic drones and ostinati over rhythms for the newly developing Orff instruments that were to recur later in the volumes of *Music For Children.*

As the Schulwerk instrumental and dance teaching developed, so also did the musical materials designed for it. All the dancers were expected to play all the instruments and all the instrumentalists were expected to dance. Günther and Orff believed that, as a result of this interchange, sensitivity to the elements of music was heightened and response made more dynamic. This process, in which players moved and movers played, established the artistic alliance which became the essence of the educational philosophy in *Music For Children* when it was published in 1950: "Out of movement, music; out of music, movement."[5]

The cycle of music→movement→more creative movement→more creative music reflected the musical experiences of earliest cultures in which there were dancers who played and players who danced, and in which the creativity of the dancers led to further creativity instrumentally.

The beginning of serious work specifically for children came as the re-

[4]This compilation is Gunild Keetman, *Orff-Schulwerk—Elementare Musikübung* (Mainz: Schott, 1931).

[5]Dorothee Günther, quoted in Orff, *Schulwerk,* vol. 3, p. 150. Translation by Lee Choksy.

sult of an invitation to Orff to compose music for the opening of the Olympic Games in Berlin in 1936. Six thousand Berlin children were trained by Dorothee Günther to perform dances accompanied by an orchestra from the Güntherschule under the direction of Keetman. The presentation was a huge success. As a result of this performance Orff was asked to demonstrate his Schulwerk in major universities and colleges throughout Germany, and his publications began to be known. However, recognition of his work was interrupted by the political situation and by censorship of the arts in Germany at that time. The Güntherschule continued until 1944 when the building was confiscated by the Nazi regime in response to alleged nonconformity by Günther. In 1945 the school was bombed and all of the instruments and materials were destroyed. However, the underlying artistic philosophy could not so easily be suppressed or destroyed.

In 1948 Dr. Walter Panofsky, an official of Bavarian Radio, discovered an out-of-print recording from the time of the Güntherschule and played it for the national director of school programming. They called Orff and asked him to consider writing instrumental music for children, music that could be performed on radio for other children to hear. This gave rise to a whole new educational adventure with ideas that had up until then been the exclusive property of adults.

Orff was clearly aware that the singing voice and the spoken word were not used at the Güntherschule. Yet he recognized that speech and song *must* be the natural starting point for children:

> I was well aware that rhythmic training should start in early childhood. The unity of music and movement that young people in Germany have to be taught so laboriously is quite natural to a child. It was also clear to me what "Schulwerk" had so far lacked; apart from a start, in the Güntherschule we had not allowed the word or the singing voice its fully rightful place. The natural starting point for work with children is the children's rhyme, the whole riches of the old, appropriate children's songs. The recognition of this fact gave me the key for the new educational work.[6]

In 1948 the first of the Orff radio programs was aired to a largely nonexistent audience, since few people had access to radios in those early postwar days. But the materials for these broadcasts were the pioneer works, opening the way to many educational possibilities. The programs slowly but surely became known. Schools that had radios tuned in to the Orff programs, and these programs excited in children a desire to become involved, to play the instruments they were hearing. The rising demand for instruments resulted in the founding of Studio 49 (by Klaus Becker, a cabinetmaker by profession), the first center to produce such instruments commercially for the schools. Studio 49 became the strong support system of the Orff-Schulwerk.

The high point of the broadcasts over Bavarian Radio was the presentation of a Christmas play for children, *Die Weihnachtsgeschichte* ("The Christmas Story"). It was this work by Orff and Keetman that truly brought the meaning of

[6]Orff, *Schulwerk*, vol. 3, p. 214. Translation by Avon Gillespie.

Orff-Schulwerk to the people. Its performance is still an annual event throughout Austria and Bavaria. (A film of this work, produced by Peter Grassigner, was made in 1975 for Bavarian Radio.)

In 1949 Eberhard Preussner, Director of the Mozarteum in Salzburg, as a direct result of his acquaintance with Orff and the Schulwerk, engaged Keetman to teach children's music classes. Traute Schrattenecker, a former dancer and student at the Güntherschule, was at that time conducting a respected school of gymnastics and dance in Salzburg. Opportunities were made for Keetman and Schrattenecker to combine the forces of their children, and, in the tradition of the old Güntherschule, they brought together once more the process of music and movement begun by Dorothee Günther and Carl Orff—this time, however, for children.

In 1953 a demonstration of the children's work was seen by Dr. Arnold Walter of the Royal Conservatory of Music in Toronto and Professor Naohiro Fukui, Director of the Musashino Music Academy in Tokyo. The impression on these two observers was strong enough to start what was to be the international spread of the Orff-Schulwerk—Music for Children.

In response to the many demands for seminars and courses for both children and teachers, the Orff Institute was established in Salzburg in 1961 and this became, in 1963, the music education division of the Mozarteum, with its own building and staff.

THE ORFF PROCESS

The word *process* is paramount in Orff-Schulwerk, and the keys to the Orff process are *exploration* and *experience*. The elements of music are explored first in their simplest, almost crude, forms. Gradually, through experience, these elements are refined and elevated to more complex levels of exploration and experience.

EXPLORATION OF SPACE.   Children are encouraged to explore the qualities of movement—light, heavy, down, up, in, out, smooth, jagged. Body positions and motions are explored and experienced, without discussion and without teacher-imposed definition. There is a cyclical exploration leading from

> outer motivations of movement (the actions done naturally: walking, running, skipping, hopping, crawling)
>
> to inner motivations of movement (moving with the breath, feeling the heartbeat, recognizing the pulse)
>
> back to outer motivations of movement, at a higher level (taking that breathing and heartbeat and incorporating them into stylized walking, running, skipping, hopping, crawling)

Inner motivation thus becomes part of outward expression. Movement is fundamental to all Orff process. It is the foundation on which all other learning rests.

EXPLORATION OF SOUND.   The exploration of sound begins with environmental sounds and sounds without organization: a dog barking, a door slamming, a plane passing overhead, an object dropping. It moves then to organized sounds: patterns of drumbeats, sticks tapped together. Children play and experiment with sound qualities: hard sounds, soft sounds, wood sounds, metal sounds, rattle sounds, solid sounds. The first instruments are not of necessity any standard ones, but rather natural instruments found or invented by the children: gourd rattles, hollowed logs, dried pods. The sounds produced on these crude instruments are organized into simple forms that demand beginnings and endings and involve a sense of duration within defined limits. Sound sources are grouped into families of like sounds and the whole is worked into "pieces" not for performance but for growth and development to the next stage of exploration.

The voice, too, is treated as a sound source to be explored. Children discover that there are many ways to manipulate sounds from the mouth, and these sounds become a vocabulary which will support speaking and singing later. Children play with speech sounds:

Nonsense words and sounds delight children and adults as well. Their use becomes one more step toward a full musical experience. Much vocal play of this sort precedes the introduction of standard material for speech and singing.

EXPLORATION OF FORM.   The exploration of form occurs concurrently with the exploration of space and sound. Movements are organized into patterns, and patterns into dances. Sounds are organized into compositions with like and unlike phrases, introductions, and codas. The shapes of movement and sound are diagramed and symbols are invented to represent them. This is the crude but effective beginning of notation. Results often resemble drawings of the Stone Age, but this simply reflects the elemental aspect Orff referred to in the learning process.

IMITATION TO CREATION.   In Orff-Schulwerk *imitation* is used to insure a role model for creativity. Imitation is the oldest mode of learning. The medieval craftsman was an apprentice before becoming a master; the drummer in African society has a long apprenticeship before becoming a master drummer. The teacher in Schulwerk is like the "master" or major role model. The role of the teacher is gradually lessened as children exhibit more and more independence and finally demonstrate the ability to solve their own problems and answer their own questions through the process. This pattern,

Observe →Imitate→Experiment→Create,

is repeated for each new concept presented. Wilhelm Keller says of this process, "It is the main task of the teacher and educator gradually to make himself superfluous."[7]

INDIVIDUAL TO ENSEMBLE.   Although children must discover the qualities of space, sound, and form for themselves, each individual simultaneously contributes to the group as a whole, and that community of individuals becomes the *ensemble*. Working toward this community or ensemble is a major goal of Orff-Schulwerk. The individual is *most* important when he or she is part of the group. This ensemble consciousness makes its demand at every level of the Schulwerk. Music cannot be made where there is no community.

MUSICAL LITERACY.   Each stage of development within the Schulwerk constitutes a part of the whole which has as its ultimate goal the complete musical experience. Just as children learn to read words only after years of speaking, children in Orff-Schulwerk approach music reading only after much experience with musical sound. Music reading and writing is not systematized in Orff practice; that is, when, where, and how certain literacy skills must be introduced is not predetermined. The reading of standard notation usually begins with the introduction of the recorder and comes only after a number of years of other musical experiences. The task of systematizing music reading is left to the imagination and sensitivity of each teacher. The child who can sing, play, and dance to music, as well as read and write it, is the ultimate aim of the process.

Support Systems for the Process: Orff Instruments

VOICE AND BODY.   The most important instrument in Orff practice is the *body*, and the second most important is the *voice*, since it is contained in the body. Any part of the body can be used to express both a fundamental beat and phrase awareness. The body can be the principal accompanying instrument for speaking and singing at the early stages, without the addition of any other instruments. The model for this comes from early cultures; it is "elemental."
Later, the body instrument is used to express four types of sound at different spatial levels:

---

[7]Wilhelm Keller, *Introduction to Music for Children* (New York: Schott, 1974), p. 47.

These sound gestures are introduced in a systematic way that is consistent with physical development.[8] They can be used separately and in combination to accompany chant or song.

Next, speaking and singing should become the basis for an exposure to the building blocks of music. From such simple sources as children's names, familiar phrases, foods, and natural surroundings, the elements of time and melody may be discovered. Musical forms may be used to put together these elements to create compositions. In actual practice, the singing voice, while very important in Schulwerk, has been given less attention in process development than movement and instrument playing. Some teachers have begun to incorporate singing exercises and songs in the Orff style, which are designed to aid in the development of the voice. Good vocal technique is essential to the overall musical development of children and to the best performance of the Schulwerk.

THE INSTRUMENTARIUM.   The set of instruments used in the Orff process offers a variety of timbres, colors, and textures, and may be easily played by children. These instruments, referred to as the *Instrumentarium,* include

Barred instruments
> Xylophones, producing the mellow, dry sound of wood; of African descent; bass, alto, and soprano;
> Metallophones, producing the mellow, lingering, "wet" sound of metal; of Indonesian descent; bass, alto, and soprano;
> Glockenspiels, producing the sharp, crisp, bell-like sound of metal; of German descent; alto and soprano.

Recorders
> Sopranino, in F; soprano, in C; alto, in F; tenor, in C; bass, in F

[8]Young children can pat accurately long before they can clap accurately. Finger-snapping is the last body sound acquired.

Drums and other percussion instruments descendent from drums
> Bass drums, bongo drums, conga drums, snare drums, hand drums, tambourines, tympani, tom-toms.

Woods
> Claves, wood blocks, slit drums, guiros, temple blocks, maracas, wood rattles.

Metals
> Hanging cymbals, crashing cymbals, finger cymbals, cowbells, sleighbells, wrist and ankle bells, triangles, metal rattles, wind chimes.

Strings
> Guitars, double basses, cellos

The exploratory process used throughout Orff-Schulwerk is used in the instrumental work as well. Improvisation comes before the introduction of written material. Form is introduced as an aid to improvisation.

When first working with a barred instrument a child may be asked to drop both of the mallets lightly on the bars, playing notes in random order but to a specific beat and phrase length given by the teacher. This can be followed by having the child play randomly in an alternating left hand–right hand pattern with instruction to end on a specific tone, thus establishing awareness of tonal center. Later, chants and songs become the basis for instrumental improvisations. A level of proficiency is expected from even the youngest children. The child should play well, and should *know* it.

Children love the Orff instruments and delight in making music on them. However, the approach does not *demand* a set of instruments. The process is more successful in an empty room with a knowledgeable teacher than with a less able teacher in a room full of instruments. When an Orff program is working and the process is clear, the moment for introducing instruments becomes obvious; the need for instrumental expression becomes apparent. Indeed, at this point instruments support the process.

Recorders (sopranino, soprano, alto, tenor, bass) are introduced after the other instruments and are among the chief tools for introducing standard notation to children.[9] However, even with the recorder the approach used is basically an improvisational one.[10]

The Musical Materials

Orff and Keetman wrote five volumes of *Musik für Kinder,* in addition to a number of supplemental works. These volumes offer a rich source of music for performance as well as models for improvisation and composition. They do not present the material in sequential order, although in each book there is a range from very simple to very complex music; choices may be made from any of the

[9]Techniques for teaching music reading in an Orff program may incorporate such Kodály and Jaques-Dalcroze techniques as rhythm syllables, *solfa,* and hand-signs, or may use other traditional note-reading methods. There is no Orff music-reading method.

[10]An excellent source for the recorder is Carol King, *Recorder Routes: A Guide to Introducing Soprano Recorder in Orff Classes* (Memphis, TN: Memphis Musicraft, 1978).

volumes for use at any level. Thus, the process, as such, does not exist in the *Music For Children* volumes. What *does* exist is the basic musical material through which the process may be realized.

There are a number of guides, introductions, and manuals available to the teacher.[11] However, none of these imply that it is possible to become an "Orff teacher" without formal and intensive training in the Schulwerk.

Freedom of choice and its concomitant individual responsibility to the process are zealously guarded by teachers of Orff-Schulwerk. The teacher must be thoroughly grounded in the process if the work is to be successful. Systematic and methodical materials are shared, demonstrated, published, and otherwise distributed to support the Schulwerk, but the individual teacher must be able to make choices with understanding of the process, and this can come only with training. The Orff teacher is taught as he or she is later expected to teach. The program of teacher training leading to certification provides extensive experience with those very elements the teacher will be expected to use with children: exploration and experimentation with space, sound, and form; movement and instrumental experience; and imitation leading to creation. It is a never-ending experience; like all music, it involves lifelong learning. Not every teacher of music is or can be comfortable with the demands made in the Schulwerk. Its roots are in experimentation and improvisation. It is theatrical and it is elemental.

The physically, mentally, and spiritually prepared individual who has had sufficient training in the Schulwerk finds the loosely woven fabric of the Orff approach enough of a system or "method" with which to transmit to children the aesthetic satisfaction of making music.

SUMMARY

The Orff process at every level includes

> exploration of space through movement
> exploration of sound through voice and instruments
> exploration of form through improvisation

At each step of the process the learners move

> from imitation to creation
> from part to whole
> from simple to complex
> from individual to ensemble

all of which supports Carl Orff's ultimate goal of making music live for children.

[11]Doreen Hall, *Teacher's Manual, Music for Children* by Carl Orff and Gunild Keetman. (Mainz: Schott, 1960); Gunild Keetman, *Elementaria: First Acquaintance with Orff-Schulwerk* (London: Schott, 1975); Wilhelm Keller, *Introduction to Music for Children* (Mainz: Schott, 1963); Jos Wuytack, *Musica Viva* (Paris: Alphonse Leduc, 1970, 1972).

6

COMPREHENSIVE MUSICIANSHIP: An American Technique and Philosophy for Teaching Music

Comprehensive Musicianship (CM) is a concept about the teaching and learning of music based on the premise that all facets of music study should be integrated and related. It is an approach to musical study in which the source of all music learning is the literature of music. CM encourages students to grow in musical knowledge and skill at all levels of instruction by synthesizing the musical materials they are working with and by making conceptual connections through performance, analysis, and composition. The principles and philosphies of CM emerged from the Young Composers Project and the Contemporary Music Project for Creativity in Music Education.

In 1957 the Ford Foundation decided to examine the place of the arts in the social and educational environments in the United States. Several successful and respected artists were asked to observe school and community programs and to identify problems and to suggest solutions. The well-known American composer Norman Dello Joio (1913–) observed school music programs and recommended to the Ford Foundation that young composers be placed in the public school systems to compose for performing groups and classes and to encourage the creative process within the academic environment. Dello Joio con-

cluded that the emphasis of public school music programs was on the performance of music and not on the creation of music or on the analysis of the music
performed. By placing composers directly in the classrooms and in the instrumental and choral rehearsals, students would benefit from sharing in the creation of new compositions and from seeing the creative process in operation. The
composers would benefit early in their careers from having specific performing
groups to write for and by being exposed to the realities and problems of school
performances. In addition, the repertoire of school music materials would be
expanded and upgraded.

The Young Composers Project

Based on the recommendation from Dello Joio, the Ford Foundation funded
the Young Composers Project (YCP) in 1959. The project was administered by
the National Music Council with a committee of selection which was chaired by
Norman Dello Joio. This committee consisted of both composers and music educators and was one of the first examples of successful communication and
cooperation between these two segments of the music profession. From 1959 to
1962 the committee placed thirty-one composers in public schools throughout
the United States. The experiment generated enthusiasm for the creative process and provided valuable composing and performing experiences for the students in the selected schools. However, the YCP also pointed out some serious
deficiencies in the public-school music programs. It was discovered that very few
music teachers at that time knew about contemporary techniques of composition. It was also discovered that music teachers lacked the pedagogical skills necessary to incorporate the new compositions within a teaching and learning setting in the classrooms or in the rehearsals. The evaluation of the YCP resulted in
the conclusion that teachers needed to have more training so that present-day
music could be used more widely in the public schools in the United States. In
1962 the Music Educators National Conference (MENC) submitted a proposal to
the Ford Foundation suggesting that (1) the YCP be continued and (2) the program be expanded by including clinics, workshops, and seminars on contemporary music in the schools and by organizing pilot teaching projects in elementary, junior high, and high schools.

The Contemporary Music Project

In 1963 the Ford Foundation granted $1.38 million to the MENC to design and
implement a program called the Contemporary Music Project for Creativity in
Music Education. The name was soon shortened to Contemporary Music Project
(CMP).

In the initial proposal to the Ford Foundation the MENC identified five
basic purposes for the CMP.

1. To increase the creative aspect of music in the public schools
2. To create a solid foundation or environment in the music education profession for the acceptance, through understanding, of the contemporary
   music idiom
3. To reduce the compartmentalization which now exists between the pro-

fessions of music composition and music education for the benefit of composers and music educators alike

4. To cultivate taste and discrimination on the part of music educators and students regarding the quality of contemporary music used in the schools

5. To discover, when possible, creative talent among the students in the schools

The name of the Young Composers Project was changed to Composers in the Public Schools Program of the Contemporary Music Project and between 1963 and 1968 forty-six more composers were placed in the public schools systems. These composers continued to write for performing groups in the schools and continued to share their creative approaches, talents, and outcomes with the school children.

After the CMP was established in 1963, sixteen workshops and seminars were held at colleges and universities throughout the country to help teachers build a better understanding of the analysis, performance, and composition of contemporary music. Six pilot projects were also set up in elementary schools so that models could be developed which demonstrated possible ways for teaching contemporary music to children and also demonstrated workable approaches of utilizing creativity and composition in the classroom.

THE COMPREHENSIVE
MUSICIANSHIP APPROACH

In April, 1965, the CMP sponsored the Seminar on Comprehensive Musicianship at Northwestern University. Composers and music educators at this seminar focused their attention on defining and describing Comprehensive Musicianship. The participants also recommended steps for the improvement of teacher training and recommended ways to improve and upgrade teaching and learning music in classrooms and rehearsals in elementary, junior high, and high schools, colleges, and universities throughout the country. It was at the Northwestern University seminar that the general thrust of the CMP changed from an emphasis on contemporary music in the schools to an emphasis on broad-based and total music teaching. The Comprehensive Musicianship Approach was born.

The curriculum recommendations and suggestions formulated at the Northwestern University seminar led to the establishment of Regional Institutes for Music in Contemporary Education. These institutes developed specific ways of applying and implementing the principles of CM. The following five general aims helped to guide the regional institutes between 1966 and 1968:

1. To relate directly each component of basic music studies to one or several other components; for example, theory to history; or ear training to analysis, writing, performing, sight singing, and conducting

2. To use materials illustrating techniques and styles from all periods and types of music repertoire

3. To devise a continuity between a course on one level and that which precedes and follows it. The totality of the music program from kindergarten to graduate school is viewed as a responsibility shared by all involved in the educational process
4. To help students develop self-direction in music, to exercise imagination, and to sharpen critical judgment in a broad perspective of music
5. To enable the student to generalize from particulars and to deduce particulars from generalizations[1]

The regional institutes helped to establish two-year experimental programs in CM at thirty-six educational institutions throughout the country. Seminars, clinics, and workshops in comprehensive approaches to the teaching of music were also held as in-service training for music educators.

In 1968, the Ford Foundation continued its support of the CMP by giving a five-year grant of $1.34 million to the program. The MENC decided to supplement this by contributing $50 thousand per year during the five-year period. The resources of CMP were divided among three major programs: Program I, Professionals-in-Residence to Communities; Program II, The Teaching of Comprehensive Musicianship; and Program III, Complementary Activities.

Program I—Professionals-in-Residence to Communities—was an expansion of the Composers in Public Schools program. Between 1969 and 1973, thirteen professional musicians were placed in communities of various sizes. The composers served the cultural interests of the communities and encouraged cooperation among the artistic, educational, and civic organizations in the community. The composers gave recitals and concerts and wrote over one hundred compositions.

Program II—The Teaching of Comprehensive Musicianship—focused on the development of teaching skills and techniques in CM. Between 1969 and 1973, twenty-one teachers received project grants to write and to implement experimental programs of music teaching and learning in the elementary and secondary schools, colleges, and universities. Programs at the elementary level were designed to develop content and comprehensive teaching procedures in elementary music classes and to expand the competencies of music specialists, classroom teachers, and students preparing to be elementary music or classroom teachers. At the secondary school level programs were designed to implement comprehensive methods of teaching general music and to implement specific approaches for adapting CM to the instrumental or choral rehearsal. Programs at the college and university level focused on the revision of theory courses and the utilization of CM for the entire music curriculum in higher education.

Program III—Complementary Activities—provided the dissemination of the principles, techniques, and materials of CM through workshops, courses, seminars, CMP publications, the development of films, and the publication of CMP newsletters.

The projects, seminars, and programs of the Young Composers Project and the CMP were directed by the Project Policy Committee. The members—

[1]Contemporary Music Project for Creativity in Music Education," College Music Symposium, VI (Fall, 1967), p.34.

music, educators, scholars, historians, composers, theorists, and performing musicians—served on the committee for varying lengths of time.

In May, 1973 the CMP ended ten years of work and research in music teaching and learning. Its definition, description, and experimentation with CM has been felt in every corner of the world. A variety of outcomes has emerged from the myriad of activities sponsored by the CMP. One of the most important outcomes has been the establishment of the CMP Library.

The composers involved in the Young Composers Project and the Composers in Public Schools program wrote over a thousand different works in a variety of styles and for many different media. The works were all composed for specific groups of young musicians representative of contemporary school ensembles. The most successful of these works have been collected and are available to music educators and musicians through the CMP Library and its catalog, which contains compositions published in *CMP Editions* by University Microfilms of Ann Arbor, Michigan. It is an important source of contemporary choral and instrumental compositions composed specifically to meet the needs of the school ensemble.

Through the various activities, projects, and innovative experiments sponsored by the CMP, CM has emerged as a vital force in American music education. CM, as an educational concept, can be implemented in classrooms, private lessons, class instrumental lessons, class voice lessons, instrumental rehearsals, and choral rehearsals at any instructional level. The CM framework of teaching music can help students gain specific insight into the nature of music, help students relate and synthesize the isolated facets and areas of musical experience, and help students view music with a global perspective.

CM is based on principles that are divided into three broad categories which include common elements, musical functions, and educational strategies.

Common Elements

Through the common-elements approach to the comprehensive study of music, students can gain an awareness and understanding of the structural elements of music common to any culture, tradition, or style. In basic music study, according to the CM approach, these essential properties serve as the carrier of common terms and principles among all music. Commonalities of musical structure can be found in very diverse musical styles such as the Japansese *gagaku* (traditional court music), a hymn, or a popular rock composition. A comprehensive structure of the common elements of music begins with the premise that music is sound. Sound has essential properties which help to describe it:

> frequency (pitch)
> duration
> intensity (loudness)
> timbre

The organization and the interaction of these structural elements produce music which is organized in the following three ways:

1. Horizontal organization: movement of sound and silence through time continuously or in separate units.
   Rhythm: the durational division of sound and silence into long, short, regular, and irregular groupings.
   Melody: the horizontal organization of pitch frequencies as they interact with rhythm.
2. Vertical organization: vertical organization of sounds in a simultaneous unit.
   Harmony: sounds that are played or sung simultaneously
   Texture: qualities created by the density of the simultaneous pitches or the accumulation of individual lines.
3. Expressive qualities: aspects of musical production that contribute to the uniqueness of the sound.
   Intensity: energy that gives sound its qualities of loudness from very soft to very loud. Intensity is often referred to as volume, dynamic variance, or amplitude.
   Timbre: the specific tone qualities or tone color of the sound. Such qualities can be derived from a number of sound sources, including voices, band and orchestra instruments, folk instruments, non-Western instruments, synthesizers, nonmusical sources.

Musical form or structure is the shape that results from the organization of these elements of music.

The resulting musical form always occurs within a musical context which in turn is influenced by other contexts such as historical, social, and aesthetic. Music has a historical background which has influenced its development as well as its initial conception. Historical developments in instrument making and in instrument invention have influenced the quality of sound and the sound possibilities available to the composer. Social trends and practices have often influenced the style of music and the musical techniques employed. The artistic developments and the aesthetic requirements of a society or a culture have also had profound influence on the compositional style of music.

These common elements can be used as the basic units within a curricular structure. Although music should always be studied in the Gestalt, or in the total perspective, the individual structural elements can provide a curricular framework for the teacher to use in planning comprehensive programs of musical instruction. For example, the four properties of sound (frequency, duration, intensity, and timbre) can be the fundamental teaching units for the musical study of primary-age children.

Frequency: high and low pitches
Duration: short and long durational values
Intensity: loud and soft pitches
Timbre: the quality of sound produced from various sound sources

In a comprehensive setting, these four properties are studied, analyzed, performed, and used in sound organization by the primary-age children. Relationships are made to these properties within the musical context or within the musical materials being used by the teacher. The understanding of these common elements of music is expanded at the various educational levels by exposure to more complex musical material.

Musical Functions

A CM approach to music study from preschool through university advocates that students develop personal musical competencies through a balance of experience in

>Performance: reading and recreating music written by a composer
>Analysis: describing the music through perceptive listening
>Composition: understanding and utilizing compositional and improvisational techniques

CM approaches in classrooms and in rehearsals emphasize the common elements of music through actual performance, through listening and description, and through compositional and improvisational activities. Through these experiences, the students take on the roles of performer, listener, and composer. Each role remains within the comprehensive framework, but the actual activities center around the major role, with emphasis on its interrelationship to other roles.

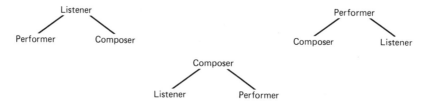

The student in a CM class or rehearsal assumes all three of these major roles and participates in related activities of a creative nature. The teacher and the student probe for meaningful individual and group activities in which the student can participate as either a listener, performer, or composer. During the planned activity the student is careful to note the important, although supportive, roles of the other two components. A listener, to be a comprehensive listener, should also be a composer and a performer. A performer, in order to be a comprehensive performer, should also be a listener and composer. The composer, in order to be comprehensive, should also be a performer and a perceptive listener. The teaching process is usually an indirect one which leads the student to an awareness of the comprehensive totality of music.

Major emphasis in the classroom or in the rehearsal on one of the three basic musicianship functions depends on the educational focus of the class or the ensemble. It is likely that students in a concert choir at the high-school level would emphasize performance while the students in a high-school music theory class would emphasize analysis and composition. However, in both situations the students would actively participate in the subordinate musical roles as well. The concert choir member in a comprehensive setting would describe the music being sung and would be exposed to activities which emphasize composition or improvisation. The music theory students at the high school level would sing or play the compositions being written or analyzed.

Educational Strategies

Derived from the Contemporary Music Project experimental program initiated from 1963–1973, the CM approach stresses music instruction that is integrated and that shows the relationship of one facet of music to another. Theory is related to historical performance practice and to specific musical literature, and musical elements are related to each other. Music is always viewed as a totality of learning with focus on the connections of the constituent parts of the musical materials. In the comprehensive setting, music is also related to all other art areas.

CM approaches also emphasize depth and breadth of study. Students in CM classes or performing groups are encouraged to study the individual musical elements or a series of musical concepts as completely and as thoroughly as possible by examining them within a variety of musical contexts. This in-depth approach to musical study helps to reinforce and expand musical understanding and skill development. Students are also encouraged to study the breadth and variety of music. CM programs of study are based on all types of music from all countries and cultures. Emphasis is on using musical literature from all time periods, including contemporary music, music of the masters, folk music, and global music. Music from this broad spectrum is approached through the common elements and is performed, analyzed, and composed or improvised by the students.

In a CM structure, non-Western music is often performed by the students, it is described and analyzed by the students, and its unique qualities are used in compositional and improvisational experiences and activities. Contemporary music, too, is used as a basis for improvisation, composition, analysis, and performance. Folk music is also analyzed using the common elements of music and is performed in the folk style from which it came. Folk music is studied thoroughly and its compositional and constructional aspects are used as a basis for improvisation and composition.

Some educators have mistakenly thought that CM, since it emerged from the Contemporary Music Project, deals exclusively with contemporary music. Certainly the understanding of music composed in the twentieth century is of great importance in CM programs but the comprehensive curriculum promoted by the Contemporary Music Project includes music played or sung anywhere on this planet—the music of primitive people, ancient oriental music, the music of American youth, and folk and composed music of all times and places.

A CM class or rehearsal is active and many times project oriented. The concept is founded on the premise that students enjoy learning best and learn more if they find their work immediately useful and if they have the opportunities to directly apply the ideas and principles through composition, performance, and through analytical listening. In a CM setting the students are actively involved in the learning process.

The CM approach stresses that students should become actively involved in the common elements of music through participatory experiences as performers, listeners, and composers, and through educational activities that require their personal interaction, involvement, discovery, and interpretation of music of all times, places, and cultures. These CM principles can be applied to all classrooms, ensemble rehearsals, and private lessons. The guidelines of the approach allow the teacher and the student a great deal of flexibility in the selection of materials for pedagogical use and in the selection of the method or the technique of teaching the basic concepts of musical understanding.[2]

SUMMARY AND CONCLUSIONS

Comprehensive Musicianship is a total and integrated approach to the study of music through the common structural elements. These elements are experienced in

performance

perceptive listening, analysis, and evaluation

compositional and improvisational processes and techniques

Students acquire musical knowledge and gain understanding through

active involvement in musical learning

a study of the music of all cultures and time periods

an in-depth study of major concepts or a series of concepts in music

personal discovery and the immediate use of and application of music concepts, skills, and information

Students of Comprehensive Musicianship assume increased responsibility for their own learning and they develop the capacity to formulate and express their own musical judgments and values.

[2]There are two invaluable curricular sources for the CM approach. The first is the *Hawaii Music Program* designed and written by the Curriculum Research and Development Group of the College of Education at the University of Hawaii. The final materials of the program were published in Leon Burton, (ed.), *Comprehensive Musicianship Series* (Menlo Park, CA: Addison-Wesley, 1972). This book includes course and class outlines, materials, and suggested activities for the elementary music class, the general music program in the junior high school, band, orchestra, and choral programs, and the music theory program at the high school level.

A curricular taxonomy of educational concepts, goals, objectives, strategies, and evaluation procedures in a CM context, which is found in Stefan Edelstein, Lois Choksy, Paul Lehman, Njall Sigurdsson, and David Woods, *Creating Curriculum in Music* (Menlo Park, CA: Addison-Wesley, 1980). This source is particularly valuable to those teachers who are designing comprehensive curricular structures for their own school systems or districts and who need a taxonomical guide of goals and objectives for CM.

7

ACHIEVING GOALS AND OBJECTIVES IN SCHOOL MUSIC PROGRAMS VIA THE PRINCIPLES OF JAQUES-DALCROZE, KODÁLY, ORFF, AND COMPREHENSIVE MUSICIANSHIP

The Music Educators National Conference (MENC), the 50,000-member professional organization of American music teachers, has adopted the following statement of goals and objectives for school music programs:[1]

GOALS FOR MUSIC EDUCATION

The National Council of State Supervisors of Music endorses and supports the following goals for music education adopted by the Music Educators National Conference in 1970.*

[1]National Council of State Supervisors of Music of MENC, *Guidelines in Music Education: Supportive Requirements* (Reston, VA: MENC, 1972). Copyright ©1972 by Music Educators National Conference. Reprinted by Permission.
*These goals were derived from the intensive efforts of hundreds of music educators who worked together on the Goals and Objectives project of MENC.

MENC shall conduct programs and activities to build

a vital musical culture
an enlightened musical public

Goals of the profession are

comprehensive music programs in all schools
involvement of persons of all ages in learning music
quality preparation of teachers
use of the most effective techniques and resources in music instruction

The same forces that demand a changing curriculum for tomorrow require changing conceptions of the music education program. The National Council of State Supervisors of Music recommends the following general guidelines in planning or revitalizing programs of music instruction.

The comprehensive music program should

1. be planned and administered to give *every* student opportunities to develop his musical potential to the fullest. Varied and flexible music experiences, geared to meet the divergent abilities, interests, and socio-cultural conditions of the total school population, should be offered from kindergarten through adulthood.

2. begin at the beginning. Emphasis must be placed on in-depth rather than superficial music experiences in early and middle childhood years.

3. be conceived and designed to maintain the interest and involvement of all students in music beyond early and middle childhood years. The practices of exclusivity and selectivity as evident in many music programs of the past are detrimental to the function of music in the curriculum. The myth that musical talent belongs to only a select few must be abandoned.

4. be planned and implemented on the basis of clearly stated objectives for the total program as well as for each level and section of the program. All music staff members should communicate and coordinate their efforts toward common goals.

5. encompass the teaching of music of all periods, styles, forms and cultures.†

6. employ new teaching–learning techniques and technology.†

7. provide an environment which encourages innovation, experimentation and research among its staff members.

8. make use of the products of research in music education.

---

†These statements are quoted or adapted from the MENC Objectives cited for priority attention in 1970.

9. be *student-centered* rather than music-centered or teacher-centered.
10. develop programs of study that correlate performing, creating, analyzing, and listening to music and encompass a diversity of musical behaviors.†

OUTCOMES OF THE MUSIC EDUCATION PROGRAM

As a result of experiences in the comprehensive music program, the graduating student should be able to

1. participate in some kind of musical performance either as an individual or as a member of a group.
2. listen to a wide variety of music with understanding and enjoyment.
3. associate the music score with what is heard or performed.
4. improvise and create music of his own.
5. use music for recreation.
6. recognize the importance of the musical contributions of all regions, cultures, historic periods and ethnic groups to the present world culture.
7. value music as a form of communication and self-expression.
8. actively support music as a vital part of education and of community life.
9. continue to grow musically.‡

FRAMEWORK FOR A MUSIC EDUCATION PROGRAM

The comprehensive music education program provides opportunities for the individual to develop skills, knowledge, understandings, and attitudes for his personal enjoyment, expression, and musical growth in contemporary society.§

The basic elements of music (rhythm, melody, harmony, form, tone color, dynamics, and tempo) are presented to students through various cycles of experiences involving singing, playing instruments, listening, movement, creative expression, and music reading. A continuous sequence of learnings at all grade levels involving these basic experiences will be presented in the student's education so that he can develop usable concepts about the structure of music.

---

†These statements are quoted or adapted from the MENC Objectives cited for priority attention in 1970.

‡These outcomes are adapted from the Curriculum Revision Outline, State of Kansas, 1971, and the Position Paper of the Georgia Music Educators Association, 1972.

§From the Music Section of a Curriculum Bulletin, State Department of Education, Charleston, West Virginia, 1971.

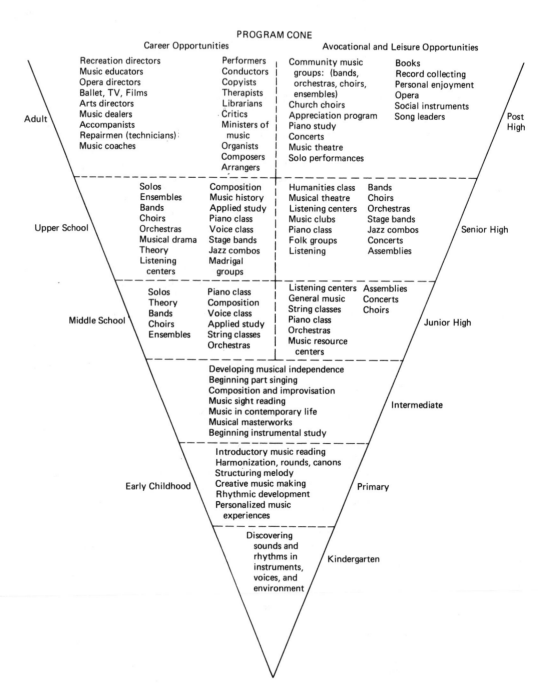

PROGRAM CONE

Career Opportunities   Avocational and Leisure Opportunities

Adult

Recreation directors
Music educators
Opera directors
Ballet, TV, Films
Arts directors
Music dealers
Accompanists
Repairmen (technicians)
Music coaches

Performers
Conductors
Copyists
Therapists
Librarians
Critics
Ministers of
  music
Organists
Composers
Arrangers

Community music
  groups: (bands,
  orchestras, choirs,
  ensembles)
Church choirs
Appreciation program
Piano study
Concerts
Music theatre
Solo performances

Books
Record collecting
Personal enjoyment
Opera
Social instruments
Song leaders

Post High

Upper School

Solos
Ensembles
Bands
Choirs
Orchestras
Musical drama
Theory
Listening
centers

Composition
Music history
Applied study
Piano class
Voice class
Stage bands
Jazz combos
Madrigal
groups

Humanities class
Musical theatre
Listening centers
Music clubs
Piano class
Folk groups
Listening

Bands
Choirs
Orchestras
Stage bands
Jazz combos
Concerts
Assemblies

Senior High

Middle School

Solos
Theory
Bands
Choirs
Ensembles

Piano class
Composition
Voice class
Applied study
String classes
Orchestras

Listening centers
General music
String classes
Piano class
Orchestras
Music resource
  centers

Assemblies
Concerts
Choirs

Junior High

Developing musical independence
Beginning part singing
Composition and improvisation
Music sight reading
Music in contemporary life
Musical masterworks
Beginning instrumental study

Intermediate

Early Childhood

Introductory music reading
Harmonization, rounds, canons
Structuring melody
Creative music making
Rhythmic development
Personalized music
  experiences

Primary

Discovering
sounds and
rhythms in
instruments,
voices, and
environment

Kindergarten

These goals and objectives could be achieved through any of the four approaches explored in this book. The curriculum within each method may be framed in terms of the basic elements of music—rhythm, melody, harmony, form, tone color, dynamics, tempo—listed by MENC. Each approach is cyclic or spiral in its treatment of skills, and each is geared to the development of "usable music concepts." Each relies on such activities as singing, playing instruments, listening, movement, creative expression, and music reading as the means through which to further skills and lead to concept inference. Clearly, *the choice of means must rest more on the individual teacher's talents, capabilities, and training than on any examination of goals and objectives.*

Two further kinds of knowledge could be helpful in making curricular choices: (1) an understanding of the teaching style and lesson planning technique implicit in each approach, and (2) the curriculum framework and types of lessons used in each approach to achieve goals and objectives. These are dealt with in subsequent chapters.

PHYSICAL SETTINGS, EQUIPMENT NEEDS, LESSON PLANNING, AND TEACHING STYLES

Implicit in the practice of any teaching method are certain space requirements, materials particular to that method, lesson planning techniques, and teaching styles unique to it. No examination of method in teaching would be complete without attention to these factors as they pertain to the Jaques-Dalcroze, Kodály, Orff, and Contemporary Musicianship programs in North American classrooms.

JAQUES-DALCROZE

Teaching Style

As a general rule, teachers of Eurhythmics are trained to talk very little and to use valuable class time for music listening and performance. Directions like *begin, stop, go, walk, run, listen, sing, think, make a circle, line up* are given by gestures rather than words. Certain verbal signals are used as commands or directions to introduce changes during an activity. Words like "change" (to indicate a change of direction, changing movement of hands to movement of feet, or replacing one pattern or activity by another) are uttered with an appropriate speech-melody. Eurhythmics teachers convey fairly complicated information even to very young students by using only a few words spoken with precise rhythm, dynamics, and melody, combined with clear and powerful gestures. In easier exercises, in order to allow time for students to prepare for a change, commands are given on the anacrusic beat of a measure. As exercises become more difficult and the students more expert, commands are given first only slightly before the crusic (first) beat and then at various other points in the measure. This demands a quick and accurate response from the student even under stressful rhythmic conditions. Since the teacher can vary the placement of the commands, students are forced to be attentive and self-disciplined.

Commands may also be given by flash cards, chalkboard graphics, or physical signals (nods of the head or other gestures). Finally, purely musical commands are given from the keyboard or by percussion or voice: a chord, a trill, a particular tone, accent, subdivision, playing in bass or treble range, harmonic progression, or melody fragment may be used to alert the students to change to a different movement. A command can be used also to create counter-

point between students and teacher: "If I play ♩, you demonstrate ♪♩

by movement; if I play ♪♪, you demonstrate ♩."
In Europe the verbal commands most frequently used are "Hip!", "Hop!" and "Hup!" Each command indicates a different predetermined action to be performed by the student.

The Jaques-Dalcroze manner of using group dynamics emphasizes freedom of exploration and the many possibilities of individual solutions to rhythmic problems. The greatest value is placed on the student's discovery of interesting and unusual solutions rather than on imitating the teacher's solutions. Such solutions are then shared by the group and become one source of a larger vocabulary of ideas for the group and the teacher.

The Eurhythmics teacher must be sure that students are never treated simply as an audience which reacts to the thrills engendered by the teacher's artistic manipulations. Instead, students are viewed as young artists and are expected to develop their own thoughtful and personal artistic responses to the teacher's rhythmic stimuli. The best teachers in this method are those who are able to help students transmute raw feelings into cogent techniques of expression which discipline action. The problem of balancing technique with expressive feeling is basic to all artists and is central to the Jaques-Dalcroze method.

Since one goal of lessons is to produce personal responses to musical challenges, students from many different levels of musical sophistication can work together. Each individual's solutions to a Eurhythmics exercise may be correct, but the solutions within a class may vary in imagination, depth, intensity, and clarity.

A summary of the Jaques-Dalcroze teaching–learning style is given on p. 119.

Space, Equipment, and Costume

Comfort, hygiene, and safety are primary concerns to the Eurhythmics teacher. Ideally, lessons require a spacious, well-ventilated classroom with an immaculately clean wooden floor. Students should wear comfortable, washable clothing suitable for freedom of movement and should either wear soft gym or dancing shoes or go barefoot in order to enhance balance by direct contact with the floor and ensure flexible use of the arches and toes. A well-tuned piano, simple percussion instruments, chalkboard, balls, ropes, and hoops are the ideal equipment.

Since these ideal conditions are rarely found in North American schools,

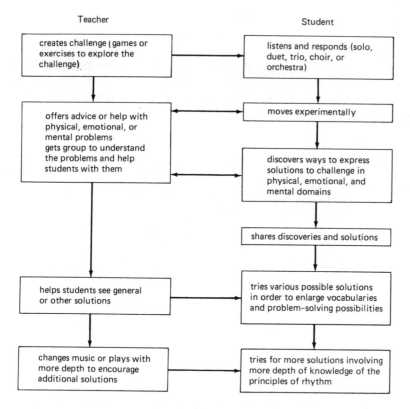

Teacher | Student

many Eurhythmics teachers have been forced to modify Jaques-Dalcroze's original plans and practices and have developed new movement and music exercises and games or have modified old ones to suit rooms with little open space. Some teachers have moved classes into gymnasiums, libraries, or cafeterias where furniture can be moved to provide open space. Others have used corridors of school buildings or playground areas.

Physical safety is realized by special exercises in spatial awareness, energy matching, energy discipline, ensemble, and social integration. Students learn to deal quickly and efficiently with spatial formations (circles, letters, lines, files, teams); these exercises are extended to help students learn to handle traffic problems involving bumping, pushing, following, and leading. Classes too large for the available space may be divided into group formations, such as concentric circles, or into particular combinations, such as movers and clappers, or movers, clappers, and singers.

Musical Materials

A Eurhythmics lesson can begin from speech, percussion, song, or piano improvisation and lead to ear training and analysis by movement; or it can begin with movement and lead to ear training and music making. The teacher may use music ranging from play-party songs through all varieties of folk, popular, and classical song and dance music. The styles may include all periods, and all instrumental and vocal performance media. A lesson could begin with stories or poems, or with observations of rhythmic movement in people, nature, dance, sports, architecture, drawings, sculpture, and visual designs, as well as the mechanical rhythms of machines, toys, and imaginative science-fiction creatures. By means of this wide range of rhythmic sounds and ideas, the students and teacher can engage in exploratory activities which lead to skill, understanding, and knowledge.

Lesson Planning

There are certain major presumptions necessary in order for any teacher effectively to implement Eurhythmics practices. They might be viewed as the teaching cornerstones of the Jaques-Dalcroze method.

The teacher should assume that

1. children may have little formal knowledge, but are brilliant, sensitive and artistic and can learn anything they need or want to know;
2. what children are helped to discover for themselves is most memorable;
3. if children seem confused, it is not because they are stupid—it is because the teacher has not found effective ways to present the material;
4. if children meet with success by working at each step along the way, they will enjoy the process of learning and want to discover more.

When implementing lessons the teacher should

1. teach in many small steps rather than one big step;
2. encourage the whole class to think about the problem if a child makes a mistake, and have the whole class help to find ways to correct it;
3. review old games so that children can see the results of their work and enjoy their own progress and skill;
4. stay alert for signs of fatigue and tension and deal with them quickly by changing to a counteracting activity;
5. always check the orchestration of the body: is the body part chosen appropriate for a particular rhythm or tempo? (not all rhythms are appropriate for full locomotion, not all gross body movements are easy, not all smaller muscle movements are difficult);
6. practice skills in many varieties of tempo; use dynamics and phrasing to develop concepts as to effective and correct usage of these in performance.
7. choose an appropriate tempo for each musical activity (this requires great care since the wrong tempo can make a simple activity difficult or impossible);
8. change game rules: even the slightest change in the rules of the game makes it a new game and renews interest;
9. speak rhythmically and dynamically, but remember that demonstration saves both time and words;

10. repeat activities, since repetition aids memory, but remember that repetition in a slightly varied form fights boredom.

The process of Eurhythmics moves from simple to difficult movement, from outer to inner movement. The beginning position, sitting down, is limited in spatial range but safe and free of balance problems. After sitting comes kneeling, standing, movement in place, and movement in space—a progression of increasing difficulty. The final goal of movement activities is for the student to extinguish all outward movement while recalling, reliving and performing the musical experience vividly.

The specific instructional objectives of such a positive movement approach are to help children to

use all their faculties when learning
explore the movements of their bodies
use their imagination and creativity
become aware of the space around them
become flexible and agile and develop coordination and motor abilities
develop a complete sense of body awareness
express feelings through body movement and sound
develop listening capacity
use their minds to control their bodies
develop skills in following directions
develop thinking processes
acquire musical concepts
develop techniques for musical expression
develop attention and concentration abilities
perceive and express the slightest nuances of rhythm and pitch
feel relaxed while at the same time having a positive and constructive outlet for physical energy

Though there are both published and unpublished volumes of Eurhythmics exercises by Jaques-Dalcroze,[2] they were written only to remind his students of their lessons; though suggestive, they can be used neither to learn to teach his methods nor as a guide to building Eurhythmics lesson plans.

Teachers of Jaques-Dalcroze's Eurhythmics are expected to create their own exercises, games, and materials, and, by presenting all of these in a logical developmental sequence, to create a form for the lesson. Since a lesson might last thirty minutes and deal with many subjects or, on the other hand, might last several months and deal with only one subject, a single lesson plan may be complete

[2]The published volumes are *Méthode Jaques-Dalcroze*, Pts. I et II; *Gymnastique Rythmique* (Paris-Neuchatel: Sandoz Jobin, 1905) and *The Jaques-Dalcroze Method of Eurhythmic Movement* (London: Novello, 1916). The unpublished works, originally at L'Institut Jaques-Dalcroze in Geneva, are now being transferred to the Geneva Conservatory.

or be merely part of a larger plan. The lesson is itself a creative process. Lesson plans are rarely repeated since they must be tailored to the needs, abilities, and talents of the students. Because Eurhythmics teachers receive special training in vocal, instrumental, and movement improvisation, they are accustomed to discarding or surrendering all or part of a lesson and even to inventing a new plan on the spot when necessary, with suggestions and help from the students. This is done to satisfy the special needs or interests which grow out of sudden discoveries made during the lesson.

All Eurhythmics lessons are based upon one or more of Jaques-Dalcroze's 34 elements of rhythms. The first step in designing a lesson is to think deeply and broadly about the element or elements to be taught, in a way that connects that rhythmic element or elements with the students' physical, emotional, mental, and musical life. One way the Eurhythmics teacher could examine the possible scope of a lesson is outlined below.

1. Title: subject (chosen from the 34 elements of rhythm)
2. Musical definition of the element (or elements), with musical examples from the literature; improvised examples on piano or percussion instrument or with speech or song.
3. Physical definition of the element (or elements)
    a. What kind of movement, what orchestration of body parts might express the qualities of the element?
    b. Which possibilities are easiest? more difficult? more complete? incomplete?
    c. What physical problems of body technique, time, space, energy, direction, weight, balance, and geometry (straight, curved, $\triangle$, $\bigcirc$, $\square$) must be studied in preparation for various parts of the lesson?
    d. What tempi would be best? what dynamic level?
4. Emotional definition of the element (or elements)
    a. How does the element affect feelings of performer or audience? Will it make them excited or quiet?
    b. How do composers use the element to produce mood (relaxed, quiet, excited, releasing, suspenseful)?
    c. What emotional problems might emerge because of the element? How will the teacher and students handle them?
    d. Can the students learn to feel and express without simply acting out?
5. Cognitive (mental) definitions: what symbols, graphics, language, judgements, willpower, imaginative techniques, life examples, or analogies will be needed for development of automatisms (automatic responses) to solve the problems of the games?
6. Life sources for subject
    a. What life, nature, mechanical experiences, situations, objects, and behaviors can be found and used for developing activities in the lesson—music, songs, stories, movements connecting the subject to students' lives?
    b. What live materials might be used to enhance the lesson?

c.   How can the teacher improvise imaginatively on these associations?

7.   Baseline for lesson and training: what kind of preparation must students have in order to solve the challenges proposed in the games and other activities of the lesson? (For example, a lesson on rests requires the ability to initiate or inhibit motion quickly while maintaining balance and to stay alert and responsive during rests. If students have not been trained in this behavior, the tension of rests can produce difficulty in breathing or even intense, painful muscular contractions and spasms.)

Exercise and Game Plans

In planning lessons, five basic exercises and game plans are used, at varying levels of complexity:[3]

1.   the quick reaction
2.   the follow
3.   the replacement
4.   the interrupted canon
5.   the continuous canon

THE QUICK REACTION.   This is the opening game of the classic Jaques-Dalcroze lesson plan. In this exercise the students listen to the musical stimulus and decide which of two or more rhythmic ideas is being presented, then quickly select the appropriate movement responses. Its purpose is to induce attention, concentration, and analysis. It often introduces the basic content of the lesson—sound or silence (interpreted as moving or being still), walking or running, accented or unaccented beats, high or low, loud or soft, with or against the beat. The teacher begins the lesson on an easy level by cueing changes or giving the changes in a simple sequence (for example, every 8 beats or every 4 beats). Then the teacher begins to raise the level of the game by giving the changes in a compound sequence (for example, every 8 beats, then every 2 beats, then every 4 beats, and so on). The game is raised to its most difficult level by giving arbitrary changes or by setting up a regular sequence (for example, every 4 beats) for a considerable period and then suddenly breaking the sequence, in order to discover if the students have gone into "automatic" reaction instead of conscious decision-making. The quick response, when three or more rhythms are presented simultaneously, is more difficult. Verbal commands such as "Hands," "Feet," "Left-right," "Walk," and "Stop" can be used instead of musical signals. Visual signals, such as flash cards with music notation, can be used in all these games.

THE FOLLOW.   The follow calls for accurate response to constant changes of tempo, accent, dynamics, phrasing, and articulation. It forces the student to respond to the slightest nuance of the teacher's performance or conducting by appropriate movement changes. It is useful in producing flexibility in a given rhythmic behavior. It requires generalization of a pattern in spite of sub-

[3]For specific games see Robert M. Abramson, *Rhythm Games for Perception and Cognition* (Hialeah, FL: Columbia Pictures Publ., 1978).

tle or obvious changes within the pattern itself. A sense of balance is a prime requirement. An overly emotional reaction will destroy this equilibrium. In these exercises the students are encouraged to combine emotional reactions with thought about the best way to express these feelings. This leads to the development of aesthetic judgment. For example, the simple rhythmic figure

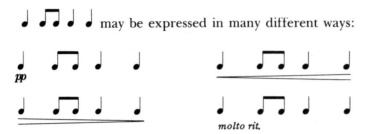

Each of these implies a totally different shading of feeling. The student must express these different shadings in movement response to the teacher's performance. This type of exercise can promote a vitality of musical expression that is often lacking in the performances of music students whose expression is otherwise almost always chosen and directed by the conductor or teacher.

THE REPLACEMENT.   The replacement exercise is a game in which one item is replaced in a rhythmic pattern which is already learned. If students have

learned | ♩ ♩ ♩ ♩ | and then replace beat 4 with a rest, they have created a

new pattern, | ♩ ♩ ♩ 𝄽 |. The new pattern demands a new physicality; it requires that the movers be prepared to stop toward the end of beat 3 and wait for the length of the fourth beat to resume the pattern. A new expressive quality develops (the effect of removing beat 4 is very powerful, it being the anacrusis, a moment of growing energy) and the rest becomes a particularly powerful silence. In this game the teacher and class could insert the variable in either a serial or random order and study the correct physical performance and expression in each new case. Verbal commands in the form of numbers ("one," meaning

𝄽 ♩ ♩ ♩; "two," meaning ♩ 𝄽 ♩ ♩; and so on) tell the student which beat must be replaced. This exercise is often converted into a memory-training study, by choosing a series of patterns and performing them in any random order commanded by the teacher. Commands of the patterns memorized, identified by letter (pattern A, pattern D, etc.), are practical and remind the student which pattern is affected. It is as definitive a method of training as lists of verb endings in language study.

THE INTERRUPTED CANON.   The interrupted canon is commonly called the "echo canon." It is used to develop fast memory for a pattern without much attention to analysis. The teacher claps or otherwise performs a rhythmic pattern and is immediately "echoed" by the class. The teacher then continues with a new pattern. This activity aids short-term memory. If the patterns are chosen carefully and performed musically, employing dynamic variation, articulation, and phrasing, they are very valuable. However, when they are performed as noisy or unmusical clapping without nuance, they are studies not in rhythm but only in time. In Jaques-Dalcroze's Eurhythmics the material in an exercise such as the interrupted canon is always based on the subject of the lesson—in other words, the rhythmic element (or elements) being studied. Thus, a lesson on rests will include a variety of patterns using rests, and the students will have to discover the expressive purposes and deal with the physical problems created by rests. Directions for the interrupted canon (telling the students either to listen or to imitate) are most often given by body cues such as a smile or a lift of the head on the preparatory beat. Patterns longer than one measure may create canons of the length of a phrase or period, and require longer intervals of concentration and memory. Interrupted canons using replacement-exercise techniques can be used to induce analysis simultaneously with performance. This brings hearing memory and performing memory together and aids the development of extended memory. Interrupted canons can be used to develop visual memory, by creating rhythms in movement without sound. Canons can also be performed as movement echoed by sound.

THE CONTINUOUS CANON. The continuous canon is a more difficult game. As with all canons, there is a leader and a follower. Usually the teacher leads by performing a rhythmic pattern of movements or sounds or both. The students are directed to begin to follow after a specific number of beats or measures ("Begin four beats after me," "Begin two movements after me," and so on). The students must live in three worlds of memory; analogously to the spirits in Dickens's *A Christmas Carol*, memory past becomes performance present, listening present becomes performance future. There are three major problems for students performing continuous canons. First, they must keep an internal count of beats, especially of the crusic (down-) beats. Even if they cannot perform all the patterns given by the teacher, they must be encouraged to keep a sense of balance and order under stress. Second, they must develop an ability to continue after an error and to find a new starting place that makes musical sense. A student may falter during a continuous canon, but should not give up. Instead, he or she must keep counting beats, listening for the anacrusic and crusic beats to a new measure performed by the teacher, and enter again in the proper place. The third problem in the performance of continuous canons occurs with the introduction of real counterpoint. Dealing with opposing ideas and movements, keeping the inner world together while the outer world seems totally different, is a particularly difficult problem for students who have always been trained to work in unison with teachers or groups. Assertive and independent action with an understanding of interdependent relationships is one hallmark of good part singing and ensemble performance. The study of canon is often placed at the end of a Eurythmics lesson, as a summation of the skills and knowledge gained in the lesson.

Three Types of Lesson Plans

The lesson plans used in a Eurhythmics class are enormously varied, but frequently they take the shape of a musical composition. Sometimes the teacher shapes the lesson in theme-and-variations form, in increasingly complex order. Sometimes the form is symphonic and consists of an introduction, two themes, development, recapitulation, and coda. The best lessons have an introduction, development, and climax. In this way the lesson plans themselves are a kind of artistic musical composition. Each lesson should provide for the development of physical, emotional, and mental skills, the formation of concepts through analysis, identification and manipulation of symbols, and the application of learning through student improvisation, using movement, percussion, speech, song, and traditional or folk instruments. The goal is constant and intense ear training.

Among many possibilities, let us look at three basic types of Jaques-Dalcroze lesson plans. All are based on the 34 elements of rhythm.

PLAN 1.   This type of lesson provides many experiences with a single element of rhythm or on a simple level of skill.

a.   quick-reaction exercise using the element or pattern
b.   five different quick-reaction and follow exercises using different body orchestrations and various locomotion activities on the same element or pattern
c.   chalkboard or flash-card work involving reading and writing the element or pattern
d.   improvisation with the element or pattern
e.   interrupted canon or dance game using the element or pattern

PLAN 2.   In this format the teaching process is the same from the beginning to the end of the lesson, but many rhythmic elements are experienced on a very simple level.

a.   quick reaction or follow on an element
b.   quick reaction or follow on a new element
c.   quick reaction or follow on a new element or on combined elements
d.   quick reaction or follow on two new elements

PLAN 3 (THEME AND VARIATION TYPE).   This lesson format is used to present one or more rhythmic elements in order of increasing difficulty.

a.   quick-reaction games on the elements or patterns being taught, in order to stimulate attention, to start the kinesthetic process, and to familiarize the students with the elements or patterns
b.   follow games, in order to develop flexibility of response and to study the effects that the variables (tempi, accents, dynamics, phrasings) have on the elements or patterns being studied
c.   replacement games, in order to stimulate memory, to study the effect of variations on the elements or patterns, and to develop vocabulary, automatic responses, and short-term memory recall
d.   interrupted canons, using the elements or patterns of the lesson to produce continuity of musical form

   e. use of chalkboard, for reading and writing music notation, dictation, and improvisation with the elements or patterns

   f. student conducting of the elements or patterns

   g. group improvisation, using speech, percussion, or singing, separately or in combinations, conducted by the students

   h. creating canons, dances, or games, using the elements or patterns

Emile Jaques-Dalcroze's special gift was his ability to imagine and express musical quantities as movement qualities. Imagination is of the greatest importance to the successful use of his method. The methods and the lesson plans teach facts about music, but, more importantly, they teach what sensitive musicians think and feel when performing. The facts themselves are less important than how musicians use facts and feelings—not *what* to think and feel but *how* to think and feel is what Eurhythmics training seeks to convey.

The Process of Eurhythmics

The *process* of Jaques-Dalcroze's Eurhythmics is the manner in which experiences are converted into perception, information, and cognition. Observers and students in a Eurhythmics class often confuse the process with

> the teaching style: what the teacher and students do and how they share; for example, teacher plays, student walks
>
> the content: what exercises and activities are used; for example, quick reaction, follow, replacement, canon
>
> the medium: the ear and body; for example, walk, run, sing, speak, conduct; full body or small parts of body movement in place or in space
>
> the concepts or subject matter: for example, tempo, beat, duration, phrasing
>
> the curriculum: the ordering of exercises and concepts

All of these aid the process, but they are not the process itself.

The process of Eurhythmics requires the use of fresh, interesting, and aesthetically satisfying music to induce intense directed listening. This listening experience is the exact opposite of the types of hearing employed when music is used for three purposes common today: to cover noise; to accompany other more important activities; and to produce pleasant, dreamlike states in order to escape reality. The listening experience in a Eurhythmics class does not permit any nonthinking behavior.

The process begins when listening evokes a kinesthetic response connecting body and mind through aural and physical sensation. Impression becomes expression; sound becomes physical memory. Musical memory must be quickly available both as sensation and as sound. Since students cannot predict the teacher's improvised music, they must remain alert, in a state of concentration. The entire process of Eurhythmics is based on the musical challenge to listen carefully and to find ways to express what is heard, felt, understood, and known.

A representation of the process might be:

STAGE 1

The teacher may manipulate the material (speed up, slow down, etc.). Such spontaneous manipulation of musical material during the game creates constant novelty, which stimulates more involvement of the brain and nervous system. The challenge may also be offered by the students, using music or movement of their own invention.

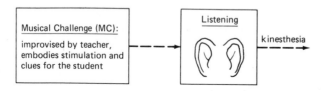

STAGE 2

In Stage 2 all faculties of the student are engaged in solving musical challenges. Feelings and ideas are expressed simply and may be gross responses rather than specific ones. The movement may be in place, in preparation for the more difficult problems of gross motor movement in space, where weight and balance bring new problems of performance and body technique.

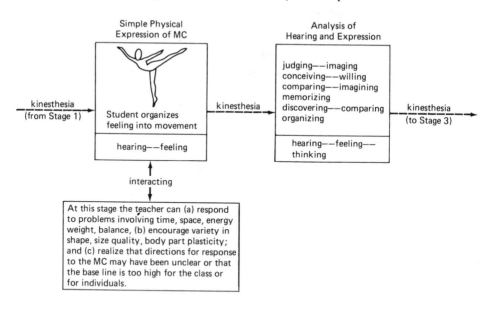

STAGE 3

The teacher's role is to lead the students to improved responses and expression. The teacher's ability to observe and resolve problems of expression are important at this stage. Students may need to stop to work out a problem, or the teacher may have to revise the challenge.

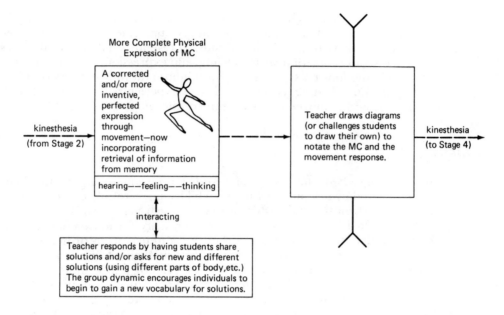

More Complete Physical
Expression of MC

A corrected and/or more inventive, perfected expression through movement—now incorporating retrieval of information from memory

hearing––feeling––thinking

kinesthesia
(from Stage 2)

Teacher draws diagrams (or challenges students to draw their own) to notate the MC and the movement response.

kinesthesia
(to Stage 4)

interacting

Teacher responds by having students share solutions and/or asks for new and different solutions (using different parts of body,etc.) The group dynamic encourages individuals to begin to gain a new vocabulary for solutions.

STAGE 4

The use of graphics and symbols to represent experiences follows Jaques-Dalcroze's rule of *experiences before abstraction.* The eye is as capable of producing kinesthetic sensations in the nervous system as the ear, since even more of the students' faculties are involved. However, the temptation to use the eye without body movement to interpret the symbols of music should be avoided. Though the final goal is to see and hear internally and to feel all the motions and emotions of the music, this should not be attempted too early. If it is rushed, there is

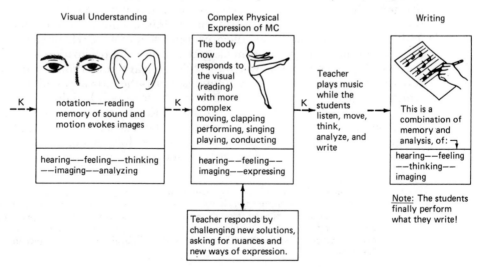

Visual Understanding

notation––reading memory of sound and motion evokes images

hearing––feeling––thinking
––imaging––analyzing

Complex Physical
Expression of MC

The body now responds to the visual (reading) with more complex moving, clapping performing, singing playing, conducting

hearing––feeling––
imaging––expressing

Teacher plays music while the students listen, move, think, analyze, and write

Writing

This is a combination of memory and analysis, of:

hearing––feeling
––thinking––
imaging

Note: The students finally perform what they write!

Teacher responds by challenging new solutions, asking for nuances and new ways of expression.

a risk of developing technically impressive yet unmusical performers. When reading is introduced into singing, speaking, or movement, students may tend to perform with an accurate but dulled musical response. The use of the eyes can lead to a disconnection of hearing, feeling, and expression. The eyes, ears, body, brain, and emotions must act as one continuous and fully expressive unit. This will happen only if there has been sufficient experience at Stages 1, 2, and 3 of the process and if movement is continued into Stage 4.

KODALY

The only ingredients necessary for a Kodály program are a good musician well trained in Kodály teaching techniques, children, a carefully chosen core of folk songs and art music, and sufficient time to teach and learn music.

While it is very pleasant to have open space for movement, it is possible for the Kodály teacher to work within the confines of an ordinary classroom without too much difficulty. In practice the usual school "music room," with its lack of desks and proper surfaces for music reading and writing, presents a far greater problem to the Kodály teacher than a normally equipped classroom.

Even a piano is not a necessity for good Kodály programs. While the Kodály teacher will occasionally use a beautiful Bach, Brahms, or Bartók accompaniment for singing with a fifth or sixth grade, the piano is never used to accompany really young voices. Until in-tune singing is firmly established and part singing is secure, no accompanying instruments are used. It is the belief of Kodály practitioners that secure intonation and accurate vocal intervalic performance are best developed using vocal models.

The Kodály teacher must, of course, be extremely sure of his or her own pitch perception, since he or she is the principal role model for the children. The A–440 tuning fork, always in hand, has become the badge of the Kodály teacher.[4] The good "Kodály teacher" is one who is at home with relative solmization and secure in the many worlds of rhythm, is knowledgeable about theory and musical forms, and knows the great musical literature. He or she is probably involved in the adult life in some aspect of musical participation and performance. Such a teacher enjoys watching children learn and is content not to interfere, not to give quick and easy solutions, but rather to allow children space in which to discover principles and time in which to polish skills.

The teaching style of a well-trained Kodály teacher involves very little speaking and no "telling" or "explaining." The teacher may sing a phrase of a song, indicating with a conducting gesture where children are to begin; he or she may indicate simply by doing that the children are to

[4]It was Zoltán Kodály himself who inaugurated the use of tuning forks for finding starting pitches, among the Hungarian choral teachers who first worked with him on the evolution of the method. He objected strongly to pounding out starting notes on a piano for a choir about to sing an *a cappella* number. If the director used a tuning fork unobtrusively, choirs could be given the key note softly, vocally, and could begin singing full voice in many parts "as if by magic."

      tap the beat
      clap the rhythm
      perform an ostinato while singing

When the teacher does speak it is to ask questions designed to guide analysis:

> *Is the new note higher or lower?*
> *Can you find the I chord outlined in the melody?*

to offer support and help to a child experiencing difficulty:

> *Clap it with me.*
> *Try to make your voice match mine.*

or to give simple directions:

> *Now construct the first phrase on your felt staves.*
> *Read the first phrase silently with inner-hearing.*

Nothing is ever told in a Kodály class if it can instead be demonstrated by the teacher or inferred and derived by the students.

> *Is the ostinato we are clapping the same as the rhythm we are singing? Where is it different? How could we change the notation of our ostinato so that when we per-form it, it will sound the same as the rhythm we are singing?*

    Certain information can be imparted only directly. The *name* of a new tonal or rhythmic element cannot be inferred or derived, it can only be told. Only the teacher can name the new note *re* or the new rhythmic figure *tum–ti*. But the *place* of that new tone in relation to tones previously learned can be identified by the students as "higher or lower." Its probable position on staff can

be inferred. The relative durations of notes in the new pattern ♩. ♪ can be

derived if students compare it aurally to the previously known pattern ♩ ♫.
    The teacher in a Kodály class is unobtrusive. He or she is never a *per-former* in front of children; rather, children become the performers while the teacher quietly guides and directs the learning experience, helping those who need help, praising those who deserve praise, expecting and usually getting 100 percent of the children's attention to the tasks at hand. This high level of expec-tation in Kodály groups is one key to the total involvement of children in such groups.
    The intellectual challenges, the emotional satisfaction derived from such teaching and learning make most behavior problems disappear—children are simply too involved to be mischievous. A sense of "I can do it!"—of positive self-

image—is developed in this type of teaching–learning model that is conducive to good behavior.[5]

Lesson Planning

The major goals of all Kodály training are:

1. to develop musical literacy—the ability to think, read, write, and create with the traditional language of music
2. to impart a sense of cultural identity through use of the students' own folk-music heritage and to further the understanding of other peoples and cultures through knowledge of their folk music
3. to encourage the performance abilities of all students—to sing in classes and choirs, to participate in ensembles and orchestras—to use such participation in musical groups as a way of enriching their lives
4. to make the great art music of the world the property of the students

In planning to accomplish these goals it is necessary to focus on a number of different musical functions in each lesson: singing in unison and in parts; musical reading and writing; ear training, inner hearing, and memorization skills; recognition and use of musical forms; moving to music; listening to music; improvisation and composition.

As security with each new skill is developed within these musical functions, the teacher moves from (1) demonstrations by the class as a whole to (2) demonstrations by smaller groups and, finally, to (3) demonstrations by individual students. Assessment of skill learning can take place only at the third, the individual, level of performance. The teacher cannot be sure that Johnny can sing in tune or Susan can hear the beat and step to it correctly until he or she has heard Johnny sing alone and seen Susan step alone. Classes do not learn, individuals learn; and they learn at differing rates. It is vitally important that the teacher be sure that one concept has been acquired, that one skill level has been mastered, before expecting students to move on to another, more involved concept level, to yet another higher skill level.

Pedagogical Process

The pedagogical process through which concepts and skills are developed always begins with the total musical experience and moves gradually to the abstractions for that experience—from known to unknown, from sound to symbol.

The teacher proceeds through a four-stage process in presenting each new learning to the children. First there is a long period of (1) *preparing* the children for the new concept or skill to be acquired. This is accomplished through the performance of many rote-taught songs containing the unknown element. When the children are sufficiently prepared—when they can perform the new element completely—it is (2) *made conscious knowledge* to them—it is aurally

---

[5]The final report of the San Jose Project quoted numerous interviews as evidence of the influence of this kind of teaching on children's self-image. Randolfo P. Pozos, *Kodály Music Education Program. San Jose Unified School District* (mimeographed and bound) (Oakland, CA: Holy Names College, 1978), 60 pages.

identified by the children in response to questioning, and then named and shown in notation by the teacher. This is followed by another long period of (3) *reinforcement,* during which the teacher leads the class to examine all songs studied in the preparation stage to discover the newly made-conscious element and to sing new songs also including the new element. Finally, the teacher presents new song material containing the new element to determine whether the children have acquired the new concept or skill sufficiently well (a) to read new material including it independently, and (b) to improvise or compose using the new element. This is (4) *assessment.*

The teaching process is

prepare → make conscious → reinforce → assess

The whole is interwoven, so that while the teacher is at stage 3 (reinforce) of a new melodic learning he or she may at the same moment be at stage 1 (prepare) of a rhythmic skill and at stage 4 (assess) of a harmonic one. The planning involved is complex, but once understood, extremely rational.

Concurrently with the above the learners are moving through a five-stage process. They (1) *hear and perform* the new element in a rote manner in numerous songs; they are then led to (2) *discover and derive* the new element and to *infer* concepts; after which they (3) *write or construct* the symbols representing it, then (4) *read* it in familiar and in new songs and, finally, (5) *create* music using the new element.

The learning process is

hear/perform → infer/derive → hear/construct/notate → read → create

The two sides of this one teaching-learning process fit together in the following manner.

The Teaching-Learning Process of the Kodaly Method

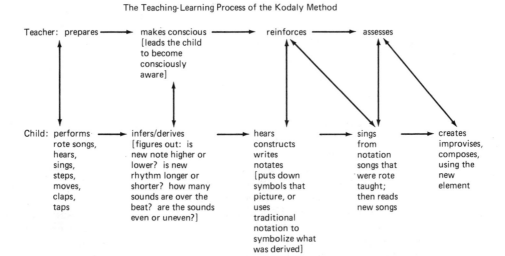

Week No.	PREPARE NEW LEARNINGS		MAKE THE CHILDREN CONSCIOUSLY AWARE OF THE NEW LEARNING		REINFORCE NEW LEARNING THROUGH SKILL ACTIVITY			
	Rhythmic	Melodic	Rhythmic	Melodic	Hand Singing	Constructing or Writing	Reading	Inner Hearing and Memorization
15		*la* in *s-l-s-m* patterns. Songs: *Bounce High, Here Comes a Bluebird, Lucy Locket, Icka Backa.* ♩ ♩ ♩ ♩ (l l l m)			*s-m* phrases of known songs: *Snail, Star Light.*	Construct on felt staves the first phrases of *Snail* and *Star Light* in F-do	Read rhythm of *Bounce High* from chalkboard:	Inner hear the 'B' phrases of *Here Comes a Bluebird*; then the 'A' phrases.
16				*la* in *s-l-s-m* patterns. Make Conscious Song: *Bounce High* / Other songs: *Here Comes a Bluebird, Lucy Locket, Icka Backa.*	New handsign for *la*. Practice showing & singing patterns of *s-l-s-m* in songs	Construct on felt staves the first phrases of *Bounce High* & *Lucy Locket* in F-do	Read & sing from own felt staff notation	Rhythm drill on 'board to be spoken, memorized, erased, spoken again, & reconstructed on 'board by class
17	Song: *Who's That?*	new pattern *s-m-l-s-m.* *Bye Baby Bunting, Rain, Rain* [2nd phrase]			Start class with *s-l-s-m* handsinging. Lead into songs: *Icka Backa, Lucy Locket,* to be sung completely in solfa & with handsigns.	Construct on felt staves the first phrases of *Bounce High* & *Lucy Locket* in G-do		Inner hear & identify the song *Here Comes a Bluebird* from seeing the first phrase shown in handsigns.

This process is repeated for every new rhythmic learning, every new melodic idea, for each new harmonic concept, and for learning about form, tempo, timbre, and dynamics.

It is almost impossible to deal effectively with complex long-range planning through the usual lesson-by-lesson format used in most teacher-training programs. Instead, there must be some way of showing over a series of lessons the progression of a specific learning from the preparation stage through the moment of making it conscious knowledge to the students and on to the reinforcement and assessment stages, while at the same time showing other skills, other concepts, other learnings being dealt with during the same time span.

	REINFORCE NEW LEARNING THROUGH SKILL ACTIVITY				ASSESS CONCEPT INFERENCE AND SKILL ACQUISITION	
Improvisation	Recognition of Musical Forms	Part Work	Moving to Music	Analytical Music Listening	Reading	Improvising and Composing
Improvise melodic responses on *s-m* to teacher's melodic question	Arch arms to show phrases of *Here Comes a Bluebird.* Diagram the form using circles, squares, rectangles.	Clap ostinati [rhythm notation] and while singing *Lucy Locket*	Singing games *Here Comes a Bluebird, Snail*	Listen to ballad: *Fox Went Out.* Children tell story in own words		
Rhythm conversation game. Teacher gives a *4-beat pattern;* child "answers" with a different 4-beat pattern, clapping & speaking the pattern in *ta*'s & *ti*'s	Children arrange a set of rhythm *flashcards to* show the order of phrases in *Lucy Locket*	Clap ostinati [rhythm notation] while singing *Icka Backa*	Singing games *Here Comes a Bluebird, Bow Wow Wow*	Children first re*call & describe the story;* then listen to correct or add to their recollections: *Fox Went Out*		
Melodic conversations using *s-l-s-m* pitches in any order. Word questions, word answers; example: "Who is wearing red today?" ([rhythm notation])	Identify the form of *Hot Cross Buns* from seeing, saying & clapping its rhythm shown on 'board. Use letters to diagram the form [notation with A A B A]	New ostinato [rhythm notation] with *Bounce High*	Singing game: *Bow Wow Wow.* Sing the song, step the beat & clap the rhythm for *Icka Backa*	Act out the story of *Fox Went Out* as teacher sings. Children join the singing on chorus parts		
				At a later time:	Read a new song built on the tonal pattern *s-l-s-m*	Improvize *solfa* answers using *s-l-s-m* to teacher's question phrases

Hungarian teachers faced with the complexity of such planning developed chart forms which clearly showed the progression through pedagogical stages over a given period of time.[6] Further refinements of this lesson-planning technique have been made by a number of North American teachers.[7] The format preferred by the author (L.C.) separates skill development from concept acquisition. Concepts are stated for a six-week or two-month period, rather than

[6]For examples of these see p. 131 of Choksy, *Kodály Method* and p. 171 of *Kodály Context.*

[7]The chart that follows is adapted from planning forms used by Sharyn Favreau, music specialist, Calgary Catholic Schools, and Karen Taylor, music supervisory staff, Prince George, B.C.

lesson by lesson. Skill development is shown in chart form that is really an analysis of the teaching task. The preceding chart covers three weeks during the second half of Grade 1. The movement of one new learning—the new note *la*—is shown from preparation through conscious knowledge of reinforcement and assessment. New learnings for this three-week period are as follows:

> In melody: The new note *la* is made conscious knowledge.
> (Concept: Pitches can be higher or lower.)
> In rhythm: Preparation is begun for teaching the half note.
> (Concept: Some sounds last longer than one beat.)
> In form: Phrases are diagrammed and labeled with A's and B's.
> (Concept: Phrases can be the same or different. Patterns of same and different can be shown with letters A, B, C.)

Such diagrammatic planning does not give the actual ordering within lessons; rather, it gives content and musical functions. The purpose of such planning is to ensure that no important concept or skill area is overlooked. The chart itself must be changed from time to time to accommodate differences of focus in instruction. For example, "part work" did not appear on this chart in the first half of first grade since children were not yet ready or able to demonstrate two musical ideas at the same time. Dynamic and tempo concepts were listed in its place; children were involved in distinguishing between faster and slower, softer and louder, and in making appropriate tempo and dynamic choices. These activities will reappear at a later date, but they are not part of the focus of this time period.

Musical Materials

The quality of the songs and listening examples to be used in teaching is of vital importance to the Kodály teacher. They must be either authentic folk songs or art music of unquestionable quality. On this point Kodály was adamant. He believed deeply that the inculcation of musical taste must be a primary goal of music education and that children would learn to love good music only if they were taught through good music. This maxim of Kodály has been one of the least observed in North American adaptations of his work.[8]

There are a few excellent sources of North American folk songs, both published and unpublished, analyzed for teaching purposes,[9] and many other sources in which the songs have not been organized or analyzed by teaching pur-

---

[8]Numerous series books have organized their song materials in Kodály skill sequences. To the extent that these materials are authentic folk songs or art music, these books are usable in Kodály programs. However, in some series books a large portion of song material is comprised of author-composed ditties or of pseudo-popular music, styles not acceptable to anyone seriously attempting to implement Kodály's principles.

[9]Peter Erdei and Katalin Komlos, *150 American Folk Songs to Sing Read and Play* (New York: Boosey & Hawkes, 1974), 118 pages; Ilona Bartalus, *Sing, Silverbirch, Sing* (Willowdale, Ont.: Boosey & Hawkes Canada, 1980), 64 pages; Lois Choksy, *The Kodály Method* (Englewood Cliffs, NJ: Prentice-Hall, 1974), 221 pages; and Lois Choksy, *The Kodály Context* (Englewood Cliffs, NJ: Prentice-Hall, 1981), 281 pages.

pose but which, nevertheless, are goldmines of folk song for the interested teacher.[10]

A basic teaching repertory generally consists of thirty to forty-five folk songs for each year. Additional songs may be used, but this will be the core through which concepts and skills are developed. They must be carefully chosen, with the children for whom they are intended as much in mind as the quality of the music itself.

Art music for teaching is chosen from the great masterworks. Selections are made from the music of Monteverdi and Palestrina, Bach, Handel, Haydn and Mozart; from Schubert, Beethoven and Brahms, Debussy, Bartòk, Britten, and Stravinsky, among others. All periods and styles are included in the systematic study that begins in grade four and continues throughout the rest of the school years. All works are studied first through singing and memorization of thematic material and later through detailed analyses. Music is never listened to superficially but always studied in depth to the extent that the maturity and musical knowledge of the children will allow.

In later grades fewer folk songs are sung (although they are never totally omitted) and an increasing amount of fine composed song literature is included. Motets by William Byrd, duets by Bach, choruses by Beethoven, and similar musical materials make up the largest part of the teaching core for older students.

ORFF

"Magic" is a word often used to describe the finished product of an Orff workshop or student demonstration. In the Schulwerk an illusion is created in which the musical experience appears to have taken place effortlessly and instantly. Participants realize that without much technique or theoretical background they are making music; they are experiencing an ensemble feeling of a kind normally reserved for professional musicians.

In truth, there is no magic. There is only a well-trained, knowledgeable teacher who has mastered the tools of music and then used those tools to release the natural latent musical powers of the child. Well-worked-out progressions of skills aid the student slowly but surely toward sensitive exploration of the ingredients necessary to make music.

The tools of rhythmic speech, body gestures, movement, singing, and instrumental techniques are woven together around simple musical forms. These forms, in turn, provide a context in which students can participate fully and freely at whatever levels of competency they may have attained. The tools—speech, movement, gesture, instruments—then act as building blocks in a spiral of increasing complexity. There is no pressure of having to succeed, but rather the reassurance of *instant* musical success at each level.

For the teacher, working within the Orff approach demands great

---

[10]Richard Chase, *American Folk Tales and Songs* (New York: Dover, 1971), 240 pages; Edith Fulton Fowke and Richard Johnston, *Folk Songs of Canada* (Waterloo, Ont.: Waterloo Music, 1954), 198 pages; Alan Lomax, *The Folk Songs of North America* (Garden City, N.Y.: Doubleday, 1975), 656 pages; and Helen Creighton, *Maritime Folk Songs* (Toronto: Riverton Press, 1972), 210 pages; Richard Johnston, *Folk Songs North America Sings* (Toronto: E. C. Kerby Ltd., 1984).

flexibility and, as in all good teaching, energy. The constant exchange of ideas between students and teacher enhances and encourages a clear definition of the process. Many questions are asked, many possibilities are explored, even in the simplest exercises. Questions are designed to encourage open-ended, student-discovered, rather than teacher-directed, answers. "What is happening?" "What are the possibilities?"—questions continuously asked in American Orff classes—are parallel to the German "Was ist möglich?" used at the Orff Institute in Salzberg.

This is not to say that the overall musical learning experience is not directed by the teacher, but rather to indicate that in presenting a new learning, such as duple meter, the teacher does not "explain" it, but offers the students a variety of ways to discover its properties; its effect on the body, words, songs, dances, and instruments; its dynamic and tempo possibilities; and the possible devices of time manipulation within it.

This process, while easy in appearance, demands careful and detailed planning by the teacher. He or she must be able to make instant shifts and be ever sensitive to obscure but perhaps correct student answers to the questions. There must be an awareness of the different levels of achievement within the class, a watchful eye for the child's body language that suggests success or a need for remedial work or reinforcement. The teacher must have a well-trained and -tuned ear in order to be able to hear everything happening in a class or ensemble and must be prepared to correct mistakes instantly and positively in order to assure good performance. Correction is always done for the group, not just for the individual. Helping one student offers opportunity for positive reinforcement with the rest.

Lesson Planning

In the Orff Approach there are large central ideas that are essentially the "hidden agenda" around which the curriculum is organized. These are the goals in the teacher's mind as he or she leads the students through Orff experiences.

The first of these is *community.* In order for music to exist there must be an exchange and a contribution by individuals within a framework of form. One natural form is the children's game. Games which engage and include everyone tend to give children a sense of community, of belonging to the group, of being a contributing member. In successful game playing *all* the children—the community of the class—must listen, watch, follow, lead when chosen, and support and respect the place of others. Since a primary goal of the first musical experiences is to develop that sense of community, the processes and materials of the teaching method reflect the needs of communal music making.

A second goal of Orff practice is the development of a sense of musical *organization*—a sensitivity to beginnings and endings, to longness and shortness of thematic material. Recognition and use of forms is a skill necessary for working intelligently with music. In this second goal area a consistent working vocabulary is established. Clear and systematic use of words in giving directions or in leading performance is essential. Speech should be straightforward and uncluttered. From teacher to teacher, with the Orff process, there can and will be variation in vocabulary; however, within a classroom such variations are counterproductive and should be avoided.

Comprehension of music as an art is the third goal in Orff practice. The more the child knows about music the better able he or she is to use that knowledge. When dealing with elemental music there is no need for secrets (the attitude that the teacher knows, so the students don't have to know). Everything should be accessible and easily assimilated. Any concept released into the context of music can be played with, enjoyed, and made personally identifiable to the child. As within any community, the less one is confused, the more one can contribute.

The fourth goal, *musical independence,* is fostered through such activities as conducting a class or ensemble, contributing a rhythm or a melodic figure which can be expanded by the group into a new composition, or offering alternative steps to a previously known game or dance.

A fifth goal is *personal growth.* Individual strengths are necessary for the community to grow. The systematic development of techniques necessary for accurate speaking, singing, instrument playing, and dancing must be a part of any Orff curriculum. Only through mastering these skills can the individual be freed to grow and create.

The sixth goal of Orff instruction is *performance.* The personal satisfaction of performance is fundamental to the continued growth of a child in music. Performance is a major focus in Orff practice—not performance for an audience, but performance for the personal satisfaction of completing a piece, whether it be simple or complex, in a musically pleasing way. The sense of being one part of the whole, of ensemble, is vital to learning and making music.

The seventh goal is the development of a *positive self-image.* When the child feels good about his or her contribution to the whole, an obvious result of participation may be seen in the increased sense of personal worth—the self-esteem—that ensues.

To summarize, the major goals of all Orff practice are as follows:

1. sense of community
2. understanding of the organization of music
3. comprehension of music as an art
4. musical independence
5. personal musical growth
6. performance ability
7. self-esteem

These goals are not exclusive to music, but they are basic to teaching with the Orff Approach. Each of them appears in some way at every level in the Schulwerk. They are the unspoken organizational elements which, when added to the traditionally necessary competencies for learning music, become a means to education of the total person—a Gestalt approach to music.

The role of the teacher is made clearer as lesson plans are constructed. Lessons cannot be entirely made of vertical listings, even though such listings are necessary for basic skills. Instead, lessons must be organized along linear planes, providing for chance as a necessary and ever-present ingredient. The objective of a lesson may be as simple as building a sense of community—a collection of play-party and ring dances which offer relaxation and supportive participation for everyone—or it may be as complex as using an extended poem, myth, or story and discovering ways to express it musically. Obviously, this more complex experience involves skill building over a long period of time in the areas of moving, singing, speaking, and playing instruments. These skills, once acquired, become the tools of creativity and discovery.

In planning for either simple or complex experiences there are expectations of skill competencies which must first be prepared for with any class. For example, the beginning use of the Instrumentarium should be the end result of one whole series of physical and mental preparations and the beginning point of another. Students should be able to walk the beat accurately and to sing in turn long before being introduced to instrument playing. Singing is a most necessary skill for correct playing. Knowledge of forms should also precede instrumental experience. Students must work with patterns that become motives and then themes that are organized into forms, or pieces. These pieces are performed through body, speech, and voice before the student ever approaches a xylophone or glockenspiel.

Because of the importance of skill development to the Orff process, lessons must be carefully structured to provide sufficient practice. Lesson planning begins with a search for the "kernel"—the pattern, aspect, or part of music to be discovered, experienced, and explored. Examining this kernel, the teacher must find a thread which will lead to many possibilities within the discovery process. There is no specific set of sequential steps by which to design an Orff lesson, but there are some distinct priorities:

1. Preparation: a progression of events designed to provide necessary skills
2. Synthesis: use of these skills in planned and improvised play
3. Integration: repetition of the skills and combination of these skills with others previously learned
4. Transfer: relating the newly learned skill or skills to another performance medium or material

All lessons follow a basic continuum from "imitation of the teacher" to "creation by the students." For example, an ordering for a single lesson might be as follows:

1. an exercise or game which contains the kernel of the element to be explored
2. conversation or communal play with the kernel by the students, until competency with it is demonstrated
3. play or ensemble work with the kernel within forms and in various media
4. creation of "The Piece" from the kernel
5. performance (this must be at a high level for even the simplest of experiences)

However, the experienced Orff teacher does not plan lesson by lesson, but plans a series of lessons related by their material and content. A sample progression of events in such a series follows.

LESSON 1

1. The children enter the room, remove their shoes and place them in a designated spot, then join the teacher in the free space on the floor in a large semicircle.
2. A speech piece (nursery rhyme or short poem in simple duple meter) is introduced. It may be, but does not have to be, accompanied by gestures or bodily percussion. The piece is learned by imitation of the teacher, phrase by phrase.
3. The piece is "played with." At each repetition the group introduces some new aspect of performance to the piece. Tempo changes, vocal color, different dynamic levels are all experimented with. It may be performed in canon, or perhaps with a series of spoken ostinati invented to support the original line.
4. The piece is rehearsed with its various additions.
5. The piece is performed.

The next lesson would grow from these activities.

LESSON 2

6. Teacher and class review the poem as performed in the previous lesson.
7. They explore the use of small percussion instruments as a possible support for the text.
8. They expand the piece by adding an instrumental introduction and coda.
9. If the text has a melody, it is taught in the same phrasewise rote manner as the text was in Lesson 1. Attention is given to vocal performance, tonal production, articulation.
10. Small percussion are added to the singing, to produce a performance.

Again, this is a natural stopping point.

LESSON 3

11. If the rhyme or song has a game or dance, the steps are now taught. Using a consistent dance vocabulary, the teacher sings the actual movement descriptions phrase by phrase until the dance is learned. If there is no traditional game or dance associated with the rhyme/song, one may be created by the class.
12. A small percussion instrument introduction and coda are added to the song and dance and the whole piece is performed.

LESSON 4

13. The barred instruments are now discussed and approached. Teacher

and students prepare the instruments for the tonal system in which the piece is to be played, by removing bars to form pentatonic scales or by adding the sharps or flats necessary for specific keys or modes.

14. When the instruments have been prepared, the students "search" for the melody they have been singing—they strike bars at random—attempting to discover the tune.

15. The teacher asks those students who were successful to demonstrate individually.

16. Students reinforce the "find" by singing the tune with letter names before playing.

17. To reinforce the performance, notation for the melody may be written on a chart or chalkboard.

18. The melody is performed again vocally in a variety of ways—as solo, duet, quartet, and with the whole group.

19. Instrumental accompaniment is added to the singing—possibly an open fifth drone on a bass xylophone or an ostinato on soprano and alto barred instruments.

20. Instrumental performance of the melody is added to the drones and ostinati and the form is expanded by the addition of an introduction and a coda.

LESSON 5: THE PERFORMANCE

Choose
> Players for instruments
> Dancers
> Singers
> (All students should at some point during the lesson experience being players, dancers, and singers.)

Expand the form
> Introduction A (sung and danced)
> Interlude A′ (played on instruments and danced)
> Interlude A″ (sung and played on instruments)
> Coda (sung, danced, and played)

Each teacher must judge the time needed by the class in order to prepare for each new step along the way toward performance. A piece could take a day to prepare from introduction to performance or could take a month, two months, or longer, depending upon the age of the students and on the skills they bring to the experience.

A lesson series should become more interesting and involving with each additional step. Because it is the basis for work over a possibly long period of time, the quality of the text chosen for use in this process is of prime importance. Further, although the illustrative lesson series given here is intended for use with a single poem or rhyme, often, while one piece is being developed, other songs and games may also be included in the lessons to provide contrast and variety or to reinforce skills needed for the ongoing piece.

The success of the Orff process is evident when students can transfer the concepts and skills acquired in one experience to another new experience, and adapt what they have learned to new situations and new materials.

Musical Materials

Materials for teaching may be chosen both from the culture of the children and from other cultures around the world. The teacher must choose carefully, keeping the children who will use the material in mind. Folk songs and games comprise a large part of the teaching repertory, with the addition of arranged and composed songs from the five volumes of *Music For Children* and its many supplements. The American edition of *Music For Children* provides teachers with a wealth of materials from American sources. However, none of these books is suggested for cover-to-cover use, and they are best utilized simply as wellsprings of ideas. In the Murray edition of Volume I:Pentatonic Music, many simple songs are coupled with accompaniments too complex for any but the most accomplished students, while the texts—often based on nursery rhymes—are inappropriate for students old enough to be at that reading and playing level. Having younger children sing the songs while older students play the accompaniment is a satisfactory way of incorporating these materials and provides an illustration of the spiral nature of the Orff curriculum.

Other materials, ranging from folk sources to art music and popular music, may also be used in Orff programs. The Schulwerk provides no series of books and does not dictate specific sequences as to when certain musical materials should be used. Each teacher must design programs directed at the children served. The ordering from simple to complex is the key to selection for every age group. There is need for three-note tunes and simple rhythms for both the six-year-old and the fifteen-year-old. There is need for the pentatonic melodies that can be so easily and beautifully accompanied with descants and ostinati; and there is need for experiencing diatonic and modal material in the more advanced classes.

The music in an Orff classroom should be live when at all possible. Learning to respond to musical cues and live stimuli is paramount in the Schulwerk. While recordings may be used to reinforce or support a learning principle, their use should be minimal. The major function of the recording is to offer colors, sounds, and instrumentations otherwise unavailable to the children. Such listening experiences might include authentic recordings of folk music for dancing, examples of another composer's use of a rondo form, or another performer's rendition of a learned piece. Elemental music is best learned by live performance whenever possible.

Physical Setting

The ideal Orff classroom is an open space with a floor designed for movement in bare feet. (If state or local laws prohibit bare feet, gymnastic shoes with textured soles are acceptable. Street or tennis shoes do not allow for freedom in moving.) If Orff instruments are available, an area in the room should be set aside large enough to have them arranged in a wide semicircle. There are times when the dancers may wish to face the players. Most activities are done in the semi- or full circle, so that all the participants can see and hear one another. Instruments should be placed on stools or small tables which afford comfortable access for correct playing. The piano may be used in the Schulwerk, but its use is limited. *A cappella* singing is considered most desirable. Accompaniments to singing can be performed on unpitched percussion or on barred instruments. When a piano is used it should be the last instrument added in the process of making a total piece. Only after children have demonstrated independence and security in instrumental playing can the piano be added to provide another instrumental color.

The typical Orff classroom might be arranged as follows:

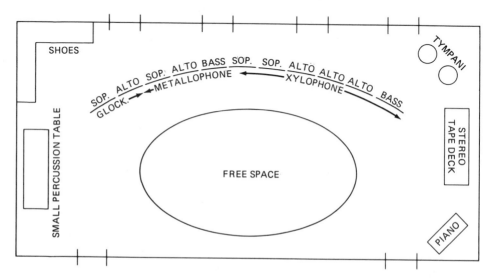

Ensemble is a key element in the Schulwerk: ensemble in speaking, singing, dancing, and playing. The space reflects the need for flexibility with opportunity for formation of large or small ensemble settings.

As lesson plans are developed, the space needs become more evident.

In the Schulwerk, space and content are closely related. Both must be considered in order to have a strong and credible program.

COMPREHENSIVE MUSICIANSHIP

Comprehensive Musicianship (CM) is a flexible philosophy which does not dictate a particular technique or learning approach such as *solfège*, rhythm syllables, or the use of specific instruments. Rather, it suggests learning roles and teaching roles within any methodological context.

At any age level or in any musical area (band, vocal, or general music), the structural elements of music are presented to the students by many avenues and are guided by experiences in composition, analysis, and performance.

The goal of CM is to help students gain insights into the nature of music, its variety of styles, and the many uses it has in the lives of people everywhere. In

CM these insights are developed through a study of the common elements of music as experienced in composition, analysis, and performance.

Classroom Objectives

The objectives are as follows:

1. To provide meaningful and complete musical experiences which emphasize the importance of spontaneity, self-motivation, and creativity in each student regardless of aptitude, achievement, or training.
2. To allow the student individual freedom in musical exploration.
3. To allow for individualized instruction and informality in musical learning without losing sight of the fundamentals of musical understanding.
4. To emphasize analysis (the description of the musical process), composition (the creation and organization of music), and performance of music (the recreation of musical composition) in all classes and in all instrumental and choral rehearsals.
5. To provide creative, performance, and analytical experiences for the student planning to enter the field of music as a vocation.
6. To provide aesthetically fulfilling musical experiences emphasizing performance, analysis, and composition for those students who are primarily involved in general education.
7. To relate musical experience to the students' own culture and environment.
8. To initiate experiences that will not be terminal with the classroom but will continue with life-long musical involvement.
9. To provide a synthesis of musical elements in every musical experience.
10. To avoid isolating any aspect of music, its elements, and its functions, out of a musical context.
11. To focus on competencies achieved in musical learning rather than the materials covered.
12. To encourage the use of classroom materials and experiences from a plurality of music, including jazz, rock, popular, non-Western, traditional, folk, and electronic music.

Role of the Teacher

During the final years of the existence of the Contemporary Music Project it became apparent that any meaningful and long-lasting change of music curricula must depend on the individual teacher in the classroom who is implementing and applying the CM philosophy and procedures. At this time the project began to focus activities and funding on the development of teaching skills and abilities in individual music teachers, which would help them construct viable and valuable comprehensive and broad-based classes and rehearsals.

Faced with the magnitude and diversity of instructional responsibilities, the music teacher often spends countless hours concerned with the tools of his or her trade—basic series books, specific methods and approaches, books, contest lists, and even more mundane daily concerns. All too often these "means" become "ends" in themselves. Robert Werner, Director of the CMP in 1969, wrote: "It is the desire of the CMP to assist the individual musician/teacher in developing his goals and setting his priorities in such a way that items of tactical support are used as a means of obtaining meaningful objectives."[11] The CMP shifted the educational emphasis of the program from specific projects and seminars to the development of teaching and learning skills.

The emphasis of teacher education and teacher training in the CM model is on developing the knowledge and understanding of music in all areas and on expanding individual performance, analytical, and compositional skills. In order for a teacher to teach comprehensively, he or she must be a *comprehensive musician*—all other matters of daily teaching should be secondary. The teacher's skills of performance, composition, analysis, and communication must be extended through vital educational experiences that require application, integration, and synthesis of what is known.

The CM teacher must develop pedagogical techniques for integrating the various aspects of the art of music in every teaching situation. The teacher must synthesize the common elements of music during a learning experience and must guide the students into the important roles of listener, performer, and composer, based on the students' individual comprehension levels, abilities, and interests.

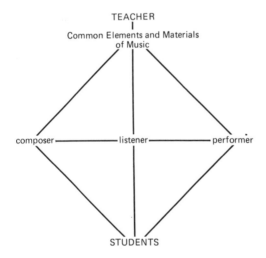

According to the CM concept, the students in music classes and in rehearsals at any level of instruction discover musical principles by actually doing. Students learn concurrently to perform music, to compose music, to listen to music, to analyze music, and, ultimately, to communicate effectively what music

[11]Robert J. Werner, "The Individual Teacher and CMP," *Music Educators Journal,* 56 (January 1969), 47.

actually is. The teacher guides this process, based on an expanded knowledge and interest in all music, including the Indonesian *gamelan,* the Japanese *gagaku,* the *ragas* and *talas* of India, the rich heritage of European art music, and music produced in twentieth-century North America. A true CM teacher will teach music comprehensively in every class.

Planning for Musical Learning

A CM program in the elementary school emphasizes an integrated approach to music study and strives to reduce fragmented teaching and learning by providing opportunities for students to see relationships in music. The various activities within the elementary music sequence reinforce each other and promote conceptual unity and cohesion. All activities and song materials are connected by the threads of the common elements of music. Elementary students experience song materials, games, chants, movement activities, and exploratory activities through varying degrees of emphasis on improvisation and composition, analysis, and singing and playing. One specific activity can include many concepts for in-depth study and allow the students to be improvisers, performers, and perceptive listeners.

The CM process begins with the literature of music and actively involves the child in music making, discovery, and conceptual awareness. One series of experiences in a comprehensive lesson for six-, seven-, or eight-year-olds might be as follows:

1. The children, sitting in a circle, are led by the teacher to say a rhyme while tapping the beat on their laps.
2. A melodic line is added to the chant and the children continue to demonstrate the beat by tapping or clapping while singing.
3. The subject of the song is discussed and some children leave the circle to find sound sources in the room that might be used to illustrate or amplify the ideas contained in the song. [For example, to accompany the popular folk song "There's a Little White Duck" the children might make quacking, buzzing, dripping, wind, bubbling, splashing, raining, rustling, or bird sounds,—any sounds that might be associatd with a duck, a pond, or a meadow.] For this the children may use classroom instruments, mouth and body sounds, or any objects in the room that their imagination may conceive; for example, crumpling paper, scraping a ruler along an uneven surface, twanging a rubber band.
4. The singing is stopped and the children in the circle listen to the sounds being produced by those outside the circle. Without looking they try to identify the type of sound heard and the instrument or sound source used to make each sound.
5. An ostinato pattern is created using rhythm instruments or other sound sources and is added to the singing and beat tapping.

In this CM setting in the primary grades, children are being exposed to the following concepts and musical ideas:

beat	sound sources
rhythmic pattern	texture of sound
acoustical space	ostinato patterns
environmental sounds	

The children participating in the activity are involved in clapping the beat, chanting the rhythmic pattern, creating sounds, and improvising ostinato patterns; they are playing and singing and describing sounds through perceptive listening. The elements of music are being experienced through the musical functions of performance, analysis, and composition, in an active educational setting.

In another lesson at the primary level children might

1. learn a new rhyme by rote from the teacher
2. keep the beat by swaying, clapping, or snapping
3. learn traditional motions to accompany the rhyme
4. vary the tempo of the rhyme from very slow to very fast while using the motions
5. try the rhyme in canon, with the motions
6. invent a tune to fit the rhyme or invent another rhyme or chant based on the one just learned, and create motions to accompany it.

In this lesson children are being exposed to the following musical concepts and ideas:

beat	tempo changes
tempo	canon

The children are performing, analyzing the tempo and tempo changes, and creating their own chant canons, melodies, and movements.

Application of CM in the Upper Elementary Grades and in the Junior High School General Music Program

A CM program should afford students opportunity to discover musical principles and concepts through actually doing. Students in the general music classes should concurrently learn to perform music, to compose it, to listen to it and analyze it, and to communicate effectively what music is. In a CM setting the general music curriculum encompasses a variety of activities which ultimately leads the student to a mastery of the fundamentals of music. Self-discovery and self-advancement in an individualized framework are essential to the comprehensive core of the music program. CM is based on the premise that each student is a unique human being who learns in his or her own particular way, and thus stresses individualized instruction. Such individualized approaches to musical learning have been influenced by the research and experiments of Friedrich Froebel, Johann Pestalozzi, John Dewey, and Francis Parker.

In addition to traditional classroom approaches, the major systems of CM studies through individualized instruction include the learning contract, the learning activity package, and the learning center.

THE LEARNING CONTRACT. The learning contract used in the CM setting is a written agreement, drawn up by the student with guidance from the teacher and signed by the student, that obligates the student to complete a specified number of tasks leading to a terminal goal or musical project. These tasks involve the student as a performer, a listener, and a composer. The student is responsible for setting time limits, for organizing materials, for setting short-term goals, and for evaluating his or her progress toward the terminal goal.

Projects suitable for contractual learning in CM classrooms are suggested by the teacher for consideration by the students. These project lists are conceptually oriented and are designed to provide viable options and alternatives for specific skill development and musical understanding. In the contractual learning process the students are also given the opportunity to design original projects and experiments.

The learning contract provides a flexible and individual format for musical development. Students work by themselves or in small groups during the music class to discover and to explore the common elements of music through performance, composition, and listening. The teacher often offers assistance, direction, and suggestions to the individual students during the learning contract work sessions.

THE LEARNING ACTIVITY PACKAGE. The learning activity package (LAP) in CM classrooms provides a clear set of directions and instruction for the student to use at his or her own pace in order to develop a conceptual understanding of a specific idea or set of ideas in music or to develop specific musical skills. Learning activity packages in CM should have activities for the students as composers, listeners, and performers.

The primary goal of the LAP is behavior modification. Students follow a set of procedures designed to give them the information necessary to complete a task. These instructions include self-evaluation procedures. The LAP instructions include:

> title of the instruction
> time allotment
> musical concept or concept cluster being presented
> behavioral objectives
> grade and criterion levels
> materials needed for completing the LAP
> suggestions for follow-up activities, research, or post-testing

LAPs can be used for remedial activities, extended activities in CM for talented and gifted students, modified activities in CM for handicapped students, reinforcement activities for those students needing additional experience and assistance with a concept or a skill, and expanded activities for those students who are interested in a wider scope of activities related to a specific topic or subject.

LAPs can also be used in the comprehensive core of activities to introduce new instruments, introduce alternative fingerings and bowings, suggest procedures for repair and maintenance of instruments and equipment, provide instructions for using electronic devices, assist in note reading skill development, instruct vocal or instrumental technique, provide experiments in musical and environmental sound, apply the principles and the concepts of the common elements of music, and instruct students in music history and music theory. Individual LAP topics are only one part of the total musical education. They involve the student both in conceptual and in skill development.

THE LEARNING CENTER. Learning centers in the CM setting are units or modules which are constructed in various areas of the classroom or the school. Students experience the activities and the tasks of the units and modules as their personal schedules dictate and at their own learning rates. Instructions for the student are provided in each learning unit or module on cards, instruction sheets, or in packets. Objectives for the educational experience are identified in the instructions. Learning centers are designed for specific comprehension levels and achievement levels.

Learning centers can include experiences in instrument building, instrument playing, musical composition, musical games, music research, theoretical and historical study, music listening, and in other areas related to music.

The following example of a module card involves the student in experimental composition using twelve-tone technique, performance, and analysis. The student experiencing this activity would be exposed to the following concepts and musical ideas: (1) twelve-tone row; (2) ABA form; (3) retrograde.

TWELVE-TONE ROW CHANCE GAME
Module Card

Write a seventeen-syllable Japanese haiku.

Add your own simple rhythmic pattern to the haiku.

Shuffle and deal a deck of twelve cards with one note of the twelve-tone row written on each card.

Place the notes of the row on the board or on a piece of paper in the order of the cards.

Use the twelve tones for the syllables of the haiku. Use all twelve notes before repeating them.

Examine the like phrases and label the sections as ABA.

Play the resulting chance composition on an instrument or sing the words and music.

Play or sing the song backwards.

[Back of card]

Record your results of the experimentation and describe the sounds created.

Listen to Ernst Krenek's Opus 22 (Society of the Performing Arts, Number 4). Compare the techniques used by Krenek to those you used. Write these out on paper.

The poetry gives structure to this Comprehensive Musicianship activity but the cards give the element of chance and allow the student to explore twelve-tone chance composition.

Learning contracts, learning activity packages, and learning centers are individualized approaches to music learning and teaching which can be utilized with traditional approaches of music teaching in a CM framework.

Application of CM in the Secondary School Performing Ensembles

Although performance is the primary goal of instrumental and choral ensembles, students should also experience analysis and composition as supportive roles to the major performance role. The following techniques can be used in secondary school performing groups to encourage a comprehensive totality of musical learning. These techniques are helpful in the development of musical skills and understanding but should be used sparingly in the performing ensemble rehearsal. (They can be used interchangeably with instrumental and choral performing groups.)

1. During rehearsals of specific musical literature, students should be encouraged to make musical decisions based on their personal musical knowledge. These decisions should be alternatives to critical judgments and suggestions given by the ensemble director.

2. Decisions regarding dynamic markings should be made by the students in relationship to the underlining musical reasons and purposes for the variation in intensity. Students should know why, for example, they are getting loud or why they are getting soft.

3. Compare the styles of the literature performed and make the appropriate performance adjustments.

4. Have students in various instrumental or choral sections of the ensemble know what is musically happening in the other sections.

5. Have students notate melodic parts or chordal structures on manuscript paper or on the chalkboard.

6. Have students rewrite or rearrange endings or sections of a piece. Make comparisons of these compositional alterations to the original ending or section written by the composer.

7. Relate the performance of the composition to specific historical and social contexts.

8. Select a student or several students to listen to a particular piece during a rehearsal and to analyze the problems and weaknesses which occur. Have the students identify specific musical concepts and musical ideas being performed correctly as well as incorrectly.

9. Have sections direct with simple conducting patterns while other sections are rehearsing.

10. Have individual students direct the ensemble after careful score preparation and analysis.

11. Have members from various choral or instrumental sections perform

entire works as a small ensemble. Have the parent group listen to, evaluate, and analyze the performance.

12. Record on a tape recorder or a video recorder the rehearsal of a particular composition. Have students listen to the tape and encourage the identification of performance problems.

13. Extract a specific musical problem, such as interval singing, and have the students write it, sing or play it, use it in other contexts, and analyze it before putting it back into the original musical context.

14. Compare the blend and balance of one piece of music to that of another piece of music through the use of recordings.

15. Have students develop aural skills by getting starting pitches from previous pieces.

16. Have instrumental students sing their parts before playing.

These sixteen activities can help students in performing groups gain experience in analysis and composition. The responsibility of musical achievement and musical development in the CM rehearsal rests with the individual student. They are encouraged to make musical decisions and judgments based on their comprehensive understanding and knowledge of music. They are encouraged to be active participators in the music-making process.

CONCLUSIONS

A number of commonalities emerge from an examination of lesson planning techniques and teaching styles among these methods. Each requires detailed long-range planning to achieve specified goals. Each considers the good teacher one who does little talking, one who teaches by example rather than by explanation. Each emphasizes the importance of student exploration and discovery. Each begins with music as sound, and moves from sound to analysis skills and to creative activities.

However, certain differences also emerge clearly in teaching style:

The teacher in a Jaques-Dalcroze class must be facile at piano and other improvisations and should be comfortable with movement.

The Orff Schulwerk teacher must possess skill at speech, melodic, and harmonic improvisation and must have mastered the instrumental techniques required by the Instrumentarium.

The Kodály teacher must sing well with a voice that is a model in pitch and intonation for children's singing, must possess a wide folk-song repertory, must be knowledgeable about the art music of the western world, and must also be comfortable with movable-*do solfa*.

The CM teacher must be at home with the world's contemporary music and music of non-Western peoples as well as with the technique of composition as a teaching device.

It is obvious that certain teaching modes are better suited to one method than another. Anyone entering teaching would do well to examine his or her own tastes, talents, and capabilities carefully before making a choice among these methods.

8
GRADES K–1–2

INTRODUCTION

The Program Cone developed for the Music Educators National Conference in 1970 (see p. 116) lists the following desired musical experiences for the early school years:

> discovering sounds and rhythms in instruments, voices, and environment
> personalized musical experiences
> rhythmic development
> creative music making
> structuring melody
> harmonization, rounds, canons
> introductory music reading[1]

Each of these areas is incorporated to some extent within each of the four methodologies—Jaques-Dalcroze, Kodály, Orff, Comprehensive Musicianship—in the early grades. The differences among the methods are more ones of emphasis than of inclusion or omission. An examination of curricular content and some sample lessons in each method at the primary level may

---

[1]National Council of State Supervisors of Music of MENC, Guidelines in Music Education: Supportive Requirements (Reston, VA: MENC, 1972), p. 5.

help in determining which goals are actually being stressed in each methodology.

JAQUES-DALCROZE

Jaques-Dalcroze, in speaking of the method he developed, stated its goals:

> . . . to establish an intimate correlation between the functions of our body and those of our mind . . . to make the child understand himself, to make him conscious of his innate rhythms.
>
> I have based my method on music because music is both a regulating and a stimulating agent, able to adapt the motor habits of men to all different degrees of tempo and space; to harmonize his nervous system and to imprint on his mind a lasting image of his physical sensations rhythmically regulated and balanced.
>
> Music, in the Greek meaning of the word, is a pedagogical element of first importance, and it is in this sense that my method remains essentially musical.

How can experiments in music teaching undertaken at the turn of the century be relevant to today's children?

Preschool

According to recent medical research, the child is capable of hearing even prior to birth. One of the first sounds heard is the mother's heartbeat; her coughing and her eating also penetrate the unborn child's world. Recent research also shows that the unborn child is most uncomfortable when the mother's movements are tense, jerky, and unrhythmic. They cause the child to kick and turn, as if to offset the disturbances. Immediately after birth the child is more conscious of sound than sight. Soon parent's voices are recognizable and vocal and instrumental music is responded to.

When a child begins to learn to move, the crawling, bouncing, and other leg and arm movements are done with a regular tempo which the child soon discovers is its own. Walking, however, is more complex, with its balancing and transferring of body weight. It does not become rhythmic until the child's technique is secure, often not until the second or third year. Thus, from before birth the child has been using the ear and the body, consciously or unconsciously, as he or she learns the natural patterns of movement.

Nursery School through Grade 2

Since the basic instrument of Jaques-Dalcroze's method is the ear, and the basic means of expression of what one hears is through movement of the human body, the earliest Jaques-Dalcroze training consists of simple and short experiences in learning to listen and move to music. Two different kinds of experiences are introduced: a relaxed, casual type of listening, and a concentrated analytical musician's listening. The materials used are singing games, finger play, percussion play, and stories with a musical accompaniment that invoke rhythmic mime activities.

CONCEPTS AND SUBJECT MATTER. In general, teachers of Jaques-Dalcroze's method create their own curriculum. Various activites led by music are directed toward experimental play on the subjects of tempo, dynamics, accents, rhythmic patterns, measures, durations, instrumental timbres, and phrasing articulations. Concepts are generally grouped in opposing pairs of high–low, loud–soft, fast–slow, straight–curved, smooth–sharp, sound–silence, start–stop, big–little, long–short, thick–thin, wood–metal (in instrumental timbres). Next, the same concepts are studied through listening and moving to gradations and orderings of opposites: high to low, low to high, and so on.

FURTHER DEVELOPMENTS. By Grades 1 and 2, listening and analysis by movement will extend to combinations of concepts and gradations of concepts occuring simultaneously. Children will be led to measure and express nuances and shadings with more precision. The ability to discriminate will require the simultaneous development of a vocabulary that includes "more than," "less than," as well as "a little more than" and "a lot more than." There will also be special exercises in the ability to remember and reproduce longer patterns of rhythm and more complex changes in the sequence of accents, rests, measures, and tempi in a rhythmic composition. Special exercises will be used to break down the natural tendencies that equate fast with loud and slow with soft, in order to permit tempo and dynamics to be heard and performed in many different combinations.

BODY TECHNIQUES. Since musical phenomena and musical performance, whether singing, reading music, or playing an instrument, are produced by physical activity, many body techniques, play songs, games, and exercise are taught at this early period. These musical stimuli are used to develop the ability to use both sides of the body together and then slowly produce the bilateral symmetry and equality that the human body is so perfectly designed to exploit. Games and activities with the music are introduced to help children learn to select different body parts to perform rhythmic activities and to replace quickly one body part with another or to combine and coordinate different body parts.
This training paves the way for the more advanced movement techniques. Through these techniques the method coordinates the three basic questions of musical rhythmic study:

1. What is music made of? (theory)
2. How may one physically reproduce and use musical materials? (technique and composition)
3. What are the effects of the above on singing and playing music? (musicianship)

Breathing and posture games are used in the early study of Eurhythmics to prepare the children for good singing and movement. Some of these exercise "games" introduce experiences in relaxation, contraction, and extension of various groups of muscles, which are the basis of all rhythmic skill. Others help children learn to use separate parts of their bodies alone and in combination with each other. This aspect of the training teaches children how to use the laws of gravity—time–space–weight–energy—in order to get maximum variations in expression in their movement. These same exercises are also used to demonstrate those parts of the body in which a movement begins, continues, and ends. For example, a swing can begin with a movement originating in the shoulder, travel through the upper arms, through the forearms and wrists, and finally end in the hands.

Games of imaginative movement are introduced in each lesson to help children find many ways to express the varieties of beat and the gradations of accent, dynamics, and tone color found in even the simplest music. The goal of such exercises is the development of physical and expressive skills that will allow the body to express complicated artistic effects with little effort.

RHYTHM: READING, RECOGNITION, AND MEMORY. Through clapping, marching, running, hopping, jumping, turning, swinging, galloping, skipping, and by using the infinite variations of weight and energy, the youngest children develop memory of basic tempi and of simple rhythmic combinations. By combining such movements and music with games using flash cards on which the notation of movement patterns are shown, visual identification of rhythmic figures is established. Cards may then be joined together to produce simple patterns which, in turn, are performed in movement.

RHYTHM: WRITING. The idea that sound and movement can be converted to picture writing to produce musical graphics is first introduced by free drawing or painting while listening to music. At this stage children create their own expression to convey information to the teacher and other class members. Next, children may experiment with art materials (crayons, markers, paper collage) in order to translate muscular and emotional responses to musical experiences into visual interpretations of specific musical qualities and concepts. Later, simple geometric shapes and lines are used to produce graphic equivalents of actual musical rhythmic notation.

Children who have already had Eurhythmics training in nursery school[2] become more involved with Eurhythmics activities requiring the use of the newly developing skills of the body, mind, and nervous system as they move through the primary grades. New games and exercises demand quicker, more detailed and skillful musical-movement analysis, a longer attention span, and the ability to stabilize and maintain an inner beat and tempo. This skill is developed slowly to include counterpoints of dynamics, accents, and even polymetrics. At first, individuals acquire the ability to produce two different rhythms simultaneously, then teams produce three- and four-part counterpoint.

Reading and writing are begun with linear shorthand which is then translated into traditional notation on a one-, two- or three-line staff. Children create simple improvised compositions for speaking, singing, percussion orchestra and movement choir, recorders, and piano. These are notated and reinforced by class rehearsal and performance.

THE LESSON PLAN. Eurhythmics lessons often begin with a *tune-up* of students' mental, physical, and emotional faculties. It has the same purpose as an

---

[2]In New York City Eurhythmics is now being taught to classes of two-year-old children, along with their parents.

athlete's warm-up or a musician's tuning of an instrument. This is followed by exercises in body techniques to teach students skills they will need in order to express the musical ideas in the latter part of the lesson. Next, the musical concepts to be worked on are introduced in the form of listening activities, games, experiences, and exercises. These are followed by reading, writing, and improvisation exercises built on the main concepts of the lesson. A lesson may be repeated or may form the basis for a series of lessons on the same concept. Although the strategies given here are designed for young children, they could be used with any age group. The differences are purely in the style of presentation, not in content or order.

In the sample lesson offered here suggestions have been placed throughout to help teachers avoid problems. However, teachers are cautioned to use both the plan and the music for it carefully, in order to make every movement musical. Above all, teachers should not hesitate to modify the plan according to the needs of students. There is no single perfect formula for a lesson. The following are merely suggestions.

Lesson for Primary Grades

STEP I: "TUNE-UP" FOR THE DEVELOPMENT OF
ATTENTION

1. The teacher greets the students outside the classroom.

> Teacher: *Let's make a follow-the-leader line.*

The teacher uses appropriate gestures to show direction and straightness of line. A line on the floor with tape or chalk helps to cue students to make this shape.

> Teacher: *We are going to take a space walk. Everybody follow all my movements. I may walk, run, stop, or anything. Are you ready?*

2. The teacher chooses a good walking tempo for the children and then, in the tempo chosen, says

Here   we   go,   now!

3. The teacher leads the space walk into the classroom, changing positions of arms, hands, elbows, and head while travelling in various floor patterns—lines, curves, squares, triangles, spirals, circles, shapes of letters, or shapes of numbers. Simultaneously, the teacher watches the students who are following and uses verbal and gesture cues for students who are having trouble (*Watch my fingers! Arms! Head!*).

4. The teacher at times stops gradually or, at other times, suddenly, using cues to indicate a change of activity. The students try to follow. The teacher may change from a walking to a running tempo, back to walking rhythm, then to

hopping rhythm on one foot or both feet, or to galloping and skipping rhythms. The students try to follow.

> [It is important not to expect immediate results. Perfection requires experience and practice, and this is only a tune-up.]

5.   The teacher changes the level of space-walking to high, with a lifted body, lifted arms and feet on tip-toe; or to low, with arms pulled down, knees bent, and feet flat.

> [During the space walk the teacher can begin to observe and study the different levels of speed of response and the various levels of physical skills of the students. The first responses may be slow and clumsy. After a few practice trials the students will become more comfortable and skillful.]

6.   The teacher ends the exercise by leading the line into a circle formation, facing inward, and stops all movement.

Teacher: (Slowly extending arms open) *Let's float our arms down.* (Spoken gently while making appropriate arm gestures) *Now let's float ourselves down and sit on the floor.*

STEP II: DEVELOPING ATTENTIVE LISTENING

Orientation to space and the movement of sound in space. All sitting in a circle.

1. Teacher: *Let's look around the room. Let's point to the windows.* (Students point.) *Where are the lights? the piano? the desk? the chalkboard?*

The teacher mentions all the visible things in the room, including specific colors (blue table, green wall) or the number of items (three windows, ten chairs). Students respond by pointing.

2. Teacher: *Close your eyes and let us find out what we can remember about the room space. Can you point, without looking, to the window? the piano? the chair? the table?*

3. Teacher: *You have very good eyes and very good bodies* and *good memories. Now let's try to listen to all the sounds we can hear in the world around us. Close your eyes, be very quiet, and listen.*

Teacher and students listen.

4. Teacher: *Good! Open your eyes! I heard a car. What did you hear?*
    Students: *A truck; children playing in the yard; a dog barking; water running; rain on the roof; someone singing; a door closing.*

5. Teacher: *Good! Let's close our eyes and listen again.*

The teacher gets up and moves to a different part of the classroom.

Teacher: *Keep your eyes closed. I'm here now. Can you point to where you hear my voice?*

Students point. The teacher hums or signs while moving to another position.

Teacher: *Can you point to my sound as I move, while you still have your eyes closed?*

Students point and follow the sound.

[Learning to listen is the prime skill of musicians.]

STEP III: SPATIAL ORIENTATION

Spatial memory and tempo variations.

1.   The teacher places a round piece of colored paper or draws a chalk circle in front of the students sitting in a circle.

Teacher: *This will help us to remember our circle when we leave it.*

2. Teacher: *Stand up, everyone! Can you draw the whole circle slowly with your finger and your arms?*

Students follow, using a finger as a pointer.

Teacher: *Can you draw a big circle slo—w—ly on the ceiling over your head? in front of you? around you? in back of you? Can you make a circle with your elbows? shoulders? wrists? knees? feet? head? bottoms? hips? everything at once?* (After each of these, sufficient time is given for the physical response.)

[This exercise encourages movement exploration and improvisation and helps to develop an inner feeling of the smoothness, roundness, and completeness of circular movement. This is turn becomes the foundation for future studies in legato, whole notes, slow durations, compound meters, triplets, and phrases requiring flowing, curved motions. It also serves as a physical warm-up and a tempo and spatial transition from the stillness and small movements of the previous sitting exercises and prepares the way for the new tempi of the next theme.]

STEP IV: WALKING TEMPO AND
SPATIAL ANALYSIS

1. Teacher: *When I say "Go," let's walk away from the circle and travel all around the room. Are you ready? Go!*

The students walk throughout the room, all at their own walking tempo.

2. Teacher: Ready . . . Stop!

The students stop in place.

> Teacher: *Let's walk back to a place on our circle. Are you ready? Let's go back!*
>
> > [The signals "ready," "go," "stop" give young children time to think in order to make their actions objective and purposeful. During this exercise the teacher studies the class to determine the average walking tempo chosen by the students. Using these observations the teacher can select the best starting tempo for the class. (Children's tempi are usually faster than adults'.)]

3. Teacher: *Let's try it again. Get ready to walk anywhere in the room. Are you ready?* (At this point the teacher checks the alertness of the ensemble before giving the signal.) *Let's go!*

> [Again the teacher studies the walks of the individual students and the average tempo chosen by the group. It is important that the teacher note the kinds of problems the students have while walking. If these problems are not corrected in subsequent lessons, they may interfere with the students' progress in attaining rhythmic skill using full body movement.]

4. The teacher begins to use speech, singing, drum, or piano to accompany the students' walk, being careful to follow their tempo, dynamics, and flow characteristics.

> [This is the first time that music is used to match the students' own movements. It represents the first announcement of the basic theme of Eurhythmics: Human motion and musical rhythmic motion are a wholeness, two sides of the same coin, analogues of each other.]

5. Teacher: (Stopping music or speech)

Let's   stop   right   now!

Students try to stop. With practice students will learn to stop without extra beats or steps.

6. Teacher: *Let's walk back to the circle. Are you ready? Go!*

Students walk back to the circle while teacher accompanies them, following their tempo, dynamics, and flow.

STEP V: RUNNING TEMPI

1. Teacher: (With increased energy and excitement) *Let's take a run away from the*

circle all around the room. Are you ready? (The teacher checks for readiness.) *Don't bump anyone! Go!*

Students run all over the room.

> [In this game students begin to organize traffic flow and to be aware of other people's safety. If there is a lack of space, one group can run, another can simulate running with their fingers, and some can run in place, others in space or in circles. Soloists or partners or teams of three or more can run to designated places to stop there.]

Teacher: *Get ready to stop . . . Stop!*

Students stop as quickly as they can.

> [The ability to start and stop is fundamental to good ensemble playing and to the study of rests. This ability to initiate and inhibit motion or sound needs a good deal of practice at every level.]

2. Teacher: *Let's run back to the circle. Are you ready? . . . Run!*

Students run back to the circle and stop.

> [Running tends to be awkward in young children because they often use a flatfooted run. Help them to use the ball of their foot.]

STEP VI: FINDING STUDENTS' AVERAGE RUNNING TEMPO

1.   The teacher observes the students to find their average running tempo and begins to accompany them at that tempo with clapping, speech, singing, percussion of piano. At the command "Stop!" all sound and motion stops.

STEP VII: SLOW TEMPO

This tempo change acts as a transition to the next exercise.

1. Teacher: *Do you remember our big, slow circles? Can you make one with your arms?*

2. Teacher: (Showing the movement) *Can you make your hand walk slowly all over your other arm?*

3. Teacher: (Demonstrating) *Can you take a slow, deep breath? Can you exhale slowly?*

Students explore slow breathing, walking-speed breathing, and very short running-speed breathing.

STEP VIII: SLOW TEMPO IN SPACE

1. Teacher: (Spoken slowly) *Let's see how b–i–g a sp–a–ce we can take when we walk away from the circle. Can you lift your legs high and slow; put them down slow?*

   [The idea of slow as "spaciousness" has already been planted in Step IV. Slow is a new and difficult concept for most young children. They usually associate "slow" with "small" rather than the musical concept of slow as spaciousness. Slow tempi require a good deal more control of balance and weight than young children are capable of without training.]

2. Students experiment with sliding, slow walks, dragging, pushing, pulling, imagining they are carrying heavy stones, and so on, trying a slow tempo while moving around the room.

   Teacher: *Can you slide your legs and feet like an ice skater in slow motion?*

Students experiment with this idea as they walk.

3. Teacher: (Slowly) *Get . . . ready . . . to . . . stop!*

Students stop slowly.

   Teacher: *Lets do slow, sl–i–dy walks back to our circle.*

The teacher picks up the class average for slow tempo and accompanies the students' walks until they all get back into a circle.

STEP IX: RECEIVING AND RESPONDING TO TEMPI

1. Teacher: *Let's all melt down to the floor like this.* (Very slowly and gently floats downward to a sitting position.)

2. Teacher: (In a walking tempo) *I've got a walking song. Sing it with me.*

In the children's walking tempo the teacher sings "Twinkle, Twinkle, Little Star," emphasizing the walking qualities of words and music.

3. Teacher: *Walk your hands all over your body as we sing it again. Are your hands ready to walk? Good!* (In tempo)

Let's   walk   right   now!

4. The teacher sings, students listen, then sing and follow the movement.

   [This is the first time students are asked to *follow* a tempo by listening—a complete reversal of the experience of being accompanied; it is the first important move toward regularization of sound and movement through response to an outside sound source.]

5. **Teacher:**   (In a running tempo) *I have a running song. Listen.*

In the children's running tempo the teacher sings "Yankee Doodle." Students join in.

6. **Teacher:**   *Let's make two fingers run all over our arms; all over our bodies; on the floor, all through the song. Are your fingers ready? Get them ready.* (In tempo) *Here we go!*

7. **Teacher:**   *Can we sing and use our fingers to run?*

The teacher and students repeat, using singing and movement together.

8. **Teacher:**   (In a slow tempo) *I have a sl–o–w song. Listen, and we'll swing our arms from side to side very slowly. Can you push the air away as you swing?*

The teacher makes gestures of controlled swing starting from the fingers and extending through the arms in the children's slow tempo and sings

You   can   move   slow,   I   can   sing   slow.

9. **Teacher:**   *Let's take slow breaths while we sing.* (Sings again.)

10. **Teacher:**   *Let's sing and swing! Get your arms ready! Get your voice ready!* (In tempo) *Here we go—now!*

The teacher and students sing and swing.

> [Throughout this lesson the teacher has chosen to start from ordinary-life tempo sources and then to move toward musical versions of life activities.[3]]

STEP X: LIVING DICTATION

1. **Teacher:**   *My drum can speak and sing too! It can say "walk walk" or "run run run run" or "sl–o–w." Can you tell what my drum is saying? Listen.*

The teacher points to an ear and, at the average walking speed of the class, plays (The dynamics adds to sense of forward motion.) Students walk.

Tempo of class:

[3]For more tempo games and activities see Robert M. Abramson, *Rhythm Games for Perception and Cognition* (Hialeah, FL: Columbia Pictures, 1978).

2. **Teacher:** (Continuing to play) *Good! But can you speak just like the drum: "walk walk walk walk"?*

Students speak in tempo.

3. **Teacher:** *Good! Get up and follow the drum all around the room.*

Students walk around the room following the drum beats.

4. **Teacher:** (Still playing the "walks") *Listen to my drum say "Stop!"*

The teacher plays
and stops.

5. **Teacher:** *Listen to what my drum says now.*

The teacher plays

The tempo should be exactly twice the walking tempo. The dynamics add phrasing and rhythmic motion to the tempo.

Students: *Running!*

[The teacher should make sure that each note has forward momentum; the rhythm must not be played as ♫ ♪ ♫ ♪ ♫ ♪ ♫ ♪ —this gives too much feeling to the quarter-note beat. In this exercise students for the first time begin to hear the relationship of 2 : 1 in the change from ♩ to ♪♪ and from ♪♪ to ♩. From this point on, the relationship will be maintained by the teacher and will soon be internalized as sound and feeling by the students.]

6. **Teacher:** *Can you say "run run run run"? Good. Let's run around the room with the drum.*

The teacher continues the pattern and ends with the signal and verbal cue

Stop.

7. **Teacher:** *What does my drum play now? Listen.*

The teacher plays

using a large arm stroke to show continuity and spaciousness of sound.

    Students: *Slow!*

8. **Teacher:** *Can you make the sound "slow" last as long as it does on my drum? (Continuing to play the pattern) Follow the drum around the room.*

Students try to follow. Not all students will be able to perform a continuous slow tempo in their first experiences. The teacher can help by verbalizing cues: "Slide," "Stretch,' "Big,", or can make the exercise easier by reorchestrating, by using arms, breathing, swings, pulls and pushes, instead of feet.

9. **Teacher:** (Continuing to play) *Listen for the drum's signal to stop.*

The teacher plays [musical notation] to end the exercise.

STEP XI: THE GALLOP

1. **Teacher:** *Let's gallop all around the circle!*

The teacher plays

Students and the teacher gallop until the drum announces the "stop" with

[musical notation] . The gallop acts as a rhythmic contrast to all the

controlled concentration of Steps VIII and X.

STEP XII: RELAXATION

1. **Teacher:** *Let's all melt down and rest on the floor. Let's lie on our backs. We've been*

working very hard, so relax and let the floor hold you up. Make yourself as limp as a piece of cooked spaghetti!

2.   The teacher picks up a student's arm and slowly moves it to test relaxation.

Teacher: *That's good. Just let it be limp and heavy and I'll hold it for you.*

3.   The teacher then checks the other arm, the head and the legs, while moving them, and also checks the other students' bodies for looseness and relaxation.

[In order to perform rhythms physically, students must be able to consciously direct muscles into many different flows of tension and relaxation. Later, one part of the body may have to be relaxed, while another is tensed. This is the first exercise in conscious tension and relaxation.]

4.   Teacher: *While we're resting, let's listen to the drum* (or *piano* or *song*). *Your body can relax and follow with just the fingertips tapping on the floor. Are you ready? Listen.*

The teacher, softly and in any order, plays ♩ , ♫ and ♩ , the tempo changing every eight beats, while students follow by tapping the floor. If students do not respond accurately, the teacher asks them to stop and "listen" again.

STEP XIII: NEW PHYSICAL RESPONSES

TO ♩ , ♪, ♩ ; INTRODUCTION OF THE WORD "TEMPO"; TEMPO MEMORY

1.   Teacher: *Listen to the drum say "sit up.*

The teacher plays ♩ ♩

[The teacher can invent many drum or clapping rhythms to indicate *sit down!, start!, stop!, are you ready!, ready, go!, change movements!,* and so on, purely rhythmic commands without any verbalization.]

2.   Teacher: *Who remembers the walking speed—the walking* tempo?

[This is the first time the word *tempo* is used.]

Students: *I do! I do!*
Teacher: *Show me how you move it.*

One student demonstrates the tempo (walking, clapping, singing, moving arms, legs, etc.).

Teacher: *Let's all do it John's way.*

Students try.

3. **Teacher:** *Let's find a new way to show a walking tempo.*

The teacher waits. (It is important not to cue unless absolutely necessary; the students must be given time to work it out in their own way.) Students show some ways, using hands, jumps, torso swings, knees. If shy students do any movement at all (wiggle knees, brush nose with hands), the teacher should accept these. The purpose of this exercise is to develop and express tempo memory.

Teacher: *Let's do it Helen's way . . . Let's do it George's way.*

The teacher accompanies each particular movement by finding the proper rhythmic qualities in speech, singing, percussion, or piano:

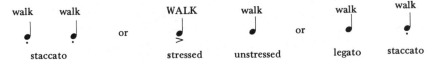

Teacher: *Let's find another part of the body or another way to clap it (jump it, swing it, etc.).*

One student demonstrates; the class follows.

Teacher: *Another way?*

If students tend to imitate others too often, the teacher may have them do this exercise with eyes closed.

4. **Teacher:** *I'll show you my favorite way to clap.*

The teacher claps ♩ by tapping fingers of one hand into cupped palm of the other. Students follow.

5. **Teacher:** *Let's change hands.* (Demonstrates.)

Students follow.

> [The reversal is important for developing a clear bilateral symmetry. At first students find it awkward; later it is easier. This step must not be omitted.]

This exercise introduces one of the many preferred styles of clapping. One hand is cupped and remains still in front of the middle of the chest while the clapping hand and arm move sideways away from and back across the body into the cupped hand. The clapping begins with the tips of the fingers of the clapping hand tapping the base of the cupped hand. The clap is performed with a gentle rebound of the wrist.

[This method of clapping, once mastered, avoids painful, noisy and unartistic sound and automatically introduces a sense of rhythmic life into an activity that otherwise may produce a flat, unmusical sound.]

6. **Teacher:** *Who remembers the slow tempo?*
   Student: *I do.*
   Teacher: *Show it, with our new clap.*

Student demonstrates, using a large movement (and no sound).

   Teacher: *Let's all do it.*

The teacher helps those who do not at first get the details and the quality of resistance and the flow of the movement.

7. **Teacher:** *Who remembers the running tempo?*
   Student: *I do! I do!*
   Teacher: *Let's get up and do it until the drum says "stop."*

The teacher plays, the students follow and stop when the drum speaks

STEP XIV: QUICK RECOGNITION AND RESPONSE TO TEMPO CHANGES

1. **Teacher:** *Let's see how quickly you can follow the drum. Walk when it says "walk," run when it says "run," swing when it says "slow," and stop when it says "stop."*

The teacher alternates patterns of ♩, ♫, and 𝅗𝅥 without breaks in between.

[This is a quick-reaction exercise using changing sequences of the tempi studied in the lesson. It will take the students a few beats to change with the drum. Later, students will match changes more quickly. Help in the form of cues can be given by dynamic changes in drumming.]

STEP XV: FINALE

1. The teacher sings the song "Looby Loo" while making gestures demonstrating movement in and out of the circle. Students follow and learn the song and dance movement.

2. **Teacher:** *Let's do it very slowly. Let's do it really slowly. Let's do it at a walking speed. Let's do it faster. Faster still!*

The teacher increases speed until it becomes impossible. Students collapse in laughter and squeals of delight.

3. Teacher: "Let's make our line for a space-walk out."

The teacher or a student leads the space-walk out of the classroom, using songs of the lesson.

KODÁLY

In Kodály classrooms singing is the basis for all musical learning. Because of this, considerable time must be spent with the youngest children to develop in-tune singing and pitch consciousness.[4] Many of the teaching strategies for the earlier grades have in-tune singing as their primary objective. Until security with singing is established, few other skills are stressed, although children may perform beat and rhythm accurately even without being able to sing well, and can deal also with use of the expressive qualities—softer-louder, faster-slower, and timbral differences—at a quite early age.

First lessons are designed to teach children a basic repertory of songs, many of which will be used later for skill development and concept inference. These songs may be drawn from the three-note chants of early childhood, from simple pentatonic folk songs, or from songs with a wider range (always being careful that the song material remains within the range of the young child). When this core of songs is being sung well, when the beat can be tapped and stepped accurately and the rhythm clapped correctly, the first connections are made with musical notation.

Lesson For An Early Stage

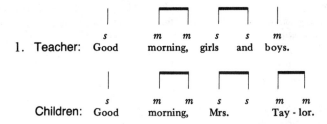

1. Teacher: Good morning, girls and boys.

Children: Good morning, Mrs. Tay - lor.

Then the teacher singles out one or two children for individual response.

Teacher: Good morning, Er - i - ca.

Erica: *Good morning, Mrs. Taylor.*
Teacher: *Good morning, Johnny.*
Johnny: *Good morning, Mrs. Taylor.*

2. The teacher then sings

---

[4]See Lois Choksy, *The Kodály Context* (Englewood Cliffs, NJ: Prentice-Hall, 1981), pp. 17–22, for a detailed description of techniques for the development of in-tune singing.

loo, loo, loo, ...

Children identify the song as "Hey, Betty Martin" and sing it through, tapping the beat on their laps.

Hey, Betty Martin

Hey, Bet - ty Mar - tin,   tip - toe, tip - toe;   hey, Bet-ty Mar - tin,   tip - toe fine;

Hey, Bet -ty Mar - tin,   tip - toe, tip - toe;   hey, Bet - ty Mar - tin,   please be   mine.

Teacher: *Listen to my new tempo.* (The teacher taps the beat faster on the desk.) *Who can sing "Betty Martin" at this tempo?* (Jimmy performs the song alone at the new tempo.)

Teacher: *Was the new tempo faster or slower?*

Children: *Faster.*

Teacher: *Here is another tempo.* (The teacher taps the beat slower on the board or desk.) *Is it faster or slower?*

Children: *Slower.*

Teacher: *Who can give us a good tempo for "Betty Martin?" John? Mary? Susan?* (Each sings alone.) *Which tempo did you like best?* (All sing it at the tempo chosen.)

Teacher: *Is there any place in the song we could make more interesting by singing louder or softer?*

Michael: *We could sing "tiptoe" very softly each time.*

Class again sings "Betty Martin" at the tempo agreed upon, with the dynamic change to soft on the word "tiptoe" each time it occurs. The children then play the game, changing "tiptoe" to "run run," "skipping," "hopping," and "sliding." To return to their seats they (a) put the song in their voices, (b) put the beat in their feet, and (c) put the rhythm in their hands.

3. New song: "Hush, Little Minnie," taught by rote.

Hush, Little Minnie

Hush,   lit - tle   Min - nie,   don't   say   a   word,

Pap-pa's gon - na buy   you a   mock - in'   bird;   It   can   whis - le and

it   can   sing;   It   can   do   'most   any   -   thing.

The teacher sings the whole song and discusses the words with the children.

Teacher: *What kind of song is it?*
Children: *Lullaby.*
Teacher: *How should it be sung?*
Children: *Softly.*

The teacher then sings the song phrase by phrase, with the children repeating after her, until they are singing the whole song correctly. Attention is given to phrasing and expressive singing.

Teacher: *Who can sing another lullaby we know? Alice?*

4. Alice sings "Bye, Baby Bunting."

Bye,   Ba - by   Bun - ting,   Dad - dy's gone   a - hun - ting   to

catch   a   lit - tle   rab - bit   skin   to   wrap the   Ba - by   Bun - ting   in.

Teacher: *Put the beat on your laps softly as you sing.*
    Class sings and taps beat.
    Where is the end of the first phrase? Where is there a good place to take a breath? (After "bunting.") *How many beats go by in the first phrase?*
    Class sings just the first phrase and taps; counts the beats (4).
Teacher: *Carl, would you put hearts on the feltboard to remind us of how many beats go by the first phrase?*
    Carl does this:

Heart

Teacher: *Let's check to see if this is correct.*
         Class sings the first phrase as Carl points to the beats (hearts).
Teacher: *This time as we sing the first phrase, put the rhythm in your hands.*
         The class claps and sings

Bye,   Ba - by Bunt - ing

Teacher: *Was there any beat with more than one sound?*
Children: *Yes!*
Teacher: *Which beat?*
Children: *The second.*
Teacher: *How many sounds were on the second beat?*
Children: *Two.*
Teacher: *How could we show that on the feltboard? I have some felt buntings here.*
         A child places the buntings to show how many sounds are on each
         beat.

Bunting

Teacher: *How could we show that pattern with* ta's *and* ti's?
         Another child places felt strips to show the rhythm:

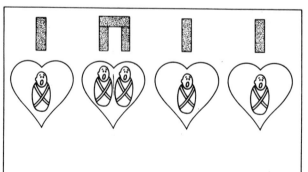

Felt strip

All sing the phrase (a) with words, and (b) with *ti–ta's*, to check that it is correct.

Teacher: *Build the first phrase of "Bye, Baby Bunting" with your rhythm sticks at your desks.* (Each child has a bundle of sticks [coffee stirrers, ice cream sticks, tongue depressors, counting sticks, etc.] for this purpose.) *Be sure to check your work by singing the first phrase with words and with* ti–ta's.

Several individual children are called on to point to their patterns and sing; then all point and sing: *ta ti - ti ta ta* . At this point a flash card

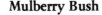

containing the pattern is shown and the rhythm is *spoken.* (Taking the known melody away from the rhythm pattern adds a level of difficulty.)

Teacher: *What other song begins with this rhythm?*
Children: *"Hey, Betty Martin," "Hush, Little Minnie."*

The class sings to determine whether these answers are correct, while one child points to the rhythm on the feltboard and all others point to the patterns on their desks.

Children: *"Frog in the Meadow."*

Frog in the Meadow

The class sings to determine whether the answer is correct.

Children: *"See Saw, Up and Down,"* (or some other incorrect answer).
Teacher: *Put the beats on laps. Now put the rhythm in your hands while I point to the beats on the feltboard.* (In this way the mistake is quickly discovered.)

5. Game song (after a concentration activity). The teacher claps the rhythm of the song "Mulberry Bush."

Mulberry Bush

Teacher: *What is it? Who can sing the first phrase? Is it a skipping song or a stepping song?* (This is to distinguish between compound and simple meters.)

The children form a circle and play the game.

6. Quiet listening song, "Cock Robin," is used to end the class.

CONTENT OF LESSON. The lesson included seven songs, four of which were used for skill development or concept inference, two of which involved movement, and one of which was for quiet listening.

TYPES OF SONGS. The songs included two lullabies, two game songs, one lyric song, and one other (depending on which one children suggested).

PRIMARY PURPOSE OF LESSON. The primary purpose of the lesson was the first derivation and notation of the pattern ♩ ♫ ♩ ♩.

SKILLS PRACTICED. The skills practiced included singing in tune; beat tapping and stepping; rhythm clapping; phrase identification; tempo judgement; appropriate use of dynamics; aural rhythmic derivation; rhythm reading from flash cards; rhythm construction with sticks; ability to recall songs beginning with the rhythm pattern, which have been sung in previous lessons; identification of a song by its melody sung on a neutral syllable.

In the course of the three years from ages five to seven, children in Kodály programs learn to read and write simple rhythms and pentatonic melodies in three key placements—F, C, and G—and in simple and compound duple meters. They learn to identify song forms and to hear and perform more than one musical idea at a time. Musical memory skills are sharpened and the abilities to visualize what is heard and to inner-hear what is seen are systematically developed.

Lesson for the End of Grade 2

1. Teacher sings a greeting, using notes from the known tonal vocabulary, ending with an implied V chord—musically, a question phrase.

s   l   s   m   d   r
Good   morn-ing, boys and girls

Children respond, using the same rhythm and the same tone set, but ending on *do*—providing a musical answer to the musical question (in the same key as the greeting).

s   l   s   m   r   d
Good   morn - ing, Mrs.   James

2. The teacher shows hand signs for

s   m m m   r   r   r   m   s

The class sings silently (with inner hearing) following the hand signs and identifies the song as "Hey, Come Along Jim, Along Josie."

Hey, Come Along Jim

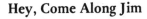

Hey, come a-long   Jim, a-long Jo - sie,   Hey,   come a-long   Jim, a-long Joe!

All sing the familiar song and tap the beat.

3. On the board is

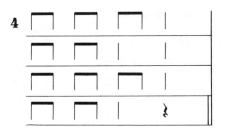

Teacher: *Which phrases are alike; which are different?*
Children: *The first and third are alike. The second is different and the fourth is different.*
Teacher: *What is the form then?*
   Class: *A–B–A–C.*
Teacher: *Let's say it in ta's and ti's.*
          (The class reads the example.) *Now memorize it. Which parts are easiest?*

Class: *The A parts, because they happen twice.* (A short time is given for children to reread and internalize the rhythm.)

Teacher: *Close your eyes.* (The teacher erases the A phrases.)
Open your eyes. (Establishing the beat) *One–two–ready–read!*
The children recite the exercise, including the missing parts.

On the board now is

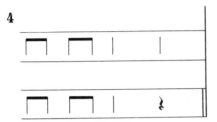

Teacher: *Close your eyes again.* (The rest of the exercise is erased.)
Open your eyes. One–two–ready–read!

Looking at the blank form the children recite the entire rhythm from memory.

Teacher: *John, put the third phrase back on the board; Mary, the second; Susan, the fourth; Alex, the first. Are they all correct? Let's say them to check. Fine! Do you know a song with that rhythm? Not sure? If we come to one during this class be sure to tell me.*

4. Teacher sings on a neutral syllable

Loo   loo   loo   loo   loo   loo   loo   loo

The children sing the known song back with words

Who's That?

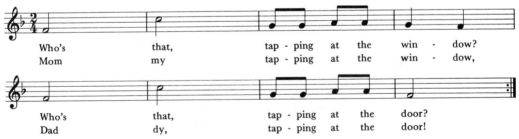

Who's   that,   tap - ping   at   the   win - dow?
Mom   my   tap - ping   at   the   win - dow,

Who's   that,   tap - ping   at   the   door?
Dad   dy,   tap - ping   at   the   door!

Teacher: *As you sing, show the phrases by arc-ing your arms. How many phrases are in the song?* (4) *This time put the beats in your lap and see how many beats go by in the first phrase.* (8)
A child diagrams the beats on the board with magnetic symbols.

Teacher: *Now, tap the* accented *beats. How is the music moving?* (In 2s.) *John, put the bar lines in to show how the music is moving.*
John does this:

Teacher: (Sings "Tapping at the Window") *Sing this part in ta's and ti's.*
Children: Ti–ti, ti–ti, ta, ta.
Teacher puts the given rhythm on the board:

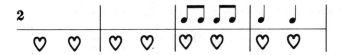

Teacher and class now sing "Who's That?"

Teacher: *How many beats go by on each word?* (2.) *How can we show that?*

The children have not yet seen the half note, so they draw on what they know. Several ideas may be put forward, but the most frequent one is usually:

♩ ₹ ♩ ₹ . The teacher should sing the song as:

♩ ₹ ♩ ₹ ♫ ♫ ♩ ♩ .

Teacher: *Are our voices really resting in these places? Is that the way we usually sing this?*
Children: *No; put another "ta" in each measure!*

Teacher complies, and performs the result.

Who's Who's | that that |

Teacher: *No. You can see that won't work.*

Through further discussion the children are led to the conclusion, "We need one *longer* sound, not two shorter ones."

Teacher: *Let's* tie *the two shorter sounds together to make one longer sound.*

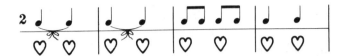

(Concept: Shorter sounds can be tied together to produce longer sounds.) The two-beat sounds are sung as *too*. Children sing the rhythm as: *too–, too–, ti–ti, ti–ti, ta, ta,* etc.

Teacher: *Put this rhythm in your manuscript books.*

[At later lessons the half note will be given as an alternate way of showing

♩♩ = ♩. However, *this* lesson is on the function of the tie.]

4. The teacher sings a known song and the children join in.

Here Comes a Bluebird

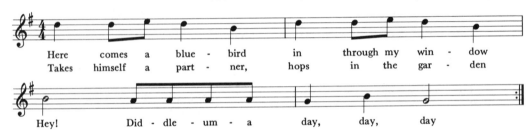

Here	comes	a	blue -	bird	in	through my	win -	dow
Takes	himself	a	part -	ner,	hops	in the	gar -	den

Hey!   Did - dle - um - a   day,   day,   day

As the children sing, they step the beat and form a circle to play the game. (This has previously been established as the way to get ready for a game.) After playing the game, they return to their seats, stepping the beat and clapping the rhythm as they go.

Teacher: *Are there any tied notes in "Here Comes a Bluebird"? Any notes that last longer than one beat?*

The children sing again to locate the two-beat sounds on "Hey" and "day" and show on the board the notation ♩♩.

5. The teacher presents a new song, "Sleep, Baby, Sleep":

Sleep, Baby, Sleep

Sleep   ba - by,   sleep;   Fath - er   tends   the   sleep.

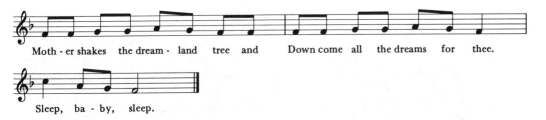

Moth - er shakes the dream - land tree and Down come all the dreams for thee.

Sleep, ba - by, sleep.

The children learn the song by a rote process, with attention given to text, dynamics, and phrasing.

> **Teacher:** *Is there any place in this song where we could use a tie?*
> **Children:** *On the second "sleep"; on "sheep"; on the last "sleep."*

Teacher illustrates on the board:

and the children sing the rhythm as:

> ta ti–ti too—
> ti–ti ti–ti too—

6. Teacher sings the opening phrase of the familiar song "Great Big House in New Orleans" and the children join in. Immediately, several recognize it as the rhythm-erase exercise done earlier.

Great Big House in New Orleans

Great big house in New Or - leans, For - ty stor - ies high.

Ev - 'ry room that I've been in, Filled with pump - kin pie.

The class sings the song, plays the circle game, and then claps an ostinato

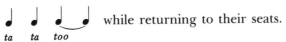 while returning to their seats.

ta ta too

7. Teacher sings a ballad for listening, "Fox Went Out on a Chilly Night."

Fox Went Out on a Chilly Night

Fox went out on a chil-ly night, Prayed for the moon to give him light,

He'd ma-ny a mile to go that night be - fore he reached the town - o,

the town - o, the town - o, He'd ma-ny a mile to go that night

Be - fore he reached the town - o.

Children join in on the chorus parts that they know.

What has happened in this lesson? Children have

improvised in question–answer phrases
demonstrated ability to arrive back at the tonal center
demonstrated memory of songs sung on a neutral syllable
read a rhythm from the board
derived the new rhythmic notation
analyzed the form of a song
aurally identified the meter of a song
identified phrases and illustrated them physically
written a rhythm in staff books
performed two folk dances

Conclusion

It is evident from these two lessons that in Kodály classes there is a great deal of emphasis on skill development and musical literacy at even early ages. However, it should be equally apparent that children are singing, dancing, and creating and that musical reading and writing, though important, are not necessarily the predominant activities of a Kodály class with young children. Musicality—the *feeling* for music—is fostered above all else in every class.

ORFF

For the youngest children in Orff programs, curriculum may be effectively organized around three basic areas: movement, voice, and form. Each of these areas demands specific objectives, processes, and materials.

Movement

OBJECTIVES. The children should (1) explore space with and without the beat being present; (2) move rhythmically in a variety of ways, alone and with others; (3) experience the beat in many tempi and to a number of different external stimuli; (4) develop gross and fine motor skills in a rhythmic context, and (5) demonstrate movement in twos and threes (duple and triple meter). Children should be able to move with ease and awareness of themselves and others, in circles, semicircles, lines, free formation, and independently.

PROCESSES. Language is used to motivate movement. Children say what is being done and do what is being said. They combine (1) language and movement of body parts; (2) language and actions; and (3) language and dance. There is continual verbal reinforcement of movement.

MATERIALS. The materials used are: say-and-do games, rhymes, and chants; play-party games; and jumprope chants.

Voice

OBJECTIVES. For poems, rhymes, or chants, the texts should be recited clearly and distinctly with sensitivity to expression and dynamics. Children should be able to sing, alone and with others, simple melodies in a two- to six-note range. They should demonstrate good phrasing.

PROCESSES. Songs, poems, chants, and rhymes are taught a phrase at a time by an echo-response process. There is much repetition in order to ensure clarity and correctness. Solo and ensemble performances are used to reinforce learning.

MATERIALS. The materials used are nursery rhymes, poetry in simple and compound meters, and nursery tunes with limited ranges (from three notes for the five-year-olds to six notes for the eight-year-olds).

Form

OBJECTIVES. Children should be able to identify forms being used and should be able to organize musical ideas into song forms, rondos, and canons. They should be able to think and act in musical phrases and to recognize and perform the conducting gestures for downbeat, upbeat, and cutoff.

PROCESSES. Children are led to discover the patterns of like and unlike in speech, song, and dance. Pictures, children's invented notation, and standard AB form designations are applied to these patterns.

MATERIALS. The materials used are nursery rhymes, poetry, chants, nursery songs, and dances.

Suggested Orff Experiences

Each of the following experiences touches on some aspect of each of the above objectives, processes, and materials that might be used in class work with five-, six-, or seven-year-olds.

MOVEMENT ACTIVITIES.   The body is the first instrument. It moves through space, like sound moving. Each body is sound waves in motion.

The children play a familiar singing game that encourages action improvisation.

Little Red Wagon

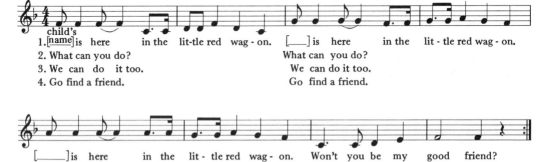

1. [name] is here   in the   lit-tle red   wag - on.   [____] is   here   in the   lit - tle red wag - on.
2. What can you do?   What can you do?
3. We can do it too.   We can do it too.
4. Go find a friend.   Go find a friend.

[____] is   here   in the   lit - tle red   wag - on.   Won't you be   my   good   friend?
What can you do?
We can do it too.
Go find a friend.

The class forms a circle. During the first verse the child who is "it" steps the beat inside the circle. On the second verse he or she shows an improvised action which is imitated by the group, and during the third verse he or she points, on the beat, to different children in the circle. The child being pointed to on the last note of the song becomes "it." At the end of the game the children remain standing in a circle.

Teacher:

What   are   the   parts   of   the   feet   that   can   keep   the   beat?

The children mention heel, ball of the foot, base and sides of the foot, and toes. The class tries each.

Teacher: *Without using your toes, walk around the room.*

Many children will walk with stiff legs and outstretched fingers to fill in for toes. (Remind them that they still have knees!)

Teacher: *Stretch, grab the floor with your toes, one foot at a time.*
Walk, feeling your feet; go all the way through the big toe.

Walk, tucking your bottom under, shoulders down. Walk with your feet guiding your body—heel, ball of your foot, toe.
Walk backwards and do the same thing in reverse order—toe, ball of your foot, heel.
Rock backward and forward. Change, and rock with the other leg back. Use your knee and sink forward and back. Keep your back straight, shoulders down, and bottom tucked under.
When you're moving, let your feet guide you.
Relax all parts of your body, starting with your head.
Let different parts of your body show the music at different parts of the song.

At this point the teacher may improvise an instrumental accompaniment as children continue to move.

MIRRORING.   In this exercise, the class, which is sitting, becomes the teacher's mirror image. The class is divided into pairs and each child takes a turn being the mirror image of the other.

QUALITIES OF MOVEMENT.

Teacher: *Show without touching anybody how you can move. Go from [here] to [there].*
See where your stopping point is. Go back to your first space. Go faster or slower; use a different part of your body to go back; use a different direction to go back. At your arrival place, freeze, and really show how you can be there.
Go, return in another level; change the quality of your movement.
Find a way to go across in a straight line.
Choose a partner: (a) move in your own way to your partner; (b) use your partner's way of moving across and change to your own way halfway across the space.

PARTS OF THE BODY.

Teacher: (Head) *Move your head in the "rhythm of the day"* (the specific rhythm pattern being worked on). *Feel that your head is so huge that your whole body moves with it.*
(Neck) *Try to move your neck forward and back, and put the rhythm of the day in it. Try different directions and tempi.*
(Shoulders) *Feel movement in your shoulders, raising them and lowering them. Move one shoulder at a time.* (Isolating parts is difficult.)
(Upper arm) *Try to lift with your shoulders down. This area is flowing and graceful.*
(Elbow) *Make sharp, mean motions with your elbow.* (The teacher uses the rhythm of the day.)
(Forearm) *Swing in $\frac{3}{4}$ time. Let the motion swing you and turn you around the room.*
(Wrist) *Show high and low motions with your wrists.* (The height should correspond to the instrumental sounds produced by the teacher.)

(Hands and fingers) Move your fingers in all possible ways. Make them become worms communicating with each other. Have them show tension by moving away from your body, then return relaxation back to your body.

Movement may be used to teach or to underline important musical concepts. Here is one way the understanding of meter might be developed in an Orff class.

Teacher: *What is heavy on the body? What would your body look like and feel like if it were five hundred pounds? How would you move it? Do it!*

The movement is basically downward. The floor is used, heads are hung down, lifting is a chore. The teacher beats a low-pitched timpani with a steady pulse. The students respond with grotesque gestures. Some transform themselves into monsters. Great creatures from the past and new ones break out of tiny bodies.

Teacher: *Freeze!*

All around the room are examples of what the feeling of *heavy* is to children.

Teacher: *Relax!*
What is light on your body? What would your body feel like or look like if it were three pounds?
Go!

Immediately hands go up in the air; bodies are supported on toes; lifts are tried; the whole atmosphere is alive with airy, open, free movements. The teacher adds a high-pitched timpani to accompany the movement. The movement takes a rhythmic sway, not as a unit, but rather like leaves on a tree being moved by the wind.

Teacher: *Freeze!*
Is everything in the world heavy? Is everything in the world light? (The answers are "No," for both cases.) *Everything is a combination of these things. So let's play with these qualities. Listen to the sound of the timpani. Show me what you hear.*

The thump of the low timpani begins. Bodies are heavy. After eight pulsations the teacher switches to the high timpani. Bodies fly. The switching continues until there is nothing left except the play between the heavy sound and the light sound. The feeling is heavy–light, heavy–light, heavy–light. Bodies are bobbing and weaving, up and down to the sounds of the timpani. The drumming stops.

Teacher: *What did you hear and feel?*
Class: *Down and up. Heavy–light. Strong and weak. Out–ins. Push and pull. One–two.*

They heard and felt the contrasts and a definite grouping of sounds.

> Teacher: *Let's give this grouping of twos a name: "Duple meter." Let's try it again, the duple meter.*

Off they go again; however, this time within a sixteen-bar phrase. Now there is the possibility of a dance. The children look for movements which best say "duple"; combine a few of them, rehearse them for a while, then perform the latest dance, the "Duple-Meter Stomp." A suggestion of music is added; mouth music (neutral nonsense syllables and sounds) is enough. In the next lesson, perhaps, the class can listen to a series of compositions which would best fit the new dance. The teacher returns to the timpani. This time the sound is heavy–light–light, in other words, groupings of threes, or "triple meter." This time a different instrument is used for demonstration. The recorder, in contrast to the timpani, is by nature lighter, but it can also produce a feeling of heavy–light–light. The children strain to listen for the metric grouping. It is there and they feel it.

> Teacher: *As you move this time, try to feel the energy coming from your friends around you. You may join their energy, but do not touch. Like mirrors, reflect what you see and feel. Listen for the beginning.*

Individuals begin; soon couples form, then trios. Partners change and new reflections are made. There is much stretching and reaching, as well as use of different levels and directions. The children may not touch, so their actions appear to be pure dance. Their faces as well as their bodies are fully engaged. They are totally involved in play and fantasy in the triple meter. At a later time this game can be enlarged to include mixed meters.

VOICE.

> Teacher: *The mouth can make all kinds of sounds. Try to make sounds without words. (The children experiment and come up with numerous mouth sounds.) Now try your sounds in the rhythm of the day. Mix and match your sounds to other people's.*

Choosing two contrasting sounds, the teacher divides the children into two groups. Either the teacher or a child conducts the two groups in a performance of the rhythm of the day in the two contrasting mouth sounds. Beginning and ending sounds are added and the middle is elongated. Tongue clicking is added and alternated with the other sounds. Low and high pitches are added. Finally, the class is divided into three groups: low-voice (growl), medium-voice (speaking pitch), and high-voice (squeak), and the whole is performed.

The singing voice too must be trained:

> Teacher: *Your voice comes from air. Breathe. Put your left hand on your chest and your right hand on your tummy. Breathe out and in:*

Now put the syllable "sh" ("s," "pl," "ts," "rr") on the out-breath.
Now try this:

(breathing on the rests). *Do this also with the syllable "ha" ("hey," "yah," "ho").*

AN EXPERIENCE INVOLVING MOVEMENT, VOICE, AND FORM.

1. A rhythm is clapped by the teacher and repeated by the children, phrase by phrase, until it is known.

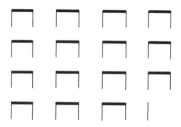

2. **Teacher:** *What did I clap?* (Some of the children may recognize the rhythm as "Peter, Peter, Pumpkin Eater"; others will not know the rhyme.)

3. Teacher teaches the rhyme, having children echo a phrase at a time until all know it well.

> Peter, Peter, pumpkin eater,
> Had a wife and couldn't keep her,
> Put her in a pumpkin shell and
> There he kept her very well.

4. The children then clap and say the rhyme in order to decide on the meter, beat, and pulse. They discover the meter as duple.

5. The children step the beat while saying the rhyme and clapping the pulse

6. The teacher teaches a melody to go with the rhyme, a phrase at a time, by the echo technique.

Put her   in   a   pump - kin shell and   there he kept her   very   well.

7. The teacher next focuses attention on the meaning of the story. One half of the group tells the other half the story. Facial expressions are encouraged. Different children in the class tell the story as if they (a) *were* Peter or (b) are telling about Peter. The subjective (doing) brings into play different emotional qualities than the objective (judging). Some attitudes expressed by children in one class were:

DOING (SUBJECTIVE)	JUDGING (OBJECTIVE)
defensive	sarcasm
despair	disgust
feeling of "last resort"	disbelief
	questioning

8. **Teacher:** *Now sing the song and step the beat again. This time show in your face and body and stepping how you really feel, either as Peter or as someone else who is talking about Peter.*

9. **Teacher:** *Can we do it in another meter? Triple. Say it to yourself and do body percussion.*

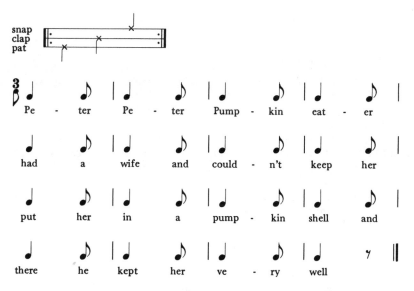

This creates a different mood altogether.

10. **Teacher:** *What if we combine the duple and triple meters?*

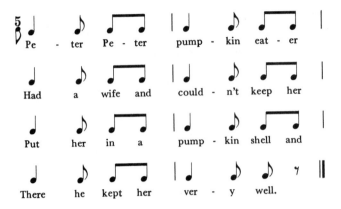

Pe - ter Pe - ter pump - kin eat - er

Had a wife and could - n't keep her

Put her in a pump - kin shell and

There he kept her ver - y well.

Introduce body percussion.

snap
clap
pat

Say the rhyme and accompany it with body percussion.
Sing the song through in this new meter with body percussion.

11. Ideas are put forward by the children for a dramatic piece based on a "trial" of Peter. For this, the piece could be put into the following form:

    a.   The theme is sung by the class.
    b.   The theme is spoken in duple meter with each child speaking at a differ-
         ent tempo. The speech is treated as gossip, beginning at one end of a
         semicircle and spreading through it getting louder and louder. Peter ap-
         pears and everyone is hushed: "Sh!"

Return to a. In an innocent, childlike manner the original version is sung, then silenced.

    c.   The theme is then performed in triple meter and in minor to represent
         the nightmare quality—Peter telling his version of the story.

Return to a. Sung as at the beginning.

    d.   The piece is recited in mixed meter with new improvised words
         describing the jury's decision: "Peter is guilty!"

Return to a. The theme as sung originally.

        The final dramatic "composition" is an experience in rondo form. It has utilized speech, song, movement, and body percussion. It has benefited from contributions by individuals, small groups, and the whole ensemble. In this it is a typical Orff experience for young children.

COMPREHENSIVE MUSICIANSHIP

Learning Objectives

The overall goal for the youngest students in a Comprehensive Musicianship (CM) approach could be stated, "to explore sound and discover the parameters of sound in time and in space." In order to accomplish this goal a number of learning activities are offered in the areas of pitch, duration, intensity, and timbre, as well as in the organization of these elements.

PITCH.   Children play, sing, and experiment with high, low, and medium sounds. They arrange and organize pitches from the environment and from a variety of sound sources into melody. They sing melodies and analyze and describe through movement and visual representation the melodic contours apparent in musical composition. Children begin to conceptualize and to shape concepts of pitch organization into scales and melodic patterns. They listen to music, sing, and play on classroom instruments. Using pitches of specified scales, the students arrange them into compositions and improvisational pieces.

DURATION.   Children perform, listen to, and create rhythms, meters, and tempi. Emphasis at this beginning level is on basic beat and pulse, simple rhythmic patterns, and the metric divisions of two and three. Movement is stressed to reinforce the perception and conceptualization of beat and pulse, metric organization, and tempo variation. Children explore rhythmic groupings, identify the basic meters employed, and use the basics of beat, tempo, and meter to create chants, speech canons, and ostinati. Emphasis is on the listening, singing and playing, and creating, and on the direct application and implementation of basic concepts.

INTENSITY.   Dynamic variation in song materials is identified through singing and listening. Children decide on the utilization of louds and softs in familiar and unfamiliar songs. They experiment with and explore sounds which are soft and those which are loud in the environment. Environmental compositions with a variety of loud and soft sounds are composed and analyzed.

TIMBRE.   Sound awareness is stressed. The timbres from sound sources from the environment, the body, the traditional instruments, the electronic instruments and synthesizers, the folk instruments, and non-Western instruments are performed, described, and used in the creation and organization of simple compositions or improvisational experiences. World music is the source of CM timbral exploration, discovery, and learning.

THE ORGANIZATION OF PITCH, DURATION, INTENSITY, AND TIMBRE. The interaction and arrangement of pitch, duration, intensity, and timbre create specific organizations of music in the CM model.

HORIZONTAL ORGANIZATION.   The horizontal organization of pitches and durations create melodies and rhythms which can be explored, performed, created, and described by the children. At the beginning levels children are exposed to a division of sound and silence into long, short, regular, or irregular groupings. Through compositional activities, analysis, and performance by singing and playing, children are made aware of the interaction of rhythm and pitch frequencies found in melody. These frequencies are heard and classified as white sound, sounds of indefinite pitch, single pitches, or as divisions into scale units.

VERTICAL ORGANIZATION.   Even at the beginning level of the CM model, children listen to, identify, perform, and create the simultaneous sounds known as harmony. At this point in the teaching-learning spiral of CM the experiences in vertical organization occur through simple melodic ostinato patterns, partner songs, and simple two-part playing and singing. Children are also exposed to the concept of texture through the differing densities of simultaneous sounds or the accumulation of individual lines. They explore various textural possibilities and add and subtract sounds to build a compositional whole.

FORM.   The result of the interaction of the above elements of music is form. Children explore form by identifying like and unlike phrases and sections and by identifying ABA organization, song form, and simple rondo form.

MUSICAL CONTEXTS.   The exploration of these elements and organizations of sound is done within social, aesthetic, and historical contexts with a variety of world music materials.

Lesson Plans

The following examples of lesson plans for primary age children are taken from a CM curriculum. It should be noted that in the school environment, these activities would relate to other musical activities at all levels of instruction and would supply the readiness for certain musical concepts and skills and reinforcement for others. The materials presented in the following lessons should not be isolated or fragmented; instead, they should relate to the total music program.
The CM application of the following activities and experiences allow for active participation in conceptual development through performance, analysis, improvisation, and creativity.

LESSON PLAN A

1. Perform and analyze
    a.   Teach by rote the folk rhyme "Ordinary Clapsies," and ask the children to perform the appropriate movements as they chant

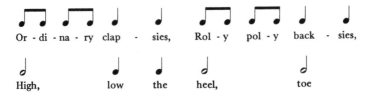

Or - di - na - ry clap - sies,   Rol - y   pol - y   back - sies,

High,   low   the   heel,   toe

Clip,   clop,   and a - way   she   goes.

Suggested movements:

Ordinary clapsies	Clap on the beat.
Roly-poly backsies	Circle or roll the hands.
High, low	Reach high and bend low.
the heel, toe	Tap the heel and then the toe.
Clip, clop, and away she goes	March in place.

    b.   Ask the children to vary the tempos of the rhyme as they repeat it.

    c.   Have the children use specific words (fast, slow, medium) to describe the tempos used.

    d.   Have the children chant the rhyme as a three-voice canon, after they are familiar with it.

2.   Create

    a.   Ask the children in the class to contribute to a class rhyme.

    b.   Write the suggested lines of the rhyme on the chalkboard and have the children chant them with the precise rhythm.

    c.   When a short class rhyme has been formed, have the children suggest appropriate movements for the various phrases and sections of the rhyme.

    d.   Have the children chant the class rhyme with the suggested movements in canon.

3.   Perform and analyze

    a.   Teach by rote the English folk song "A-Hunting We Will Go."

    b.   Have the children determine which beats in the song are stressed as it is sung. Ask the children to clap the stressed beats as they sing.

A-Hunting We Will Go

Oh!   A - Hunt - ing   we   will   go, _____   a -

hunt - ing   we   will   go; _____   we'll   catch   a   fox   and

put   him   in   a   box,   and   then   we'll   let   him   go.

4.   Create: Have the children create a new text for "A-Hunting We Will Go" by substituting new words for "fox" and "box." The new words should rhyme with each other. (The substitute word for "fox" should be an animal.)

Some possibilities are

> We'll catch a *dog* and put him in a *bog*.
> We'll catch a *duck* and put her in a *truck*.
> We'll catch a *raccoon* and send him to the *moon*.
> We'll catch a *cat* and put him on a *mat*.
> We'll catch a *quail* and put her in the *mail*.
> We'll catch a *hen* and put her in a *pen*.

5. Analyze
   a. Ask the children in the class to go on a sound search in their homes and to locate sound sources, or objects which can be played loud or soft, high or low, and long or short.
   b. Have the children bring several of these sound sources to the music class to place in a *sound box*.

      The sound sources could include bolts and washers, dried leaves, plastic bottles with rice or macaroni placed inside, an old toothbrush or scrubbrush to be rubbed on another object, a piece of paper to be ripped, coins to be jingled.
   c. Have each child present his or her sound objects to the class and demonstrate the sounds that can be made with the objects.
   d. Ask the students to describe the sounds made as loud or soft, long or short, and high or low.
   e. Experiment with various sound textures by having the children select several of the sounds to play at one time. Have the children gradually build the texture by adding one sound at a time until several sounds can be heard at once.
   f. Give each child in the class a blank piece of newsprint or drawing paper. Also give each child several crayons or markers to use. Ask the children to represent the sound textures on paper as they are played. For example, if a can filled with beans is played, then a few seonds later a toothbrush is drawn over a plastic bottle cap, and then a small rubber ball is bounced on the floor, the graphic representation could look like this:

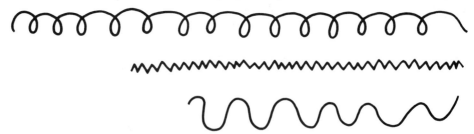

6. Perform and analyze
   a. Ask the children to sing the familiar folk song "Little Tom Tinker."
   b. Have the children identify the place in the song where the words should be sung loudly. ("Ma")

c. Have the students begin the song softly and then increase the dynamic level on the words, "Ma! Ma! What a poor fellow am I."

Little Tom Tinker

Lit - tle Tom Tink-er got burned with a clink - er and he be-gan to cry.

ma____ ! ma____ ! what a poor fel - low am I____

LESSON PLAN B

1. Perform and create
   a. Teach by rote the folk song "London Hill."
   b. Have the children create their own verses to the song. Have them include interesting and unusual activities that they could do on London Hill. For example,

   I drove my car on London Hill.
   I ate a pear on London Hill.
   I washed my hair on London Hill.
   I played baseball on London Hill.

London Hill

As I went o - ver Lon - don Hill, Lon - don Hill, Lon - don Hill,

As I went o - ver Lon - don Hill on a cold, fros - ty morn - ing.

2. Perform
   a. Teach by rote the Omaha Indian song "Follow My Leader."
   b. Select a child to play the steady beat on tom-tom or hand drum as the class sings the song. Ask the child playing the drum to vary the tempo each time the song is repeated.

Follow My Leader

Fol - low my Lead - er wher - e'er he goes;

What he'll do next, no - bod - y knows.

3. Create
   a. Ask the children to form a line behind the leader who is at the head of the line. Have the leader perform unique movements and actions for the other children to follow as they sing the song "Follow My Leader."
   b. Have one child play the steady beat of the song on a tom-tom or a hand drum as the other children move.
   c. Repeat the song a number of times before changing leaders.
4. Create and analyze
   a. Have several large tuning forks available for the children to use as they experiment with sound and vibration.
   b. Strike one of the tuning forks sharply and hold it close to the children, so that they can hear the sound made by the vibrations.
   c. Strike the tuning fork sharply and place the vibrating end in a shallow pan of water. Have the children explain what made the water splash so violently as the tuning fork was placed into it.
   d. Place a handful of split peas or rice on a drum head and then strike the drum or have a child strike the drum. Have the children watching the experiment explain why the split peas or the rice danced on the head of the drum.
   e. Explain to the children that vibrations caused the tuning fork to sound, vibrations caused the splashing of the water, and that vibrations also caused the movement of the split peas or the rice on the drum head. Explain that vibrations are fundamental to sound production.
5. Create
   a. Provide each child with a half-pint empty milk carton which has been cleaned and dried and has the top cut off. Supply each child with a rubber band and instruct each child to place the rubber band across the open end of the carton and around the bottom of the carton.
   b. Have the children pluck the rubber band and produce sounds.
   c. Have the children explain what caused the sound made by the rubber band.
6. Perform and create
   a. Teach by rote the folk song "Here Stands a Red Bird" and have the children form a circle holding hands.
   b. During Verse 1, select one child to be the "red bird" and to stand in the middle of the circle singing the verse as a solo.
      During Verse 2, ask the children in the circle to sing while the "red bird" in the center demonstrates a specific movement with his or her body.
      During Verse 3, have all the children sing and imitate the movements shown by the "red bird."
      During Verse 4, the "red bird" selects a partner and the two children then walk around the inside of the circle stepping on the beat as they both sing the verse together.

The "red bird" returns to a place in the circle and the selected partner becomes the new "red bird" as the singing game is repeated.

Here Stands a Red Bird

Here stands a red bird   tra - la - la - la - la-la,   Here stands a red bird
tra - la - la - la - la-la,   Rice,   su - gar, and   tea!

Verse 2
> Let me see a motion, tra-la-la-la-la.
> Let me see a motion, tra-la-la-la-la.
>> Rice, sugar, and tea!

Verse 3
> Very pretty motion, tra-la-la-la-la.
> Very pretty motion, tra-la-la-la-la.
>> Rice, sugar, and tea!

Verse 4
> Get yourself a partner, tra-la-la-la-la.
> Get yourself a partner, tra-la-la-la-la.
>> Rice, sugar and tea!

7. Perform
    a. Teach by rote the folk song "Old King Glory."
    b. After the children are familiar with the song, ask them to form a circle and to clap on the beat as they sing. Have the children face the inside of the circle.

    Choose one child to walk on the beat around the outside of the circle as the song is sung. On the words "first one, second one, third follow me," have the child walking around the outside of the circle tap three other children in the circle in succession. The third child tapped should then follow the leader and do the tapping as the song is repeated. Continue the circle game until all of the children are walking together on the beat of the song.

Old King Glory

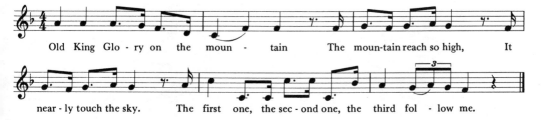

Old King Glo - ry on   the   moun -   tain   The moun-tain reach so high,   It
near - ly touch the sky.   The first   one, the sec - ond one, the third fol - low me.

Summary

In Lesson A the children are exposed to the following musical concepts:

    beat
    tempo
    stress beat
    dynamics
    duration
    pitch
    texture

The children are involved in performance, movement, analysis, sound exploration, and creativity.

In Lesson B the children are exposed to the following musical concepts:

    beat
    tempo
    sound production
    pitch

Again, the children are involved in performance, movement, analysis, sound exploration and discovery, and the creation of text for the songs. Children are given opportunities to be listeners, to be performers, and to be creators and discoverers. In this lesson, the children use song materials from the American Indians and from the English and American folk song literature.

CONCLUSIONS

In this chapter all four approaches have illustrated in their sample lessons an awareness of child development characteristics. Singing ranges are appropriate; movement experiences are geared to the ages of the children involved. There is an effort within each to inculcate basic concepts of pitch (higher–lower), dynamics (louder–softer), and tempo (faster–slower). All introduce the principle of organizing music into forms.

Still, these lessons are very different from each other. Even at this beginning level the underlying emphases of each method are clearly evident: movement (Jaques-Dalcroze), singing (Kodály), dramatization and ensemble (Orff), and sound exploration and discovery (Comprehensive Musicianship).

9

GRADES 3–4–5

INTRODUCTION

The Program Cone developed for the Music Educators National Conference in 1970 (see p. 116) lists the desirable musical experiences for intermediate grade children as the following:

> developing musical independence
> beginning part singing
> composition and improvisation
> music sight reading
> music in contemporary life
> musical masterworks
> beginning instrumental study[1]

As was true of the suggested experiences for the earlier grades, these experiences are possible within the framework of any of the methods discussed in this book. However, the differences in emphasis begin to be more apparent at this level.

[1]National Council of State Supervisors of Music of MENC, *Guidelines in Music Education: Supportive Requirements* (Reston, VA: MENC, 1972), p. 5.

JAQUES-DALCROZE

Rhythmics

Children in Grades 3, 4, and 5, who have had a Eurhythmics background in their earlier years, will have experienced at least the first twelve elements of rhythm (pp. 40–43) in some appropriate form. Listening skills will have been translated into living dictation, simple graphics, and chart reading of exercises of four-measure patterns in two-, three-, four-, and five-beat simple meters and in two-, three-, and four-beat compound meters. They will have mastered simple controls and physical techniques of weight shifting, control of balance, and movement backward, forward, and sideways using various spatial designs (circles, lines, squares) and conductor's arm swings in two-, three-, and four-beat measures in regular and mixed meters. They will also have acquired the ability to perform in speech, song, and movement (silent or sounded) the relationship of

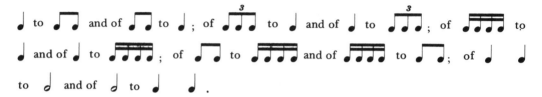

Students will have become aware of patterns that produce or require crusic, dynamic, and agogic accents. Durations as long as eight beats can be controlled and measured accurately with or without spoken subdivision. Left and right body sides and changes from right to left or left to right will be smooth and quick. Changes from movement in the arms to movement of legs will be accurate. Rests up to fifty beats will be maintained. Patterns of crusic and anacrusic measures will be performed and students should show considerable skill in the ability to create, conduct, or follow a percussion improvisation ensemble.

Singing and pitch skills will include an appropriate repertoire of songs, proper posture, and breathing, and the ability to phrase a period without words, the ability to learn a two-measure phrase in one hearing, and the ability to follow contours indicating pitch, direction, position, and function by tracing a melody with fingers and arms. The memory of middle C should be about 75-percent accurate, as well as the ability to hear, show, and sing whole- and half-steps.

Students will have had a good deal of experience singing major pentatonic and major diatonic scales on any one-measure rhythmic pattern given by the teacher. Students should be able to locate tonality in any major scale by responding to the teacher's question:

Teacher:

Student:

Students will have experienced reading a one- and two-line staff locating *do* on any line or space assigned by the teacher and locating the names of the other lines and spaces in ascending or descending order.

In improvisation, students have experienced exercises is creating, conducting, reconstructing (remembering), analyzing forms, and graphing: movement improvisations of up to ten gestures; improvised choreographies to songs; songs of up to four phrases; and short percussion or piano improvisations.

Lesson Plan

SUBJECT.   How rests, as active silences, are used to produce patterns, phrases, periods, melodies, and musical forms (Rhythmic element 10, p. 42).

STEP I: TUNE-UP—STARTING AND STOPPING
CONTROLS

1. **Teacher:** *Clap the beat, but stop clapping as quickly as you can when the music stops. Listen carefully! Are you ready?*

The teacher plays or sings any music featuring a clear quarter-note beat in a

moderate tempo ♩ = 120 . Jazz pieces and folk-dance music are extremely effective. (If the teacher prefers, a recording or tape may be used.)

2. **Teacher:** *Listen! Have you got the beat? Are your hands ready?*

The teacher scans the group for a good starting position and readiness, which are important to ensemble performance.

Teacher: (Speaking in tempo) ♩   ♩
             Let's   go.

The students clap the beat using relaxed wrists and good sound, but softly enough to hear the music.

> [Many students get carried away by their own energy when clapping, playing, or singing and are unable to hear the other parts of the ensemble.]

3. **Teacher:** (As students clap beat) *Not too loud or you won't hear the stops.*

The teacher stops the music suddenly. The students try to stop.

[Most students will stop one or two beats after the music stops, since their movement tends to become automatic rather than to follow thoughtful listening.]

4. Teacher: *I caught everyone. Let's try it again. I'll make it easier. This time keep your eyes on me. I'll clap without music. Follow me and stop when I stop. I'll even say "Stop."*

[This heavy cue may be necessary for the tune-up. It may be eliminated later in the lesson as students gain more skill.]

5. Teacher: (Speaking in tempo, without music) *Let's get our hands ready*

Here   we   go   now!

The teacher and students clap. The teacher suddenly says *Ready, stop!* loudly. Everyone stops.

Teacher: *Let's try it without the word "ready." I'll only say "Stop."*

[This is a slight withdrawing of the cue. Students should try this exercise several times. Some students will have difficulty putting on their brakes. They often simply give in to the momentum of the beat, producing a lifeless and thoughtless performance of time elements without rhythmic flow or forward drive. Performing rhythms with vitality and authority requires the ability to brake or move with equal facility.]

6. Teacher: *Let's try our first exercise again. This time I won't call out "Stop." You must listen for the music to stop.*

The students try the exercise several times. The teacher makes stops in the music at 16-beat intervals and then switches to stops at 8-beat intervals to check if students are really listening or have gone on automatic. If students are successful, the teacher then challenges them by using stops at a large variety of 8-, 4-, 2-, 5-, 1-, or 20-beat intervals in regular or irregular sequences.

STEP II

1. Teacher: *When I call a number we'll try to stop the clap and count the beats silently. Like this.*

The teacher demonstrates, using finger clapping into palm:

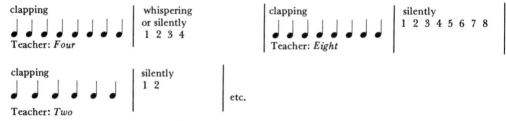

Teacher: *Let's try it. Get ready.*

The teacher sets a tempo by clapping, speaking, singing, or playing. The students follow the teacher's calls.

2. Teacher: *Let's do this again with silent counting, but this time we'll show the beat in other parts of our bodies.*

The teacher repeats the previous exercise.

> [Keeping an internal beat going during silences is an absolutely essential requirement for developing rhythmic skills. It is the rhythmic equivalent of perfect pitch.]

STEP III

1. Repeat the above exercises with silences demonstrated at walking, running, or slow tempi, while moving around in a circle.

STEP IV

1. Teacher: *Let's do some reading now.*

The teacher writes on the chalkboard

Teacher: *The circled numbers are the silences; the notes are the claps. Let's try it at this tempo. Get your hands ready.*
Setting up a very moderate quarter-note tempo, the teacher speaks in tempo,

Ready,   here   we   go   now.

The teacher points to the notes on the board. The students clap the beats, count aloud for the silences, and then resume clapping beats.

2. Teacher: *Good. Let's try it this time with silent counting.*

The teacher points, in tempo, to the beat notation. The students try it, mouthing numbers.

Teacher: *Good. Let's try it without any external movement on the silences, not even your mouths.*

The students continue to work on the exercise until they are able to perform it skillfully.

> [This process of eliminating outward movements is designed to increase inner memory and inner controls.]

3. **Teacher:** *Let's try a new speed. Let's go through at a running speed.* (The teacher sets the new tempo at twice as fast as the quarter note of the previous exercise:) *Are you ready for this tempo? We can count the silences out loud.*

> [It is important to learn how to erase one tempo and prepare for the change to another. In general, the ability to perform in one tempo does not automatically give the ability to deal with many tempi. Speaking, singing, moving, or playing an instrument all involve restrictions on tempo experience and experiment, but this can be counteracted by the teacher's awareness and skill in presenting a large variety of tempo experiences. Staying too long in one tempo can give rise to tension, boredom, or even an inability to use the body and mind in a new tempo when called upon to do so: an *arrhythmy*[2] instead of eurhythmy.]

Teacher: (Speaking in tempo)

Let's try   it   a - gain. Now, GO!

The students clap the eighth-note beat and count the silences in the new tempo.

4. **Teacher:** *Try it again; this time without counting out loud. Show the silences by movements.*

The students try it.

5. **Teacher:** *Now we'll make it more difficult. Try it without any movement during the silences. We'll count inside.*

The students try the exercise.

6. **Teacher:** *Counting silences is even harder at a slow tempo. Here is a new beat. Erase the old one and try this.*

The teacher sets the half note as the beat, making it exactly twice as slow as the quarter note of the original exercise. The teacher demonstrates a large space between claps by slowly pulling arms apart, then pressing arms in to clap. The demonstration starts with the preparation (anacrusis) of the clap, not the clap itself.

[2]For additional information see E. Jaques-Dalcroze, "Remarks on Arrhythmy," *Music and Letters*, 14, no. 2 (1933), 138–145.

[It may be necessary to give some resistance exercises so that students can maintain a slow tempo. Movements must be sustained and releases must be as controlled contractions. Pulling an imaginary rubber band is one helpful technique to encourage use of pectoral, side, and back muscles.]

7. **Teacher:** *I think we're ready.* (Speaking in tempo,)

Here   we   go   now.

The students clap the beat, then stop, replacing clapping by speaking silent beats, in the new tempo. The teacher encourages accurate attack of consonants and elongation of vowels of the spoken numbers to produce slow legato speech.

Teacher: *Let's repeat the exercise, replacing speech with movements and gestures.*

The students practice with gestures replacing speech and try to find different gestures for each silent beat.

Teacher: *Now try it without external movement or speech.*

The students work silently, without external movement, and practice until skillful performance is attained.

STEP V

1. Teacher: *Will someone replace the silences with different numbers and conduct us? Yes, Harry.* (Harry erases the old numbers and replaces them with a new series.) *Will you conduct us at a walking tempo?*

Harry conducts the class, indicating starts and stops. The teacher selects another student to conduct at a running tempo and another to conduct at a slow tempo.

STEP VI

1. Teacher: *Let's work with the silences in a new way by using a ball-passing game.*

[The ball is used to avoid an inhibiting self-consciousness. It encourages good movement by focusing the eyes and mind on an object outside the body itself.]

The teacher directs the class to make a circle.

[If the class is a large one, it may be broken into two or more circles with eight to ten students in each. If the space is small, the teacher may use concentric circles or lines.]

The teacher demonstrates passing direction and tempo by moving the ball around the circle. When the teacher calls a number, the ball is stopped until the beats of silence are concluded. During the silence the students show continuation of beats and tempo by motions of knees, hips, head, shoulders, or other body part. The signal "Stop!" involves four different mental motor commands: (1) stop passing, (2) continue beating, (3) count beats, and (4) resume passing.

2. **Teacher:** *Let's try this game now. Are you in a good starting position? Here is the tempo:*

1   2   3   4   *Let's   pass   the   ball,   now!*

The students listen to the beat of the teacher's speech, song, drum, chant, piano, or record and pass the ball until the teacher calls a number. Then the students stop passing the ball and speak the silent beats.

Teacher:

Pass,   pass,   pass   the   ball,   Pass   a - round   the   cir - cle,

Pass,   pass,   pass   the   ball,   Pass   a - round   the   world.

Teacher: *Ten!*
Students and teacher count out loud, in tempo, *1, 2, 3, 4, 5, 6, 7, 8, 9, 10;* then resume singing, in tempo,

Pass,   pass,   pass   the   ball, ...

Teacher: *Eight!*
Students and teacher count out loud, in tempo, *1, 2, 3, 4, 5, 6, 7, 8;* then resume singing.

3. **Teacher:** *Let's pass the ball in another direction.*

Students and teacher repeat the exercise.

4. **Teacher:** *Let's try the game in running tempo.*

Students and teacher repeat the activity at the eighth-note tempo. The teacher reminds the students to make the passing gestures small and light for control of poise and balance under the stress of fast stops.

[Teachers wishing to aid students to experience skillful performance at fast tempi must help them learn to handle the musical, physical, emotional, and mental excitement induced by fast tempi. The first experiences may be clumsy, but the use of very small movements will help develop control.]

5. **Teacher:** *Let's take more space so we can swing our arms to pass the ball in a slow tempo.*

The teacher sets a half-note tempo and students pass the ball, count silences, and show beats with body motion, then with silent counting, next with small body movements to show counts, and, finally, with no external movement at all, using only internal counting.[3]

[As students gain body technique this game will be translated to moving and stopping going around a circle in quarter-note, eighth-note, or half-note speed.]

STEP VII: CREATING PATTERNS WITH RESTS

1. **Teacher:** *Let's sit down. Now we'll see what else we can do with beats and rests. We'll clap a measure of four beats across our body from left to right, like this.* (The teacher claps from right to left as a mirror image to the students. The teacher continues to demonstrate.) *Be sure you show the power of the first beat, the rebound and flow of the second and third beats, and the lift after the fourth beat to return to the left side and renew your measure energy.*

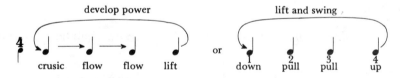

[These directions are very important for the proper experience of meter and rests.]

2. **Teacher:** *Let's all try it.*

Students and teacher do the exercise together. The teacher corrects any errors of performance.

[The most difficult movement is the return to the first beat. Students need to move quickly in order to do this at the correct moment. Later, this exercise will help students read past the bar line.]

[3]Music for these games is available on tapes 1A, 1B, 2A, and 2B of the cassette accompanying Robert M. Abramson, *Rhythm Games for Perception and Cognition* (Hialeah, FL: Columbia Pictures, 1978.)

3. The teacher writes 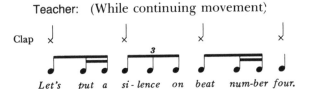 on the chalkboard. Students and teacher continue clapping.

Teacher: (While continuing movement)

The teacher makes a gesture on beat number four but does not clap on it:

Students and teacher repeat the pattern several times. The gesture made by the teacher must show that the rest still has a lifting (anacrusic) feeling and makes beat number one stronger, possibly using such words as "pull" or "lift" to help.

4. The teacher then writes ⎮♩ ♩ ♩ 𝄾 ⎮ the chalkboard.

Teacher: *Let's return to what we did before. Let's clap all four beats.*

[The important point in this exercise is that rests have different qualities which affect the beats that follow them. This difference can be experienced only by comparing patterns with rests to patterns without.]

The students follow.

5. Teacher: *Please continue.* (Writes ♩ ♩ 𝄾 ♩ on the chalkboard and points

in rhythm and continues pointing to the beats.) *Let's leave out beat number three and see what happens and what we feel.*

Students and teacher perform

Teacher: (Continuing to clap the pattern) *Do you feel a difference when the silence is on beat number three? What has happened to our nice flowing fourth beat? It has changed and become very strong. It doesn't seem to flow as much.*

[The general rule could be stated as: "After a rest new energy is asserted (unless a composer indicates a different interpretation by some special symbol)."]

6. **Teacher:** *Let's go back to all four beats and continue.* (The teacher writes

 on the chalkboard and points in rhythm.)
Let's leave out beat number two.

Students and teacher perform

   Teacher: *What has happened to beat number three? It has become strong and beat
   number four is very gentle now.*

As students continue to clap the pattern the teacher notates it on the chalkboard
and points in rhythm.

7. **Teacher:** *Let's go back to our regular four-beat pattern.*

The teacher demonstrates ♩ ♩ ♩ ♩ and students follow.

8. **Teacher:** (While all continue to clap) *Now for a really difficult pattern.*

Let's leave out the first   beat.

The teacher and students perform the new rhythm using a vigorous gesture,
pulling the hands apart for the rest on the first beat.

   Teacher: *A first-beat silence is most powerful; the second beat is very strong now, and
   then everything gets tired and quiets down.*

As the students continue to clap the pattern the teacher notates it on the
chalkboard. The chalkboard should now show the following patterns:

STEP VIII: READING BEATS AND RESTS
RHYTHMICALLY

1. **Teacher:** *Let's read the whole group.*

The teacher and students read the five patterns from the chalkboard.

Teacher: (Pointing to the chalkboard)

Here's   *the*   *beat*   *now.*

The students clap and speak or sing the rhythm as the teacher points and chooses patterns.

> [The rhythms may be chanted on "walk," "ta," or the beat number. The choice of syllable may differ depending on the consonant or vowel sounds desired and the tempo and quality of rhythmic attack preferred by the teacher. The word "rest" is whispered whenever there is a rest. If words are used for the beats, they must be spoken in ways that convey the changing qualities of flow and stress created by the patterns and not in the dry monotone sometimes heard in such exercises. It is easy to feel these qualities when clapping, but much more difficult to put them into rhythmized speech or singing. Beats may be equal in time, but they are seldom equal in quality.]

The teacher must offer suggestions to help the students discover various qualities of speech, whispers, and other vocal sounds to convey musical information instead of timing only. Reading in this sense is for musical and rhythmic comprehension and not just for correct placement of rests. Hands can press, glide, lift, and slide to express the plastic qualities of these patterns.

2.   **Teacher:** (Speaking in tempo)

Let's   *do*   *the*   *first*   *one.*

    Teacher and students: (Clapping as they speak) *WALK, walk, walk, waLK.*

This exercise must be repeated until a satisfactory performance is obtained.

3.   **Teacher:**

Let's   *do*   *the*   *next*   *one.*

Teacher and students:

WALK walk   walk   rest   WALK walk   walk   rest
                     cresc.

| | Teacher: | *Remember to whisper the rest with a crescendo.* |
| | Teacher: | (Speaking on the fourth beat until a good performance is obtained) *Again!* |

4.   Teacher: (Speaking in tempo)

Let's   do   the   next   one.

Teacher and students:

WALK walk   rest   WALK

Teacher: (Speaking on fourth beat until good performance is obtained) *Again!*

[Commands must always be given in an appropriate rhythm to produce flow and continuity. This adds great power to a Eurhythmics lesson and also to choral, band, and orchestral conducting. It helps to avoid constant stopping and starting when flow must be maintained during the corrections in spite of the urge to stop and relax when probing the changing sequences of a problem.]

5. The teacher continues this process until all the patterns are done with clarity and musicality.

STEP IX: RANDOM MEMORY AND RECOGNITION

1. The teacher points to the patterns on the chalkboard in random order. The students read and clap; read and speak; then read, clap, and speak at the same time.

2. The teacher then shows the students how to read in retrograde (right to left).

The normal,   ♩ ♩ ♩ ≀   when read in retrograde becomes
      1   2   3   4

| ≀ ♩ ♩ ♩ | The teacher points to patterns, indicating the direction of read-
  4   3   2   1
ing, and the students perform each, once in normal order and once in retrograde.

STEP X: LONGER CONTINUOUS READING AND RESPONSIVE PART READING

1. **Teacher:** *Now let's read continuously any pattern forward or backward that I choose for you.*

The teacher separates the group into two choirs. The teacher then points to the normal or retrograde version of a pattern slightly in advance of the choir making the performance change.

STEP XI: PERFORMING A PRESET SEQUENCE

1. The teacher establishes an order for performance and a tempo.

Teacher:

Here's the tem - po. Let's go!

Choir I reads and performs pattern 1; Choir II immediately does pattern 2. Choir I reads and performs pattern 3; Choir II immediately does pattern 4. Choir I reads and performs pattern 5; Choir II immediately does pattern 1.

The exercise repeats. (It can also be done with soloists taking some of the patterns.)

In these exercises the choirs or soloists must keep the beat and tempo going *at all times,* not just on their own turns. Later, more difficult ensemble games can be developed by having student conductors choosing new sequences. The choirs must remember the sequence each time.

STEP XII: DICTATION

1. **Teacher:** *I'll choose a pattern. Will you echo me? Get ready to listen and echo.*

The teacher indicates beats and tempo with body, head, shoulders, or other body part and claps one pattern from left to right, being sure to show the flow and dynamics. The students echo the pattern.

Teacher: *Where is the rest?*
Students: *At the end. On the last beat. The fourth beat.*
Teacher: *I'll do it again. You echo my clap and analyze by speaking the word "walk" and whispering "rest."*

The teacher claps the pattern again and the students echo:

♩ ♩ ♩ 𝄽

WALK   walk   walk   rest

Teacher: *Let's write it on the chalkboard.*

One student notates the exercise on the chalkboard and all read back the dictation.

2. The teacher chooses another pattern and the students follow the same process.

3. The procedure followed for each of these dictations is as follows:

1. listen
2. echo with movement
3. listen again
4. analyze where the rest is placed
5. notate the exercise
6. read from the notation
7. read the exercise in retrograde
8. read the first pattern again and join it to the new one
9. read pattern 1 normal
    read pattern 2 retrograde
    read pattern 3   ?
    read pattern 4   ?   , etc.

Steps 7, 8, and 9 help students who have memorized the patterns to refocus their energies back to reading. Such exercises demand more than a good ear memory.

STEP XIII: A LONG SEQUENCE OF PATTERNS
WITH RESTS

1. **Teacher:** *Let's finish with a game. A magician makes things disappear, sometimes little by little. Let's take four beats and make their sounds slowly disappear . . . like this:*

Echo my clapping.

The teacher demonstrates by moving hands left to right across the body. After each four-beat pattern is demonstrated, the students echo it. They clap the quarter notes and use silent gestures for the rests. To complete the exercise teacher

and students together perform ♩ 𝄽 𝄽 𝄽 . Students continue this exercise

poof

until they are proficient in it.

STEP XIV: WALKING PATTERNS WITH RESTS

1. **Teacher:** *Let's do this exercise with walking in place. Get ready to echo me. Watch!*

The teacher steps in place, exaggerating the steps:

1   2   3   4
♩   ♩   ♩   ♩
>   Go

The students echo.

2. The teacher then steps ♩ ♩ ♩ 𝄽 . On the third beat the teacher puts
            >

hands on the knee and presses the leg down to the floor to consciously prepare the rest. The torso and head continue to move during the rests to show the silent beats. The students echo, imitating the teacher's actions and rest preparation.

3. The teacher performs ♩ ♩ 𝄽 𝄽 , preparing the rests by consciously
            >

pressing the knee down on the second beat to stop the leg. The torso and head move twice to show the two beats of rest. The students echo the actions.

4. The teacher performs ♩ 𝄽 𝄽 𝄽 , using hand pressure on both knees.
            >

The torso and head swing to show the three rests. The students echo.

5. Finally, the teacher presses knees alternately—left, right, left, right—to show

the silence of 𝄽 𝄽 𝄽 𝄽 , while torso, head, or hips move to show the

four beats of silence. The students echo.

6. **Teacher:** *Let's do the whole series together.*

The teacher and students perform the series.

7. **Teacher:** *Let's do it walking in space. Make a circle and we'll go around clockwise. Ready?*

Here   we   go   now.

STEP XV: ADDING SINGING

1. **Teacher:** *Now we'll finish with clapping, stepping in space, and singing.*

The teacher sings

STEP XVI: COMBINING REST RHYTHMS WITH SCALE PATTERNS TO CREATE MELODIES

[Any of the one-measure patterns or combinations of patterns studied in this lesson may now be put together with known scales to create melodies. Both the teacher and students may experiment singing or playing different scale arrangements.]

1. Example based on a *do*-pentatonic scale:

STEP XVII: DEVELOPING RECALL FOR A SPECIFIC PITCH; USING THE DIATONIC MAJOR SCALE

1. **Teacher:** *Let's sing the C-Major scale.* (Syllables, numbers, or letters may be used.) *Who remembers the sound of our C tonic? Before we sing it, let's think about it. Can you feel it in your body? Can you hear it in your mind? Let's try to sing it together.*

The teacher and students sing middle C.

Teacher: (If students sing it correctly) *Good!* (If students are not correct) *Is it too high? (too low?)*

The students try to judge and answer.

Teacher: *Let's try it again. Can you feel it?*

The students try again. If they do not succeed, the teacher sings as a question

so   so   so   la   ti

The students find and sing the answer

do

The teacher and students sing the scale ascending and descending, using hand and arm movements.

do   re   mi   fa   so   la   ti   do   ti   la   so   fa   mi   re   do

2. **Teacher:** (Clapping) *Now let's sing it using*

The students try it, singing the scale in the rhythm given, as follows:

Teacher: *Be careful to sing a crescendo ascending and diminuendo descending.*

[Notice the anacrusic phrasing produced by this rhythm. Students finish when they reach middle C on a strong (first) beat of a measure. The teacher should have the students try this on other patterns for new melodies.]

This entire series of lesson strategies may now be repeated using different meters. Two-, three-, and five-beat patterns with rests should each, in turn, be practiced.

Conclusion

The example of Jaques-Dalcroze work given here was a series of exercises on one subject: rests. It included Eurhythmics, *Solfège* and *Solfège-Rythmique* techniques. Children were moving, reading, writing, and singing. They practiced analytical skills, worked on memorization, and created new patterns from known elements. It was a complete Jaques-Dalcroze *experience.*

KODÁLY

Children in Kodály programs generally enter third grade secure in their singing voices and with a reading and writing knowledge of pentatonic music in three key placements—F, C, and G. They are at ease performing individually, since such performance has been a part of their musical experience from first grade. They can perform a variety of rhythmic and melodic ostinati and can keep to a part in easy canon singing. They have been introduced through live experiences to at least one orchestral instrument from each family and have been led to draw conclusions about the effect of size, shape, and material upon pitch and timbre.

In the three years from eight through ten (generally, the third, fourth, and fifth grades) these children will leave the repertory of infant and early childhood songs—the "Bye, Baby Bunting"s and the "Rain, Rain, Go Away"s—and draw their musical learning instead from the world of adult folk music—of their own culture and, later, of others—and from art music of the Western world. They will make the step from pentatonic to diatonic music and will extend musical reading and writing to all keys.

Lesson for Grade 3

Following is one lesson taught to third-grade children early in the school year.

1. **Teacher:** *Who can give me the A today? John?*

John sings a pitch; all sing it with him. The teacher taps the A–440 tuning fork and all listen to determine whether John's pitch was too high, too low, or accurate. (Most of the time children can give the pitch of A accurately by third grade if it has been used as the class starting pitch throughout grades one and two.)

2. **Teacher:** *Call the A re and sing do. Now find so. Follow my hands. The right side of the room follow this hand (showing) and the left side, the other hand (showing).*

right hand

left hand

[This should be done slowly and deliberately with intent listening to the intervals formed at each pitch change. Then the parts should be reversed.]

3. The teacher points out a melody on a tone ladder on the chalkboard in the key and tone set just practiced:

s

m

r

d

[Note that there is an implication of interval size in the vertical spacing of the tone set.]

By thinking (inner-hearing) the melody as it is pointed out on the tone ladder, the children identify the song as "Rain Come Wet Me":

Rain Come Wet Me

The children sing the song and conduct it in 4s:

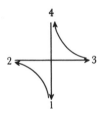

4. Teacher: *This time, as you sing, listen to me. See if you can hear my part.*

As the children repeat "Rain Come Wet Me" the teacher sings an ostinato:

Teacher: *Who can sing what I sang? John? Susan?*

Several individual children sing the ostinato part.

Teacher: (To the class) *You sing the song. (All sing.) Jane's and Tom's groups sing the ostinato, while Mary's and Don's sing the song. (After they do) Now reverse the parts. (Later) Mary and Ellen, can you sing the two parts? Ellen, sing the ostinato and Mary, sing the song?*

The two perform together and the class helps if and where help is needed.

5. **Teacher:** *Look at the rhythm on the chalkboard. What is the form?*

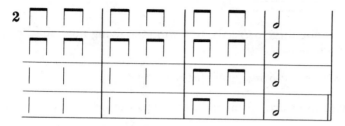

Children: *A–A–B–B.*
Teacher: *Read it in ta's and ti's. Here is your beat:*

one,   two,   rea - dy,   read

(Later) *Now face away from the chalkboard and say it again. One, two, ...*

6. **Teacher:** *Open your books to page 11. What can you tell me about this new song?*

Rocky Mountain

Yes, the rhythm is the one we had on the chalkboard. Look at the last note. What pitch is it? (G) Let's practice reading it in G-do. Follow my flying note.

With a board staff and a notehead attached to a pointer the teacher leads the children through the intervals and melodic turns they will need to read the new song successfully.

When they are singing these correctly, following the flying note, they look again at the song in their books.

Teacher: *Read the first phrase with inner hearing.*

The teacher gives the starting pitch, G, and taps the beat audibly on a desk.

Teacher: *Now sing it aloud. One, two, ready, sing* (sung on G).

The class sings the first phrase in *solfa*. If the preparation has been sufficient there will be no problem. The reading is guided in the same manner, phrase by phrase. Children notice that the third and fourth phrases are similar but not identical—the third a question phrase ending on *re* and the fourth an answer phrase ending on *do*. After having read the entire song in *solfa* as a group, several children sing it individually while the rest of the class follows the notation. When the melodic lines are secure the *solfa* is "taken away" and the melody is sung on a neutral syllable—"loo." If it is sung correctly the text is then added and attention is given to phrasing and dynamics.

7.   The teacher sings a familiar song, "Whistle, Daughter, Whistle," and the children join in, singing and conducting in 2s:

Whistle, Daughter, Whistle

Teacher: *Has anyone a new verse today? Emmy?*

Emmy sings the new verse she has created:

> Whistle, daughter, whistle,
>   And you shall have a moose.
> I can't whistle, mother,
>   Because my tooth is loose!

Several others have invented new verses that they also sing for the class.

[This song has been taught as part of the aural preparation for the next scale tone to be introduced, *fa*.]

8. **Teacher:** (Silently, showing handsigns) *What song is this?*

Children: *"Frère Jacques."*

Frère Jacques

Are you sleep - ing,   Brother John?   Morning bells are ring-ing,   Ding, dang, dong.

Teacher: *Alice's group, sing voice 1; Mary's, voice 2; William's, voice 3. Put the beat on your desks softly with your fingertips and be sure to listen to each other. One, two, ready, sing* (given on F pitch).

[The children are expected to enter at the right place and carry their parts without any signals from the teacher. All their training in canon singing is directed toward such independence. The teacher maintains an attentive listening attitude, but does *not* help vocally. If there is a problem, it is discussed afterwards with the class: "Where did the problem occur?" "The third phrase." "Which voice part had trouble?" "The middle." "What was the problem?" "The tempo got faster." Only by analysis of difficulties *with* children can such problems in part-singing be eliminated.]

9. **Teacher:** *This time sing the song in unison and listen to what I do.*

The teacher *claps* the rhythm in canon, a phrase behind the children's singing.

Children: *You clapped the second voice.*
Teacher: *Can you clap the second voice while I sing the first?* (They do.) *Now, can you sing the first voice and clap the second at the same time?*

The teacher demonstrates. The children attempt this, some with success, others with less. (Within three lessons all will have mastered it.)

10. The teacher sings on "loo":

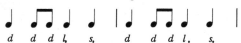

The children respond by singing the first phrase of the familiar dance song "I've Been to Haarlem" in *solfa* and then with words.

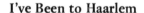

I've Been to Haarlem

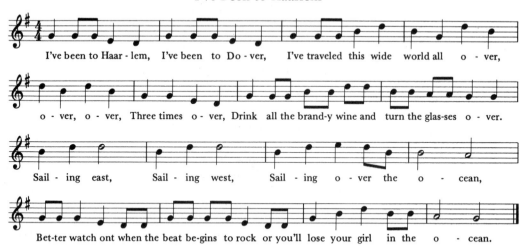

They form a double circle around the chairs or desks in the room and perform the dance—one of several in their repertory that are actually circle forms of square dances. At the end of the dance they are told, "put the beat in your feet,

put this ostinato— ♩ 𝄽 ♫♩ —in your hands, and sing the song." They do this, while returning to their places.

11. **Teacher:** *On your desks you'll find the music for "I've Been to Haarlem." Let's sing it through in* solfa.
    Children: *But there are some measures mising!*
    Teacher: *Oh, dear, so there are! We'll have to fill them in.*

The children sing the whole song in syllables from memory and, with guidance, fill in the notation of the missing measures.

> [It is easier to notate parts of songs in beginning music writing; the given parts act as models for note formation and spacing in the missing parts.]

12. **Teacher:** *Put your papers and pencils away now. I have a ballad I'd like to sing for you, "Once a Canadian Lad." (This is a new song to the class.)*

Once a Canadian Lad

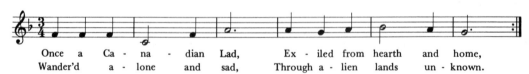

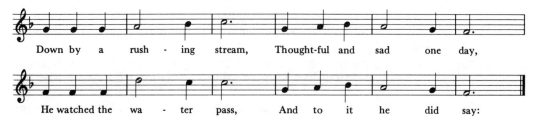

Down by a rush - ing stream, Thought-ful and sad one day,

He watched the wa - ter pass, And to it he did say:

Verse 2
> If you should reach my land,
>   My most unhappy land,
> Please speak to all my friends
>   So they will understand.
> Tell them how much I wish
>   That I could be once more
> In my beloved land
>   That I will see no more.

The children discuss the text; the word "exiled" and what "exile" seemed to mean to the "lad" in the song. They will eventually learn the song, but it is intended only as a listening experience in this particular lesson.

CONCLUSION. In this lesson children have worked on the following skills:

> aural acuity (specific pitch recall and interval singing)
> musical reading and writing
> identifying forms
> inner hearing
> memorization
> conducting 2s and 4s
> independent part singing,
> listening
> creating (text)
> performing two musical ideas simultaneously (ostinato and song;. singing and clapping in canon after)
> moving to music

The musical materials were:

> part of a known early-childhood song, "Rain, Rain, Go Away," used as an ostinato,
> two easy folk songs of small range and pentatonic character—"Rain Come Wet Me" and "Rocky Mountain"
> two songs in a *s–f–m–r–d* scale (pentachord) to prepare the ear and voice for the as yet unknown note *fa* and to give experience in singing the

mi–fa half step—"Whistle, Daughter, Whistle" and "Frère Jacques"

one song for dancing—the American play-party game "I've Been to Haarlem"

one song for listening—a ballad from French-Canada in triple meter and with unusual three-measure phrases: "Once a Canadian Lad"

In the third and fourth years of the program children are taught a number of new rhythm patterns and figures: ♩. ♪, ♪♩ ♪, ♪♩., ♬♬, ♬♩, ♩♬, ♩., and 𝅝.   Their tonal vocabulary is extended to include *fa* and *ti* and with these notes key signatures are introduced. The musical materials used for teaching are expanded as well, with more folk songs from other cultures being included and with an increasing emphasis on art music.

Lesson for Grade 5

Below is a lesson taught to a fifth-grade class.

1. **Teacher:** *Who can give us the A today?*
   Brad: (Sings)

A

The teacher taps the tuning fork and holds it against the chalkboard to resonate so that the whole class may check the accuracy of the pitch sung.

2. **Teacher:** *Call A* mi. *Sing* do. *What key are we in?* (F) *What is the key signature* (one flat)?

   [Children at this level identify notes both with *solfa* and with absolute letter names.]

   Teacher: *Follow my hands* (showing hand signs for the following pattern):

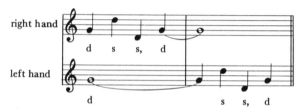

right hand   d   s   s,   d

left hand   d   s   s,   d

(This is done to tune the voices on the intervals needed for the canon to follow.) The teacher hums a phrase of "London's Burning" and students identify the familiar canon. One student is called on to sing the first phrase alone.

London's Burning

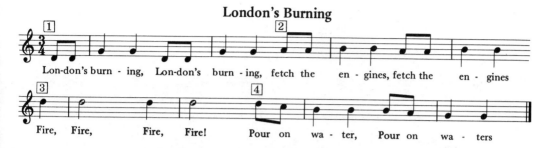

3. Teacher: *Sing it in unison and show the meter by conducting.*

All sing and conduct:

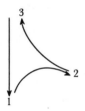

4. Teacher: *In canon now. Bob's group sing voice 1, Mary's, voice 2, Ellen's, voice 3.
   Continue to conduct; it will help you keep together.*

The class performs without the teacher's help.

5. Teacher: *Who would like to sing the first voice alone? Jane? The second voice part?
   David? The third? Pat? Remember, all of you sitting near Jane must help
   by singing with her silently, inside your heads. If she has any problems, sing
   aloud to help her. David's group and Pat's group, help aloud if help is
   needed.*

   [This approach to individual part singing gives the students who are performing great security and also ensures that the students listening are
   concentrating rather than simply waiting.]

After the trio sings, both teacher and class evaluate their performance. Such
evaluation must be positive but truthful: "Jane got lost on the third phrase, but
she got back in by the end. Maybe it would help if we all sang the third phrase
with her this time." The trio sings again, correcting mistakes that occurred the
first time.

Teacher: *On what note does this canon end? (Do, F.) Yes, we are in the key of
F-Major. F-do is the tonal center. Let's put a rhythm to the tonal center and
use it as an ostinato throughout the song.*

Various suggestions come from the class:

Fire!   Fire!   Fire!   Fire!

Call the   en - gines, Call   the   en - gines!

Put   it   out!   Put   it   out!

Each is tried with the song and the whole is performed as a three-part canon with ostinato.

> Teacher: *What degree of the scale is* do? (The first.) *We can show that in music with the roman numeral I* (putting it on the chalkboard).

[This is the first step in the study of harmony.]

6. Teacher: *Look at the mystery rhythm on the chalkboard. Read it silently. When you think you know what it is, raise your hand.*

one,   two,   read - y,   read.

When a number of students appear to recognize the song, the teacher gives a starting pitch:

One,   two,   read - y, sing!

Most begin; the others join in as they recognize it.

I'se the B'y

I'se   the b'y   that   builds   the boat.   I'se   the b'y   that   sails   'er,

I'se the b'y that catch-es the fish, And brings 'em home to Li - za!

Hip yer part - ner Sal - ly___ Ti-bbo! Hip yer part - ner Sal - ly Brown!

Fo' go, Twil - lin-gate, Mor' - ton's Har - bour, All a-round the cir - cle!

Verse 2
    Sods and rinds to cover yer flake, Cake and tea for supper.
Codfish in the spring o' the year Fried in maggoty butter.
Chorus

Verse 3
    I don't want your maggoty fish, That's no good for winter;
I could buy as good as that Down in Bonavista.
Chorus

Verse 4
    I took Lizer to a dance, And faith, but she could travel!
And every step that she did take Was up to her knees in gravel.
Chorus

Verse 5
    Susan White, she's out of sight, Her petticoat wants a border;
Old Sam Oliver, in the dark, He kissed her in the corner.
Chorus

Teacher: *Put the beat in your feet and the ostinato ♩. ♩. , in your hands. Make the formation for our reel dance.*

[The children form the well-known double-line formation and move through the steps of the reel while singing. This dance form has been known since third grade and has been performed with many different songs.]

At the end of the dance students return to their seats, clapping, stepping, and singing.

7. **Teacher:** *How is this song moving? (2s.) Conduct it as you sing.*

On what note did it end? (G, do). How could I show that in numbers?
Students: *With I; it is the first degree of the G scale.*
Teacher: *Our ostinato on I worked well with "London's Burning." Let's make one for "I's the B'y". How shall we do it?*

The students give various suggestions:

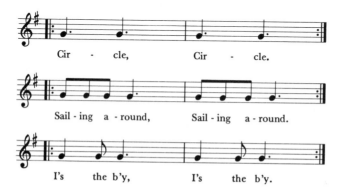

One of them is tried to accompany the song by the class.

[It will not sound good to the students. The melody of the first song, "London's Burning," is built almost entirely on the tonic chord (I) *do–mi–so* and so can be accompanied with *do*, I, throughout. The melody of "I's the B'y" is built on the tones of the dominant (V) chord *so–ti–re'*. When an accompaniment is played or sung on *do*, major and minor seconds result. Even inexperienced listeners can tell that this dissonance does not seem right or suitable for this song. This is not to say that fifth-grade children do not *like* dissonance. Actually, they like it very much in the right setting. A well-loved folk song is not the right setting.]

8. Teacher: *You are right; it doesn't sound as good with this song as it did with "London's Burning." Perhaps we need another note in some places. Try so. If the first degree of the scale, do, can be called I, what do you think we could call so? (V.) We won't put a rhythm pattern with it yet. Let's just see where in the song do (I) sounds best and where so (V) sounds best. I'll sing the song, you sing the do (I) or so (V). Change whenever your ears tell you to.*

[Two attempts are usually enough for any class to find the pattern of implied chord changes.]

At a later lesson, when these changes are being made quickly and automatically, a rhythm may be added to them to create a second part:

I's   the B'y,   I's   the B'y,   I's   the B'y   I's   the B'y.

9. **Teacher:** *Look at your music papers.* (These were placed on desks before the period began.)

What key is this in? (G, second line *do.*) *What is our starting pitch?* (B, mi.)

The teacher gives the starting pitch and the class reads the notated parts of the example in *solfa*, tapping the beat lightly on their desks with their fingertips.

Teacher: *Do the two phrases given sound finished? No! They are question phrases. Who can improvise answer phrases to go with them?*

Several possibilities are sung:

Teacher: *Listen to how Bach answered that question phrase* (playing a recording of a chorale from the *St. Matthew Passion*).

Lamb of God

After listening, the class sings from memory the Bach answer phrases and notates them on their papers.

Teacher: *Now let's see where I fits and where V fits as a second part with the Bach. I'll sing the melody while you sing* do *or* so.

When the class has agreed on the best change points from *do* to *so*, they write I and V under the notation of the melody in the appropriate places.

[In later lessons the I and V chords will be sung and played from this notation to accompany this piece.]

10. **Teacher:** *How could we vary this music? What could we do to make it different without changing the melody?*

Suggestions will be made about tempo, dynamics, and meter. Each suggestion should be tried by the class.

Teacher: *Which meter shall we try? Three? Conduct as you sing.*

Bach, too, tried it in triple meter. Listen. (Play recording of "Jesu, Joy of Man's Desiring.")

Jesu, Joy of Man's Desiring

J.S. Bach

Children listen, singing softly with chorale sections.

Teacher: *How is it different in this setting? Yes, it is in triple meter; and yes, there is another melody with it—a countermelody.*

[In later lessons children will see, read, sing in *solfa*, and memorize the countermelody, and then perform the two parts together. Children taking instrumental lessons will play the chorale part on flute, violin, and piano, while the class sings the countermelody.]

11. **Teacher:** *Let's finish with our Kodály* Bicinia, *no. 3.*[4] The children know this short two-part work well.

---

[4]Zoltán Kodály, *Bicinia Hungarica*, vol. I, rev. Eng. ed. by Geoffry Russell-Smith (London: Boosey & Hawkes, 1968).

The Blackbird

CONCLUSION.   In this lesson children have

aurally identified tonal centers and related them to key placements

sung in canon as a class and as trios

conducted in 2s and 3s

invented melodic ostinati

identified a known song by its notated rhythm

identified *do* as I (the tonic) and *so* as V (the dominant) in major, and aurally determined where each is implied by a melody

improvised answer phrases to a musical question phrase

listened to two Bach compositions

notated a phrase from a Bach composition

changed the meter of a melody from quadruple to triple and performed it in the new meter

sung a two-part song by Kodály

ORFF

For children in intermediate grades the Orff curriculum is still organized primarily around movement, voice, and form. The Instrumentarium is introduced at this level if it has not been before. In general, the skills developed in the earlier grades are now transferred to areas outside of the self—to instruments, part singing, ensemble preparation, choral experience, group dancing, and intergroup experience. Emphasis is on the social aspect of music within the regular classroom activities. As in the lower grades, there are specific expectations in the areas of movement, voice, and form, and there are additional expectations now in the area of instrumental experience.

Movement

OBJECTIVES. The children should acquire a vocabulary of dance steps and styles. There should be exploration of body movement within spatial and time limits. Rhythmic accuracy is expected with duple, triple, and mixed meters, and movement should reflect tempo and dynamic changes.

PROCESS. Language is still the principal motivator for movement. However, there is an expectation that the movement will show greater sensitivity to the straightness and curvedness of the body, to the fastness and slowness possible within specific actions, and to the physical demonstration of phrasing.

MATERIALS. American and international folk songs and dances, rhythmically demanding games, and theater games are used.

Voice

OBJECTIVES. The children are expected to speak clearly and with expression and to sing with a clear open sound. They should be comfortable singing alone and with others and willing to try improvised singing. They should be able to recognize intervals and patterns of the pentatonic scale—5–3 (*so–mi*), 6–5–3 (*la–so–mi*), 5–3–2–1 (*so–mi–re–do*), and 5–1 (*so–do*)—by sight and sound.

PROCESS. There should be increasing attention given to good vocal production; the teacher must be the model for accurate articulation and techniques.

MATERIALS. American and international folk songs and games and composed works for voice and instruments are used.

Form

OBJECTIVES. The children should be able to identify and use the following forms: AABA, rondo, and canon. They should also be able to create and use ostinati, introductions, codas, recitatives, and melodic progressions. Most of their work with forms will be done in the context of major and minor pentatonic scales.

PROCESS. Work with forms is largely improvisational. The children are led to invent musical patterns and then to organize these patterns into forms with introductions and codas. Notation may be introduced as part of the process.

MATERIALS. Folklore, stories, poems, rhymes, etc., set to music by the students.

Instruments

OBJECTIVES.   The children should play accurately and with security, at whatever level of skill they possess. They should be able to play musically, alone and in ensemble, showing an awareness of the other instrumental parts in the latter.

PROCESS.   Singing experiences are transferred to mallet or barred instruments first, and later to recorder. Techniques for good playing are presented and reinforced continually.

MATERIALS.   Compositions for voice and instruments and for small and large ensemble are used. Exercises for instrumental proficiency are improvised and composed.

READINESS FOR INSTRUMENTS.   If much time is spent developing a readiness for instruments, then when instruments *are* introduced, the skill transfer is easy, and students are ready for further learning. The teacher who is overeager for the children to experience the sound of the Orff instruments might leave out vital steps, which will surely retard and may possibly eliminate the possibility of success for children. Orff instruments are intended as an extension of the body and voice, not as ends in themselves.

There is no single time frame by which a teacher can judge readiness. It is possible that in some cases instruments would not be introduced until the beginning of third grade. The individual teacher must take the responsibility for recognizing the readiness of his or her class.

One activity that could aid the teacher in determining the readiness of children for the Instrumentarium involves the use of "found instruments." The teacher asks the class to find any noninstrument to use. The children experiment to discover what kinds of sounds they can make with their objects. The found instruments are divided into types of playing technique.

In one third-grade class the instruments were divided into

> metal scrapers
> metal shakers
> nonmetal shakers
> thumpers
> squeakers (balloons)

The sounds of these instruments were then organized into a rondo form:

RONDO NO. 1 FOR STUFF

Introduction balloon squeaks
> A eight-bar rhythmic pattern performed on thumpers
> B metal shakers improvise eight bars
> A (repeated)

C metal scrapers improvise eight bars
A (repeated)
D nonmetal shakers improvise eight bars
A (repeated)
Coda balloon squeaks

Children who can make timbre choices, identify the sound type and best playing mode, and organize a performance on instruments in a recognizable form are probably ready for the real instruments of Orff practice.

INTRODUCTION TO THE INSTRUMENTARIUM.   It is important that the students feel a strong sense of right and left before being introduced to instruments. Readiness for mallets parallels natural growth and development. Exercises in gross motor development must precede small motor skills, of which mallet technique is one. Some mallet preparation exercises, in order of increasing difficulty, might be

1. parallel patching on thighs, shoulders, heads, desks, to four-beat patterns at different tempi and dynamic levels in response to both live and recorded music
2. patching in two parts, hands acting separately on different parts of the body: thigh-shoulder, shoulder-head, thigh-floor, etc.
3. patching with crossing at the midpoint: side-side, shoulder-shoulder, left hand to right side and right hand to left side, etc.

The process then becomes one of transferring skills from one medium to another.

MALLET TECHNIQUE   Children may be told, "Hold the mallets as if they were the handlebars of a motorcycle. When you play, the touch should be nice and free, light and bouncy, drawing the sound out of the instruments instead of pounding the sound in. The smaller bars are higher in pitch and the larger bars are lower in pitch." Hands moving in unison, the children play low and high, randomly playing anywhere.
Given the specific rhythm pattern

children may be told to "play anywhere on the instrument, but alternate left and right hands each time."
A next step might be to have the children play a gradual movement from low to high, alternating hands, with the left hand playing the lower notes and the right hand the higher notes. To make the sound more interesting the teacher may improvise a melody on the recorder to accompany the barred instruments.

All these activities are generally performed on prepared instruments—the bars making diatonic half steps have been removed to produce a pentatonic scale (G A B D E, F G A C D, or C D E G A). Without minor seconds the combinations produced randomly tend to go well together.

The teacher should draw from children their perceptions of the timbral qualities of the barred-instrument families:

> xylophones: sounding wood, warm, hollow, ferns, corn chips
> metallophones: water, rain drops, silver, stars, sustaining sound
> glockenspiels: crystal, sugarplum fairy

Following is a sample score for early instrumental experience.

C PENTATONIC: RHYTHM OF THE DAY
FOR PITCHED
AND NON-PITCHED INSTRUMENTS

Introduction: two bars of timpani

f = floor
s = shoulder
(alternating hands)

Lesson Cycle

The following is a lesson cycle that might be performed by fifth-grade students, on a Halloween theme. In this series of Orff experiences the class progresses through several stages. First there are warm-up activities, then vocal experimentation with the chant. Next, form is added to the piece and some parts are transferred to instruments. The final performance becomes a small theater piece with chanters, singers, dancers, and instrumentalists all contributing to the ensemble.

Chant

Witch-es go 'round the sun,— Witch-es go 'round the moon,—

Witch-es go 'round the chim-ney pots on Hal-lo-we'en af-ter-noon.—

1. Warmup
   a. learn poem by echo
   b. emphasize sounds, use clear diction, change dynamics.

2. Vocal experimentation
   a. canon in two parts at one measure
   b. canon in four parts at the half measure
   c. canon in seven parts at the half measure
   d. any of the above repeated three times with crescendo
   e. augmentation by lower voices while higher voices say *cantus firmus* (the chant in its original time values) twice
   f. diminution by higher voices two times with others on *cantus firmus*

3. Speech form
   a. *cantus firmus* in six-part canon, with high voices in diminution and low voices in augmentation (in menacing tones)
   b. coda: everyone, on cue, finishes on "nooo–n" while a conductor directs crescendo, diminuendo and pitch variations, with some students adding "ch" sounds at random

INSTRUMENTS

1. Preparation
   a. put chant on D; put chant on A; put chant on D again
   b. for warmup:

$$BX^5 = low\ D \qquad AX = low\ D \qquad AGl = low\ A$$
$$BX = low\ A \qquad AX = high\ A \qquad SGl = high\ A$$

2. Instrumental canon
   a. canon at full measure with bass, alto and soprano xylophones, glockenspiels
3. Improvisation at the end of witches' celebration
   a. random notes on all barred instruments
   b. add hanging cymbal
   c. timpani comments infrequently
   d. gradual transition to "Alleluia." During transition the bass and alto metallophones play C's.
4. Additive orchestration (Each time the chant is repeated a new instrumental part is added. Note also that letters *a* through *f* here correspond to letters *a* through *f* in the score that follows.)
   a. bass xylophones play chant
   b. alto xylophones play chant
   c. timpani
   d. bass metallophones
   e. five percussion voices
   f. choir

Witches Go 'Round the Sun

Instrument Set-up

| C | D | E | F | G | A | Bb | B | D | E | F | G | A |

Key

☿ timpani

⌒ hanging cymbal

🗿 gong

⊟ slit or log drum

▭-▭-▭ temple blocks

▦ Ratchet

⁵The following abbreviations are commonly used in Orff practice:
BX = bass xylophone
AX = alto xylophone
SX = soprano xylophone
AG1 = alto glockenspiel
SG1 = soprano glockenspiel
BM = bass metallophone
AM = alto metallophone
SM = soprano metallophone

After the complete performance by all players of the above score, there is a period of transition signaling the approaching dawn of All Saints' Day. This is followed by:

"ALLELUIA"

1. Preparation
   a. sing melody
   b. sing chant (text) on octave C's
   c. sing a sixth above the melody
   d. low voices sing only melody or middle C's
2. Performance: additive orchestration
   a. transition (from witches' celebration): bass and alto metallophones on octave C's
   b. "Angelus" (call to prayer)
   c. bass and alto metallophones
   d. sing melody
   e. glockenspiels and chant on C
   f. sixth above melody

a. Transition
b. "Angelus"

Arr. Gillespie

"Angelus"
3x for a total of 9
Bells: Call to prayer

ia.   Let all Saints praise the   Lord.   Al - le - lu - ia.

THE DRAMA

The contrast to Halloween is All Saints' Day. We need some witches, but we also need some saints. (For our performance many will take part in both sections.)

1. A coven of witches comes from the four corners of the earth to the center of the room, as though drawn by a special power. As they come, it is the close of day; the fog comes in—slow glissandos starting on the basses, moving up the Instrumentarium. Vocal ad libs (mysterious sounds) are added.

2. An instrumental canon of "Witches Go 'Round the Sun" is performed in unison, then in canon. "Dies Irae" is added by the choir. The witches dance and posture for position.

3. Day is breaking; sounds are dying away. To depict this, an accompaniment is improvised (see item 3 under "Instruments"). The witches return to their corners and fade away to hide from the light.

4. The transition from night to day is indicated by instruments playing octave C's (see item 3 under "Instruments").

5. "Angelus" (call to prayer). It is now All Saints' Day, following the revelry of the witches' night. Witches become saints now, entering from corners (these could be a second group of youngsters).

6. Bass and alto metallophones and chimes are added.

7. The vocal group adds the "Alleluia" melody, once in unison, then with an added harmony line and chanting voices on C's.

8. Glockenspiels are added.

9. Steps 6 through 8 are displayed through drama as the saints show praise to a high monarch on a mountain top. Dancers' movements circle around a central point.

Many of the above ideas for both orchestration and dramatization came from children. A true Orff experience cannot be written down in advance but must evolve in the classroom with the children.

COMPREHENSIVE MUSICIANSHIP

The exploration of sound sources and the discovery of specific musical foundations in the early grades lead to the implementation and application of more complex musical ideas in Grades 3, 4, and 5. Students continue to experience a balance of activities in composition, performance, and analysis appropriate to their individual levels of comprehension, achievement, and aptitude.

Learning Objectives

PITCH. At this level of CM, students are introduced to the symbolic association of pitches and pitch patterns through visual representation, graphic notation, mapping techniques, or traditional notation. They develop an ability to hear what they see and to see what they hear in performance and in listening activities. Composition in short forms is written using major and minor scales, whole tone scales, the pentatonic scale, twelve-tone scale, synthetic scales, and all of the modes.

The organization of pitches into scale units and forms should be explored, performed, and identified. Song materials from contemporary popular music, traditional art music, non-Western music, and folk music are used as the basic material for pitch exploration and identification. Students develop the skills of interval recognition and analysis within a musical context and utilize this understanding in performance and in composition. Intervals are related to patterns of pitches and patterns are related to scale structures used in a variety of musical styles.

DURATION. Students are introduced to the notation of rhythm through experiences in listening, score reading, musical composition, and performance. Beat and pulse are fundamental to the listening, performance, and organizational experiences at this level of the CM model. The activities are expanded to include an understanding and application of accent, meter, polyrhythms, polymeters, and more complex rhythmic patterns. Original rhythmic accompaniments are written by the students and free rhythmic composition and improvisation are encouraged. Multimetric systems are added to the duple and triple meters utilized in the listening, performance, and compositional activities. Opportunities for rhythmic growth include basic conducting and body movement to complex rhythmic patterns and metric organizations.

INTENSITY. Variation in intensity as an expressive quality in music is experienced by the CM student through improvisation, composition, listening activities, and performance. Students develop their understanding of dynamics through individual judgments as composers, listeners, and performers. A variety of music from Boston play-party songs to the steel-band music of the Caribbean is utilized in activities emphasizing the dynamic expression found in music.

TIMBRE. The exploration of sound sources and the textures produced by these sound sources are extended to specific categories of sound and specific instrumental families. Instrumental and vocal timbres are explored through listening and performance activities. Improvisational and compositional activities on a variety of instruments (folk, traditional, non-Western, and electronic) are encouraged. Timbral differences are noted, identified, and described.

The Organization of Pitch, Duration, Intensity, and Timbre

The organization of pitch, duration, intensity, and timbre within a compositional structure creates melodic and harmonic arrangements of sound.

HORIZONTAL ORGANIZATION. In association with pitch development in scale forms, the horizontal organization of sound is extended to include the contemporary techniques of random frequency, pointillism, computer interfaced electronic synthesized sound, and aleatoric pitch and rhythmic arrangements. These arrangements are not only listened to, but also are performed by the students and are utilized in composition and in improvisation.

VERTICAL PITCH ORGANIZATION. The recognition of chordal movement and direction is developed by using a number of listening, performance, and compositional activities employing progressions and cadential settings. Multiple sounds in singing are expanded to a variety of instruments including the piano, guitar, banjo, autoharp, and other classroom instruments. Compositions written by the students should include specific aspects of the cadential formulas and progressions that have been studied. Through these activities involving performance, analysis, and composition, the student develops abilities in reading harmonic musical notation. All primary and secondary chords are introduced in the listening and performance experiences and utilized by the students in compositional activities.

FORM. More complex musical forms are introduced at this level of the CM model. Repetitive and contrasting melodies and rhythmic patterns are made obvious to the student through analysis. Students are guided and encouraged to use these musical concepts in their own compositions. Dance and movement to music are encouraged. Song form, rondo form, sonata form, fugue, and symphonic form are explored.

MUSICAL CONTEXTS. The music used in performance, listening, and composition at this level of the CM model comes from the culture of all the periods and geographical areas, including our own. The study of this music is within its aesthetic, historical, and social contexts.

***Lesson Plans Emphasizing the
Comprehensive Musicianship Approach to
Teaching in the Intermediate Grades***

The following examples of lesson plans for children in Grades 3 to 5 emphasize the exploration of specific musical concepts with a variety of musical materials. In these lessons the students continue to experience a balance of activities in composition, performance, and analysis.

LESSON PLAN A

1. Create and analyze
    a. Have the children experiment with chance compositions by using a *composition box* as a source for musical material.

        Prepare in advance several sets of 5 × 8 cards with musical information on each card. Color code the cards by musical element (yellow for melody, red for rhythm, green for meter, orange for form, blue for timbre, pink for dynamics, and purple for tempo).

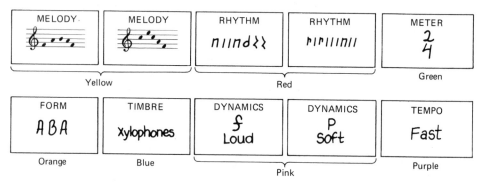

        Place each set of the musical information cards into a composition box. (A shoe box is about the right size for this activity.)

        Tape the following message to the top of each composition box:

        Inside this box you will find cards of different colors corresponding to a musical element. Use the information or terms written on the cards to compose a short piece for your group to perform for the class.

        You may combine the items in any manner you choose. You may also add items not listed on your cards, as long as you use everything listed.

        You will have fifteen minutes to design and rehearse your piece.

    b. Divide the children in the class into small groups and give each group a composition box. Allow fifteen minutes for each group to compose their piece.

2. Perform and analyze
   a. Ask each group in the class to perform and to explain their final box composition to the other members of the class.
   b. After each performance ask the children to suggest modifications to specific elements in the piece which might improve its total musical effectiveness. Have the groups incorporate the suggestions and perform the pieces again.
3. Perform
   a. Provide the children in the class with copies of the Mayan Indian song, "Xtoles."[6] This Mayan Indian song is from the Yucatán peninsula of Mexico, where the descendants of the great Mayans continue to speak their ancient language. The text of this song refers to the sun as the King of Heaven.

Xtoles

Edited by Theodore Grame

Mayan

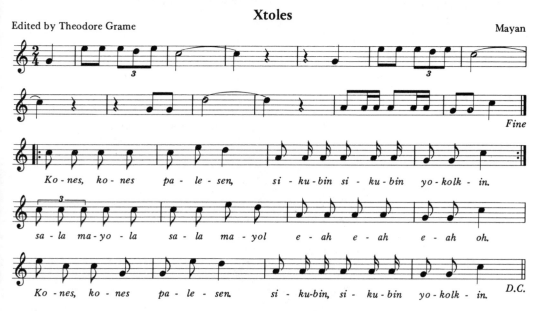

Ko - nes, ko - nes   pa - le - sen,   si - ku - bin si - ku - bin   yo - kolk - in.

sa - la ma - yo - la   sa - la   ma - yol   e - ah   e - ah   e - ah   oh.

Ko - nes, ko - nes   pa - le - sen.   si - ku-bin, si - ku - bin   yo - kolk - in.

Ask the students to pronounce the words phonetically as they sing.
   b. Have the introduction and coda section of "Xtoles" played by selected children on soprano recorders, soprano glockenspiels, and/or alto xylophones.
4. Analyze
   a. Ask the children to identify each interval used in the introduction and coda of "Xtoles." Have the children write the intervals in their scores and ask them to identify the intervals as major, minor, perfect, diminished, or augmented.

[6]Juilliard Repertory Library (Cincinnati, OH: Canyon Press, 1970), p. 232.

    b. Make a list of the intervals identified by the children in the class on the chalkboard.

5. Create

    a. Using the intervals identified in the introduction and coda of "Xtoles" by the children in the class, have them each compose an alternate introduction and coda for the song. Ask the children to keep the same meter and the same key as the original Mayan song, but to change the melody, using a different combination of the intervals identified. Ask the children to keep their alternate introduction and coda to twelve measures in length.

    b. Have the children perform their compositions on soprano recorders, soprano glockenspiels, or alto xylophones for the other members of the class.

    c. Have the children in the class select several composed introductions and codas to use with the main section of the song. Compare these compositions with the original.

    d. Ask the students to supply dynamic markings as well as phrase markings to the entire song. Perform the song with a selected introduction and coda with the added dynamic and phrase markings.

6. Create

    a. Using the following rhythm patterns taken from the song "Xtoles," have the children create a rhythmic ostinato pattern to be played on hand drums, tom-toms, wood blocks, or finger cymbals throughout the song.

    b. Ask the students to notate their rhythmic ostinato patterns.

    c. Have the class perform "Xtoles" with the added rhythmic ostinato pattern.

7. Perform

    a. Teach by rote the American folk song "Turkey in the Straw."

    b. Ask the children to perform a stamp–snap–stamp–snap sound gesture on the beat of the song as they sing it.

says   day   day___ to the   wa - gon   tongue.   Tur - key   in   the   straw,_____

_____   Tur-key   in   the   hay,_____   Roll'em   up and twist 'em   up   a

high   tuck - a - haw,   And___   hit 'em   up   a tune___ called___   Tur - key   in   the Straw!

Verse 2

    Went out to milk and I didn't know how,
    I milked the goat instead of the cow.
    A monkey sittin' on a pile of straw
    A-winkin' at his mother-in-law.

Verse 3

    Met Mr. Catfish comin' downstream.
    Says Mr. Catfish, "What does you mean?"
    Caught Mr. Catfish by the snout
    And turned Mr. Catfish wrong side out.

Verse 4

    Came to the river and I couldn't get across.
    Paid five dollars for an old blind hoss.
    Wouldn't go ahead, nor he wouldn't stand still,
    So he went up and down like an old saw mill.

8. Analyze and explore

    a. Provide three children in the class each with a glass jug. Have one child play his or her jug to match an F below middle C on the piano. Have the second child blow his or her jug to match a B-flat below middle C on the piano. Have the third child match middle C with his or her jug.

    b. Have the children in the class determine which tones on the jugs (F, B-flat, or C) should be played on the first beat of each measure of the refrain of the song.

    c. Have selected children notate this accompaniment pattern for the refrain on the chalk board using the chord symbols I, IV, and V.

9. Perform: Have the children with the jugs play their assigned notes during the refrain of "Turkey in the Straw" as the other members in the class sing.

10. Move

    a. Ask the children in the class to form circles of four partners (boy-girl) in each. During the first four measures of the verse of "Turkey in the Straw," have the children join hands and circle clockwise stepping on the beat. During the second four measures of the verse, have the children reverse directions and circle counterclockwise holding hands while stepping on the beat. During the first two measures of the refrain ask the partners to swing. At the beginning of the third measure of the refrain ("Turkey in the hay") have the boys walk around their partners, passing them on the right. Have the boys take the left hand of the next girl with their own left hand and have the boys and girls pass each other. Have the boys take the right hand of the next girl with their own right hand and again have the boys and girls pass each other. Have the children continue this movement until the original partners are back together. Have the partners swing, cross hands, and promenade clockwise around the circle.

When the partners are back in their original positions, have them clap and stamp on the beat until the end of the refrain.

b. Have the children sing as they dance this modified square dance.

c. Ask three students to play the jugs as accompaniment to the refrain for the song and the dance.

LESSON PLAN B

1. Listen and analyze.
   a. Play a recording of the "Viennese Musical Clock" from the "Háry János" suite by Kodály.[7]
   b. Ask the students to determine how many times the first section of the "Viennese Musical Clock" is repeated as they listen to the piece.
   c. Ask the children to determine how many different sections there are in the piece. (A B A C A D A)
   d. Have the following tagboard signs at the front of the room. Ask a child

   to arrange these signs in the appropriate rondo-form order as the recording of the "Viennese Musical Clock" is played once again. (A B A C A D A)

2. Move
   a. Ask the children to create a movement to use with the A sections of the piece. Then, ask the students to also create different and unique movements for the B, C, and D sections of the piece.
   b. Play the "Viennese Musical Clock" again for the students and have them perform their movements during the various sections of the rondo. (The same movement should be used for all of the A sections.)

3. Create
   a. Ask the children to bring seven plastic containers, such as margarine

[7]"Adventures in Music," Grade 2 (RCA Victor—LE1002).

cartons, from home. Have the students label the top of the cartons in the following manner:

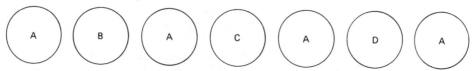

Have the children find sound-making ingredients for the cartons such as small pieces of chalk, pebbles, sand, rice, macaroni, coins, bells, or nails. Have the children place the same type of ingredient in all of the cartons labeled A. Have them put different ingredients in each of the cartons labeled B, C, and D.

b. Have each child in the class create a sound piece in rondo form using the cartons. Ask the students to notate specific rhythm patterns for each of the sections of the rondo form. The A sections should always be the same rhythm pattern.

4. Perform and analyze
   a. Have each child in the class perform their compositions in rondo form using the cartons labeled A, B, C, and D.
   b. Ask the children to discuss how the choice of the ingredients of each carton made the various sections of the rondo distinct or similar. Have them decide whether or not "contrast" is important in composing rondos.

5. Listen and analyze: Place the following cards in random order at the front of the room.

Have a selected child in the class arrange the cards in the appropriate rondo form for the "Colonel Bogey March" by V. Alford as a recording of it is played.[8] (The cards should be arranged in the following manner at the completion of the march: A B A C A.)

6. Move
   a. Divide the children into five groups representing the five sections of the rondo form on the "Colonel Bogey March": A B A C A.
   b. Play the recording of "Colonel Bogey March" again and ask group 1 to make movements during the A section. Have group 2 move differently during the B section. Have group 3 move on the repeat of section A using the same actions as introduced by group 1. Have group 4 move differently on Section C and have group 5 move on the final A section of the march using the same actions as introduced by group 1 and repeated by group 3.

[8]"Marches," Album no. 54, Bowmar Orchestral Library (Los Angeles: Bowmar/Noble).

7. Perform and create
   a. Have the children in the class create a sound-gesture rondo using the movements snap, clap, patsch, and stamp. Ask the students to use the following form for the class rondo: A B A C A D A E A.
   b. Ask the students to create a sound gesture to be used for all of the A sections of the class rondo. Have a class member place the sound gesture for the A section on the chalkboard. For example:

Patsch   patsch   patsch   clap   clap   Clap   clap   clap   clap   snap

Stamp   stamp   stamp   snap   Clap   clap   clap   clap   snap   snap   patsch

   c. Select several children to improvise the B, C, D, and E sections of the rondo using the sound gestures of snap, clap, patsch, and stamp.
   d. Perform the rondo in class.
   e. Ask the children to experiment with changing meters, changing tempos, and changing dynamics as they improvise the contrasting sections of the rondo. After the performance of the rondo, have the children who improvised the contrasting sections explain what specific musical elements they used in their improvisations.

8. Perform
   a. Teach by rote the Jamaican folk song "Stone Pounding."
   b. Have the children sit in a circle on the floor. Give three of the children two small stones each and have them sit in the center of the circle. Have the children with the stones hold one in each hand and perform the following ostinato pattern by tapping the stones on the floor using alternate hands, as indicated (R= right hand, L= left hand).

R L   R L   R L

Have the three students perform this ostinato throughout the song as the children sitting in the outer circle sing it.

Stone Pounding

Transcribed by Helen H. Roberts
Edited by T. Grame

Jamaican

♩ = c. 112

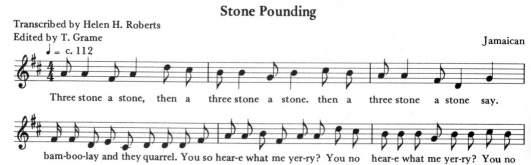

Three stone a stone, then a   three stone a stone. then a   three stone   a stone   say.

bam-boo-lay and they quarrel. You so hear-e what me yer-ry? You no   hear-e what me yer-ry? You no

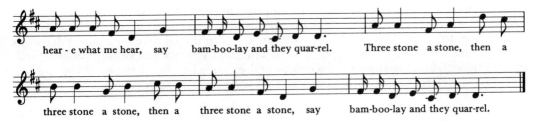

hear - e what me hear,   say   bam-boo-lay and they quar-rel.   Three stone a stone,   then   a

three stone a stone,   then a   three stone a stone,   say   bam-boo-lay and they quar-rel.

9. Analyze
    a. Ask a student in the class to write the rhythm of the ostinato part on the chalkboard. Have the three children with the stones play the ostinato pattern written on the chalkboard. Have the class compare it to what was originally played by the children in the center of the circle.

10. Create
    a. Divide the class into groups of three and have each group create a rhythmic ostinato pattern to be played with the "Stone Pounding" song.
    b. Have the children notate their rhythmic patterns on manuscript paper to use as they play, but caution them to avoid letting others in the class see the patterns.
    c. Have the assigned groups take turns sitting in the center of the circle playing the ostinato patterns with the stones.
    d. After each group has performed the pattern with the song, ask the children in the outer circle to write the pattern on the chalkboard or on separate pieces of paper. Have the children check to see if their patterns are correctly written.

Summary

In Lesson A, the children are exposed to the following musical concepts:

> melody
> rhythm
> meter
> form
> timbre
> dynamics
> tempo
> introduction
> coda
> rhythmic ostinato
> intervals
> harmonic accompaniment

In Lesson A, the children are involved in an experimental activity with the composition box, which provides individual exploratory experiences with the specific elements of music and their relationship to each other. In this lesson, the children are exposed to music of the Mayan culture as well as music from the American folk song literature. The children are encouraged to make musical decisions based on their knowledge and skill. The children encounter compositional, analytical, and performance activities and experiences in all facets of the lesson.

In Lesson B, the children are exposed to the following:

rondo form
contrast in musical composition
rhythmic ostinato

The children listen to the "Viennese Musical Clock" by Kodály and the "Colonel Bogey March" by V. Alford. The children analyze the rondo form of both pieces and are given opportunities to apply their knowledge and understanding of rondo form through compositional activities and through improvisatory movement activities. The children also create sound-gesture pieces in rondo form. In this lesson, the children are given opportunities to develop aural skills through the creation and subsequent dictation of rhythmic ostinato patterns used with the Jamaican folk song, "Stone Pounding." In this lesson, the children are again involved in a balance of composition, performance, and analytical activities.

CONCLUSIONS

The preceding experiences within the frameworks of Jaques-Dalcroze, Kodály, Orff, and Comprehensive Musicianship illustrate clearly the extent to which each may contribute to musical skill development and concept inference. Obviously, worthwhile musical objectives may be achieved through use of any of these approaches in Grades 3, 4, and 5.

However, it should be equally obvious that the kinds of lesson examples offered here are in each case totally dependent on earlier experiences within the same method. It would be difficult, if not impossible, for the child with three years of CM background to be successful if suddenly thrown into a situation in which all the other children had had an equal amount of Jaques-Dalcroze training. The vocabulary is different. The two approaches are almost diametrically opposite in their degree of teacher-centeredness. Similarly, the child who has done much dramatization and chanting, less singing, and little or no musical reading and writing (Orff) would surely be lost if placed in with children able to sing easily in parts and to read and write music (Kodály); and the child used to singing as the basis of all musical learning (Kodály) would not have the necessary manipulative skills for Orff instrument playing—and would also bring to such playing a level of literacy that might actually impede rather than aid the Orff improvisational process.

The principal goal of each of these methodologies—to develop musicianship to the fullest extent possible—is evident in all the lessons. The paths to that goal are extremely divergent by fifth grade.

10
GRADES 6–7–8

INTRODUCTION

At the middle school level, for the first time in the MENC program cone (see p. 116) a separation is made between those students headed for careers in music and those who will more likely enjoy music through amateur participation or as audiences.

Preprofessional Training

For the career-directed students the suggested programs include piano, voice, and string classes, as well as "applied study" (the private study of a specific instrument), theory, and composition. Performing media suggested are bands, choirs, ensembles, and orchestras.

In point of fact, few schools except those in the largest urban centers offer these possibilities to their students. While wind classes abound, and almost every junior high school has its band, string study and orchestral experience are rare indeed on a national level; and most serious music students receive the major part of their training from private teachers outside the school system. The schools can often claim little credit beyond providing performing experience.

Avocational and Recreational Training

The great majority of students do not want a career in music. These are the students who will or will not choose to be the audiences of future symphony orchestras and symphonic bands; the ones who will or will not choose to sing in community choruses or church choirs; the ones who will or will not feel it worth their while to vote tax support for music in the schools for *their* children. To them, many of the activities suggested in the program cone are, at best, nebulous. "Listening centers"?—To listen to what? and with what level of direction or understanding? "Music resource centers"?—Resources for what, if musical capabilities have not been and are not being developed? *"General* music classes"?—Is there an adult who does not recall the waste of time he or she spent in junior high school "general music" class? Is there a junior high school music teacher who does not at times react with frustration when trying to appease and amuse thirty recalcitrant adolescents six times a day with school music texts that are irrelevant to the age group, following curricula that assume a level of musical background that few, if any, of the students possess?

It is possible to carry on music classes with children from three to ten years of age, keeping them happy, satisfying administrators, supervisors, and parents simply by maintaining order and putting on two or three shows a year. The sheer pleasure of seeing young children performing is often enough to make adult audiences deaf to the sounds being produced and blind to the lack of educational value in the activities being pursued.

As students from such programs enter adolescence, however, the situation changes. It is no longer the teachers, parents, supervisors, or principals who must be pleased with the musical product, it is the students themselves. And if there has been no real musical training in the lower grades, it is going to be very nearly impossible to offer this satisfaction to students not in the preprofessional stream in the junior high or middle school.

Teachers faced with this situation often take the course of least resistance. They steer students who play instruments well or sing well into performance groups where those students will perhaps learn something, where they will build repertory and develop some feeling for ensemble. Those more talented students become a sort of elite in most school situations: they enter competitions, they tour, they play at athletic events.

The other students, the great majority, take the usual *required* general music courses that are often assigned to the least experienced member of the staff. Students and teacher alike may end up hating what they think of as school music (as opposed to real music).

This is not intended to be a scathing indictment. The problem outlined here is not attributable to or solvable at the middle school level. Both the problem and the solution lie much earlier—in elementary school.

If there is a *coordinated, sequential, developmental* program of music instruction by qualified music teachers in the lower grades, teachers of eleven-, twelve-, thirteen-, fourteen-, and fifteen-year-olds can continue teaching music as a subject with skills to be mastered, concepts to be inferred, competencies to be developed—a subject with information to be imparted, discovered, absorbed, and applied.

The teacher of junior high school mathematics or French seldom has the kinds of behavior problems encountered by the teacher of junior high school music. The problems encountered in music are of the music-teaching profession's own making. A cohesive curriculum, continuous from kindergarten through Grade 12, exists in most academic areas. It must similarly exist in music.

Each of four approaches being considered in this book has such a structure. The child who has come through a properly taught program in Jaques-Dalcroze, Kodály, Orff, or Comprehensive Musicianship will enter middle school with musical skills and competencies. If the teacher receiving these students has sufficient training to make use of this knowledge and these skills, musical training for the adolescent can become a truly rich, rather than a frustrating experience, and the "general" music class will no longer be *general,* but will be a *specific* continuation toward musical independence. The class will make use of and further develop the participation skills that all music teachers surely want for their students.

The following lessons are samples of the kinds of activities that take place in middle schools committed to the principles of Jaques-Dalcroze, Kodály, Orff, or CM. They are extremely different from each other in their content and teaching process, yet each is in direct line from similar activities in earlier grades. Each builds skills and competencies in the subject of music. It should be stressed, however, that none of these lessons could be successfully implemented with youngsters who have *not* had the requisite previous training in the method.

While it is possible to begin a Jaques-Dalcroze, Kodály, Orff, or CM program at the middle school or junior high level, that is not the focus of these examples.

JAQUES-DALCROZE

By middle school, students studying Jaques-Dalcroze's techniques are comfortably able to use the musical language expressively through improvisational speech, song, percussion, ensemble, recorder, and piano. Physical and musical skills have been combined smoothly and harmoniously. Students are able to demonstrate oppositions of direction, tension, and release, and counterpoints between different sides and different parts of the body—*disordination.*[1]

One of the more common problems of musical training—that is, equating loud with fast and soft with slow—has been resolved, so that tempo is independent of dynamics, accent, and pattern. The ability to distinguish and express foreground, background, and middleground in musical structures makes it possible for students to perform independent contrapuntal parts in ensemble activities. Exercises of opposition have led to the ability to stabilize tempo, beat, and place within a measure during performances of two- and three-voice canons. Students are expected by this age to do a reasonably clear performance of a piece at first reading.

Conducting of tempo, beat, and measure is now automatic. Upbeat (anacrusic) and downbeat (crusic) versions of measures, patterns, and phrases can be performed by conducting with appropriate arm gestures. Conductor's arm beats and arm swings in two-, three-, four-, and five-beat simple or compound measures may be demonstrated using music with unequal measures, such as those in folk songs and dances of France, Spain, Mexico, or Hungary.

Rhythmic reading is advanced to eight-measure periods in simple, compound, and mixed meters. The ability to read and perform rhythms with proper

---

[1] A French word, with no English equivalent, meaning "the harmonizing of two, three, or four different movements of different qualities."

phrasing, articulation, emphasis, and expression should now be fairly well developed. Rhythmic dictations of four measures in length should be performed easily, and ear training involving critical listening and correction of a performance and a score should be quick and accurate within four hearings. The challenge of performing syncopations against a regular metric pattern is also appropriate for this age group.

Students should be encouraged to apply the techniques learned earlier in Eurhythmics classes to musical problems that may occur now in choral, band, or orchestra rehearsals or in private voice or instrumental lessons. They must be taught techniques for helping themselves: how to scan music for rhythmic sense, how to apply the movements of pitch groups, tonalities, cadences, and modulations. They must be taught to make quick and comprehensive interpretations of musical scores.

At this age students are ready to tackle more involved *Solfège* and *Solfège-Rythmique* games and to develop a deeper understanding of the role of pitch in melody, harmony, and counterpoint. More advanced literature can be used for analysis of vocabulary and musical processes, and this vocabulary and these processes can then be transferred to student improvisations.

Rhythmic and pitched compositions may be improvised in forms using various lengths and qualities of both phrase and cadence. Part forms, theme and variations, and the various rondo forms are all studied to determine the compositional uses of balance, unity, and contrast. The ability to move from solo to group improvisation should be fluent and comfortable.

The Jaques-Dalcroze lessons in this chapter and the next represent an extrapolation of various techniques Jaques-Dalcroze wrote about in his own methods.

A complete lesson on one of Jaques-Dalcroze's subjects can last an hour, a week, or a month, since rhythm is an immense domain. Lessons are concept oriented and rhythm supplies the binding thread that connects the study of pitch to musical analysis, understanding, and musicianship. The Jaques-Dalcroze approach relates Eurhythmics to *Solfège* and *Solfège* to Improvisation in order to explore one subject in many dimensions.

Some of the techniques in the following lessons may be useful for choral, band, or orchestral work; others are more suitable for a general music class. All activities are designed to enable students at various levels of skill to participate together, yet each doing so at his or her own level of development. All will receive stimulation and nourishment appropriate to their age, interest, and skill.

Lesson on Group Improvisation

Subject: ♩ → ♫ and ♫ → ♩ as subdivisions and as tempo changes

(twice as fast; twice as slow).

Equipment: Chalkboard, percussion instruments, piano.

Starting position: Students with untuned percussion instruments should be sitting in groups according to instrument type.

STEP I: IMPROVISATION WITH RHYTHM ALONE

1. Warmup: (♩ **and** ♫) using movement to generate sound.

> Teacher: *Watch.*

The teacher improvises four repeated gestures in a moderate quarter-note tempo at a moderately quiet dynamic level, using a moderate level of energy and moderate space.

> Teacher: *Follow me.* (Repeats the gesture).

The students follow the demonstrated movement by playing instruments in the correct tempo.

2. The teacher begins to develop the gestures, using terraced dynamics (pp; p; mf; f; ff), then sudden extremes (subito p; subito f), and finally gradual dynamic nuances (diminuendo, crescendo) of one-, two-, three-, and four-measure lengths. The students follow, demonstrating each variation.

3. Next the teacher adds sudden sharp accents on different beats or combinations of beats (♩ ♩ ♩ ♩ ; ♩ ♩ ♩ ♩); then regular accentuation by repetition of accent pattern

; etc.).

The students repeat the patterns as given.

4. The teacher uses changes of level (low, middle, high) and calls out names of instrument groups (*drums, wood, bells*) to bring different groups in or out of the piece.

5. The teacher develops the piece to a climax and begins a long diminuendo as a coda. The ending can be very soft and die away with a final gesture to produce silence, or the piece may end with a sudden loud beat and a gesture of silence.

STEP II: CONSCIOUSNESS OF MUSICAL EVENTS

1. Teacher: *Did our piece have a beat? What speed was the beat?* (Walking.) *Yes, we used a walking beat. What did we do with it? Can you remember the ways we performed it?*

The teacher helps with gestural cues and the technical name (crescendo, accent, etc.) if necessary.

2. **Teacher:** *Who remembers how the piece began? Can you play the beginning?* (Gives a starting gesture.)

The students try to remember and replay the correct tempo. They then try to recall and reconstruct the entire piece as they played it, with all its nuances and variation.

STEP III: STUDENT IMPROVISATION BY GESTURE CONDUCTING

1. **Teacher:** (Choosing a student to conduct) *Show us a gesture that means stop.* (The student demonstrates a gesture.) *Now choose a four-beat gesture pattern of your own. Start, lead, and stop the orchestra. When you get tired of one sound, use variations to develop interest. Start softly and build this piece with a long, slowly developing crescendo.* (The teacher speaks these directions at the dynamic levels being suggested.)

2.   The teacher then joins the orchestra and takes an instrument while the student conducts an improvised piece. The teacher must remember the general structure of the piece so that it can be discussed afterwards. If the piece begins to lose interest, the teacher may suggest the introduction of variations; if the piece seems to go on too long, the teacher may coach the conductor by speaking in rhythm: *Get ready to finish the piece and . . . stop.*

3. The teacher then questions the class about the general structure of the improvisation.

Teacher: *Who played when, and what happened at the beginning, middle and end of the piece? The form of this piece was*

At this point the teacher may play a listening example in which one of the principal unifying qualities is a gradual crescendo; for example, Ravel's *Bolero.*

STEP IV: IMPROVISATION BASED ON CONTRAST

OF *cresc.* ff AND ♩ *and* ♪ ♪

1.   The teacher chooses another student to conduct a piece which starts with a walking speed and later changes to a running speed. Gestures are decided on for the two speeds. The student conducts the improvisation while the other students and the teacher follow.

2.   After playing the piece the teacher and students discuss the shape of it and try to graph it.

Part I all   ♩

Part II all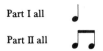

Part III some 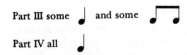 and some

Part IV all

STEP V: IMPROVISATION WITH A DOUBLE CHOIR

1. **Teacher:** *Let's divide the group into two choirs: Choir I will be walking speed; Choir II will be running speed. If I conduct and point to Choir I, it is to play; if I conduct and point to Choir II, it is to play. Be alert! I may point to both at the same time, or I may stop suddenly and start again. When it is over we'll see what we can remember.*

The teacher conducts an improvised composition, using one arm for ♩ and the

other for ♫ . He or she uses additional gestures to create dynamic changes, accents, and rhythmic patterns. The result might be

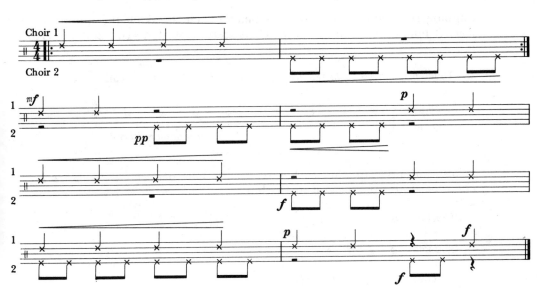

2. After playing, the class tries to recall the improvisation.

    Teacher: *Which group started the piece? Then what happened? How did it end?*

The teacher continues to question as long as necessary to reconstruct the piece.

3. The teacher then chooses a different student to improvise a short new piece,

but asks Choir I to perform the ♫ and Choir II to perform the ♩ . The conductor should be reminded that Choir I and II can be alternated or combined, and that the music can be stopped and restarted. If further help seems needed, the teacher can whisper a suggestion for the shape of the piece into the conductor's ear, so that the others cannot hear; for example, "Start very softly and each time you change groups, change the dynamics." Again the students are asked to try to remember what events took place during the performance of the piece.

STEP VI: GENERATING PATTERNS FOR
IMPROVISATION, USING TWO
RHYTHMIC ELEMENTS

1. **Teacher:**   *Let's develop some new patterns from ♩ and ♫ . Put your instruments down and clap with me in four-beat time, like this.*

The teacher claps four beats in place across the body from right to left (if the teacher is facing the students), counting 1, 2, 3, 4. The students follow, clapping from left to right (mirror image) while speaking the numbers. The teacher notates this pattern on the chalkboard as students continue to perform it.

2. **Teacher:**   *Get ready to replace any beat I call with a ♫ clap.*

Students: { ♩ ♩ ♩ ♩ |♩ ♩ ♩ ♩ ‖: ♩ ♩ ♩
Teacher: {   *Change beat number 4*

While students clap, the teacher places the new pattern ♩ ♩ ♩ ♫ on chalkboard and points to it in rhythm.

Teacher: *Back to normal.*

Students: ♩ ♩ ♩ ♩ .

Teacher: *Change beat number 3.*

The teacher writes the new pattern and the students read and clap it.

Teacher: *Back to normal*

The teacher and students continue in this manner until they have thought, felt, performed, and read the following patterns placed on the chalkboard by the teacher:

3. **Teacher:** *Now let's play these patterns.*

The teacher sets a tempo. Students read and play the patterns on their instruments as the teacher points to specific rhythms or calls for pattern 5, pattern 2, and so on. Next the teacher may choose students to go to the chalkboard and build new pieces by pointing to different arrangements of patterns.

STEP VII: EXERCISE TO IMPROVISE
RHYTHM AND REMEMBER RHYTHMIC
COMBINATIONS

1. **Teacher:** *I'll play (clap, speak) a pattern with ♩ and ♩ ♫ in a four-beat measure.*

When I point to one of you, you improvise a new pattern using ♩ and ♫ in a four-beat measure. Remember, don't echo me; choose a pattern different from mine.

The teacher claps from right to left in front of the body and speaks:

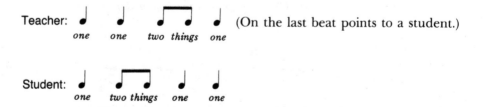

The teacher continues this technique until each student has given a response.

2. Teacher:

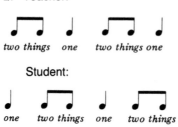

two things   one   two things one

Student:

one   two things   one   two things

This exercise continues until all have had a turn. If a student misses an entrance, the teacher waits four beats and repeats the pattern. It may prove helpful to have students silently mark four places, left to right, during the teacher's part.

3. Teacher: *This time, after I improvise one measure, the whole class should echo that measure. Then I'll point to one of you. That one must improvise a new measure and the whole class must repeat it.*

[This exercise is designed to improve and lengthen memories.]

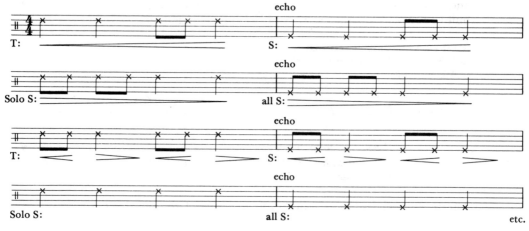

4. Teacher: *This time I'll do a pattern; one of you will do a new one, and the whole class must perform both.*

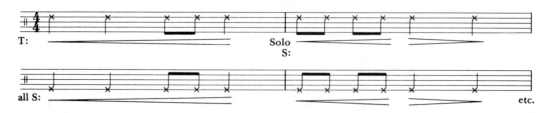

STEP VIII: IMPROVISED RONDO

1. **Teacher:** *Let's build a more formal piece, a rondo, by alternating patterns.*

The teacher builds an improvisation, alternating pattern 1 with other patterns and combinations; always returning to 1. Then the teacher chooses one student to improvise a new pattern to be used as the repetitive element. The student conducts by pointing to rhythms on the chalkboard in rondo form, which the whole group must play. Later, a conductor may choose soloists to perform the alternating parts while the group performs the repetitive element. Again, the students should be expected to recall what happens within the piece each time.

STEP IX: IMPROVISATION OF LONGER
PATTERNS, PHRASES, AND PERIODS

1. **Teacher:** *We can improvise another way. Follow me. We can choose the rhythmic ges-*

ture   ; repeat it,   ; develop it by making

it more active,   ; and then repeat the first gesture for

an ending. Let's try it.

The teacher conducts. The students play:

2. **Teacher:** *Let's experiment by starting with lots of activity and ending with a quieter gesture.*

The teacher demonstrates:

Individual students choose and experiment with different rhythmic combinations and orchestration, and explore different possibilities. Others listen and repeat the phrases invented, then analyze the choices verbally. For example:

      Student: *He started with gesture 1 and repeated it and then chose gesture 4 and repeated it. It felt and sounded balanced.*

STEP X: STRIATED COUNTERPOINT
(LAYERING TEXTURES)

1. Teacher: *Let's see what happens to the texture if we slowly add layers of rhythmic counterpoint. Drums, will you repeat pattern 1* 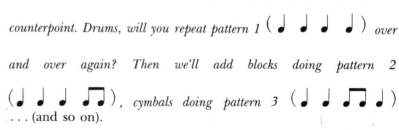 *over and over again? Then we'll add blocks doing pattern 2* *, cymbals doing pattern 3* *... (and so on).*

The students add the layers one at a time, until all are playing different patterns. The teacher then signals the layers to drop out one at a time.

2. Teacher: *We have a lot of material now. Let's experiment with improvising a piece with thin layers and thick layers* (thin and thick textures).

STEP XI: IMPROVISING A
CANON THEME

1. Teacher: *Let's improvise a short canon or round. We can choose four gestures from the rhythmic patterns on the board to make a subject. Which pattern shall we start with?*

The students choose four patterns and decide on the order in which they should be played.

    Teacher: *Let's play that whole series.*

The students play the four phrases in unison.

2. Teacher: *Now let's make another choice. Which instruments shall we have begin* (bells, blocks, etc.)? *Which instruments will come next* (tambourines, drums, etc.)? *The* (first instrument) *will begin; then the* (second instrument choice) *will begin at the first phrase after four beats. That will give us an interesting way of creating a duet.*

Groups I and II play the entire example in canon.

3. Teacher: *Let's try a thicker texture. Choose a third instrument group. Group III will begin after Group II has finished the first gesture. Then we shall have a trio.*

Groups I, II, and III play in canon.

4. Teacher: *Let's make another choice and create a four-part canon.*

The students choose the fourth instrument and play through the canon several times. Various conductors experiment with entrances of parts at the distance of one, two, or three beats, then at two or three measures. Other conductors may experiment with ordering entrances by range of sound; for example, they might begin the canon with high-voiced instruments, follow these with low-voiced instruments, and have middle-voiced instruments perform the third part.

STEP XII: PITCH AND RHYTHM
IMPROVISATION—DEVELOPING MELODIC
IMPROVISATION BY DIMINUTION AND
ALTERATION

1. Teacher: *Let's do some improvised variations on "Frère Jacques." Sing it in C Major with syllables (or words or numbers). Sing each measure once at normal tempo and then repeat it twice in a tempo twice as fast to find out what it sounds like.*

The students perform as follows:

2. Teacher: *Let's try it,* singing *a measure and then* playing *the measure twice as fast.*

Sing   Play   etc.

3. Teacher: *Let's try the opposite way. Play the original, then sing the tempo variation, but sing each note of the melody as two eighth notes.*

do   do   re   re   mi   mi   do   do

4. Teacher: *You sing the first measure of "Frère Jacques" and I'll insert a tune based on one of our rhythmic patterns joined to patterns of the major scale.*

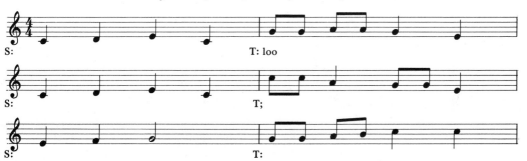

S: T: loo

S: T;

S: T:

S: T: etc.

5. **Teacher:**   *I'll sing "Frère Jacques" and you invent a new measure in the pentatonic scale. First let's experiment with combining our rhythmic pattern with shapes in C-pentatonic scale.*

etc.

The teacher and students explore cell combinations, write them on the chalkboard, and then read them.

6. The teacher sings "Frère Jacques," indicating student soloists who choose cells to produce variation at every other measure. (All of these pitch and rhythm studies can be performed on the recorder, piano, or any other pitched instrument.)

STEP XIII: NOTECLUSTERS ON BLACK KEYS
OF THE PIANO—A DUET GAME

1. The teacher demonstrates a measure of ♩ ♩ ♩ ♩

at the keyboard in the bass, answered by a measure of ♫♫ ♫♫ ♫♫ ♫♫

in the high register using repeated note clusters on black keys played with a gently closed hand or hands, using the piano as a percussion instrument. The students form two lines, one for the bass and the other for the soprano, in front of the piano. The teacher sets a tempo and the first bass student plays a musical

question phrase ♩ ♩ ♩ ♩

and then moves quickly left to the end of the line, thus being replaced by a new bass student. Meanwhile, the first soprano student plays an answer phrase

and then moves right, to the end of the line. This continues until each student has had a chance to play. The students waiting for a turn do not simply wait; *all* students must be showing the beat and tempo throughout the piece.

2. **Teacher:**   (Demonstrating) *This time use your pattern as clusters moving up from the bass toward the middle of the piano* (alternating hands, hands together, or crossing hands).

The teacher then plays ♫ ♫ ♫ ♫ in clusters, starting at the high end of the keyboard and moving leftward to the middle. The students should mime these movements simultaneously with the teacher. Using the same procedure as before, the students form bass and soprano lines and play alternating patterns moving toward the middle of the keyboard. Again it is important that *all* students show body movement, keeping the beat and tempo even when not playing.

3. Teacher: *This time choose your own dynamics and your own patterns to play from the patterns we have studied.*

The teacher sets a tempo and gives a starting signal. After the students have been through the line, the teacher asks one player to finish the piece by elongating the pattern or the last note or by shortening the last note by a staccato touch. Each student should have the opportunity to play both a bass pattern with the left hand and a soprano pattern with the right hand. The last students should use both hands for the final measure and must find a satisfactory way to finish the piece.

Conclusion

Ideally, all aspects of the Jaques-Dalcroze method—Eurhythmics, *Solfège,* and Improvisation—should be interrelated in lessons by the middle school level. Eurhythmics training, begun first with the youngest students, has been illustrated in two lessons.[2] The lesson presented in this chapter focuses specifically on the improvisational aspects of Jaques-Dalcroze practice. (*Solfège* and *Solfège-Rhythmique* will be treated in Chapter 11.) The reader must realize that Eurhythmics, *Solfège,* and Improvisation need not be taught in isolation; they can be, and frequently are taught together in a single lesson based on the rhythmic subject or concept being developed.

KODÁLY

By the time students enter seventh grade in a total Kodály program they are able to:

> sing at sight with ease
> sing fluently in movable-*do solfa* and in absolutes (letter names), switching from one to the other at a given signal
> sing in two and three parts from score
> identify binary and ternary forms, both in songs and in larger works
> aurally identify the modes: aeolian, dorian, ionian, mixolydian, lydian, phrygian
> take melodic and rhythmic dictation from voice or piano

[2]Chapter 8, pp. 157–169: Chapter 9, pp. 199–214

perform two or three musical ideas simultaneously: singing a melody, tapping an osinato, stepping a beat

identify some art music by style and period, and often by specific composer (The art music studied from fourth to sixth grade is principally from the Classical, Baroque, and Romantic periods, with some twentieth-century music.)

improvise within known scales, meters, and rhythms

compose in small forms within specific scales and meters

harmonize known melodies with I, IV, and V chords

arrange I, IV, and V chords in inversions for best voice leading

play known songs on the recorder

identify and sing intervals by number (third, fourth, etc.) and as "major," "minor," or "perfect"

identify basic scale patterns of whole- and half-step arrangements for major and minor diatonic scales

identify the key or mode of songs by examining the key signature and final note

determine where modulations occur within pieces and make the appropriate *solfa* changes

In Hungary many students at this age have already had a number of years of instrumental study, and have taken concurrently with this a required two hours a week of *solfa* and musicianship training, all free of charge or at minimal cost. In Hungary the teacher of trumpet is a trumpet performer and teaches only the trumpet; trombone is taught by a trombonist, clarinet by a clarinetist, violin by a violinist. Two private lessons a week are given to each student through the special public "Music Schools." In North America, on the other hand, private instrumental training is never free of charge and seldom of only minimal cost. In North American public schools the same teacher is usually responsible for teaching all woodwind, brass, and percussion instruments—and even strings, where such programs exist. All the students are taught in "classes" rather than in private lessons, and in the worst situations even these group lessons do not exist—all instrumental instruction takes place through band rehearsals.

The absurdity of such "teaching" hardly requires comment. Serious students give up and, if their parents can afford it, go to a music school or conservatory, or to a community music school. Public schools at this level that take training in music seriously are obviously needed: there is no lack of students. If there are now an insufficient number of trained teachers, they can surely be trained.

The relevance of all this to Kodály training is that the students who come to junior high school or high school already musically literate, with a sense of what is good and worthwhile in the musical literature, with compositional and performance skills, often simply drop out at these so-called advanced levels. They find the usual junior and senior high music program, at best, boring and, at worst, impossible to participate in for the student who has developed an acute and critical musical ear.

The lesson that follows was done with sixth-grade students. The students in this group went on in the following semester into a junior high school in which the teacher could not function at the musical level of these students. The result, of course, was a massive dropout.

Teachers at this level must be Kodály trained if they are to be able to further the musical education of their Kodály-trained students. It is no longer enough to know *ti–ta*'s and *so–mi*'s. Teachers must have studied in depth the works of Szőnyi and Hegyi; they must have worked through the pedagogical works of Kodály; and they must have thorough analytical knowledge of music literature. They must themselves be capable of intelligent listening, improvisation, and composition.[3]

The erroneous notion that the Kodály Method is something for little children stems solely from the fact that in North America only a few teachers have yet been adequately trained to take Kodály teaching techniques or sequences beyond the *ti–ta*'s and *so–mi*'s. The problem lies not in the method but in its implementation in North America.

Lesson for Twelve- and Thirteen-Year-Olds

Here is one lesson done with thirty twelve- and thirteen-year-old students[4] with a strong Kodály background at the end of grade six. The principal subject of this lesson is the dominant chord and the dominant seventh chord.

1. Teacher: *Who can sing the A today?* (One student sings it correctly; it is checked by the tuning fork and sung by all.) *Now sing the E-Major pentachord scale in* solfa *in canon.*

[The students do not see the notation of this exercise. The purpose of the exercise is to focus aurally on the thirds and triads being produced.]

---

[3]Erzsébet Szőnyi, *Musical Reading and Writing*, pupil's book, vols. 1–8 (London: Boosey & Hawkes, 1972; 1973; 1979); Erzsébet Hegyi, *Solfège According to the Kodály-Concept, 2 vols.* (London: Boosey & Hawkes, 1975; 1979); Percy M. Young, ed. *The Kodály Choral Method* (London: Boosey & Hawkes) [This is a series of books containing pedagogical exercises by Kodály.]

[4]These students came from the schools of Plano, TX, and formed a special demonstration group at the University of Texas at Dallas.

2.   Teacher: *Good! Now sing the Cherubini canon⁵ in unison with an E-do. Use your handsigns as you sing.*

Canon

Cherubini

3.   Teacher: *In three parts now. Can we have a trio? Julie? Tom? Derek? Everyone else follow with handsigns. Help by singing aloud if anyone needs help. Can you find the tonic chord (I) in the melody* (the last three measures)? *Let's sing them as a chord. I'll put them on the board.*

d'   s   m   d   I

Can you find the V chord in the melody (the ninth measure)?

The teacher places it on the board:

f   r   t,   s,

4.   Teacher: *But all our chords so far have had only three tones, 1–3–5, above any scale degree. This one has another tone. The 1 (so), 3 (ti), and 5 (re) are here. What number must the other tone (fa) be? (7.) Yes. This is still a V chord—a dominant chord—but we need to show its difference by adding the number 7 after the roman numeral V. Let's sing it as a chord:*

f   r   t,   s,   V7

5.   Teacher: *We have sung triads on each note of the major pentachord. Let's see if we can sing the seventh chords on them:*

⁵This canon, called simply "Solmization," was written without words and is customarily sung in *solfa*.

d	m	s	t		r	f	l	d′		m	s	t	r′		f	l	d′	m′		s,	t,	r,	f
I7					ii7					iii7					IV7					V7			

> *Yes, some are easier to sing than others; but we can add the seventh to any triad.*

6.   Teacher: *Let's look at a new song from Newfoundland, on page 40 in your book.*[6]

We'll Rant and We'll Roar

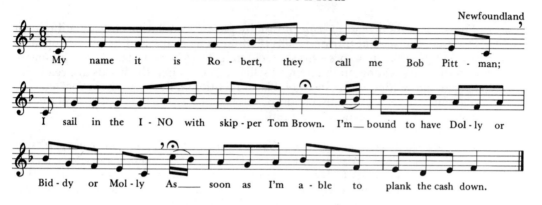

Chorus (same tune)

      We'll rant and we'll roar like true Newfoundlanders,
        We'll rant and we'll roar on deck and below,
      Until we see bottom inside the two sunkers,
        When straight through the Channel to Toslow we'll go!

Teacher: *What is the meter?* (⁶⁄₈.) *How will we conduct it?* (In 2s.) *Read the rhythm in ti–ta's, please, and keep the beat* (two in a measure) *lightly on your desks with fingertips.*

The class reads. If there are any problems they are discussed and corrected.[7]

Teacher: What key are we in?" (F Major.) *Follow my flying note to practice the intervals and melodic turns you will need in this song.*

---

[6]The book referred to here is a very useful one for older students. Ilona Bartalus, *Sing, Silverbirch, Sing* (Willowdale, Ont.: Boosey & Hawkes Canada, 1980). The song "We'll Rant and We'll Roar" may be found in many sources and in many variants in both folk song collections and in school music texts. (Sometimes it is listed under the title "The Ryans and the Pittmans.")

[7]The rhythm of this song is so easy that this preliminary rhythm reading may be omitted with most classes and the song read in rhythm immediately with *solfa.*

The intervals and turns practiced are

s – d	*f – r – t – s*
s – r	*m – r – m*
s – m – d	*t – l – t – d*

The song is then read in *solfa* phrase by phrase. Similarities are identified: for example, the second phrase recalls the first in its shape and its use of repeated notes. When the melody seems securely sung in *solfa*, the syllables are eliminated and the song is sung on the neutral syllable "loo." Then the words are read, discussed, and added to the melody. Places mentioned in the song are located on a map and there is some discussion of the life of a seafaring people living in the isolation of small island communities.

7.   Teacher   *Sing the melody again. Can you find a tonic (I) chord any place in it?* (On the words "bound to have Dolly or") *Can you find a dominant seventh* (V₇) *chord? There may be an extra note among the notes of the chord.* (For the words "call me Bob Pittman" and "Biddy or Molly", "Bob" and "or" are on F, a note not in the chord.)

8.   Teacher: *This time as you sing it, boys carry the melody, girls sing* do *where the tonic chord is implied and* so *where the dominant or dominant seventh chord is implied. Now reverse your parts.*

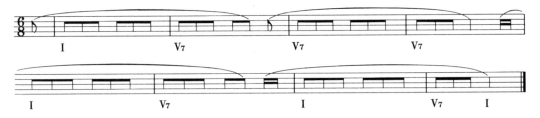

How could we chord this vocally? We know two good singing inversions from I to V:

Students: *The group singing* so *could split into two, singing* so *and* fa (a); *or the ones singing* mi *could split into two, singing* re *and* fa (b).

Teacher: *Yes, but perhaps there aren't enough of us to do that really clearly. Let's try leaving out one note. It can't be the root—that would make it a different chord—and it can't be the seventh, for then it would no longer be a dominant seventh chord. It must be the third or the fifth. Let's see which way the chord sounds most complete.*

The students experiment and discover that the character of the chord is least affected by leaving out the fifth.

Teacher: *Now let's accompany the song with chording. Use I and V₇. What rhythm shall we use?*

The students make various suggestions; for example:

Dol - ly,   Mol - ly,   Kit - ty,   Mar - y Tib-bo   Dol - ly,   Mol - ly,   Kit - ty,   Mar - y Tib-bo!

9. Teacher: *John, Louisa, Kent, and Eila sing the melody. The rest of you sing the harmony parts. Those of you on the harmony, be sure to sing softly—there are twenty-six of you and only four on the melody part."*

[The result will be imperfect, but with practice this could become part of a choral performance for parents. Programs built in this way have educational value rather than simply fulfilling an entertainment function.]

10. Teacher: *Look at the rhythm on the board. Read it with me. Here is your tempo:*

Students:

Teacher: *In your manuscript books please compose a melody for this rhythmic phrase. You may use only the notes of the tonic chord in F Major, but you may place them in any position. As you can see on the board the final note of the phrase is not in the I chord. It must be* fa. *Does that indicate a question phrase or an answer phrase? (A question phrase.) It ends on a note of the* V₇ *chord rather than on the I chord. However you choose to arrange your I chord notes to this rhythm, be sure you can sing them if you are called on.*

The students must be given sufficient time for this activity, but not too much time. Three to five minutes usually suffice. Some typical solutions are:

[By *giving* tempo, meter, rhythm, and specific notes to be used, the teacher has made this compositional task performable by even the least secure student. Other kinds of compositional experiences are given individually to students who do not need the security of an imposed structure. It is, however, a technique of the Kodály method to lead to composition through systematically withdrawing the giving of meter, rhythm, melody, form, harmony, one at a time. Students volunteer to sing their compositions. Obviously, not all can be heard in a class period, so the notebooks are collected to be read by the teacher. It is important that any mistakes be corrected and that encouraging words be written on each.]

11. Teacher: *Let's hear how Beethoven used these same notes.* (Plays a recording of Beethoven's *Symphony No. 6* (the "Pastoral"), fifth movement.)

Symphony No. 6 ("Pastoral"), 5th Movement Theme

Beethoven

Teacher: *Can we sing Beethoven's theme in* solfa?
The class tries, then listens again to correct mistakes.

[In subsequent lessons the class
        memorizes the Beethoven theme
        harmonizes it vocally with I and V chords
        listens to the recording again to discover where Beethoven used harmonies other than I and V, and sings the Beethoven harmonization in three parts

Chordal accompaniment for *Pastoral theme.*

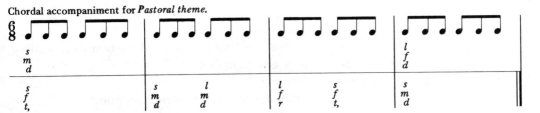

listens to, sings in *solfa,* and memorizes the bass line, singing it as a second part with the melody:

compares the style of Beethoven with the style of Bach and draws generalizations about the Baroque, Classical, and Romantic periods in music

listens to a performance by instrumental students who have studied Beethoven compositions.]

12. **Teacher:** *Let's finish up today with the Praetorius Canon. Group 1 sing it through three times; Group 2, two complete times, then finish on the second "musica" (the note A); Group 3, two times, plus a repeat of the first phrase, ending on F. What will the triad at the end be? (D–F#–A.) In the key of G, on what chord are we ending? (The dominant (V) chord.) In three parts, conducting in 4s as you sing:*

VIVA LA MUSICA

sfmrdt,l,s,f,

Praetorius Canon

①
Vi - va, Vi - va la mu - si - ca,

②
Vi - va, Vi - va la

③
mu - si - ca,   Vi - va   la   mu - si - ca.

Conclusion

The principal focus of this lesson was the teaching of a previously unknown chord, the dominant seventh. However, in the course of the lesson the children also:

sang canons in three parts
read and sang a unison folk song

conducted
harmonized a known melody
sang to discover which chord inversions produced the best voice leading
composed a melody to a given rhythm
sang a Beethoven theme in *solfa*
listened to the last movement of a Beethoven symphony

The elements of music were touched on in a way that contributed not only to musical literacy but also to the development of musical taste. Kodály's axiom that "only the best is good enough for children" was reflected in the choices of authentic folk music and composed music of unquestionable quality.

ORFF

The process in an Orff approach does not change, regardless of the age of the students involved. For junior high school students, there is an expectation of a higher level of performance, but the curriculum is still organized around movement, voice, form, and instruments. However, the area designated "Form" in the earlier grades now encompasses much more and might be better termed "Organization and Materials of Music."

Movement

OBJECTIVES.   Students should acquire an expanded vocabulary of dance steps and demonstrate sensitivity to style and performance practice. They should move securely and freely alone and with others. They should be able to analyze and execute dance steps illustrated by others, as well as imitate such movements and notate them in some graphic way. They should be able to create dances.

PROCESS.   Opportunities are given for students to see and do, read directions and do, say and do a large number of traditional and nontraditional dance steps. Students are encouraged to organize movements, formations, and steps into new dances.

MATERIALS.   Folk, popular, and classical music and dance are used at this level.

Voice

OBJECTIVES.   Students are expected to practice full open-throated singing, in tune, in an expanded range and using a head voice. They should be able to analyze, describe, and demonstrate good singing techniques.

PROCESS.   Music to be played on instruments is generally sung first. The teacher must be ready to give vocal help individually or to the group.

MATERIALS.   Folk songs still comprise a large part of the repertory. To them are added art songs, religious and patriotic melodies, and popular tunes that reflect good compositional practices.

Organization and Materials of Music

OBJECTIVES.   From simple binary and ternary forms with introductions and codas students are introduced to more complex experiences which may use

pentatonic scales
diatonic scales
the chord progression I–IV–V–I
dorian, phrygian, aeolian, mixolydian, and lydian modes
non-Western tonalities

PROCESS.   The process of learning first by rote, then speaking, singing, playing, expanding the work, and arranging accompaniments is now extended to include an increasing amount of score reading.

MATERIALS.   At this level experimentation may lead to pitched and unpitched compositions, accompaniments for solo instruments or voice; extended forms created from stories, fables, parables or long poems, even incidental music for plays.

Instruments

OBJECTIVES.   Students are expected to play with security all the instruments of the Instrumentarium. The recorder is introduced if that has not already been done.

PROCESS.   Instrumental work is generally led into by having the students first speak then sing what is to be played. For the study of recorder a number of published recorder methods are available.[8]

MATERIALS.   The instrumental music should include works for both small and large voice and instrumental ensembles. They may be drawn from published Orff arrangements or be created by students.

Evaluation

Evaluating learning in such an approach requires far more analysis of performance than the usual school report card allows for. To fill that need the following is suggested:

[8]For example, Carol King, *Recorder Routes: A Guide to Introducing Soprano Recorder in Orff Classes* (Memphis, TN: Memphis Musicraft, 1978).

MUSIC COMMENT SHEET   REPORT PERIOD 1 2 3 4   DATE _____

NAME _____   GRADE 1 2 3 4 5 6 7 8

TEACHER _____

EFFORT _____ 1—SUPERIOR   2—SATISFACTORY   3—INSUFFICIENT
(Only the checked items apply for this report period.)

RHYTHMIC COMPETENCY	ALWAYS	MOST OF TIME	PART OF TIME	SELDOM
Recognizes and responds to primary beat				
Recognizes and responds to secondary beat (pulse) and subdivisions				
Recognizes and is literate of simple rhythm patterns				
VOCAL COMPETENCY				
Sings in tune				
Sings with rhythmic and melodic accuracy				
Articulates, enunciates and uses expression				
Sings with enthusiasm and confidence				
Sings simple melodies from sight (grades 3–8)				
MOVEMENT COMPETENCY				
Moves musically and with confidence				
Uses dance vocabulary and style effectively				
ENSEMBLE				
Works well within the group				
Is supportive of others				
Demonstrates self-control				
Contributes freely				
Plays with good musicianship and confidence				
Plays recorder with good musicianship and confidence (grades 5–8)				

Comment

Lesson Cycle

In middle school, movement can be approached best through concrete images. One way to do this is to relate it to practices such as folk dances, games, or folk rituals that students of the same age do in other cultures. A theme around which a variety of activities can be planned offers both the student and the teacher great latitude to explore and experiment. If the students have had three or more years of Orff training, the experience will simply unfold once a theme has been established; however, more precise or direct instructions will be necessary if they have not grown through an Orff program.

A theme based on Mardi Gras (a holiday centered primarily in New Orleans in the United States and called Carnival in many Latin countries and the Caribbean) would offer opportunities to explore the rhythm, sounds, and dances that accompany the celebration. The exuberant atmosphere around Mardi Gras is a natural impetus to learn about the music to be made, heard, and danced to.

I.   The teaching may begin with imitation, performing warmups with body percussion, emphasizing rhythmic play. Echo patterns can be done in a variety of ways to include clapping, snapping, patting (thighs), and stamping. In preparation for movement in space, the students may use hips, shoulders, buttocks, or knees, moving in place. One such exercise is as follows:
The teacher claps

The students respond with body movement in that rhythm.
The teacher claps

Students respond to each eight beats with movement.

The class is divided into two groups. One group claps the steady beat while the teacher continues to clap rhythmic phrases which the other group echoes. The teacher should work with an eight-bar phrase, two-bar segments at a time.

Once the procedure has been understood and the rhythms are being performed accurately by the students, the teacher may ask a student to act as teacher and make up the same kinds of patterns for the class to echo. This composing by the student is an important first step toward musical independence. The teacher must make sure that the student–teacher observes the same rules of form as those observed by the teacher, and that he or she phrases the piece musically. When one student is creating phrases well, a second student may add different rhythmic phrases, thus creating a layered sound and an effect of polyrhythms. These two students must agree on a common tempo, then begin the improvisation of simultaneous patterns. At this stage the class listens to what is being created. More students may be added as security increases. As specific combinations of patterns emerge from playing the phrases, the teacher and students may isolate the more interesting ones and create ostinati from them. The patterns may then be transferred to an unpitched percussion instrument or body percussion.

At this point the sounds may be transferred to sight. Visual images may be given and, if not known previously, ways of verbalizing durations also may be given.[9] More patterns may then be developed and a list made. Patterns created by the students at this symbolic stage are then combined and rehearsed. Rests are introduced as another possibility, and students also discover the possibility of extensions of sounds over beats into longer durations. Each possibility must first be experimented with and then may be notated and listed.

Next, the teacher may introduce the eighth notes as a subdivision of the quarter note:

These rhythmic elements are all explored and named. At each new rhythm figure the "new" sound is transferred into body percussion and movement games that employ these sound gestures. Patterns are developed into ostinati and these may be scored for unpitched percussion. Students should be led to experiment with the instruments until they find the best pattern for each. Then they may begin to combine with each other and layer sounds until an ensemble is formed. They rehearse this ensemble and perform it for themselves, discussing the various colors and combinations possible.

At this point in the cycle students search for rhythmic styles and variations of sounds used in different cultures, which may be found in recordings and written music. They bring these ideas back to the classroom and try to apply them to their own rhythmic patterns. Frequently the result of such investigation and experimentation is music that is superficially Latin or African in character. More authentic patterns and styles could be introduced by the teacher at this time.[10]

II. RHYTHM AND SPEECH.   At the next step of this lesson cycle the teacher may ask the students to pat the beat on their thighs and echo the following speech piece:

There's a Dance that Everyone Does

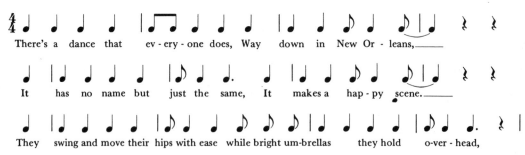

There's a dance that ev-ery-one does, Way down in New Or-leans,____

It has no name but just the same, It makes a hap-py scene.____

They swing and move their hips with ease while bright um-brellas they hold o-ver-head,

---

[9]The rhythmic vocabulary of Kodály practice—*ta* for the beat, *ti* for the pulse—is suggested.
[10]There are several resources for such material: Lynne Jessup, *Afro-Ensemble: A Beginning Book* (Ft. Worth, TX: Harris Music, 1975); W. K. Amoaku, *Orff-Schulwerk in the African Tradition: African Songs and Rhythms for Children—A Selection from Ghana* (Mainz: Schott, 1971).

Don't just stand and look a-round, But join right in the crowd in-stead!

Each phrase is repeated after the teacher until the entire poem is learned. When the text is known, the class says it while tapping the quarter-note beat, then the eighth-note pulse. They then say it while using some of the rhythm patterns practiced earlier as simple ostinato accompaniments or with contrasting rhythmic phrases on unpitched percussion as accompaniment.

III. MELODY The teacher has written the melody on the board without the text but has not drawn attention to it. The song is taught by rote, in two-measure phrases:[11]

Since the text is well known to the students by now, it is possible to move immediately to the words. The students should learn the tune thoroughly and then through experimentation choose the best dynamics and tempo for good expression. Attention to good singing techniques must be maintained throughout the process. If there has been sight singing in the classes prior to this, students will begin to recognize that the tune they are singing is shown on the chalkboard. The class may then sing the song from the score, using *solfa*, numbers, or letter names. Next, they may transfer the melody to barred instruments.

[11]Introducing a tune on the neutral sound "li" is suggested. Even though it is a strong diphthong, it promotes bright, in-tune singing.

Students are encouraged to experiment with the instruments until the piece is learned and a few have mastered the song. When the melody is comfortably in the hands, the students should sing and play it at the same time. They then add percussion, rehearse it, and perform it.

IV. HARMONY.   Because the piece chosen for this lesson cycle clearly implies a I–V harmony, a drone or bordun, such as is customarily used with pentatonic melodies, is not used. Instead, the teacher and students should explore the building of chords in root positions and discover how they are constructed in thirds. The students may experiment with major and minor chord building with instruments. Rhythmic patterns may be added to the chords. The teacher chooses a key (F) and assigns names to the chords in that key. Students identify the I chord as F A C and examine the song to discover where there is use of the notes in the melody. Next, the teacher and students identify the V_7 chord as C E G B♭ and examine the song to discover where there is use of these notes. They then create a pattern using I and V_7 chords and play their instruments, either using these patterns as block chords, alternating two tones of the chord, playing broken chords or arpeggios, or playing the chords in their root position and inversions. The use of the root as a pedal for the chord exercises is introduced.

An accompaniment built on beats

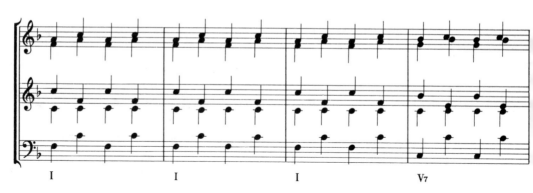

An accompaniment built on pulses

Two accompaniments built on broken chords

I   V₇   I   V₇

The song is sung *a cappella* with some of the class members singing the bass line or other chords. Numbers are assigned to the chords as they relate to the degree of the scale or *solfa* is used to relate the harmony to the singing of the melody. Countermelodies may be invented and tried, for example:

Finally, these singing experiences are transferred back to instruments. Unpitched percussion is added and the work is rehearsed and performed.

V. MOVEMENT.   The internal drive of this tune and rhythm will impel movement from the very beginning. The teacher may focus the class's attention on these movement possibilities: "Concentrate on the smooth back-and-forth hip movement without the use of your shoulders or head." "Let the backbone slip." "Keep the beat with your hips. Let your hips lead the body." "Imagine your knees on one side of the body reacting to your hips on the other side in a sort of contrary motion, shifting weight from side to side."

While stationary the class sings the song on the "li" sound. They then begin to step the beat. The teacher reminds them to "lift your leg from the hip." The "upbeat," or breath, should begin with the hip, followed by the "downbeat" in the foot. They experiment with this movement for a while. Then they try a variety of standard steps such as skipping, jumping, and hopping, but from the hip. When there is sufficient evidence that there is a strong rhythmic base in the body, the teacher encourages them to create a sequential group of movements which support the singing of the melody.[12]

Any of the possibilities suggested here could be used in a performance setting; however, they are not to be thought of as the only possibilities, merely illustrations. The fun of any Orff experience is in the process.

[12]There is a unique and colorful street dance done in New Orleans—a slow skip using the hip, while holding an umbrella—done to the music of jazz bands that accompany many of the celebrations in the city, from weddings to funerals to Mardi Gras.

Conclusion

The format of building a lesson out a of historic, cultural, traditional event such as Mardi Gras is available to any community. Finding the germ of a celebration will give substance and a *raison d'être* to the musical elements to be learned. Music that is associated with an event of any type is less easily forgotten. Other events of different moods may suggest different meters, modes, tempi, colors, and textures. Entire lesson cycles can be built during the calendar year, with either purely secular events or a mixture of sacred and secular events. The variety and contrast possible with musical elements are as limitless as the variety and contrast of seasons and celebrations.

COMPREHENSIVE MUSICIANSHIP

Students at this level of the CM model of broad-based teaching–learning take increased responsibility for their own musical involvement and growth through the individual roles of performer, listener, and composer–improviser. The search, discovery, and intellectual analysis necessary to solve the students' own musical problems and challenges in the context of the three functional roles of performer, listener, and composer lead to a greater knowledge and understanding of traditional and nontraditional practices, patterns, and forces in music.

Learning Objectives

PITCH.   As a creator–improvisor, the student at this CM level experiments with the organization of pitches and sounds in expanded compositions and in complex improvisatory experiences. Students make their own choices regarding the selection of pitch and frequency materials which best suit the compositional or improvisational problem being encountered. Musical examples from the wide spectrum of non-Western and folk music are listened to and analyzed regarding their pitch and tonal construction. Modes, tone rows, non-Western scale forms (such as the Japanese *gagaku*), synthetic scales, and major and minor scale units and patterns are identified through the listening process. These materials are then used in performance activities and in creative experiences. Attention is also given to sequence, diminution, augmentation, and other elements of alteration found in melodic structure. Comparisons are made of the use of scale units and melodic patterns from a variety of musical styles. Whenever possible, these examples are performed by the students on authentic instruments of the time period and culture. Comprehensive studies of pitch arrangement and pattern are a part of the musical whole being emphasized in the class, rehearsal, or individualized instruction.

DURATION.   The awareness of complex rhythmic patterns is extended in composition, analysis, and performance. Scores are used in listening and analytical activities and rhythmic patterns; tempi and meters are identified and defined as part of the musical tools used by the composer. Opportunities for rhythmic growth and for increased understanding of meters and tempi include basic conducting and bodily movement to complicated patterns. As a performer, the student chants or plays on a variety of classroom instruments and authentic folk and non-Western instruments rhythmic ostinatos and accompaniments to song materials. As a composer or improviser, the student utilizes a variety of normal meters, assymetric meters, polyrhythms, polymeters, and a variety of tempi, and tempo changes in compositional activities. In improvisation as well as in composition tempo is used as an aid in defining musical form. As a perceptive listener, the student is able to recognize specific and unique uses of durational patterns, meters, combinations of meters, tempi, and tempo changes in recorded music and in live performances of a wide range of music.

INTENSITY.   As performers, students play or sing using various dynamic levels and changes in dynamics and use these dynamic properties and possibilities in the expressive interpretation of music. As listeners, students analyze, describe, and compare the use of dynamics by various composers and in folk and non-Western music. As composers and improvisers, students illustrate the use of dynamic variation as a source of tension and release in music, as a source of unity and variety in music, and as an aid in defining musical form.

TIMBRE.   As performers, students have opportunities to perform on a variety of traditional, folk, and non-Western instruments. Students should be aware of specific vocal timbres and the personal changes in vocal timbre that they are experiencing. As listeners, students identify a variety of vocal timbres, electronic timbres, and environmental timbres. Students also compare and describe the influence of instrumental size and shape on the resulting overtone structure. As composers and improvisers, students utilize a variety of traditional, folk, and non-Western instruments in their compositions and improvisatory pieces. They explore new sound possibilities on traditional instruments and they experiment with various effects in the use of electronic sound (such as filtering, mixing, echoing, reverberation, and modulation). Notation, both traditional and nontraditional, is used in these compositions.

The Organization of Pitch, Duration, Intensity, and Timbre

The interaction of these musical properties and elements creates more complex melodic, rhythmic, harmonic, and textural arrangements for student involvement and exploration at this level of the CM model.

HORIZONTAL ORGANIZATION.   The interaction of duration and pitch creates melodic structures and rhythmic patterns with extended possibilities for study. Scale forms of all types are used in compositional materials and are performed and analyzed by the students. A wide range of regular and irregular rhythmic patterns, meters, and tempi are used in performance, composition, and analysis.

VERTICAL ORGANIZATION.   Students increase their understanding and utilization of inversions, chord changes, chord progressions, augmented chords, diminshed chords, noteclusters, and simultaneous environmental sounds. The students improvise, compose, perform, and analyze harmonic progressions illustrating differing degrees of tonality. Students are exposed to modulation, polytonality, freetonality, and atonality.

FORM.   Students compare binary and ternary musical forms in music they listen to, perform, and create. They become familiar with canons, fugues, rondos, sonatas, suites, symphonies, rhapsodies, ballads, intermezzos, overtures, operas, Masses, motets, songs, serial compositions, and other forms.

MUSICAL CONTEXTS.   The student should be aware of the social, aesthetic, and historical contexts of world music used at this level of the CM model.

Lesson Plans

The following examples of lesson plans for students in Grades 6 to 8 emphasize personal growth for each student as a performer, as an analytical listener, and as a creator-composer. The experiences in these lessons provide the students with opportunities to synthesize and to apply the skills and knowledge developed in music learning activities at earlier stages of the CM process.

LESSON PLAN A

1. Create and analyze. The tuned musical bow was used in many of the ancient cultures of Africa, Asia, and the Americas. Attached gourds, the human chest or abdomen, or the human mouth cavity were used as resonating chambers for the bows. The sound was usually made by plucking the string or strings on the musical bows or by tapping the strings with a thin stick.

    a. Show the students in the class the following examples of the compound musical bows:

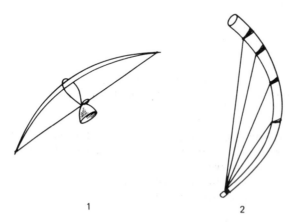

1   2

Example 1 is thought to have been created and used in West Africa to accompany folk songs and chants.

    b. Have the students in the class follow these steps in constructing the West African musical bow:

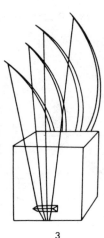

3

a. Locate a green branch or a twig about four feet long and one half inch in diameter. Bring the branch or twig to class.

b. Attach twine or nylon string to the branch to make a bow.

c. Locate a hollow gourd about four inches in diameter and bring it to class.

d. Cut the gourd in half and tie the stem to a piece of string.

e. Loop the string from the gourd loosely around the bow string.

f. Attach another piece of string to the stem of the gourd and loop it over the bow itself.

g. Have the students play the musical bow by placing the gourd against their bellies. Have the students tap the string lightly with a thin stick while slipping the bow back and forth through the string on the gourd.

2. Perform

a. Have the students play the following tones on their musical bows:

b. After the students can play the above notes with ease, have them sing and play on their musical bows the African folk song "Hey, Tswana."

c. Divide the students into two groups and have them perform "Hey, Tswana" in canon as they sing and play the musical bows.

d. Have the students experiment with several different tempi for the folk

song and have them try playing and singing the song at several different dynamic levels.

Hey, Tswana

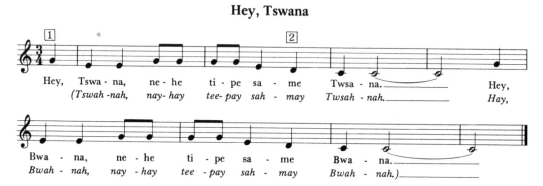

Hey, Tswa - na, ne - he ti - pe sa - me Twsa - na. Hey,
(Tswah -nah, nay- hay tee- pay sah - may Twsah - nah. Hay,

Bwa - na, ne - he ti - pe sa - me Bwa - na. Hey,
Bwah - nah, nay - hay tee - pay sah - may Bwah - nah.)

3. Analyze: Have the students in the class identify by sight and by sound the
   intervals used in "Hey, Tswana."
4. Perform
   a. Have the students clap a steady beat pattern while counting softly from
      one to twelve.
   b. Assign the following instruments to the students in the class to play
      while reading the African drumming score:

claves   triangle
conga drum   hand drum
cowbell   quiro

Have the students inner-hear the steady beat pattern from 1–12 as
they play the drumming score.

BEAT	1	2	3	4	5	6	7	8	9	10	11	12
claves	X	X			X	X			X	X		X
conga drum	X	X	X	X	X	X					X	
cowbell	X	X		X			X	X	X	X		
triangle	X		X		X		X		X	X	X	
hand drum				X		X		X	X			X

   c. Repeat the pattern several times and then shift instruments and parts
      from person to person.
   d. Have the students experiment with various tempi as they play the
      score.

5. Create
   a. Have each student draw a chart for an African drumming score.
   b. After each student has a blank chart prepared have them create an African drumming pattern on the score. The students may change the instrumentation of the score if they wish.
6. Perform and analyze
   a. Have each student in the class perform his or her own African drumming pattern for the other students. Ask each student to use a variety of tempi and dynamics throughout the performance.
   b. Have several students perform their African drumming scores at the same time in order to create rhythmic and timbral textures. Have the students discuss the difference made by the addition of the other performers.
7. Perform: Give the students in the class each a copy of the score of "The Street" by Tchaikovsky. Ask the students to sing all verses of the song with the piano accompaniment.

The Street

Translation by Anne Grossman

Piotr Ilyich Tchaikovsky

1. The thaw - ing snow makes the drip - ping roof wet. See the
   rains all day: crackl - ing reeds go swish, swish. Lit - tle

mis - tress laugh - ing so, mas - ter is - n't home yet, See the
moth-er's ver - y pleased; lit - tle fa - ther brought fish, Lit - tle

mis - tress laugh - ing so, mas - ter is - n't home yet. 2. It
moth-er's ver - y pleased; lit - tle fa - ther brought fish. 3. My die.

Verse 3
>   My little dove, little mother, I wish
>   You would quickly get the pot, make a soup of the fish.

Verse 4
>   Put parsley too, and the chowder will froth.
>   Little father loves you so, little father's fish broth.

Verse 5
>   And I will drink and I'll wander nearby.
>   When the time to live is gone, then I surely will die.

8. Analyze
   a. Have the students determine why Tchaikovsky used accents only on the first four beats of the song. Have the students analyze the text, the melody, and the harmony in order to formulate their answers.
   b. Tchaikovsky indicated only one dynamic marking in the entire song. Ask the students to suggest alternate ideas for dynamic levels throughout the piece. Have the students sing the song several times using different dynamics each time. Have the students decide on the best dynamic markings for the piece based on the text as well as the musical style.
   c. Have the students in the class determine the key of "The Street" and have them write the chord symbols under each chord in the piece. Have the students compare their chord analyses with each other.

9. Create
   a. Tchaikovsky has created pictures of events and feelings through his use of text material and the musical elements in his song, "The Street." Have the students in the class collect sounds representing feelings and events in their own environments. Have them use cassette recorders to record sound events in their homes, on their streets, and in their schools.
   b. Divide the students into small groups and have the students in each group share their recorded sound events with each other. Have each

group select five recorded events to use in a tape composition in rondo form. Have the students select one taped event to be the recurring A Section. Have the students select other taped events for the different sections of the A–B–A–C–A–D–A–E–A rondo form.

c. Have the students in each group put together a tape composition using the selected events. Have the students in the group transfer the sounds to one master tape.

10. Perform and analyze

a. Have each group present their tape composition to the class.

b. Ask the students in the class to make suggestions regarding the ordering of the events on the tape and to evaluate the contrasts evident between each of the sections of the tape composition.

LESSON PLAN B

1. Perform: Have selected students in the class perform the following quartet on recorders.

Nachtanz

J.H. Schein

2. Analyze
   a. Provide each student in the class with a copy of the score of the recorder quartet "Nachtanz," by Schein. Have the students in the class follow the score as the piece is played.
   b. Since the score does not provide dynamic indications, have the students make suggestions regarding dynamic variation for the quartet players to use. Have the students state musical reasons for their suggestions for the dynamic markings.
   c. Discuss with the students that a phrase is a division of a musical line, somewhat like a sentence in a paragraph. Most often each phrase has its own expressive or dramatic shape. That is, each phrase normally has an expressive goal or objective. Ask the students to mark the phrasing for each of the parts of the "Nachtanz" quartet. Have the recorder players perform the suggestions for the phrasing as made by members of the class. Discuss the musical goals and objectives for the suggested phrase markings.
   d. Have the students analyze each interval in each part of the first four measures of the quartet. Divide the class into four groups and assign one voice of the quartet for each of the groups. Have the students sing the first four measures of the quartet using a neutral syllable such as "la."

e. Have the recorder players perform the quartet once again and have the students in the class conduct the quartet using proper conducting technique.

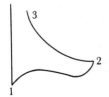

3. Perform and analyze
    a. Provide each student in the class with a score of the Latin round "Dona nobis pacem." Divide the students into three singing groups and have them perform the round in three parts.
    b. Have the students redesign the dynamic markings of the song, to allow for the best possible vocal texture when it is performed as a round.

Dona Nobis Pacem

c. Select a student to conduct "Dona nobis pacem" as the class sings. Have the student use the proper conducting technique for triple meter.
d. Have the students in the class mark the phrases in "Dona nobis pacem." Have the class sing the song several times in unison using several of the phrasing suggestions recommended by students in the class. Have the students in the class decide on the phrasing to use which best reflects a specific expressive goal in the piece.

4. Create
    a. Have each student in the class compose an eight-measure melody in $\frac{3}{4}$ meter using the words, "Dona nobis pacem" for a text. Ask the students to compose their melodies in F-Major and to use simple rhythmic patterns. Have the students indicate phrasing and dynamic markings for their melodies.

b. Have selected students write their melodies with the text on the chalkboard and have the class sing them.

c. Ask the students in the class also to perform the melodies as three-voice rounds.

d. Have the students compare their composed rounds to the original "Dona nobis pacem" round.

5. Perform

a. Provide each student in the class with a score of the Maori warrior song, "Titi-Toria." Have the students sing "Titi-Toria."

Titi-Toria

b. Ask a student in the class to conduct "Titi-Toria" using the proper conducting technique for triple meter. Have the class sing the song as the student conducts.

6. Move: The Maori warriors of New Zealand played stick games to increase their hunting skills. Have the students select partners and kneel on the floor facing each other. Give each student a pair of sticks (dowel pieces twelve inches in length and one half inch in diameter). Have the students hold one stick in each hand.

    During section A of "Titi-Toria," have the students hit the floor with both sticks on the first beat of each measure and then hit their sticks together in front of them on the second beat of each measure. On the third beat, have the students throw their right-hand stick to their partner and then catch their partner's right-hand stick.

    During section B, have the students hit their sticks on the floor on the first beat of each measure and together on the second and third beats of each measure.

    During the C section, have the students hit their sticks on the floor on the first beat of the measure and have them hit their sticks together in front of them on the second beat. Have the students throw their left-hand stick to their partner and catch their partner's left-hand stick on the third beat of the measure.

    Ask the students to sing the song as they play the stick-passing game.

7. Analyze: Ask the students to identify the form of "Titi-Toria" by noting the changes in the stick movement pattern. Have a selected student write the form on the chalk board. (A B C B A B).

8. Create

    a. Have the students create different stick patterns to use with "Titi-Toria."

    b. Have the students create stick-passing patterns for two sets of partners instead of just one.

    c. Experiment with faster and slower tempi as the song is sung and the games are played.

Summary

In Lesson A, the students are exposed to the following musical concepts:

> resonation
> sound production
> tempo
> dynamics
> intervals
> rhythmic texture
> timbral texture
> accent
> melody
> harmony
> rondo form

In this lesson, the students perform an African folk song on a musical bow which they construct in class. The students also create African rhythmic patterns and perform them, noting the rhythmic and timbral textures. The students also perform and analyze the song "The Street," by Tchaikovsky and then create environmental tape compositions based on the textual themes of the song. In these experiences and activities the students are exposed to the elements of music from a variety of cultures through performance, analysis, and composition.

In Lesson B, the students are exposed to the following musical concepts:

dynamics
phrasing
vocal texture
meter
form

The students are active participants in the music-making process in all facets of this lesson. They are involved with the basic elements of music as conductors, singers, instrumental performer, listeners, and composers.

CONCLUSION

The further up the learning cone or spiral one travels, the greater become the separations among these four approaches, each of which is, in its own different way, developing thorough musicianship.

11

METHOD IN MUSIC
FOR OLDER STUDENTS

INTRODUCTION

The Program Cone developed for the Music Educators National Conference (see p. 116) maintains at the senior high school and adult level the separation begun at the junior high school level between those people directed toward a profession in music and those for whom music is to be a leisure-time activity.

Under the preprofessonal side of the cone one finds such activities as listening, theory, ensemble, band, orchestra, music history, composition, instrumental and voice study, stage bands, and madrigal groups. But where in any public school system in North America are such choices available? They may exist, of course, in special music high schools in cities that have a population large enough to support such specialization, but they are rare even in those situations.

The special private schools, the conservatories, and the community music schools have taken over this specialized training, but they should not have to. While the public schools offer sufficient background in mathematics to those hoping to become engineers, and sufficient foreign language training for those hoping to major in French or Spanish in college, they offer little training to those who want to be professional musicians. Only in music are the preprofessionals expected themselves to obtain and pay for the education they need to gain acceptance into any good music school, university music department, or conservatory.

Career opportunities abound, as indicated in the MENC Program Cone. Not all serious music students can or even wish to be concert artists. Many more wish to teach music—instrumental, vocal, or school music. There are opportunities for well-trained musicians in recreation, therapy, ballet, opera, and films—both in the limelight and behind the scenes. There is a need for talented accompanists, coaches, and church musicians—singers, choir directors, and organists. Music librarians, music critics, arrangers, and copyists can always find employment. Orchestral performance and, of course, conducting and composing are all possible careers for the well-trained musician. Career opportunities in music today are manifold; the list above has not even touched on the increasingly widening field of synthesizer design, use, performance, and composition.

Must all the training for these many careers wait until high school graduation at age eighteen or nineteen? Why is it that automobile mechanics can receive career training at the age of 16 in most large secondary schools, while preprofessional musicians are limited to performing in the high school band, orchestra, or choir; and must receive any other training privately—and that only if their families can afford it?

The nonprofessional stream in the MENC Program Cone suggests participaton in community groups (choirs, bands, orchestras, small ensemebles), singing in church choirs, taking courses in music appreciation, studying piano (privately, or course), reading books on music, collecting records, and so on.

What in the usual general music program throughout the grades has enabled the nonprofessional to do any of these things? What church choir director wants a choir full of people who cannot read music? What level of performance can be expected from the community orchestra, band, or choir that is predominantly musically illiterate?

Who goes to concerts? People who know and love music. In addition to the professional musicians in the audience, these are generally people who have studied music privately at some point in their lives. The ones whose total musical instruction consisted of a "What would you like to sing today?" elementary school approach, followed by the usual bedlam of junior high school general music, may be found at rock concerts, may buy the latest fad record, but are most unlikely to be found in the audience of a quartet performing Brahms' chamber music, or at the Oratorio Society's performance of the *St. Matthew Passion*. And if the earlier experiences are perhaps not all that bad, it is the "pops" concert these "lost" students just *may* attend, never the concert featuring the newest work of a twentieth-century composer.

These words are written not in condemnation but in fear. Every day of a teacher's life is spent either building up or tearing down—there is no standing still in a field as vital as music. For too long the subject of music has been losing stature in academic circles. It is the first subject to be given less time in curriculum; the first to be cut when budget adjustments must be made. Too often, music teachers themselves seem to believe their subject is somehow less important than calculus or athletics. It is not! Of *all* subjects it has the most to offer the most people for the longest time—for the rest of their lives. But it must be *taught;* taught in the schools, not just in special institutions, and it must be taught to all students, not just to the few that someone has singled out as "talented." The list of stories of renowned concert artists and composers discouraged by, to put it generously, "insensitive" teachers is too long to bear close inspection. It is the music teacher's job, the music teacher's *obligation,* to teach—to encourage those who may seem talented, but to *teach all.*

With this in mind, what kinds of musical experiences are offered within the frameworks of Jaques-Dalcroze, Kodály, Orff, and Comprehensive Musicianship for the high school, college, or adult student?

JAQUES-DALCROZE

Lessons on Solfège and Solfège-Rythmique

SUBJECT. ♩ → ♫ and ♩ ♩ → 𝅗𝅥 subdivision (twice as fast; twice as slow).

EQUIPMENT   Chalkboard, piano, electric keyboard, bellchime, xylophone, or other pitched instruments.

STEP I: WARMUP—TO ELIMINATE THE TIME LAG
BETWEEN HEARING, THINKING, AND PRODUCING
SOUND

1. Teacher: *I'll sing a series of notes with arm and hand gestures. Echo me after each note.*

The teacher sings in a moderate tempo on a neutral syllable ("loo"), using hand and arm gestures and different levels to indicate variations in pitch, range, attack qualities, dynamics, and legato or staccato articulation. The teacher begins with little variation, but adds more as the exercise develops. The students respond with sound and gesture. For example:

Teacher: *Let's repeat the exercise adding* solfa *syllables* (fixed-*do* C).

The students echo not only the pitch but also the musical qualities.

2. **Teacher:**   *This time don't wait for me! Sing back and make the gesture as fast as you can.*
    For example:

[If students miss some point of musical information (dynamics, accent, or position or quality of the physical gesture), the teacher must repeat the example on the same pitch until the response if correct.]

3. **Teacher:**   *Now I'll sing two-note groups. Sing them back as quickly as you can. Don't forget to use hand and arm gestures.*

For example:

4. **Teacher:**   *Now stretch your memory. I'll sing and gesture three-note groups. Repeat them just as soon as you've heard the end of the third note.*

For example:

STEP II

1. **Teacher:**   *This time I'll play single notes on the piano (bells, xylophone, etc.). Sing them back as quickly as you can, using your own gesture and the syllable "loo."*

[This exercise is more difficult because the student must translate the range and timbre (color) of an instrument with different overtones to its voice equivalent.]

The teacher and students perform the same exercise on two-note gesture groups and then on three-note groups.

STEP III: SCALE STUDIES AND TONALITY

1. Teacher: *Do you remember the sound of* do *(middle C) in the C-Major scale? Can you feel it, hear it, sense it? Get ready to sing it with the syllable* do.

(The teacher pauses.) The students work in every lesson on memorizing this sound.
   The teacher conducts. Students try to sing middle C of the C-Major scale. (The *pitch* of C is the same in any scale, but its *quality* is not.)

Teacher: (If the ensemble is not perfect in intonation) *Let's try it again. I'll help a little. Listen! Here's the road to* do.

The teacher sings or plays

Teacher: *Hum the road to* do *and sing* do *at the end.*

The students hum

2. Teacher: *Can you do the road to C Major in your body and mind? Don't sing the road, just gesture its shape and pull. Then we'll sing* do!

The teacher conducts and students join in the silent performance of ♩ ♫♩ ♩,
                                                                        s   s s l t

then sing | o   ‖
             do

Teacher: *Good! I may ask you for that* do *anytime during the lesson, so try to remember the feeling, the place and the sound, and even the road that invites you to* do.

[The teacher does not give *do,* unless absolutely necessary, but leads the students to *do* through feeling and hearing the invitation to the tonic that the dominant gives. This feeling is essential to the performance of Western music and even helps in understanding the weaker forms of the dominant in certain types of pentatonic music. The dominant is the glue that holds a scale together.]

3. The teacher writes the ascending C-Major scale on a chalkboard, using noteheads without stems.

Teacher: *Let's sing our* do-*major scale with syllables in walking tempo. Show the position of each tone and the distance between them with hand and arm gestures as you sing.*

The teacher demonstrates the gestures, starting at hip level, raising hand and arm at each note so that the high *do* is sung when the arm and hand are fully extended above the head.

Teacher: *Can you remember and find your starting* do?

If students seem unsure or have difficulty, the teacher and students again sing "the dominant road to the tonic."

Teacher: *Let's begin.*

The teacher conducts at a moderate tempo, while the students practice the sounds and gestures of the ascending C-Major scale.

4. Teacher: *Let's do it again and show the pulls and pushes of the scale, not only in our arms but also in the energy we use in our singing.*

The teacher and students sing and gesture again, adding functional pulls and pushes between tones III and IV, using a small pushing upward gesture of the fingers and wrists while the arm makes a very small movement to show the size of the space from *mi* to *fa.* The teacher and students show an even stronger pull on tones VII to VIII, with the arms and hands extended upward.

[There is no set series of gestures, positions, and postures used by all teachers of this method. Many of the movements used are invented or suggested by the students. Standardized gestures can be used, but must be presented as movement through space and gravity and not simply as positions without function.]

5. The teacher adds the descending C-Major scale to the ascending one on the chalkboard.

Teacher: (Pointing to the board) *Let's sing our scale descending with gestures. Remember that tone VII will work and feel differently now, so make your gesture and your singing show that difference. Have you got the high-*do*? Let's hear and see it.*

The students respond.

> [If students have lost correct intonation, the teacher asks: "Is it too low? too high?" If necessary, the teacher may again sing the dominant road to reinforce tonal centering.]

The teacher and students use gestures and voice to sing the descending scale. The teacher must be careful to show the size and quality of the half-steps VIII to VII and IV to III and the tremendous pull of the cadence from II to I.

6. Teacher: *This time sing, gesture, and even move the scale with your whole body by getting up from your seats slowly; show the departures, arrivals, and passages through the scale space world.*

The teacher and students sing, gesture, and move ascending to high *do* and then descending with a molto ritardando and diminuendo on II going to I.

> [This total body movement helps students to feel the various gravitational or tonal weights, pulls, and releases of the scale.]

STEP IV: SCALE MOVEMENT JOINED
TO RHYTHMIC MOVEMENT

1. Teacher: *Do you remember our work on* ♩ ♩ ♩ ♩ *and on*

one one one one

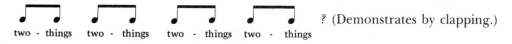

two - things two - things two - things two - things ? (Demonstrates by clapping.)

The teacher and students review the changes in tempo from ♩ to ♫ and ♫

to ♩ .

2. **Teacher:** (Pointing to ♩ and ♫ on the chalkboard) *Let's sing and gesture our*

scale ascending, using syllables first in ♩ *, then in* ♫ *, and then back to*

♩. *Remember, when you do the fast tempo, make your arm and hand ges-*
tures smaller. (Setting the tempo):

Here's   the   beat   now.

The teacher leads the students into dynamics of *crescendo* as they sing and ges-

ture:[1] 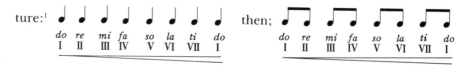 then;

do	re	mi	fa	so	la	ti	do		do	re	mi	fa	so	la	ti	do
I	II	III	IV	V	VI	VII	I		I	II	III	IV	V	VI	VII	I

3. **Teacher:** *Good! Let's try it descending in a* ♩ *tempo and feel the difference. We'll*
start strong and make a diminuendo to increase the feeling of leaving.
Make a good landing at the bottom.

The teacher sets a tempo and the teacher and students gesture and sing:

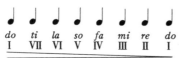

do	ti	la	so	fa	mi	re	do
I	VII	VI	V	IV	III	II	I

Teacher: *Now let's try it in* ♫ *tempo, twice as fast.*

The teacher and students gesture and sing

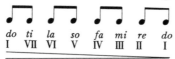

do	ti	la	so	fa	mi	re	do
I	VII	VI	V	IV	III	II	I

4. **Teacher:** *Let's join the ascending and descending versions of this scale.*

The teacher and students gesture and sing the ascending and descending versions of this scale with appropriate dynamics. After having practices gesturing
and singing the ascending and descending versions of this C-Major scale with

appropriate dynamics in the ♩ tempo, they repeat this in the ♪ tempo.

[1]In Jaques-Dalcroze practice, roman numerals are used to indicate both the degree of the
scale and the root of the chord.

STEP V: THE QUICK REACTION

1. **Teacher:** *Let's try a quick reaction game. When I say "Change," switch from ♩*

    to ♩♩ .

The teacher sets four ♩ as the starting tempo. The students sing and gesture:

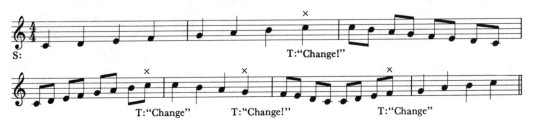

2. **Teacher:** *Let's try that while conducting in two-beat time.*

The teacher and students sing and conduct in **2** and then in **2** .

STEP VI: DEVELOPING INNER MEMORY OF PITCH
AND TEMPO CHANGES

1. **Teacher:** (Pointing to the notes on the board) *Let's sing the ascending version.*
    This time, if I say "Stop!" we'll stop singing out loud and sing silently inside
    instead. When I say "Sing!" we'll again sing outside. Let's try it at the

    ♩ tempo.

The students sing until the teacher says "Stop!" The teacher uses a pointer to
show silent notes and to give the signals for "Sing!" and "Stop!" The students
follow, singing "outside" or "inside," and using gestures throughout.

   Teacher: *Let's do it at the ♪ tempo.*

Again, the teacher gestures, points and gives verbal commands for changes, and
the students follow.

2. **Teacher:** *Now for a really tough game: "Sing!" means sing, "Stop!" means silent*

    singing, "Walk!" means ♩ tempo, and "Run!" means ♪ tempo. You may
    have to change the tempo feeling inside yourself.

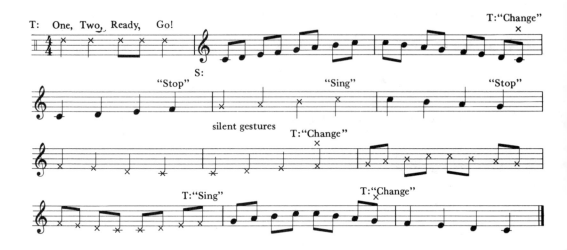

STEP VII: PATTERNS OF ♩ AND ♩♪♪ ;
DICTATION AND FORMATION OF MELODY FROM
THE SCALE

1. **Teacher:** *Listen to this rhythm pattern:*

(The teacher claps, speaks, chants, or drums, and demonstrates
arm movement right to left, mirroring what the students are to do.)
The students clap, moving arms left to right on each measure.

Teacher: *Can you analyze by speaking the "ones" and the "two-things?"*

The students clap and speak: ‖: **one two-things** :‖

2. The teacher writes the numbers "1" and "2" on the chalkboard as shorthand

for "one" and "two-things," and then notates them ♩ ♩♪ .
                                                  1   2

Teacher: *Read and clap it once again.*

The students clap and speak the rhythm.

3. **Teacher:** *Let's see what will happen if we apply this rhythm to our scale. But first, let's*

speak our syllables in the rhythm ♩ ♩♪♪ , remembering that the weight is
at the beginning of the pattern and then the rhythm moves forward towards

the next ♩ .

The students explore, speaking the scale names (♩ ♫ ♩) with a crescendo

                                                     do re mi

ascending and a diminuendo descending.

4. **Teacher:** *Now let's conduct in two-beat time as we speak the* ♩   ♫

                                                               do   *re mi*

    pattern. . . . . *Now let's sing and conduct it this way.*

The teacher points to the notated scale in rhythm, indicating at the same time the appropriate dynamics, phrasing, accents, and agogics:

[The teacher must be careful to observe the crescendo in each measure,

created by the ♫ notes, as well as the overall crescendo.]

5. **Teacher:** *That makes an interesting melody; but I think we were so busy with notes and rhythms and with reading and thinking that we forgot about the dynamic expression. That* ♩ ♫ *pattern is called a dactylic rhythm:*

♩   ♫ ♩   ♫

dac - tyl - ic   dac - tyl - ic

The students repeat the term in rhythm.

    Teacher: *Now let's do the melody again and get it all—pitches, rhythm, dynamics, phrasing, accents, agogics—and make it* music! (The teacher sets a tempo and students explore again, using singing and hand gestures.) *It feels different starting from the top and moving down. Let's try it.*

The teacher and students explore.

6. **Teacher:** *Now let's reverse the rhythmic pattern to* ♫ ♩ . (The teacher demonstrates by speaking and clapping.) *Try it with me.* (The students

practice while speaking and clapping.) *Let's add conducting beats in* $\frac{2}{4}$

time and speak the pattern.

7. Teacher: (Afterwards) *Did you notice that though there is an accent at the beginning of the pattern, the weight is at the end? Let's hear what kind of melody comes out if we use this rhythmic pattern when we sing the scale.*

The teacher uses the pointer to lead the group up and down the scale. The students sing and conduct the measures.

Teacher: *That pattern is called an anapest. Try saying it in rhythm.*
Students:

Teacher: *What happens if we join these two patterns to make a longer and new pattern?*

Students
and teacher:

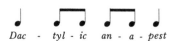

The teacher writes on the chalkboard: ♩ ♫ ♫ ♩ . The students
read and clap, then read and speak, conducting in two-beat time.

Teacher: *Let's sing and conduct the combined pattern on the scale. End the melody when we come to* do *on a strong (down-)beat.*

The students sing and conduct as directed.

Teacher: *Let's start on the high* do *and sing down the scale.*

The teacher and students experiment with new patterns of 𝅗𝅥 and 𝅘𝅥𝅘𝅥 and apply them to the scale (𝅗𝅥 𝅗𝅥 𝅘𝅥𝅘𝅥𝅗𝅥 , 𝅘𝅥𝅘𝅥 𝅘𝅥𝅘𝅥𝅗𝅥 𝅗𝅥 , etc.) .

8. Teacher: *Can we read this melody?*

The teacher writes the following on the chalkboard, first without expression marks:

Teacher: *Let's clap and speak the patterns, first without singing.* (The students speak and clap; then speak while conducting the rhythmic patterns in $\frac{4}{4}$.) *What about dynamics?*

The students repeat the reading, this time adding crescendo, diminuendo, and agogic accents (weight on long notes), thus adding correct musical variation to the phrasing.

Teacher: *Now read it speaking the syllables.* (The students say the *solfa* names in rhythm.) *Are you ready now to add the pitches?* (The students sing and conduct the melody.) *Did we forget anything? dynamics? accents? weight?* (The students evaluate their performance.) *Let's try it again for our most artistic performance.*

The students sing and try to include everything. They then analyze what they performed and add expression symbols to the notation on the chalkboard.

STEP VIII: MELODIC SEGMENTATION,
INTERVALS, AND MELODIES OF THE MAJOR

SCALE ♩ ⟶ ♫ AND ♫ ⟶ ♩

> [Jaques-Dalcroze divides scales and modes into segments or cells consisting of dichords (two adjacent note cells), trichords, tetrachords, and so on. These form the basic groups of scale tones that combine to make melody; they also determine harmony and counterpoint.]

1. **Teacher:** *Let's review our trichords going up the major scale, like this.* (The teacher points to trichord groups from the C-Major scale on the chalkboard.)

The teacher demonstrates, using syllables, quality of pointing gesture, voice intonations, and emphasis to express starting place, direction, and size of interval (half- or whole-step), size of trichord (major or minor), function (small consecutive crescendi ascending, small consecutive diminuendi descending), and the weight and pull of the dominant tones II, V, and VII. The teacher, pointing with expressive gestures, speaks: "DO–re–mi," then sings: "DO–re–mi," then writes I $\uparrow \atop 3$

and speaks: "trichord 1"; next, speaks and then sings: "RE–mi–fa," writes II $\uparrow \atop 3$ and speaks: "trichord 2."

Teacher: *Can you continue the sequence up?*

The students speak the syllables with hand and arm gestures, then sing them:

"MI–fa–so" as the teacher writes III $\uparrow \atop 3$. The teacher and students speak: "trichord

3." The process continues through TI–do–re (VII $\uparrow \atop 3$) and finishes by cadencing on do (ti–do–re–DO).

Teacher: *Let's sing all the ascending trichords in this dactylic rhythm.*

The teacher points to ♩ ♫ and sets a ♩ tempo. The students sing and gesture the trichords, finishing with a cadencing trichord ending on *DO* (I):

♩ ♩ ♩ | o . During this activity the teacher helps students to feel the phras-
ti   do   re   DO

ing, accents, and crescendo.

2. **Teacher:** *Now we'll do the descending trichords.*

The teacher points to tones in ♩ ♩ ♩ 𝄾 rhythm as the students speak the syllables in trichord groups descending to *do*.

Teacher: *Sing and follow me.*

All sing "*do–ti–LA.*" The teacher writes VI $\overset{3}{\underset{\downarrow}{}}$. As the students sing the next tri-

chord descending (*TI–la–so*) the teacher writes V $\overset{3}{\underset{\downarrow}{}}$. The students continue in

this fashion while the teacher writes the symbols for each trichord. The teacher and students continue until they reach the cadencing trichord

I $\overset{3}{\underset{\downarrow}{}}$: ♩   ♩   ♩   𝄾

    mi   *re*   *DO*
    >   –

> [In the above the roman numeral indicates the lowest note of the trichord, the arabic numeral the number of steps, and the arrow the direction.]

3. Teacher: *I'll sing the first note. You finish with the next two notes of the ascending trichord.* (The teacher sings *DO*.)
   Students: (In tempo) re–mi.
   Teacher: RE.
   Students: mi–fa.

The teacher and students continue in this fashion until they reach trichord 7 (*TI–do–re*), and then cadence to the tonic (*DO*).

4. Teacher: *Now do the same thing descending. I'll start with DO, you fill in the other notes.* (The teacher sings *DO*.)
   Students: (In tempo) ti–LA.
   Teacher: TI.
   Students: la–SO.

The teacher and students continue in this fashion until VII $\overset{3}{\underset{\downarrow}{}}$ (*re–do–TI*),

cadencing on *DO*.

> [This ordered sequence is called *adjacent trichords*.]

5. Teacher: *Let's sing the trichords again, but sing the middle note silently inside. Be sure to show how it feels by a gesture.*
   Students: DO, (*re,* silent), mi; RE, (*mi,* silent), fa, (etc.).

[This exercise aids the intonation of major and minor thirds.]

6. **Teacher:** *I'll sing the first and last notes; you sing the middle note, but show them all by active gestures.*

    Teacher: DO.
    Students: re.
    Teacher: mi.

The teacher and students continue this exercise through all the trichords, both ascending and descending.

7. **Teacher:** *Now let's apply rhythmic changes to the trichords and hear what kind of music comes out.*

The students explore, using ♩ ♪♪ and ♪♪ ♩ and other known patterns.

Teacher: (Demonstrating with hand gestures on each note) *We can sing DO,*

re, mi (♩ ♪♪) *once, or we can sing it twice, doing it twice as fast*

(♪♪♪ ♪♪♪) *. Let's try it first with the ascending scale and then*
   d r m d r m

the descending scale.

The teacher conducts the rhythm and pitch movement with hand gestures. The students follow, matching the teacher's hand signals.

Teacher: *Now let's do it in reverse. We'll sing the fast version first—*

| ♪♪♪ ♪♪♪ | *—and   then   sing   the   slow   version*
DO re mi DO re mi

once— | ♩ ♩ ♩ 𝄾 | *. Change the gestures to fit the changes in*
   DO re mi

tempo—
they must be smaller and lighter for the eighth notes.

8. **Teacher:** *Let's try it in walking tempo and then change to the running version. Conduct in* **2/4** *as you sing.*

[This exercise is conducted throughout in **𝟐**. It is important to encourage a feeling for and a knowledge of the difference between subdivision changes—

and actual change of the beat—

Notice that the crescendo marks extend through the rests and affect the conducting.]

9. **Teacher:** *Here's a new melody in trichords. Can you translate it into singing?*

The teacher writes on the chalkboard ♩ ♩ ♩ ᒐ ;   ♩ ♩ ♩ ᒐ .
do re mi   fa mi re

[To prevent purely rote reading, Jaques-Dalcroze himself used five different ways for notating pitch grouping, position, and function.
1. traditional staff notation
2. syllable notation with *do* as C
3. roman numerals with I as the first degree of the scale in each key

4. segmentation groups, such as I $\overset{\uparrow}{3}$ [*do–re–mi*]

5. pitch heads with arabic numerals

[By working with a variety of notation styles, students are forced to use their minds to hear, see, and think of relationships more clearly. Some of these techniques also offer a quick shorthand suitable for melodic dictation. They are useful from elementary grades through the most serious professional musical training.]

Teacher: *Who can come to the board and write this in noteheads?*

A student writes:

Teacher: *Let's sing it from this notehead (staff) notation.*

The students sing.

Teacher: *Now let's sing it from the syllable notation.* (Pointing to board.)

The students sing.

Teacher: *Now let's read it in code.* (Points to numbered notation.)

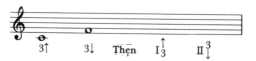

Teacher: *Let's experiment with some other ways of reading, thinking about, and analyzing a melody of trichords. Can you sing* I↑₃ *and then* III↑₃ ?

Students: (Singing) *DO–re–mi and MI–fa–so.*
Teacher: *We could show that melody like this or this or this.* (Points to the chalkboard.)

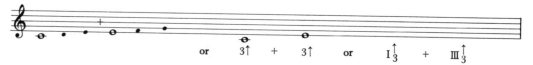

The students read the different versions, speaking, but using accents to illustrate the ascending or descending nature of the line.

Teacher: *Let's sing* so–fa–MI *and* mi–re–DO.

The students sing and then write:

Teacher: *Let's read a whole melody in code. We'll do the rhythm with gestures first, then add syllables with gestures and then sing trichord groups with gestures.*

The teacher shows

The students read and perform.

Teacher: *Can you do the same with this version?*

The students read the rhythm and then sing with pitch.

STEP IX: READING, THINKING, AND WILLING

CHANGES FROM ♩ TO ♫ AND ♫ TO ♩ .

1. Teacher: *Let's finish with two new games.* (The teacher notates "Frère Jacques" on the chalkboard in C-Major.) *Here's a tune we know.*

The students sing using rhythmic and pitch gestures.

Teacher: *Let's read each measure, once in normal tempo, and then we'll sing the same measure again twice, singing twice as fast.* (Demonstrates.)

Frè - re   Jac - ques   Frè - re   Jac - ques Frè - re   Jac - ques

The students try it.

Teacher: *Let's try the whole thing.*

The students read and sing from the music while the teacher helps by pointing to the notation.

2. Teacher: *A new way! When I say "normal" we'll sing each note as written. When I say "two" we'll repeat each note two times.*

The teacher demonstrates and the students try it:

3. Teacher: *If you listen to George Gershwin's "An American in Paris" you are going to hear as an accompaniment:*

(While playing this) *Join me, using low space claps for the bass and high space claps for the soprano.*

4. **Teacher**: *Let's end this lesson with a canon using "Frère Jacques," alternating one measure as notated, followed by the same measure two times in ♪. Start singing four beats after me. While you are singing, listen to what you must sing next.*

After the students do this successfully, the teacher divides them into two groups which then perform the canon without help from the teacher.

Conclusion

This series of activities for older students has included identifying rhythmic patterns, making tempo changes, choosing appropriate dynamics for ascending and descending melodies, inner-hearing and recalling both tempo and pitch changes, studies in scales and tonalities, work with specific intervals and scale segments, and music reading.

The activities are so sequenced that they could be used with either older beginning students or students with musical background.

However, it is important to realize that such lessons would never be done in isolation, as presented here. They would always be accompanied by work in Eurhythmics and Improvisation, the other two aspects of Jaques-Dalcroze's tripodic method that have been dealt with in earlier chapters.

KODÁLY

What has come to be known in North America as the Kodály Method had its inception in Hungary not with three-year-olds or twelve-year-olds or even with high school students, but with young adults—music students attending the Franz Liszt Academy of Music who majored in performance, composition, ethnomusicology, or music education. It was at this level that Kodály first perceived the deficiency in musicality among his students and it was then that the first major changes in teaching approach were made: the fixed-*do* of most European music schools was changed to tonic *solfa*; rhythm syllables were incorporated to facilitate rhythm reading; and two- and three-part pedagogical works were composed by Kodály to improve students' hearing, reading, and writing.

While it is true that it took only a short time for Kodály to realize the necessity of instilling musical concepts and skills in the younger child,[2] the fact remains that the Kodály Method, although effective with three-, eight-, twelve-, and fifteen-year-olds, is actually an extremely thorough way in which either to begin or to continue the musical education of adults—students at the senior high school, university, or conservatory level.[3]

This section will outline some techniques that are useful with older students who have come through Kodály programs and are now ready to continue at an advanced level with the same aspects of musicianship that were fostered in the earlier years: part singing, inner-hearing of music seen, analysis of large and small forms, performance of complex rhythms, and a musical use of dynamics, tempo, and timbre. At this level instrumental performance is often incorporated into the basic musicianship classes; for parts of their lessons students use piano, string and wind instruments—the major instruments of their study. Listening to music, always an active rather than a passive activity in Kodály classes, continues with examples from all periods and styles.

The pedagogical compositions of Kodály play a large and important part in lessons with older students, and the study of folk music continues, with less relative emphasis but in greater depth. Improvisation and composition are skills practiced regularly as a part of most lessons.

In such programs, choir and instrumental ensembles are not places for instruction in the basics of music, for students come to choir or orchestra already musicians. Rehearsals are conducted as rehearsals of professional groups: tempo, expressive qualities, and interpretation are the focuses, not notes.

At the time of this printing no program in North America is operating at this level. Secondary school and college teachers do not know how to tap the musicality and knowledge of students who have been trained thoroughly in a Kodály way. Indeed, these institutions often fail the student who, when looking at a melody line, can inner-hear the correct harmonization and can sing and name the chords. Their examinations are designed for people who have memorized rules. The student who can read anything in moveable-*do solfa* is asked in a number of respected institutions to relearn everything in fixed-*do*. The student who previously learned history and style through singing, listening, and musical analysis is suddenly faced with dull lectures punctuated with dates to be memorized.

There are, however, lights on the horizon. More and more high schools, conservatories, and university music departments are recognizing the superior-

---

[2]The first school text following Kodály's ideas was written by Kodály and György Kerényi: *A School Collection of Songs* (1943). This work was aimed at six- to ten-year-olds, and was followed shortly by a second volume for eleven- to fourteen-year-olds. Kodály himself wrote many songs and choral works for children kindergarten age and older.

[3]This section will not be dealing with the beginning older student, since that has been discussed in some depth in Lois Choksy, *The Kodály Context* (Englewood Cliffs, N.J.: Prentice-Hall, 1981), chapter 4.

ity of moveable-*do solfa*. Many are using the Kodály, Hegyi, and Szőnyi books.[4] More and more college theory teachers, who often possess perfect pitch themselves, are realizing the need for more effective teaching techniques to reach the great majority of students born without perfect pitch.[5]

It is a sad axiom that a poor teacher impedes rather than fosters learning. And it has often been observed that there is almost an inverse ratio between grade level and teaching ability. The music teacher of Grade 1 or 2, or 5 or 6, has spent many hours deciding how best to present a new idea, how to bring it to the conscious awareness of students, how best to practice using it, to reinforce it, and to assess the students' learning of it. But by the high school or college level such planning appears rarely to occur. Information is imparted—all too often through read lectures—and students sink or swim. Many, of course, sink. The loss in human resources—the loss to the world of music—is immeasurable.

Following are some Kodály techniques for use with advanced students. One lesson was done by the author with gifted children in a conservatory program. The other was observed at a high school in Hungary. Both could be done with any group of students who have had six to eight years of North American public school Kodály training.

Lesson, Example 1

This was a lesson with twenty-four students of mixed ages, all pianists or string players.[6] All were gifted students enrolled in a special conservatory program. These students had one forty-five-minute musicianship (Kodály) class weekly. The lesson below was their twelfth lesson.

1. **Teacher:** *Think the note A. Sing it for me, please.*

    [Checked by tuning fork. Since the third lesson this class has never failed to sing the A correctly.]

    Teacher: *A equals* mi. *Use hand signs, but sing inside, with inner-hearing, a descending minor scale. When you reach* la *sing it aloud. Here is your tempo:* (on A) *one, two, ready, and . . .*

The students sing the D pitch correctly together at the right moment.

    Teacher: *What key are we in?:* (D minor.) *Sing the D-minor scale from* la *to* la *in absolutes this time* (D E F G A B♭   C D). *Now sing it in*

[4]Zoltán Kodály, *The Kodály Choral Method* (London: Boosey & Hawkes) (This is a series of books by Kodály and others, several now available in English.); Erzsébet Szőnyi, *Musical Reading and Writing*, 2 vols. (Budapest: Corvina Press, 1974; 1979) (Available through Boosey & Hawkes, New York); Erzsébet Hegyi, *Solfége According to the Kodály Concept*, 2 vols. (Kecskemet, Hungary: Zoltán Kodály Pedagogical Institute of Music, 1975; Budapest: Editio Musica, 1979) (Available through Boosey & Hawkes, New York).

[5]Courses in Kodály techniques for teachers of theory are offered biannually in the United States and Hungary; an increasing number of theory teachers are also studying in Hungary or in the major training centers in the United States and Canada.

[6]The Junior Academy Program of the Mount Royal Conservatory, Calgary, Alberta, 1983–84.

solfa, *identifying the major and minor seconds. What does "major" really mean in an interval?* (Bigger.) *Minor?* (Smaller.)

la   to   ti   Ma - jor   sec - ond   ti   to   do   min - or   sec - ond   etc.

Let's sing the scale in canon this time.

Voice I   l   t   d   r   m   f   s   l'   t'
Voice II   l   t   d   r   m   f   s   l
Voice III   l   t   d   r   m

2.   **Teacher:** *What is another form of the minor scale?* (Melodic, harmonic.) *How can we form a harmonic minor scale?* (Raise the *so* a semitone to *si*.) *Let's sing it.*

la   ti   do   re   mi   fa   si   la'   si   fa   mi   re   do   ti   la

     Teacher: *What would the I chord, the tonic, be in this mode?* (1–3–5 over *la; la–do–mi.*) *The V chord, the dominant?* (1–3–5 over *mi; mi–si–ti.*) *Let's sing them.*

    la   do   mi   i   mi   si   ti   V

3.   **Teacher:** *What would be easier for singing? How could we invert the V for easier voice leading?* (Keep the *mi* on top.)

The class sings the progression with the V chord in first inversion:

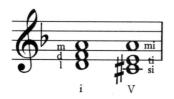

      i   V

4.   **Teacher:** *Look at the Creole folk song on your desk. What key is it in?* (D-minor.) *What kind of minor?* (Harmonic—it has a C$^\#$, a *si*.)

Don't You Cry Mam'zelle Zizi

Creole

Don't you cry Mam' - zelle Zi - zi,   Don't you cry Mam' - zelle Zi - zi,

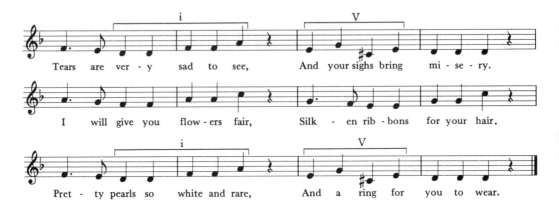

Tears are ver - y sad to see, And your sighs bring mi - se - ry.

I will give you flow - ers fair, Silk - en rib - bons for your hair.

Pret - ty pearls so white and rare, And a ring for you to wear.

5.   Teacher: *Can you find the tonic chord in minor outlined in the melody anyplace? the dominant?* (These have been bracketed in the example given here for the reader's convenience. These brackets were not shown in the students' music.) *Let's sing the first, second, and fourth phrases in* solfa. *This time when we come to a broken chord let's divide into three groups and each sing and hold one of the tones, so that we can hear the harmony.*

6.   Teacher: *Now look at the third phrase. Read it silently with inner-hearing. What can you tell me about it?* (On A.)

1   2   read - y   read

The class discovers that the third phrase is in major and contains the tonic and dominant chords in outline in the relative major key, F. Finally, a tempo is chosen suitable to the words and the whole song is sung. Dynamics are used to underline the changes from minor to major and back to minor.

7.   Teacher: *Let's practice a descending scale in minor.* (On chalkboard; sung in *solfa*):

l'   *si*   *f*   *m*   *r*   *d*   *t,*   *l*

Teacher: *Now, ascending thirds:*

l,   *d*   *t,*   *r*   *d*   *m*   *r*   *f*   *m*   *si*   *f*   *l*   *si*   *t'*   *l*

8. Teacher: *Look at the Vivaldi theme, page 12 in your Kodály* Fifteen Two-Part Exercises.[7]

Theme from Concerto in A minor

Antonio Vivaldi

In the lower part can you find the descending minor scale? Don't be confused by notes that may be between the scale notes. (For the reader's convenience the scale notes have been circled.) *Now look at the in-between notes in that line. Yes! They make a scale also—re–do–ti–la. Let's sing just those measures: 2, 3, 4, and the first note of measure 5. Putting the two scale parts together, now let's look back at the beginning; follow my hand signs—l d t⸍ r d l. Can you find these thirds hidden in the theme at the beginning? Let's sing the lower voice part through to measure 5. Good. Now sing it again as I sing the upper voice.*

[In subsequent lessons the entire work will be analyzed, worked through and, finally, sung in two parts by the group and by individuals.]

9. Teacher: *Look at* Bicinia number 4.[8] (The class has been working on this for several lessons.)

[7](New York: Boosey & Hawkes, 1952).
[8]Zoltán Kodály, *Bicinia Hungarica*, vol. 1 (London: Boosey & Hawkes, 1968).

Girls, sing the upper voice; boys, the lower.
Now all sing the upper voice and tap the rhythm of the lower.
Reverse parts.
Andrea (a piano student), *would you please play voice one while we all sing voice two; be sure you sing too.*
Good. Now, Andrea, play voice two and sing voice one alone. We'll all be ready to help if you need it.
Who else is ready to try? Gervais? Good.

[The ability to sing one part while playing another is important. It requires thought and concentration at every moment, unlike simply *playing* two parts, which can become finger automatisms.]

10. **Teacher**: *Look at the board and read the rhythm*

Memorize it. (A few moments are given and then the whole is

erased.) *Say it again.* (Corrections are made, if

needed.) *Please write it in your manuscript books, above the staff lines. Be sure to leave room for* solfa *syllables under the rhythm and above the staff.* (Three minutes are allowed for notation.)

11. **Teacher**: *Listen to the melody.* (Sung on "loo")

The class sings back the melody phrase by phrase, using *solfa,* and enters the *solfa* syllables under their rhythmic notation. Their pages look like this:

Teacher: *Sing what you have written: I'll sing something different. Be sure to stay on your part.*

As the class sings this descant the teacher sings the familiar Christmas carol "Deck the Halls." (This class had to start again because of the laughter when they realized what was happening.)

Teacher: *Now let's switch parts—I'll sing the descant, you sing the carol.*
Now, half of the class on the descant, half on the carol.
Fine. For homework, notate the descant on staff under your rhythm and solfa notation, and work on number 4 in your Bicinia. *Be able to sing either part and tap the rhythm of the other. See you next Monday!*

> CONCLUSION   There is very little obvious play in this lesson, and yet no class ever seemed to enjoy Kodály-based lessons with as intense enthusiasm as this small group of mixed ages with only their musical talent a common thread. The lesson contained far more meaningful theory than is likely to be found in the usual high school or even beginning college class, but to these youngsters the mental challenges *were* play, play that contributed to musical skills and under-standings, but play, nevertheless.

Lesson, Example 2

This lesson was with twenty-two students of approximately fifteen to eighteen years of age.[9]
> The class preceded the lesson with unison singing of a well-known and beloved folk song.
> 1. Opening the lesson with *interval identification*, the teacher played one note at a time on the piano and named an interval; individual students sang the interval from the given note using *any* correct *solfa* terminology. Since no key was established and the notes played by the teacher were random, each had several possible correct solmizations. For example:

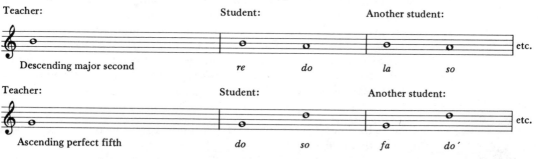

[9]The school is in Barcs, a small village in the south of Hungary. The head teacher, Vendel Bauer, is soft-spoken but dynamic.

2. The lesson continued with *absolute note name singing* in aeolian, dorian, mixolydian and lydian modes, first in comparative *solfa*, then natural *solfa*, and finally in absolute note names, all beginning on D.

l	*t*	*d*	*r*	*m*	*f*	*s*	*l'*	(comparative *solfa*)
					fi	*s*	*l'*	
r	*m*	*f*	*s*	*l*	*t*	*d*	*r'*	(natural *solfa*)
D	E	F	G	A	B♭	C	D	
D	E	F	G	A	B	C	D	

[In the Kodály approach to modes, they are all classified as either major or minor in character, depending upon whether the first three degrees of the scale are a major third or a minor third. Those beginning with a minor third may all be solmized beginning with *la* like the pure minor scale. Those beginning with a major third may all be solmized beginning with *do* like a major diatonic scale. Once these major or minor qualities are aurally perceived, attention is drawn to the *single* different sound in the remainder of the scale. That difference will *always* be a *fa* raised to *fi* or a *ti* flatted to *ta*.

Modes of Minor Character

Aeolean (pure minor)	Dorian	Phrygian
l	l	l
s	s fi >	s
f m >	m	f m >
r	r	r
d t >] m 3	d t >] m 3	d ta l' >] m 3
l'	l'	

Only after modes are thoroughly in the ear through comparative solmization are the natural modes taught, and even then, students are led to discover that the whole-step–half-step arrangement of a scale sung from *re* to *re'* is dorian mode, that from *so* to *so'* is mixolydian mode. By entirely avoiding the piano in such instruction, students are kept free of the notion that the dorian mode must always be from D to D or the mixolydian mode from G to G. From the early introduction of modes all modes are sung in comparative *solfa*, natural *solfa*, and absolute note names beginning on *any* pitch.]

3. Béla Bartók's "Don't Leave Me," a known song in lydian mode, was sung *a cappella* in three parts.

Don't Leave Me

Elizabeth Herzog (tr.)

Béla Bartók

4. The lesson continued with dictation from the piano of a four-phrase, eight-measure melody taken from a Bach chorale. The key [G major] was given and the entire melody was played first while the students listened without pencil in hand. They were asked on what note the melody ended (*do*) and on what note it began (*so*). It was then played phrase by phrase and the students notated the melody in their manuscript books, after which they sang it back first in *solfa* and then in absolute note names.

5. *Reading.* On the chalkboard was a two-part exercise shown with only rhythm and *solfa* notation:

Voice 1	$\frac{2}{4}$													
	d	f	m	l	r	s	m		d	m	s	f	m	r	d

Voice 2	$\frac{2}{4}$											
	d	l,	s,	l,	s,	t,	d		d	l,	m,	l,	s,	d

This was read in *solfa* in two parts at sight immediately. The teacher then asked the class to sing it again, in two parts—this time in the key of G Major, using absolute note names. In rapid succession the exercise was performed with absolute note names in two parts in the keys of F Major, E♭ Major and A Major.

Next, the students were asked to transform the mode from major to minor. Nothing was changed on the chalkboard, but *do* was now to become *la*, again singing the exercise in *solfa*. Then, keeping the minor mode, the students were asked to sing the exercise in absolutes in D minor.

[At none of the above tasks did the students falter. Some tasks obviously required more time and thought than others, but all were successfully completed.]

6. Along the side of the classroom were string instruments—violins and cellos. The teacher now asked those with instruments to take them out and tune them. This took remarkably little time. There were eight violinists and two cellists in the class. These students proceeded to play the above piece, with only the chalkboard *solfa* notation to follow. They played the two-part piece in D Major, G Major, and A Major; the students without instruments sang.

7. Two three-part Hungarian unaccompanied folk-song arrangements by Kodály were sung by the class next. These were obviously well known and much loved. The performance was of a professional quality, with attention to phrasing, dynamics, and general musicality—and yet these were not conducted in the sense that a choir is conducted. The teacher showed rather a careful listening attitude, and softly sang a pitch occasionally when he felt one was not as true as it should be.

CONCLUSION.   It must be stressed that this was a class, *not* a performing group. It was not a class of gifted students—no village the size of Barcs could produce that many gifted students. Of the class, not more than three or four intend to make a career of music. These were simply students who had grown up with music—music well taught—as a major part of their lives.

What has been done in Hungary can be done—and in a few places *is* being done—in North America. The only impediment to many more such classes is the dearth of teachers with sufficient training.

Kodály is not a method limited to children. It is a lifelong approach to musical knowledge, participation, and enjoyment.

ORFF

Secondary school and adult students often need to recapture a sense of childhood play. Most adults have relinquished that sense in the name of maturity. There is a need for fantasizing, dreaming, creating, trusting, and playing in the life of an adult just as much as in the life of a child. The Schulwerk teacher must seek first to uncover and then to expand the dreaming qualities present in his or her adult students, for those qualities are the touchstones of creativity.

The teacher must also retain childlike qualities. While he or she must be able formally to lead others in structured activities, if the dreaming quality—the creative bent—is missing, it cannot be replaced by any amount of instrumental facility or glossy production. Creativity itself is not enough, of course. Within any education system there are requirements for accountability—the methods employed must be validated by the results they achieve.

In Orff practice, as in any teaching approach, there can be testing, lesson plans, methods of instruction. All of these have been stated or implied in earlier chapters. However, there is no stated age at which the creative process can begin or explicitly detailed points at which certain elements of the method are introduced. The process is ongoing: both young and old, when released to play, enjoy the pleasures of learning.

Lesson Cycle

The lesson cycle given here was developed with secondary school students in California. It was designed to unite activities using movement, vocal and instrumental exploration, and improvisation, and was built on the theme of the St. Matthew account of the resurrection of Christ.

There were two basic steps in this lesson: readiness and creating the piece.

A. Readiness
　　1. Playing with a number of simple texts to encourage free chant improvisation
　　2. Improvising movement to accompany chants and songs
　　3. Improvising tunes vocally and instrumentally to fit spoken chants
　　4. Adding instrumental accompaniments to forms that use introductions and codas
　　5. Producing musical dramas with speaking, singing, and moving with instrumental accompaniment

　　[These are the steps students have gone through many times in the preceding years with other materials.]

B. Creating the piece
　　1. Students become thoroughly familiar with the biblical text Matt. 28:1–8. They must feel the natural flow of the words and express them through movement.
　　2. Students are instructed in the techniques of constructing a simple melisma—singing a whole melodic unit on one syllable—and in the use of onomatopoeia—forming words whose sound is closely associated with the object or action named. They apply these techniques to the biblical verses.
　　3. Major, minor, pentatonic, diatonic, and modal tonalites are experimented with instrumentally and vocally. The scales or modes that best suit specific parts of the text are chosen.
　　4. Melodies are invented using the chosen scales and modes.
　　5. Movement is incorporated.
　　6. Instrumental accompaniments are created and added. Chord changes are as simple or complex as the group is capable of. (The opportunity to learn more about chords and voice leading is inherent in the activity.)
　　7. The production is assembled with singers, narrators, movers, and players. It is rehearsed, refined, and performed. It can be presented in the style of a medieval mystery play, fully costumed if the group wishes.

The accompaniment may be provided solely by the Instrumentarium or it can be expanded to include winds and strings.

[The realization of this experience on the following pages is only one of numerous possibilities. To repeat, the Orff experience is improvisational and results in many different interpretations even with the same text.]

Easter Triptych

a. Procession of the Three Marys

PART I. PROCESSION OF THE THREE MARYS.   Following the canon, three verses are improvised over the same repeated bass line, which is repeated four times for each verse.

The suggested rhythm is not, of course, mandatory.

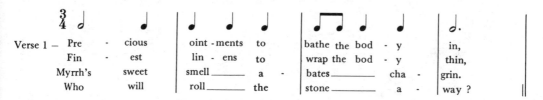

Verse 1 —	Pre -	cious	oint - ments to	bathe the bod - y	in,
	Fin -	est	lin - ens to	wrap the bod - y	thin,
	Myrrh's	sweet	smell_____ a -	bates_____ cha -	grin.
	Who	will	roll_____ the	stone_____ a -	way ?

Verse 2 —   Holy, Holy, Holy one,
              You are known as God's own Son,
              Yet you lay beneath the stone.
              Who will roll the stone away?

Verse 3 —   Grief so deep my heart does break,
              From the earth did they Jesus take,
              Never shall I His Truth forsake.
              Who will roll the stone away?

PART II. THE ANGELIC PROCLAMATION.   This consists of a vocal improvisation in chant style, in A-minor. Students should be encouraged to emphasize the meaning of the text by carefully placing long notes and melismas. The text is as follows:

> Matt. 28:2. And, behold, there was a great earthquake: for the angel of the Lord descended from heaven, and came and rolled back the stone from the door, and sat upon it.
>
> 3. His countenance was like lightning, and his raiment white as snow:
>
> 4. And for fear of him the keepers did shake, and became as dead men.

The opening lines were improvised by one student as follows:

The accompaniment for this section could be as simple as a tremolo on octave A's on all the instruments.

For the next verses, to dramatize the change in emotion from fear to hope, the class chose to move to a brighter mode—G pentatonic. The accompaniment moved in triplets, and glissandi announced the voice of the angel.

The text:

Matt. 28:5. And the angel answered and said unto the women, Fear not ye: for I know that ye seek Jesus, which was crucified.

6. He is not here: for he is risen, as he said. Come see the place where the Lord lay.

(Glissando begins here and continues randomly throughout the angel's message.)

For the next verses, to indicate the growing excitement, the tempo was increased and chording incorporated.

The text:

Matt.28:7. And go quickly, and tell his disciples that he is risen from the dead; and, behold, he goeth before you into Galilee; there shall ye see him: lo, I have told you.

8. And they departed quickly from the sepulchre with fear and great joy; and did run to bring his disciples word.

PART III. THE REJOICING.   The students wanted this section to grow out of the previous one, but to express a different emotion. To do this they chose a tonality related to the G pentatonic of the previous section, but more complete in its feeling—the mixolydian mode. The melody invented was a simple one, but it generated excitement through repetition and the addition of parts. The meter (⁷₄) also helped to carry forward the feeling of excitement.

PART IV. THE HYMN.   To end the production these students chose to improvise on the text of an old hymn, "The Strife Is O'er" (translated from the Latin by Francis Pott).

Text:

> The strife is o'er, the battle done;
> Now is the Victor's triumph won;
> O let the song of praise be sung,
> Alleluia!

(This text is traditionally sung to the well-known hymn tune "Vulpius," which could be an alternative to an improvisation at this point.)

The improvised hymn tune was followed by a coda:

CODA — All voices and Instruments:

Conclusion

Although the above Orff experience calls for much vocal improvisation, a class that has had Orff training for several years would not find it difficult. A number of factors contribute to the improvisation's simplicity, its "elemental" nature:

> There are neither key signatures nor accidentals needed. The piece moves from A-minor (the Procession and the beginning of the Angelic Proclamation), to G pentatonic (the angel's answer), to mixolydian mode (the Alleluia).
>
> The rhythmic movement is principally in quarter and eighth notes.
>
> The meters are triple and quadruple, followed by $\frac{7}{4}$, a combination of triple and quadruple.
>
> Some of the improvisatory sections are rhythmically free in the style of plainsong, while others have their rhythm strongly implied by the text.

It should be evident from the above Orff experience that the process itself does not change, whether used with five-year-olds or with twenty-year-olds. It is in the texts that the principal difference may be seen—and, of course, in the level of musical knowledge and skills brought to the creative task. To engage in this kind of total musical experience requires much of both teacher and students, but the satisfactions resulting from the final finished performance make it well worthwhile.

COMPREHENSIVE MUSICIANSHIP

One of the important aspects of a CM program is that all music classes and performing groups reinforce one another and combine their aims. Curricular offerings at the secondary school level and beyond should include courses and experiences that emphasize theory and composition, courses that explore music through perceptive listening, and a variety of performing groups for active involvement in playing and singing. It is in the performing groups at the secondary school, college, or community level that most adults will continue musical growth and development. Instead of being a mechanical practice session or drill activity, rehearsals should be opportunities for individuals to gain insights into the complex nature of music itself. People in a rehearsal should be actively involved in the use of musical elements and fundamentals through performance, analysis, and creative experience. Interpretative decisions should be made by individuals, based on personal musical understanding. Students should be allowed to conduct, and to compose original works. Rehearsals should include a historical review of the literature, analysis of theoretical and compositional aspects, and explanation of the use of expressive elements. The participant in such a rehearsal program emerges with a comprehensive background in the musical arts.

Learning Objectives

PITCH. Students at the secondary school level and beyond in CM programs will identify, listen to, and perform patterns and phrases in instrumental and vocal compositions. They will perform monophonic and polyphonic music from various periods and cultures and will identify, perform, and create appropriate descants, obbligatos, and ostinati.

DURATION.   Students should be able to demonstrate the steady beat and pulse, to perform and analyze metric, rhythmic, and melodic accents, and a variety of tempi and tempo changes. Rhythms, meters, and tempi should be explored in a cross-section of world music.

INTENSITY.   Through the performance of vocal and instrumental music, students will demonstrate various dynamic levels and changes in dynamics, describe use of dynamics in performed works, and use dynamics in original compositions and improvisations.

TIMBRE.   Adult students in the CM model will perform and listen to a variety of sound sources and timbres, including electronic and environmental sounds. They will identify, classify, and compare the timbres used in performances.

The Organization of Pitch, Duration, Intensity, and Timbre

Larger works from world music sources can be used to demonstrate the possibilities of the horizontal and vertical organizations of music.

HORIZONTAL ORGANIZATION.   Through specific performance experiences in the secondary school, college, or conservatory setting, students become aware of the melodic and rhythmic results of pitch and durational interaction. They analyze melodic and rhythmic patterns and meters and use these in original composition and improvisation.

VERTICAL ORGANIZATION.   Students identify chord changes, functional chords, and chords of various harmonic weight in compositions being performed. They should be able to identify tonal centers in harmonic progressions and to improvise, compose, and perform harmonic progressions illustrating differing degrees of tonality.

FORM.   Students should be exposed to a variety of musical forms and genres from all time periods and cultures.

CONTEXTS.   The music performed, listened to, and created at the secondary school level and beyond should relate to its aesthetic, historical, and social roots.

It is important to note that the constituent parts of this CM outline are never separated, isolated, or fragmented. They emerge within a well-integrated teaching–learning synthesis which establishes the method by which the goal of CM is ultimately achieved. It is this totality of learning from early childhood to adulthood that is the core of a CM program.

Lesson Plans

The performing ensemble is an important arena for musical learning for secondary school students. Rehearsals should provide opportunities for students to describe what they are playing or singing, opportunities for students to compose music, opportunities for students to make personal musical decisions, opportunities for students to conduct, and opportunities for students to perform music of many different time periods and cultures. The following rehearsal outlines are constructed to help the students grow as performers, listeners, and as creators of music.

CHORAL REHEARSAL OF "WHEN JESUS WEPT," BY WILLIAM BILLINGS.   The following techniques and approaches could be used during a rehearsal of "When Jesus Wept."

1. Have students consider the text. After they read it, have them consider appropriate tempi.
2. After the students consider the text and after they sing the melody line, have them experiment with different dynamic levels. Have the students decide on the most appropriate dynamic level.
3. Have students experiment with other triple meters. What are some of the reasons behind the selection of $\frac{3}{2}$ by Billings?
4. Have students map the melodic line while the group sings it.
5. Have selected students write the melody line using traditional notation.
6. The melody line can be sung by any combination of voices in the form of a round. Have students experiment with various places where it would be appropriate for the second voice to enter.
7. Have the students adjust the dynamic levels according to the entrance of voices in the rounds.
8. Obviously, "When Jesus Wept" is horizontally organized when in a round form. However, it does have a vertical organization as well. Have students listen to and describe the vertical organization of the round.
9. Have students identify by sight and by sound the various intervals used in the melodic line.
10. Using the same text, have students compose a short round. Compare the compositions to the one written by Billings.

When Jesus Wept

William Billings

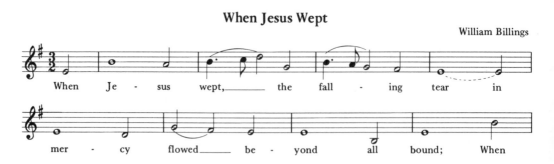

Je - sus groaned, ____ a trem - bling fear seized

all ____ the guilt - y world ____ a - round.

ORCHESTRA REHEARSAL OF "DANCE OF THE GRANDFATHERS" FROM THE NUTCRACKER BY TCHAIKOVSKY. The following techniques and approaches could be used during a rehearsal of "Dance of the Grandfathers."

1. Before looking at their assigned parts of "Dance of the Grandfathers" have the students listen carefully as the first and second flutes play the melody from the pickup of measure 2 to the first eighth note in measure 16. (The flutes should read from their notated parts.) Have all of the students in the orchestra play the melody *by ear* along with the flutes.

2. After the students have played the melody several times have them notate it for their instruments on blank manuscript paper.

3. Have the students identify the melodic intervals which are contained in the melodic fragment.

4. Have the students first sing and then play the intervals identified.

5. Have the students determine the tonal center of the melodic fragment. Ask them to explain why they arrived at their answer.

6. Have the students look at their scores and play through the piece noting the compositional form. Have a selected student illustrate the form on the chalk board.

7. Have all the students practice conducting eight measures of $\frac{3}{8}$ followed by four measures of $\frac{2}{4}$ followed by eight measures of $\frac{3}{8}$.

8. Have a selected student conduct the piece determining the appropriate tempi and dynamics.

9. Have the students play together and hold the chords found on the first beat of measures 26, 27, 28, and 29 of the score. Have the students then analyze the chords according to functional harmony and have one student write the chord symbols on the chalk board.

10. As an ensemble, have the students select a current popular song or a folk song and have them play the melody in a concert key together by ear. Have the students notate the melody for their instruments on manuscript paper and have them indicate appropriate dynamics and phrasing. Have the students identify the intervals used.

Summary

In both of these rehearsals, the students are actively involved in musical learning as related to the performance of the piece. The students analyze the musical elements, develop aural skills, experiment with dynamics and phrasing, and compose or improvise. Instead of drill sessions, these rehearsals are learning sessions in which each student has an opportunity to develop specific musical skills and to grow in comprehensive musical understanding.

CONCLUSION

The lesson examples included in this chapter, as representative of practice at advanced levels in Jaques-Dalcroze, Kodály, Orff, and Comprehensive Musicianship, are widely divergent in character. It is obvious that the more advanced the student in any of these streams, the more unique the learning experience is to the methodology being used. The next chapter will focus on the congruences and differences among these approaches and will attempt to draw some conclusions based on this information.

12
SPECIFIC METHOD OR ECLECTICISM?

Pestalozzi said, "Discover everything!"

The thread connecting Jaques-Dalcroze, Kodály, Orff, and Comprehensive Musicianship began with the application to music of Pestalozzi's principles by the Swiss musicians Nägeli and Pfeiffer. A young woman trained as a "Pestalozzian music teacher," Julie Jaques, passed the experimental ideas and ideals on to her son, Emile; and Emile Jaques-Dalcroze, in his lifetime, truly attempted to "discover everything" about the teaching of music.

His experiments, too radical for the conservative music school in which he was professor of theory and composition, were sponsored by the Dorhn brothers, wealthy German industrialists, and the Jaques-Dalcroze Institute was founded at Hellerau in 1910. During its rather short period of existence it became famous as a center for exploration and experimentation in the performing arts.

The young Carl Orff went to Hellerau, and was so influenced by the music and dance there that there is no doubt that the seeds of what was to become the "Orff Approach" to music education had its beginnings in the experience. "Discover everything" was transformed by Orff into his "Elemental" theory of music education.

Meanwhile, in the music schools and conservatories of Europe the theory books of Jaques-Dalcroze were being studied and used widely. His innovative techniques for the development of basic musicianship skills were tried, among many other places, in Hungary.

There, Zoltán Kodály believed that if universal musical literacy were ever to be achieved it would have to be through something more accessible than fixed-*do solfège*—a tool that almost demands perfect pitch. In his travels, Kodály had seen and been impressed with the choral work done in England; work based on Curwen principles and on the tonic *solfa* system. He believed this to be a far better approach to the musical education of the masses. The *solfège* techniques of Jaques-Dalcroze were adapted to meet the requirements of the English tonic *solfa* system, and the method which had begun in Switzerland as training for professional musicians ultimately became the basis for teaching music to children in the schools of Hungary.

Even in the approaches that arose in the 1950s and 1960s in North America the thread of Pestalozzi's "discover everything" may be discerned. The Manhattan Music Curriculum Project, the Contemporary Music Project and the Comprehensive Musicianship approach all viewed musical learning as best coming from experience and experimentation, with learning building on learning in a series of skill and concept spirals.

Coming as they did from the same roots, how can the four principal systems of music education that arose be so different from each other?—for different they are! And can methods so fundamentally different perhaps be combined in some way to create one "master method" that might be superior to any individual approach?

The authors of this book believe that no *combination* of methods can be as effective a teaching approach as a knowledgeable use of any *one* of them in the hands of a teacher with sufficient training. To clarify this, perhaps some basic comparisons among these four commonly used (and, unfortunately, commonly misused) approaches should be made.

In their overall goals there is no conflict whatsoever. All four have as their ultimate goal the enhancement of life; the development to the fullest extent possible of the innate musicality that exists in every human being.

That there is more than one possible route to such a goal is self-evident. The purpose of this chapter is not to suggest that one route is superior to another, but rather to examine the congruences and differences among the various methods, so that more intelligent choices can be made by teachers; and also to illuminate the irreconcilable differences, where they exist, and the futility and ineffectuality of jumping from one of these ways of teaching to another—constructing lessons with a dash of Dalcroze, a cup of Kodály, an ounce of Orff, and a soupçon of CM—a practice much encouraged by many commercial school music-series books and by college methods courses.

Let it be said that Lois Choksy is not primarily a Kodály teacher, Robert Abramson not a Jaques-Dalcroze teacher, Avon Gillespie not an Orff teacher, nor David Woods a CM teacher. The authors are all *music* teachers. Each is a music teacher who believes deeply in and follows closely one of the philosophies, principles, and pedagogies expounded in the various separate sections of this book, but all are first and foremost *music* teachers. In spite of this, the question each author is asked most often is: "Why are you a Kodály (Orff, Dalcroze, CM) teacher?" And from university and conservatory colleagues: "Don't you think you are being just a bit *narrow* in your viewpoint? Wouldn't it be preferable to use the best of each approach, each method?"

Even a superficial perusal of these methods will show the impossibility of combining them effectively. Consider the different subgoals or objectives at the core of each method:

JAQUES-DALCROZE.   Each student should develop the ability to express what is heard securely, effectively, and knowledgeably through *movement* before transferring those physical sensations into other forms of musical expression (voice and instruments) or other levels of musical knowledge (*Solfège–Solfège-Rythmique,* and improvisation).

KODÁLY.   Through *singing* every student should have the opportunity (1) to become musically literate in the sense of being able to see a score and imagine the sounds or to hear sounds and imagine the score; and (2) to know and love his or her own folk music heritage and the great art music of the world.

ORFF.   All students should find ways to express themselves through music, both as individuals and as members of a musical community (the ensemble). The *musical experience* itself is the most important objective.

COMPREHENSIVE MUSICIANSHIP.   Through discovery and experimentation with sounds and sound sources and through knowledge of music of all styles, periods, and cultures, students should be led to become composers, listeners, and performers.
    It is immediately evident that while all four approaches agree on the major goal of "enhancement of life and development of innate musicality," the subgoals indicate marked differences in what best leads to enhancement of life and innate musicality. And the differences do not end there. What is the attitude of each method toward the basic musical functions of creating, moving, instrument playing, music reading, and music writing?

Creativity

JAQUES-DALCROZE.   Movement is the first level of creativity. Movement is encouraged from the beginning, but must always be specific to the meter, rhythm, character, tempo, dynamics, and flow of the song, percussion, or piano accompaniment. There are "right" and "wrong" movement styles to accompaniments. Improvisation is expected to be thoughtful and appropriate. The philosophy of thoughtful musical improvisation is carried into classes in *Solfège* and *Solfège-Rythmique,* and to vocal, instrumental, and piano experiences.

KODÁLY.   Creativity comes from knowledge. It is necessary to have a musical vocabulary in order to create music. Just as one must know words to state thoughts, so must one know the vocabulary of music aurally and orally before improvising; just as one must be able to think and write words, phrases, and sentences before expressing thoughts on paper, so must one be able to hear, think, and write notes and know how to organize them into patterns, phrases, and forms in order to compose.

ORFF.   In order to create sound patterns it is not necessary to know notation. Sound patterns may be constructed arbitrarily and then organized into forms to create compositions. The musical vocabulary is gained aurally. The principle of "improvisation unfettered by knowledge" is upheld until very late in the process.

COMPREHENSIVE MUSICIANSHIP.   Composition need not begin with the traditional materials of music. Environmental sounds or "found" sound sources may be organized into forms to produce spontaneous improvisations. These may or may not be charted in invented graphic notation so that they may be read later (thus becoming compositions). Traditional reading and writing, while desirable skills, are not necessary for improvisation and composition.

Movement

JAQUES-DALCROZE.   All aspects and elements of music are learned first through movement. The awakening and then training of the kinesthetic sense must precede all other musical training. Improvised accompaniment (voice, speech, percussion, piano) may follow movement, or movement may be expected to follow accompaniment. While "free" in some aspects, movement must reflect the element of rhythm being studied. "Free" in Jaques-Dalcroze training never means simply "doing one's own thing."

KODÁLY.   At the earliest ages children move rhythmically to enact the words of nursery songs: they "rock the baby," "row the boat," "play on the see-saw," "go 'round the moon." This kind of movement is followed by playing traditional games of early childhood: circle games, such as "Ring around the Rosy"; line games, such as "Lemonade." Circle and line games involving chase, partner choosing, acting out, and winding are all sung and played. Later, traditional folk dances of North America are incorporated—reel dances, circle dances, and square dances. The accompaniment for all these is singing—and singing only.

ORFF.   Free, inventive, and uninhibited movement is one of the foundations of the Orff process. The impetus for such movement may be story, speech, song, or instrument, but all participants in any Orff experience are expected to move as well as speak, sing, and play.

COMPREHENSIVE MUSICIANSHIP.   With its emphasis on composing and the related roles of performing and listening, no single all-encompassing philosophy of movement has been produced by the practitioners of CM. However, within CM lessons one may find "free movement," traditional singing games and dances, and, perhaps uniquely among these methods, dances from many foreign cultures. The music of CM from the earliest grades incorporates the music of many nations, cultures, styles, and periods; and there is an obligation on the part of the teacher to ensure that both the music and the dances from these cultures, styles, and periods be authentic.

Instrumental Training

JAQUES-DALCROZE.   The ear and body are the primary instruments of instruction. Later, students will use other instruments in class instruction—voice, percussion, piano—all in improvisatory ways. Traditional instrumental study is expected to take place outside the Jaques-Dalcroze class, in private lessons: it *is* expected that most students will choose to study an instrument. Among all the methods discussed here, Jaques-Dalcroze, when practiced fully as a *three-part* method Eurhythmics, Improvisation, and *Solfège-Rhythmique*, is the most intensely preprofessional in its thrust.

KODÁLY.   No instrument may be introduced until the fundamentals of musical literacy have been established through singing. This is to ensure that musical sound will always exist in the mind, in the "inner ear," before it sounds on an instrument. Literacy is taken *to* the instrument rather than acquired *on* it. In Hungary, Kodály practices are part of private instrumental study, and in some rare instances in North America, Kodály practices have been carried very successfully into school band and orchestra instruction. Generally, however, instrumental lessons are privately given outside the school and may begin when the child is seven or eight years old. Kodály, which has as one of its professed aims the musical education of the nonprofessional—the amateur and the audience—nevertheless offers, like Jaques-Dalcroze, thorough preprofessional training.

ORFF.   The earliest Orff experiences are not instrumental; they involve movement, speech, and song. Only when certain basic skills have been mastered are instruments—the specially designed Orff Instrumentarium—introduced. This may be late in second or early in third grade. Playing is first by imitation, and moves from imitation to experimentation and creation. Notation (traditional and nontraditional) is not usually a part of the instrumental experience as this level. Expectations of performance excellence, both individual and ensemble, are extremely high, even at the beginning stages and with the simplest material. The recorder is generally introduced around fifth grade and added to the ensemble. Traditional instruments are usually studied outside the school in private lessons.

COMPREHENSIVE MUSICIANSHIP.   A major thrust in CM is the study of sound and sound sources. From the earliest years children are led to discover how size and material affect tone, pitch, and timbre. Traditional and nontraditional instruments are examined, played, and studied, not so much for playing proficiency as for the knowledge to be gained from such exposure. Instrument building is a frequent activity in classes of CM students. At advanced levels the CM student is expected to arrange or orchestrate compositions. Traditional instrumental study is still expected to be obtained primarily through private lessons, but the CM philosophy may be incorporated into ensemble, orchestra, and band rehearsals.

Musical Reading and Writing

JAQUES-DALCROZE.   Musical reading and writing are taught systematically through *Solfège* and *Solfège-Rythmique* after two to three years of training in Eurhythmics. Fixed-*do* (C-*do*) is the primary tool, combined with the use of *movable* roman numerals to represent scale steps and relationships to indicate the roots of tirads within each key. Arabic numerals are used to illustrate the size of the melodic segment being studied. A one-line staff is used first, followed by two-, three-, and, finally, five-line staff, and musical reading begins with two and three notes and extends gradually through diatonic major and minor scales to chromaticism. The voice is the principal instrument in the development of musical literacy.

KODÁLY. Musical reading and writing begin at age six with children constructing rhythmic patterns of their songs with sticks or by placing cut-out felt notes on individual felt staves to show, read, and sing in *solfa* the simple three-note melodies of nursery songs. The system used is movable-*do*. The children begin music writing with a pencil and paper on a five-line staff by the end of first grade or the beginning of second grade, and by fourth grade they are reading and writing in diatonic major and minor keys. In the upper grades modes and altered scales are added and theory and harmony are incorporated. Absolute note names are introduced in the early grades and are used interchangeably with *solfa* after that. Arabic numerals are used to indicate interval, and roman numerals, in the traditional way, to indicate harmonization. All reading, writing, and theory are taught through singing.

ORFF. There is no Orff reading method. This is not to say that Orff teachers neither expect nor train students in musical literacy; it means only that there is no Orff system for such teaching. At the Orff Institute in Salzburg, where the Schulwerk had its real beginning, the children involved in Orff classes were frequently also taking private instrumental lessons; thus, for the most part there was no need to teach them how to read music. Orff teachers in North America, however, face a somewhat different situation. For many of them literacy has become a concern. One answer is to incorporte the teaching of notation into the teaching of the recorder around the fifth grade. Other solutions have involved the use of *solfa*[1] or numbers, and still others use a traditional approach to notation. As with all the methods discussed here, many children involved in Orff programs take private instrumental lessons and acquire musical literacy in that way.

CONTEMPORARY MUSICIANSHIP. Musical literacy comes from the need to put something created down so that one can recall it later or so that others may perform it. Notation is at first representational rather than traditional. When a need is felt by the students, traditional and nontraditional notation is introduced. There is no unique CM method for teaching musical reading and writing. There is, however, a philosophy that implies value to musical literacy.

---

[1] It is this single activity more than any other that has led to the erroneous label "Orff-Kodály." *Solfa* syllables were not invented by Kodály: they predate the Kodály method by nearly one thousand years. The Kodály method can (and does in some places) exist without movable-*do solfa*. (In Estonia, for example, a totally different system of syllables is used.) The use of *solfa* and handsigns does not indicate the presence of Kodály principles and practices any more than a set of Orff instruments indicates the presence of a genuine Orff program.

Music Used in Teaching

JAQUES-DALCROZE.   In Eurhythmics, music of all periods, styles, and genres (folk, classical, popular, jazz, serious, contemporary) as well as music from all cultures may be used. There is no restriction on the type or source of music other than that it be a good example of its type and must clearly illustrate the rhythmic element or elements being studied. For the *Solfège* and *Solfège-Rythmique* aspects of this method Jaques-Dalcroze composed many exercises which are as useful today as when he composed them. However, in his writings he repeatedly urged teachers to create their own musical teaching materials— materials that should uniquely suit each different group, each different student.

KODÁLY.   "Only the best is good enough" was an axiom repeated by Kodály many times in his lifetime and illustrated repeatedly through the kinds of music he insisted on for teaching. The folk music must come from the child's own cultural and linguistic heritage and must be authentic. Where variants exist, only the best, the purest, the truest may be used—and "best" and "truest" is de-cided not by teachers, but by ethnomusicologists and folklorists. Art music plays a major role in teaching and also must be the "best." Palestrina, Monteverdi, Bach, Handel, Mozart, Schubert, Beethoven, Brahms, Debussy, Bartók, among others, are composers known to every Hungarian eighth-grade student in a Kodály program. No popular music is permitted in the classroom. Music of non-Western cultures, if touched on at all, is done so cursorily. In North American settings North American folk music is used. Beyond that, practice is sadly behind the Hungarian model. Few programs have advanced to the level of using art mu-sic as the basic material of instruction (which it should be by sixth grade); and some teachers seem to feel that as long as the skill and concept sequence is ob-served, any musical material (popular, for example) is acceptable. Kodály be-lieved that a major purpose of music education is the inculcation of a high level of musical taste—the ability to distinguish the serious from the trivial, art from amusement. No genuine Kodály program anywhere uses popular music, author-composed school-music-text ditties, or other music of questionable value. Kodály himself composed many volumes of exercises for students as well as some of the finest choral music of the twentieth century for older students and adults.

ORFF.   Nursery rhymes, chants, songs, and children's folk songs from many countries constitute the earliest Orff materials. After the introduction of the instrumentarium there are a number of published volumes of arrangements for Orff instruments on which the teacher may draw, many composed by Orff himself. But both teacher and students in Orff programs are expected to create arrangements and compositions and even total musical productions themselves. These arrangements and compositions are not limited by anything except the imaginative skill and performance levels of the groups involved. All styles and types of music may be used.

CONTEMPORARY MUSICIANSHIP   The CM model, as its name suggests, is comprehensive in its use of music from many periods, styles, and cultures; however, there is certainly an emphasis, from the earliest grades, on music of non-Western cultures and on twentieth-century idioms. Of the four methods described in this book, only in the CM classroom would one be likely to encounter a synthesizer, a sitar, or a skiffle band. All music is acceptable for teaching purposes.

Inferences

The differences among these four methods are vast—in philosophy, in teaching style, in material—in every important aspect save one: each is a legitimate and honest path to genuine musicianship.

If the authors of this book could erase one word from the English language as it is used in music education, it would be "eclecticism." Perhaps somewhere in North America there is a teacher who has spent a year or more training at the Orff Institute in Salzburg, then a year or more at the Liszt Academy of Music in Budapest, developing the skills and concepts necessary to be an adequate Kodály teacher, and has followed this by long study at the Jaques-Dalcroze Institute in Geneva, and then taken graduate work at one of the North American universities specializing in Comprehensive Musicianship. Such a teacher would have sufficient background to be eclectic. However, such a teacher would also know enough to realize that it is impossible to do so.

It is not possible to combine the approaches of Jaques-Dalcroze, Kodály, Orff, and Comprehensive Musicianship in any but the most superficial manner. How can one combine

> a system that uses rhythmic movement accompanied with voice, percussion, or piano improvisation as its earliest experiences with a system that uses *only* unaccompanied singing or folk song as its earliest experience?
>
> a system that introduces notation via singing at age six with one that introduces it at age ten via instrumental experiences?
>
> a system that makes use of jazz, pop, rock, non-Western music, and synthesizer sounds with a system that allows only authentic folk song and great art music?

How can one combine methods whose basic beginning instruments are different:

> the ear and body and voice (Jaques-Dalcroze)
> the unaccompanied singing voice (Kodály)
> the spoken word or chant, and the Instrumentarium (Orff)
> any and all sound sources (CM)

> *Any musical idea may be transformed into movement . . . any body movement may be transformed into its musical counterpart.*   Jaques-Dalcroze

> *If I had to express the essence of this education in one word, that word would be* singing.   Kodály

What, then, is elemental music? Never music alone, but music connected with movement, dance, and speech—not to be listened to, meaningful only in active participation. Elemental music is pre-intellectual, it lacks great form, it contents itself with simple sequential structures, ostinatos, and miniature rondos. It is earthy, natural, almost a physical activity. It can be learned and enjoyed by anyone. It is fitting for children.   Orff

Students [must be] *actively involved in the common elements of music . . .as* performers, listeners *and* composers.   Comprehensive Musicianship

The teacher who is not certain of his or her own goals must *become* certain of them, must read, study, and make a choice—a choice based upon both knowledge and understanding—and must then obtain sufficient training to teach well in that way.

These four approaches have one requisite absolutely in common: They demand musicianship—excellent musicianship—of the practitioner. Neither the musical nor the methodological skills required to work successfully in any of them can be acquired quickly and easily. Training is an absolute necessity, and, unfortunately, is widely available only at the graduate level. But perhaps this is not a bad thing. The teacher who has had a smattering of conflicting methodologies in undergradute training and, thus inadequately prepared, has had to try to build a music program in even one school situation, is in a position better to understand the need for training. The rewards to any teacher willing to expend the time and effort necessary to become truly professional are manifold.